Meaning and Grammar of Nouns and Verbs

Doris Gerland, Christian Horn,
Anja Latrouite & Albert Ortmann (eds.)

d|u|p

Hana Filip, Peter Indefrey, Laura Kallmeyer,
Gerhard Schurz & Robert D. Van Valin (eds.)

Studies in Language and Cognition

1

Doris Gerland, Christian Horn,
Anja Latrouite & Albert Ortmann (eds.)

2014

Meaning and Grammar of Nouns and Verbs

d|u|p

**Bibliografische Information
der Deutschen Nationalbibliothek**
Die Deutsche Nationalbibliothek verzeichnet diese Publikation in der Deutschen Nationalbibliografie; detaillierte bibliografische Daten sind im Internet über http://dnb.dnb.de abrufbar.

© düsseldorf university press, Düsseldorf 2014
http://www.dupress.de
Porträtfoto: © HHU/Foto: Ivo Mayr
Einbandgestaltung: Doris Gerland, Christian Horn, Albert Ortmann
Satz: Ekaterina Gabrovska, Timm Lichte, Friedhelm Sowa, LaTeX
Herstellung: docupoint GmbH, Barleben

Gesetzt aus der Linux Libertine und der Linux Biolinum
ISBN 978-3-943460-64-3

Preface to dup series 'Studies in Language and Cognition'

The series 'Studies in Language and Cognition' will explore issues of mental representation, linguistic structure and representation, and their interplay. Some of the research reported in the series has been carried out as part of Collaborative Research Center 991 'The structure of representations in language, cognition and science', and its predecessor Research Group 600 'Funktionalbegriffe und Frames', both of which have been funded by the German Science Foundation. This research is grounded in the idea that there is a universal format for the representation of linguistic and cognitive concepts, namely frames of the type proposed by the psychologist Lawrence Barsalou. The members of the series editorial board are Prof. Dr. Hana Filip (Linguistics), Prof. Dr. Dr. Peter Indefrey (Linguistics), Prof. Dr. Laura Kallmeyer (Computational Linguistics), Prof. Dr. Sebastian Löbner (Linguistics), Prof. Dr. Gerhard Schurz (Philosophy), and Prof. Dr. Robert D. Van Valin, Jr. (Linguistics).

For this initial volume, Prof. Dr. Löbner is not listed as a member of the editorial board, because it is a surprise Festschrift for him for his 65th birthday. The papers collected herein reflect his influence on colleagues and students, past and present, and are a tribute to him as a teacher, scholar and individual.

Table of Contents

Introduction
Doris Gerland, Christian Horn, Anja Latrouite & Albert Ortmann 11

SEMANTIC AND GRAMMATICAL ASPECTS OF NOUNS

Evidence for four basic noun types from a corpus-linguistic and a psycholinguistic perspective
Dorothea Brenner, Peter Indefrey, Christian Horn & Nicolas Kimm 21

Type shifts and noun class changes under determination in Teop
Ulrike Mosel 49

Semantic constraints on multiple case marking in Korean
Byong-Rae Ryu 77

SEMANTIC AND GRAMMATICAL ASPECTS OF VERBS AND SENTENCES

Glück auf, der Steiger kommt: a frame account of extensional and intensional *steigen*
Thomas Gamerschlag, Wilhelm Geuder & Wiebke Petersen 115

Comparative lexicology and the typology of event descriptions: a programmatic study
Volker Gast, Ekkehard König & Claire Moyse-Faurie 145

Spatio-temporal modification and the determination of aspect: a phase-theoretical account
Michael Herweg 185

The purported Present Perfect Puzzle
Anita Mittwoch 223

Phase quantification and frame theory
Ralf Naumann 237

SEMANTIC AND GRAMMATICAL ASPECTS OF NOUNS AND VERBS

She loves you, *-ja -ja -ja*:
objective conjugation and pragmatic possession in Hungarian
Albert Ortmann & Doris Gerland 269

Black and white languages
Leon Stassen 315

Variations of double nominative in Korean and Japanese
Dieter Wunderlich 339

Definiteness & perfectivity in telic incremental theme predications
Adrian Czardybon & Jens Fleischhauer 373

Referentiality and telicity in Lakhota and Tagalog
Anja Latrouite & Robert D. Van Valin, Jr. 401

List of Sebastian Löbner's publications 427

Introduction

Doris Gerland, Christian Horn, Anja Latrouite & Albert Ortmann

This volume is to honour Sebastian Löbner on the occasion of his 65th birthday. In his more than 30 years of professional life at the Heinrich-Heine-University Düsseldorf, he has substantially contributed to semantic theory, mainly to the semantics of nouns and verbs. With this book, we provide a collection of papers that were contributed by several of his colleagues and companions. It is composed so as to cover semantic and grammatical issues of nouns and noun phrases, verbs and sentences, and aspects of the combination of nouns and verbs.

1 A few nouns and verbs about Sebastian Löbner

After his A-levels ('Abitur') in Hinterzarten in 1968, Sebastian Löbner started to study mathematics as major and linguistics as minor at the University of Düsseldorf, where he graduated in 1975 with a diploma. The constant interaction with his linguistics professor and mentor Volker Beeh raised deeper interest for linguistics, especially for semantics. Sebastian Löbner combined his training in mathematics with that in linguistics when he started to study formal semantics, especially the work by Richard Montague. In 1976, he presented his "Einführung in die Montague Grammatik", which were to become a standard textbook for several generations of students of formal semantics in Germany. He further elaborated on the idea of the mathematical notion of functionality as a crucial aspect in natural language, especially as part of the lexical meanings of certain nouns which he later called *functional nouns*. In 1979, he finished his doctoral thesis titled "Intensionale Verben und Funktionalbegriffe. Untersuchung zur Syntax und Semantik von *wechseln* und den vergleichbaren Verben des Deutschen", in which he provided an analysis of verbs of change and their interaction with functional nouns in German. After that, Sebastian Löbner spent more than three years as assistant professor at the Department of German Literature and Culture, University of Tokyo.

After returning to Germany, he co-directed a project on quantifier semantics ("Quantoren im Deutschen") together with Dieter Wunderlich. The project ran from 1983 to 1986 and was financed by the German Science Foundation (DFG). In this project, Sebastian worked out central ideas that were later incorporated in his habilitation thesis "Wahr neben falsch", published in 1990. He obtained his *venia legendi* in 1989 and became a supernumerary professor in 1997. He was the Principle Investigator of the project "Verb meanings" in the collaborative research center "Theory of the lexicon" (CRC 282) at the University of Düsseldorf from 1991 to 2002. After Dieter Wunderlich retired in 2002, the chair of the Department of General Linguistics was vacant, and Sebastian Löbner acted as the interim chair until 2006. In these four years, he developed the first Bachelor's and Master's degree programme for General Linguistics in Düsseldorf. Furthermore, he developed the fundamental ideas for a DFG-financed Research Unit and brought together researchers from various disciplines to contribute to a proposal. The Research Unit "Functional Concepts and Frames" (FOR 600) commenced in 2005, with Sebastian Löbner as its speaker, and was prolonged for another three years in 2008. The topic of the Research Unit was functional nouns and their connection to the frame approach proposed by the psychologist Lawrence Barsalou. The ideas developed in the research group led to a proposal for an even larger interdisciplinary DFG-funded project cluster, that is, the CRC 991 "The Structure of Representations in Language, Cognition, and Science", again under Löbner's chair. The goal of the CRC, which started in summer 2011, is to develop a general frame theory of concepts, and for that aim, projects from linguistics, philosophy, psychology, German studies, Romance studies, and psychiatry contribute their research methods and perspectives.

Sebastian Löbner's research interests and publications[1] prove him to be a multifaceted semanticist. His main areas of research include the semantics of nouns and verbs, especially definiteness and aspect, as well as quantification. His most influential contributions are the phase quantification approach, the theory of concept types and determination (CTD), as well as his introductions to Montague Grammar and to semantics in general ("Understanding semantics"). He developed the idea of phase quantification, initially with respect to aspect on the basis

---

[1] A list of Löbner's publications is provided at the end of this volume.

Introduction

of German *noch* 'still', and subsequently extended it to other aspectual particles and further linguistic categories such as scalar adjectives and quantifiers. The principal idea of this approach is that semantic properties of certain expressions can be represented in phases, conceived of as segments on a scale connected by the concept of duality.

The theory of concept types and determination, which is based on his 1985 paper on definites, provides a systematic account of four types of nouns (sortal, individual, relational, and functional), four types of determination and the interaction between noun type and determination type. Löbner argues that the different noun types are lexically congruent with certain types of determination but incongruent with others. Incongruent uses are assumed to cause type shifts, which are manifest in the distribution of the various means of nominal determination.

The current focus of Sebastian Löbner's work lies on the connection of language and cognition. He considers frames (in the sense of Barsalou) as the general format of concepts in human cognition and conceives of the attributes in these frames as functional concepts. CTD on the one hand and the relation between frames and functional concepts on the other are being investigated more deeply in the CRC 991. Löbner is the Principle Investigator of the member projects *Conceptual shifts: typological evidence*, *Conceptual shifts: statistical evidence*, *Frames and nominal word formation*, and *Dimensional verbs*.

Besides his research it was always one of Sebastian's concerns to strengthen the role of semantics in the linguistics community. Together with Arnim von Stechow and Thomas Ede Zimmermann, he founded the Gesellschaft für Semantik (Association for Semantics), which aims at establishing a network between semanticists and other linguists. As a teacher, Sebastian often came up with innovative topics at the interface to media studies and cognitive science, thus delving deeper into the communication- and cognition-based dimensions of natural language. He supervised numerous Bachelor and Magister theses and still managed to give precise feedback to his students, all of which appreciated his friendly and helpful attitude. One of his most noticeable characteristics is his open-minded and caring nature. His door has always been open, in the literal sense (often revealing the sounds of jazz music), for students as well as for other linguists, especially young academics.

2 The contributions to this book

The papers collected in this book relate to individual aspects of Sebastian Löbner's research in the domains of noun and verb semantics, especially to conceptual noun types, tense and aspects semantics, granularity of verb meaning, and subcompositionality. We hope that the papers will serve as an inspiration for scholars working in semantics and related fields, just like many of the contributions were inspired by Sebastian's work.

In their contribution "Evidence for four basic noun types from a corpus-linguistic and a psycholinguistic perspective", Dorothea Brenner, Peter Indefrey, Christian Horn & Nicolas Kimm survey two complementing research methods, one involving statistics in text collection and the other a reaction time experiment. The overall aim is to test the distinction of four basic conceptual noun types as proposed by Löbner's theory of Concept Types and Determination. The results provide evidence for the lexical-semantic dimensions of relationality and uniqueness, which form the basis of the four basic nominal concept types.

"Type shifts and noun class changes under determination in Teop" by Ulrike Mosel is a study of the distribution of articles in the Austronesian language Teop. She distinguishes three classes of nouns, which she relates to Löbner's conceptual noun types. The mismatches between conceptual types and Teop noun classes are traced to the semantic feature [± human], which overrules the distinction between functional and relational nouns. Furthermore, the major type shifts between these classes, involving either a loss of uniqueness or the opposite, are shown. Mosel argues that the various noun classes and subclasses form a scale of individuation, with proper names representing the highest degree of individuality, and sortal nouns of the o-class the lowest.

Byong Rae Ryu ("Semantic constraints on multiple case marking in Korean") identifies 16 types of semantic relations between the referents of nominal phrases that he views as licensing conditions for identical case marking in Korean. He finds that all of these relations license double nominative patterns, while only ten license double accusative patterns. Formally, multiple case marking structures are analysed as case sharing between two consecutive NPs.

Michael Herweg ("Spatio-temporal modification and the determination of aspect – a phase-theoretical account") argues that the aspectual type of a sentence is determined by what he calls a Phase Array, which is an abstract constellation of phases defined over underlying ordered structures, such as (models of) time and space. Phase arrays allow to represent the fact that the aspectual type of verbs and

Introduction

PPs and combinations thereof may be underspecified, leaving the determination of aspect on the sentence level to various elements of the context.

In "Glück auf, der Steiger kommt: a frame account of extensional and intensional *steigen*", Thomas Gamerschlag, Wilhelm Geuder & Wiebke Petersen look at three meaning variants of the German movement verb *steigen* 'rise': manner of motion, directed movement, and intensional. The authors present an analysis in terms of Barsalou frames, which enable them to represent the event structure and argument structure, as well as the correlations holding among subevents, manner, positions and the path of the theme argument. Intensional uses of *steigen* are explained as coming about by the interplay of the lexical representation of the verb and the semantic type of the nominal argument.

On the basis of case studies from English, French, German, and several Oceanic languages, Volker Gast, Ekkehard König & Claire Moyse-Faurie ("Comparative lexicology and the typology of event descriptions: a programmatic study") discuss semantic parameters for differentiating between the individual elements as well as the language-specific inventories of verb classes such as verbs of killing, cutting and eating. They take properties of thematic relations and properties of circumstantial relations as a starting point for describing the granularity of lexical distinctions. The study reveals striking similarities and contrasts between European languages and Oceanic languages on the one hand, but also between genealogically closely related languages on the other.

Anita Mittwoch ("The Purported Present Perfect Puzzle") discusses properties of the English present perfect and the English past perfect. She argues that the English past perfect is ambiguous and corresponds to either a past of perfect or to an iterated past. By contrast, the English present perfect is argued to be unambiguous (unlike its German counterpart), but found to yield different readings depending on its use as either experiential or resultative.

Ralf Naumann's paper "Phase quantification and frame theory" aims at capturing the contribution of phase quantifiers like *still* and *already* to the meaning of sentences by combining formal semantics and the cognition-based frame theory of meaning. The latter is seen as an extension of the former. Naumann's main concern is the development of a procedural semantics in the sense of Löbner (1987) and its formalisation.

In „She loves you, -*ja* -*ja* -*ja*: objective conjugation and pragmatic possession in Hungarian", Albert Ortmann & Doris Gerland argue for a common basis of two inflectional asymmetries in Hungarian: the subjective/objective verb agreement split on the one hand, and an alienability split in possessor agreement on the other, both of which display an obvious morphological parallel. Upon analysing each of the two splits, the authors propose a common rationale, namely the expression of the presence or absence of a pragmatic component in the anchoring of the object and of the possessor, respectively.

Leon Stassen ("Black and white languages") suggests that languages tend to belong to one of only two types with opposite settings regarding five structurally independent typological parameters: (i) the order of verb and direct object, (ii) the use of the conjunction 'with' or 'and', the presence or absence (iii) of tense marking and (iv) of case marking, and (iv) the infinite construction for two clauses with different subjects. On the basis of their areal stratifications, Stassen shows that typological collocations and areal configurations of linguistic parameters tend to converge. The paper eventually challenges the view that language typology and areal linguistics should be kept apart and advocates the notion of macro-areas such as Eurasia and sub-Saharan Africa.

In his "Variations of double nominative in Korean and Japanese", Dieter Wunderlich describes the principles governing identical case marking in these two languages (as well as double accusative in the former). He stresses the similarities of double marking in both languages and hypothesises that the two systems did not emerge independently. Constituting a means to create information structure and complex sentences, possessor raising is a prerequisite of the double-nominative. Wunderlich suggests that some putatively universal principles ((i) each case domain contains the default case nominative, (ii) accusative is not available for stative verbs, and (iii) accusative is only assigned once in a given case domain) should be viewed as violable and ranked.

Adrian Czardybon & Jens Fleischhauer ("Definiteness and perfectivity in telic incremental theme predications") elucidate the respective meaning contributions of the definite article and the perfective aspect in indicating telicity in incremental theme predications. They argue that the definite article and perfective aspect, although their effects overlap, serve different semantic functions: The former has the effect of quantization with cumulative nouns, whereas the latter is used to express totality, which requires a quantized incremental theme. Evidence is provided by highlighting the non-redundant co-occurrence in the realization of telic incremental (not inherently quantized) theme predications in Upper Silesian and Bulgarian.

Introduction

Anja Latrouite & Robert D. Van Valin, Jr. ("Referentiality and telicity in Tagalog and Lakhota") examine in how far noun phrase marking and verb marking interact to generate a telic or an atelic interpretation of incremental theme verbs in the Siouan language Lakhota and the Austronesian language Tagalog, each with a determiner system and rich verbal marking. They find that a referential undergoer does not necessarily give rise to a telic reading with such verbs and that factors like the uniqueness (in the sense of Löbner) of the undergoer argument and the voice of the verb may affect the interpretation of a verb as telic or atelic.

Acknowledgements

First of all, we would like to thank those colleagues and scholars who helped the authors improve the papers with their reviews. Special thanks go to Timm Lichte, Friedhelm Sowa, and Ekaterina Gabrovska for implementing the layout. Nick Quaintmere took over the job of proofreading most of the contributions. We are also grateful to the CRC 991 for administrative support. Furthermore, we would like to thank the editors of the series "Studies in Language and Cognition", Hana Filip, Peter Indefrey, Laura Kallmeyer, Gerhard Schurz, and Robert D. Van Valin, Jr., as well as Hans Süssmuth and his team from Düsseldorf University Press (DUP) for their support during the publication process. Finally, we would like to thank all authors for being on time with their papers, which is an essential prerequisite for a festschrift.

Authors

Doris Gerland
Christian Horn
Anja Latrouite
Albert Ortmann
Departement of Linguistics and Information Science
Heinrich-Heine-University Düsseldorf
{gerland,chorn,latrouite,ortmann}@phil.hhu.de

Semantic and grammatical aspects of nouns

Evidence for four basic noun types from a corpus-linguistic and a psycholinguistic perspective

Dorothea Brenner, Peter Indefrey, Christian Horn & Nicolas Kimm

Introduction*

Löbner (2011) proposes a distinction of four basic noun types corresponding to their respective concepts (sortal, relational, functional and individual concepts). A crucial claim of his theory of concept types and determination is that the different noun types are inherently predisposed to certain modes of determination. This paper surveys and discusses the findings from current research on the topic from two research methods that complement each other. First, we report two corpus-linguistic studies on the four noun types that combines an analysis of the different modes of determination with an analysis on associative anaphors in a German text collection. Second, we present a new psycholinguistic study testing reaction times to the noun types with different modes of determination. In all studies evidence was obtained to support the hypothesis that nouns are lexically specified with respect to the conceptual features uniqueness and relationality but that a relatively high proportion of their actual uses is incongruent with their lexical specification. The data are not yet conclusive as to whether or not incongruent uses affect word recognition or involve a cognitive type shift operation as assumed by Löbner (2011).

---

* The research reported in this paper was funded by the Deutsche Forschungsgemeinschaft DFG, CRC 991, member projects C02 "Conceptual Shifts: Statistical Evidence" and C03 "Conceptual Shifts: Psycholinguistic Evidence" (www.sfb991.uni-duesseldorf.de). We would like to express our gratitude to Sebastian Löbner, Wiebke Petersen, Doris Gerland, Anja Latrouite, Elisabeth Morgner, Jessica Nieder, and Fabian Koglin. We would also like to thank two anonymous reviewers for helpful hints and valuable comments.

1 The theory of concept types and determination (CTD)

In his theory of concept types and determination, Löbner (2011) proposes a distinction of four basic noun types: sortal nouns, individual nouns, relational nouns, and functional nouns. The distinction is based on the particular values of two binary properties: inherent (non) relationality [±R][1] and inherent (non)uniqueness [±U]. The distinction between relational nouns (*leg, sister, branch, head*) and nonrelational nouns (*man, stone, snake, Peter*) has long been observed and discussed in the literature (cf. Behaghel 1923, Barker 1995, Partee 1997(1983), Vikner & Jensen 2002), the crucial difference being that relational nouns require the specification of an additional argument ("possessor argument") for reference, whereas nonrelational nouns do not. Vikner & Jensen argue that relational nouns provide an inherent relationship to their respective possessor argument whereas the interpretation of nonrelational nouns is established in the particular context of utterance and may be of various kinds ("lexical interpretation" vs. "pragmatic interpretation", Vikner & Jensen 2002: 195).

The second property ascribed to nouns in CTD is inherent (non)uniqueness. Löbner (2011) argues that nouns can be distinguished into those that are inherently unique (*father, weather, head, Peter*) and those that are nonunique (*sister, man, branch, snake*). The distinction is based on the following assumption (2011: 284): "unique nouns 'say': this is the description of the referent, in the given context of utterance there is exactly one that fits it. [−U] nouns 'say': this is the description of the referent (it need not be unique)." Löbner derives four types of nouns from the potential values of each referential property and claims that their corresponding concept types, i. e., the specific combination of the referential properties [±R] and [±U], are stored in the mental lexicon. Sortal nouns (SC; *stone, flower, car*) are [−R] and [−U], individual nouns (IC; *weather, moon, Peter*) [−R] and [+U], relational nouns (RC; *sister, branch, leg*) [+R] and [−U], and functional nouns (FC; *father, head, president*) [+R] and [+U]. In contrast to relational nouns, functional nouns provide exactly one referent if the possessor is a uniquely determined argument.

On the basis of this noun type (or concept type, respectively) distinction, Löbner (2011) develops a theory that integrates noun semantics and uses of determination. We summarize the major claims that are relevant here as follows: (1) Due to its particular combination of inherent referential properties, each noun type

---

[1] Square brackets indicate referential properties.

is predisposed to certain modes of determination in a language. (2) Many nouns are polysemous, and the different meaning variants of a noun may be of different types. (3) The different modes of determination in a language show inherent predispositions to certain noun types. Löbner classifies a selection of English modes of determination with respect to their congruency with the different noun types. However, the theory explicitly accepts uses that are not in accordance with their predispositions. (4) Matching uses of noun type and mode of determination are called 'congruent', others 'incongruent'. (5) Congruent uses preserve the noun type whereas incongruent uses lead to a type shift. Table 1 lists the modes of determination and indicates whether they are congruent (✓) or incongruent (↱) with the respective noun type.

	[–U]	inherently unique [+U]
[–R]	**Sortal Nouns** *stone book adjective water* ✓ indefinite, plural, quantifier, demonstrative ↱ singular definite ✓ absolute ↱ relational, possessive	**Individual Nouns** *moon weather date Maria* ↱ indefinite, plural, quantifier, demonstrative ✓ singular definite ✓ absolute ↱ relational, possessive
inherently relational [+R]	**Relational Nouns** *sister leg part attribute* ✓ indefinite, plural, quantifier, demonstrative ↱ singular definite ↱ absolute ✓ relational, possessive	**Functional Nouns** *father head age subject* (gramm.) ↱ indefinite, plural, quantifier, demonstrative ✓ singular definite ↱ absolute ✓ relational, possessive

Table 1: Types of nouns and modes of determination (Löbner 2011: 307), ✓ congruent determination, ↱ incongruent determination.

For illustration, consider the following examples for congruent uses in (a) and for incongruent uses in (b):

(1) a. *The father of Peter is tall.*
 b. *A father has called.*

(2) a. *The moon is shining.*
 b. *A moon is shining.*

(3) a. *Martha is a member of the club.*
    b. *Martha is the member.*

(4) a. *He found a stone.*
    b. *He found the stone of Peter's.*

Father is a functional noun and it is used congruently with the definite article and in a possessive construction in (1a). The indefinite and nonpossessive use in (1b), in contrast, is incongruent and yields a type shift of the involved nominal concept. The same contrast holds for the oppositions in (2a)/(2b), (3a)/(3b), and (4a)/(4b): *moon* (individual noun) is used congruently with the definite article and nonpossessive in (2a) but incongruently with the indefinite article in (2b). The relational noun *member* congruently takes the indefinite article in a possessive construction in (3a) whereas (3b) shows an incongruent nonpossessive use with the definite article. *Stone* (sortal noun) is used nonpossessive and indefinite in (4a) but incongruently possessive and with the definite article in (4b).

The overall question that we investigate in this paper is whether the noun type distinction is reflected in language production on the one hand and language comprehension on the other. For that, we report and discuss the results of three different studies: two studies focus on language production and employ corpus-linguistic methods. The third study on language comprehension uses psycholinguistic methods. Section 2 summarizes the method and the results of a statistical analysis of the four noun types and their co-occurrences with different modes of determination in a German text collection as presented in Horn & Kimm (submitted). Section 3 provides the results of an extension of the study (based on the same text collection) to also cover associative anaphors with nominal anchors (Kimm & Horn 2011). Section 4 presents the methods and the results of a psycholinguistic study[2] investigating whether nouns combined with congruent and incongruent determination show differences in reaction times. The investigation of the noun type distinction from the different perspectives and with the different research methods provides the basis for an overall discussion of the findings in Section 5.

---

[2] The considerations as well as the experiment presented in §4 are part of the research on psycholinguistic evidence on concept types conducted by Brenner and Indefrey as part of project C03, CRC991; cf. Brenner (in prep.).

2 Study I: a corpus-based analysis of the concept types and their grammatical use

2.1 Hypothesis and setting

The goal of the study presented in Horn & Kimm (submitted) was to investigate whether evidence for Löbner's (2011) noun type distinction can be found on the basis of a German text collection. The study tested the hypothesis that the four concept types differ with respect to their use with determination classes marking definiteness, number and possession. German is an adequate language of investigation for this task since it provides explicit modes of determination for definiteness (including a definite and an indefinite article), possession (possessive pronouns, left- and right-adjacent possessive constructions) and number (morphological alternation in most cases). The text collection consists of two short stories by anonymous authors and nine newspaper texts from websites of German newspapers. Altogether, the collection consists of 4405 word tokens subsuming 1085 noun tokens.

2.2 Method

The method for the investigation consisted of three major parts. The goal of the first part was to assign the respective concept type to all noun tokens in the texts. This task required several steps which were conducted by five native speakers of German:

(i) Identifying the given meaning variant in the context of utterance. This task turned out to be nontrivial and for unclear cases the Duden dictionary (1997) was consulted for disambiguation.

(ii) Excluding mass nouns (59 nouns) such as *water, rice, metal* since CTD is currently primarily concerned with count nouns. The nouns were assessed based on a combination of criteria such as divisibility, possible plural use, and whether a noun can be combined with the indefinite article without a meaning shift.

(iii) Excluding idiomatic uses (17 nouns) such as *Aus die Maus* 'over and done', lit: 'over the mouse' because they generally occur with fixed determination; here also the Duden (1997) was consulted in problematic cases.

(iv) Determining the referential properties and assignment of the concept type. The team of annotators jointly conducted the annotation of the respective concept type. First, inherent relationality was addressed and each annotator had to decide whether the given meaning variant was [+R] or [−R] based on semantic hints such as the existence of a nonrelational counterpart (as in *mother – woman*), the inherent kind of relationship if applicable (including e. g., part-of, kinship and body-part), or the nominalization of a ditransitive verb (as in *observe – observation*). After that, each annotator decided whether the given meaning variant was inherently unique or nonunique. For a decision on this property, relational and nonrelational nouns were treated separately. For [−R] nouns the annotator was asked whether the given meaning variant was constructed as referring to only one referent, independently of what this referent may be in a given context of utterance. For [+R] nouns the question was whether the meaning variant delivers exactly one referent when its possessor argument is saturated with a uniquely determined referent. If the annotator answered the respective question with "yes" the meaning variant was assigned [+U]. For the following steps of the analysis, only those nouns were taken into account for which the annotators fully agreed with respect to the concept type (resulting in the exclusion of 60 nouns).[3] Nouns with arities greater than two (e. g., *distance* [between A and B]) were excluded (131 meaning variants) since this study concentrated on the four basic concept types. After the application of the four steps, 818 noun tokens remained for further investigation.

The goal of the second part of the investigation was to first collect the modes of determination that occurred in the investigated texts and then classify them in order to determine their inherent congruency with the different referential properties. According to CTD, the modes of determination differ semantically with respect to their preferences for certain concept types. The collected modes of determination were sorted into six determination classes which reflect their congruency with the different predispositions of the concept types, in line with Löbner's (2011) classification of modes of determination in English. [±U] concepts are considered congruent with the following DET_U classes:

- DET_{+U}: modes of determination congruent with [+U] concept types
- DET_0: mode of determination prescribed for certain proper names in standard written German
- DET_{-U}: modes of determination congruent with [−U] concept types

[±R] concepts are considered congruent with the following DET_R classes:

---

[3] The aim of the pilot study was to also clarify the procedure and the relevant criteria, hence, inter-annotator agreement was not measured.

Evidence for four basic noun types

- DET$_{+R}$: modes of determination congruent with [+R] concept types
- DET$_{-R}$: modes of determination congruent with [−R] concept types

[+U][+R] concepts are considered congruent with the following class:

- DET$_{FC}$: modes of determination congruent with functional concept types

The modes of determination congruent with [+U] concept types are subsumed in the class DET$_{+U}$. In German these are the singular definite article, contractions of the definite article and a preposition, and singular possessive pronouns. Furthermore, singular left-adjacent genitive constructions belong to this class since they also exhibit a semantic predisposition for [+U] concepts.

The class DET$_0$ is motivated by certain subtypes of ICs which comprise various proper names such as certain toponyms, personal names and company names. They generally take the null article in written texts (but not necessarily in spoken language). Nouns of this kind are generally subsumed in the class of ICs in CTD and would hence be expected to occur with DET$_{+U}$ determination, contrary to the rules of standard written German. Hence, the group of ICs were split up to sharpen the results: (i) IC$_{+U}$ which are congruent with DET$_{+U}$, and (ii) IC$_0$ which are congruent with DET$_0$.

For all other combinations of definiteness marker and number, at least one component contributes a [−U] property: the indefinite article, demonstratives, numerals, quantifiers and all plurals presuppose nonuniqueness of the potential referent and are hence incongruent with [+U] but congruent with [−U]. Accordingly, these combinations were subsumed in the determination class DET$_{-U}$.

With respect to the [±R] concept type congruency, all modes of possession marking were classified as congruent with [+R] concepts into the determination class DET$_{+R}$. The absence of possession marking exhibits congruency with [−R] concepts and such constructions were hence grouped into DET$_{-R}$.

The class DET$_{FC}$ is inherently congruent only with functional concepts and the modes of determination in this class combine [+U] and [+R] concept congruency and are at the same time also members of DET$_{+U}$ or DET$_{+R}$, respectively. In German, these are singular possessive pronouns and singular left-adjacent possessive constructions; both not only indicate the relation between a possessor and a possessum but also mark the possessum as definite (cf. Barker 2004, Löbner 2011 for the definiteness of possessive pronouns in English; cf. Dobrovie-Sorin 2004 for the definiteness of left-adjacent possessive constructions).

On the basis of the annotated concept types on the one hand and the particular modes of determination on the other, a statistical analysis of their co-occurrences in the texts was conducted (third part of the investigation). The hypothesis investigated was that the concept types occur more often with congruent determination than with incongruent determination. However, the meaning variants were not equally represented in the text collection, i.e., some meaning variants were more frequent than others. In order to avoid the bias of high frequency nouns in the statistical analysis, Horn & Kimm (submitted) took only one occurrence of each meaning variant into account. Since most meaning variants occurred only once, their only common denominator is their first occurrence. These occurrences made up 531 noun tokens.

2.3 Results

The results of the study can be summarized as follows.

1. Both the [±R] and the [±U] distinction were reflected by the data. 59 % of the nouns in the texts were classified as [−R], 41 % as [+R]. 54.4 % of the nouns were assigned [−U] in comparison to 45.6 % as [+U]. The high proportion of [+U] nouns was surprising and to some extent due to differences in the text sorts. Among the newspaper texts, the proportion of ICs was four times higher than among the fictional texts. The second crucial difference between the two text sorts was that the SCs among the fictional texts outnumber those among the newspaper texts by roughly 50 %. The distribution of the concept types in both text sorts together was as follows: individual concepts 19.8 %, functional concepts 25.8 %, relational concepts 15.3 %, sortal concepts 39.2 %.
2. The predicted relation between the concept types and the determination classes was generally confirmed by the data[4]. The semantic distinction between [+U] and [−U] concepts was reflected in the data by their use with DET_U. The semantic distinction between [+R] and [−R] concepts was reflected by their use with DET_R.
3. The congruent and incongruent uses of the concept types were as follows: With respect to DET_U-congruency (cf. Figure 1), the 100 % congruent uses of the IC_0 was not surprising since they follow the rules of standard written German. The more interesting fact was that the proportions of congruent uses of all other concept types ranged between 59.6 % and 74.1 % (SCs 59.6 %,

---

[4] A Pearson's Chi-square test was used to analyze the data (cf. Horn & Kimm, submitted).

RCs 74.1 %, FCs 60.6 %, and IC$_{+U}$ 71.2 %). Altogether, the distribution of the data for DET$_U$ fit with the expectations depicted in CTD.

With respect to DET$_R$-congruency (cf. Figure 2), almost all SCs (93.8 %) and ICs (99.1 %) were used congruently. In contrast, the proportions of congruent DET$_{+R}$ uses dropped to only 35.8 % for functional concepts and 27.2 % for relational concepts.

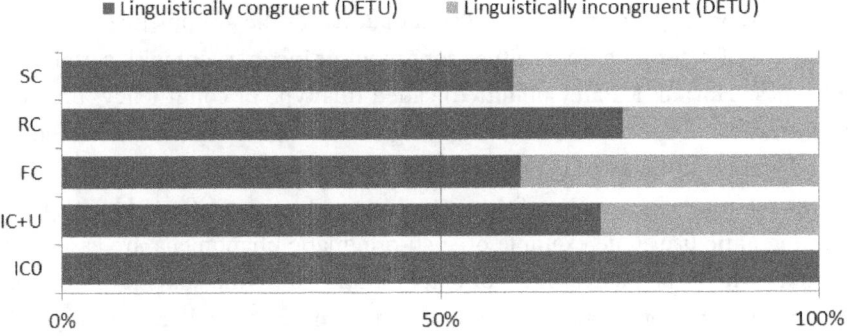

Figure 1: (In)congruent uses of the concept types w.r.t. to DET$_U$.

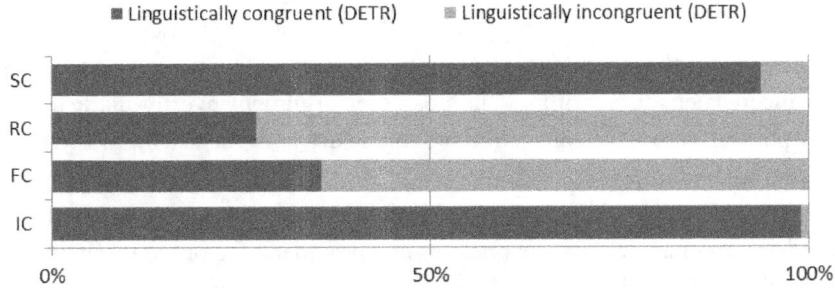

Figure 2: (In)congruent uses of concept types w.r.t. to DET$_R$.

Altogether, the results provided evidence for the assumed noun type distinction. One possible explanation for the relatively low proportion of DET$_{+R}$ uses among [+R] concepts were associative anaphors. The next section presents a follow-up study on this assumption.

3 Study II: a corpus-based analysis of the concept types and associative anaphoric use

3.1 Goal and setting

The previous section showed that two thirds of the [+R] concepts in the text corpus analyzed were used in nonpossessive constructions and hence with incongruent determination. The question arose as to how this high proportion of incongruent uses could be explained.

The kind of congruency described so far addresses the grammatical level only. Each mode of determination is either congruent or incongruent with certain concept types. Horn & Kimm (submitted) called this type of congruency 'linguistic congruency' and contrasted this with 'pragmatic congruency'. Whereas the former addresses all kinds of explicit determination, pragmatic congruency means that the referential properties of the given concept type are reflected by its particular pragmatic use. One example of such pragmatic phenomena are associative anaphors where the possessor argument is saturated by the context of utterance (cf. Löbner 1998 for an account of associative anaphors and concept types; cf. Hawkins 1978 for an account within his theory of definiteness; cf. Prince 1981 for an analysis with respect to the given-new distinction).[5] Poesio & Vieira (1998) showed that such associative anaphors constitute a frequent phenomenon among definite uses. In accordance with Grice's Maxim of Quantity (cf. Grice 1975), possessive constructions can be dropped if the hearer is able to retrieve the possessor argument from the discourse. Hence, an FC or an RC might be used linguistically incongruent (i.e., without the possessor argument overtly marked in the noun phrase) but at the same time pragmatically congruent (if it is used as an associative anaphor).

Kimm & Horn (2011) conducted a follow-up study to investigate whether the consideration of associative anaphors as one pragmatic factor would sharpen the picture for the [±R] distinction. The study focused on associative anaphors with a nominal anchor only (nominal associative anaphors, NAAs) which were defined by the following five conditions (cf. Kimm & Horn 2011: 108):

(i) The referent of the anaphoric NP is determined by associating it with a referent previously introduced in the discourse (this referent is often called the "anchor").

---

[5] Associative Anaphors are also referred to as 'bridging' (cf. Clark 1975), 'indirect anaphora' (cf. Schwarz 2000), 'inferrables' (cf. Prince 1981), and 'contiguity anaphora' (cf. Greber 1993).

(ii) The anchor is given by an NP.
(iii) The reference to the anchor is successful.
(iv) The anaphoric NP may be used with definite or indefinite determination.
(v) Both the anaphoric NP and the anchor do not corefer.

We follow Hirschman (1997) in that two (or more) linguistic expressions are said to corefer if they exhibit identical reference. An example for an NAA is given in (5) where the NP *dem Display* with the FC head noun *Display* constitutes an NAA.

(5) (Anonymous 2010)
Hannes hasste das Lachen mittlerweile, [...] mit dem <u>sein Handy</u>$_{anchor}$ *ihn immer gleich weckte. [...] Er tastete nach* **dem Display**$_{NAA}$ *[...].*
'Hannes began to hate the laughter [...] with which <u>his mobile</u>$_{anchor}$ always woke him up. [...] He felt around for **the display**$_{NAA}$ [...].' (lit.)

In (5), the possessor argument of the FC *Display* is not saturated explicitly in the NP. However, the reader retrieves it from the previous discourse, i.e., the anchor NP *sein Handy*.

Although the literature on associative anaphors primarily addresses those with definite determination (cf. Schwarz 2000), Kimm & Horn (2011) also considered indefinite uses of nouns as potential associative anaphors (cf. Cosse 1996, Löbner 1998), as considered in condition (iv). An example is illustrated in (6).

(6) (Abendblatt 2011)
[...] Ausläufer des Taifuns "Muifa" auf den Philippinen haben am Dienstag auch die <u>Hauptstadt Manila</u>$_{anchor}$ *erreicht. [...] Die heftigen Regenfälle überschwemmten* **viele Straßen**$_{NAA}$ *[...].*
'[...] Offshoots of the typhoon "Muifa" in the Philippines arrived at <u>the capital Manila</u>$_{anchor}$ on Tuesday. [...] Heavy rain flooded **a lot of streets**$_{NAA}$[...].'

In (6), based on his or her knowledge of cities, the reader interprets the referent of the NP *viele Straßen* ('streets', SC) as streets that are part of the aforementioned city Manila. The annotators classified this indefinite NP as an NAA.

3.2 Annotation guidelines

In this second study, a preliminary annotation procedure for the annotation of NAAs was set up consisting of two parts. Part A subsumed the definition of 'markables', i.e., the string on the linguistic surface that was to be annotated.

Part B covered the annotation of NAAs and coreferences. Coreferences were annotated to separate them from NAAs (cf. condition (v)).

In part A, the annotator defined the markables using square brackets. For the purpose of the pilot study, each simple and each complex NP constituted a markable. Simple NPs only consist of a determiner and a noun whereas complex NPs might also subsume pre- and post-modification (e.g., prepositional phrases). Hence, each complex NP might also include other NPs that in turn constitute markables themselves.

Part B covered several steps that were all carried out for each markable previously defined during part A. First, the annotator had to determine whether the markable exhibited identical reference with another markable in the previous discourse. If so, the annotator linked it with the respective markable in the previous discourse. Next, the annotator checked each markable to see whether an additional possessor argument was needed and if so, whether it was provided by an NP in the previous discourse. These markables constituted the set of NAAs. Subsequently, the annotator was to identify the actual anchor for each NAA. In all other cases, the annotator assigned 'other' and proceeded with the next markable.

3.3 Results

The current study was based on the same texts as the one described in Section 2. The annotation of NAAs and coreferences was conducted by two native speakers of German. As pointed out above, this study focused on the first occurrences of meaning variants only in order to analyze the extent to which NAAs can account for the high amount of nonpossessive uses for [+R] concepts. All NPs that were classified as NAAs by both annotators were entered into the study, irrespectively of the anchor chosen. The results for the NAAs are shown in Table (2).

Concept type	DET_{+R}	DET_{-R}	NAA (of DET_{-R} uses)
FC	51	101	47
	33.6 %	66.4 %	46.5 %
RC	20	64	29
	23.8 %	76.2 %	45.3 %
IC	1	108	13
	0.9 %	99.1 %	12.0 %
SC	16	223	55
	6.7 %	93.3 %	24.6 %

Table 2: Concept types and NAAs in the text collection (cf. Kimm & Horn 2011: 114)

Evidence for four basic noun types

Table 2 gives the concept types, their grammatical use regarding possessive marking, and the proportion of NAAs among those that are used with linguistically incongruent DET$_{-R}$. The proportion of NAAs among the nonpossessive uses was 46.5 % for FCs and 45.3 % for RCs. On the other hand, the proportion of NAAs among the nonpossessive uses was 12 % for ICs and 24.6 % for SCs.

The example in (5) above illustrates an FC (*Display*) being used as an NAA. An example for an NAA with an RC as the head noun is given in (7).

(7) (Berliner Zeitung 2011)
Männer in Kaufhäusern$_{anchor}$, *das geht gar nicht. [...] Während Frauen mit wachem Blick zielstrebig und elegant durch* **die Abteilungen**$_{NAA}$ *schreiten, wirken ihre Begleiter gelangweilt, sie schauen mürrisch und völlig uninspiriert.*
'Men in department stores$_{anchor}$, that's a no-no. [...] Whereas women attentively and purposefully stroll **the departments**$_{NAA}$ in an elegant way, their male companions look bored, grumpy and completely uninspired.'

The possessor required by the RC *Abteilung* ('department') is given in the previous discourse by the NP *Kaufhäusern* ('department store'). Examples (5) and (7) show [+R] concepts used as NAAs. However, the results also illustrate that this is not a necessity for a noun, as already shown in (6), where the head noun of the NAA (*street*) is classified as an SC. In (8), the NAA exhibits an IC as the head noun.

(8) (Frankfurter Allgemeine Zeitung 2010)
Computerbild$_{anchor}$ *hat unter Tarnnamen elf Computer zur Reparatur geschickt. Die Redaktion hatte ein Spionageprogramm installiert, das genau aufzeichnete, was der Techniker am PC unternahm. [...] Unabhängig von einer juristischen Würdigung* **dieses investigativen Journalismus**$_{NAA}$ *[...].*
'Computerbild$_{anchor}$ sent eleven computers for repair under assumed names. The editorial department had installed a spy program that precisely tracked what the technicians did with the computer. [...] Irrespective of a legal evaluation of **this investigative journalism**$_{NAA}$ [...].'

The annotators determined the reference of the NP *dieses investigativen Journalismus* ('this investigative journalism') by associating it with the NP *Computerbild* (author's note: a German computer magazine) in the previous discourse.

However, although both [+R] and [−R] concepts occur as NAAs, the results illustrate that the referential properties of a noun do in fact influence the probability of its being used as an associative anaphor. The proportion of NAAs was much higher among [+R] concepts than among [−R] concepts. Hence, FCs and RCs were more often used as associative anaphors in the text collection than their nonrelational counterparts SCs and ICs. Figure 3 illustrates the data for the overall congruency subsuming DET_R uses and the use as NAAs. The integration of NAAs increased the overall congruency of [+R] concepts by almost 50 % since NAAs are considered pragmatically congruent for [+R] concepts. Hence, roughly two third of the FCs and RCs exhibit overall congruency. The decrease of the overall congruency for [−R] concepts on the other hand, was only 25 % (SCs) or 10 % (ICs), respectively. The possessor argument that is retrieved by the reader from the previous discourse in case of an NAA does not match their [−R] property. However, nine out of ten ICs and roughly two-thirds of SCs still exhibit overall congruency. In summary, it turned out that the pragmatic level contributes essentially to the overall congruency of the concept types.

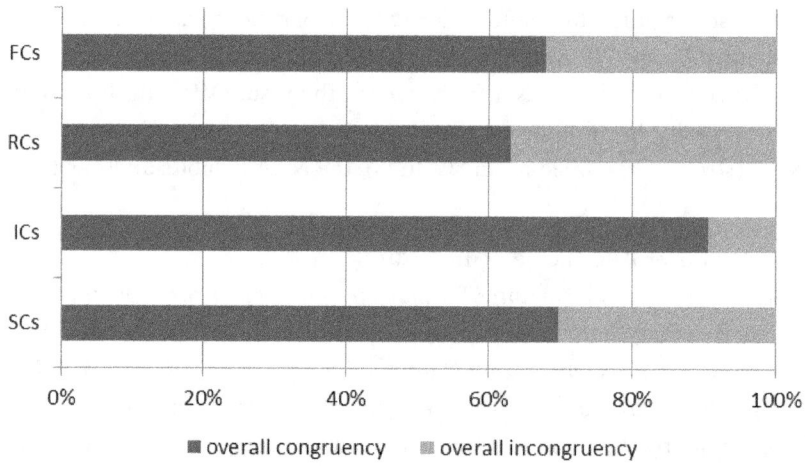

Figure 3: DET_R and NAA uses of concept types combined.

Altogether, the results presented in Sections 2 and 3 provide evidence for the concept type distinction on the basis of an analysis of texts as outcomes of language production. The following section inverts this perspective to an investigation of language comprehension. We present a psycholinguistic experiment that was conducted to detect a possible concept type congruency effect in language comprehension and thus to complement the corpus-linguistic findings from a different perspective.

4 Psycholinguistic investigation of CTD

As shown in the previous sections, nouns are used in the majority of the cases with the mode of determination corresponding to their lexically specified concept type as predicted by CTD. Nonetheless, the observed relatively high proportion of incongruent uses may be seen as evidence against a lexical specification of concept types (let us call this hypothesis 1). Then, however, the high proportion of congruent uses on the one hand and the semantic judgments by the annotators (i.e., the concept type annotation, cf. step (iv) in Section 2) would require a plausible explanation. The alternative hypothesis postulates that concept type information is lexically stored and allows for two possibilities: (i) nouns are flexible with respect to the mode of determination they combine with; CTD allows for such flexibility by assuming type shifts (cf. Section 1). Alternatively, (ii) more than one (or all) concept type(s) for each noun, ranked by their activation level, for example, due to different frequencies of occurrence (higher frequency of occurrence means faster and stronger activation in the mental lexicon) might be represented in the lexicon.

These accounts make different predictions with respect to potential processing costs arising for incongruent determination type and concept type combinations. If the concept types were not lexically specified at all (hypothesis 1), there would be no distinction between congruent and incongruent determination and hence no extra processing costs measurable for "incongruent" determination. On the other hand, if the concept types are stored in the mental lexicon (hypothesis 2), the cognitive processes involved may lead to a measurable congruency effect in language comprehension. Two predictions can be made. First, type shifts may require a cognitive operation that could be more time consuming than unshifted uses and lead to a measurable delay in the processing of incongruent determiner-noun combinations. Second, unshifted uses may profit from certain accelerating processes due to congruent determination which result in faster reaction times. In other words, there should be a concept type congruency effect with longer reaction times for incongruent uses as compared to congruent determination in certain standard psycholinguistic paradigms, such as lexical decision. A concept type congruency effect should also be observed in the case of lexical specification of more than one concept type (the higher the ranking of a concept type, the faster its processing).

A first psycholinguistic experiment[6] attempted to demonstrate the presence or absence of a concept type congruency effect. The experiment used an auditory lexical decision paradigm with German noun phrases manipulating the combination of mode of determination and the four noun types to explore the influence of (in)congruency on spoken word recognition.

4.1 Method

Materials and experimental set-up. The study tested 96 native speakers of German who were mostly students at Heinrich Heine University Düsseldorf, Germany, and who were paid a small fee for their participation (mean age 24.01 years, SD 6.78; 54 women, 42 men).

A set of 80 nouns (20 nouns from each concept type (see table 3 for examples)) was chosen based on the semantic evaluation of three linguists and native speakers of German. Between the four concept type groups frequency of occurrence in CELEX database (Baayen, Piepenbrock & Gulikers 1995), the number of phonemes and number of syllables were counterbalanced. Lexical features other than *concept type* were not taken into account, as the task was not to make a semantic decision on the nouns, where other lexical features like 'animacy' or 'concreteness' might influence reaction times, but to perform a mere lexical decision, where these lexical features do not play an equally big role for the reaction times.

To balance the number of correct 'word' and 'pseudoword' lexical decision responses, the stimulus lists contained 80 additional pseudowords (nonwords following the phonotactic rules of German). Across all four lists, each noun (or pseudoword) was combined with all determiners but was presented in only one variant per participant. The following determiners were chosen to represent examples of 3 different modes of determination (cf. Section 2): the indefinite article *ein(e)* for DET_{-U}, the definite article *der/die/das* for DET_{+U} and the 3rd person possessive pronoun *sein(e)* for DET_{+R}. For the "no" determiner control condition a 400 ms noise stimulus was used. Table 3 shows examples of the concept type and determination mode combinations that were used. Congruent combinations are marked by "✓", whereas incongruent combinations are marked by "↦".

---

[6] cf. Brenner (in prep.).

Evidence for four basic noun types

	[−U]	inherently unique [+U]
[−R]	**Apfel** ('apple') – SC ✓ *ein Apfel* ↪ *der Apfel* ↪ *sein Apfel* xxxx *Apfel*	**Papst** ('pope') – IC ↪ *ein Papst* ✓ *der Papst* ↪ *sein Papst* xxxx *Papst*
inherently relational [+R]	**Arm** ('arm') – RC ✓ *ein Arm* ↪ *der Arm* ✓ *sein Arm* xxxx *Arm*	**Mutter** ('mother') – FC ↪ *eine Mutter* ✓ *die Mutter* ✓ *seine Mutter* xxxx *Mutter*

Table 3: Example stimuli from auditory lexical decision task.

All items (nouns, pseudowords, and articles (except for the "neutral" determiner stimulus)) were spoken by a male German native speaker in a soundproof booth. For the recording of the stimuli, a Sennheiser ME64 microphone head and a Sennheiser K6 powering module that was linked directly to a PC were used. The stimuli were digitally recorded with a sampling rate of *44.1 kHz* and a 16-bit (mono) sample size using Audacity 1.3[7] software. The recorded files were stored on a computer hard drive for further processing. The sound files were edited into separate files for each stimulus and cut at zero crossings of onset and offset of each item under visual and auditory control using Audacity 1.3 and Adobe® Audition 3.0[8]. The neutral stimulus was constructed by using white noise with the same length as the mean length of the real determiner stimuli. All items were converted to WAV files for presentation. Determiner (or noise) and noun or pseudoword stimuli were combined by the experimental software (see below) according to the input lists.

The input for the experimental software consisted of four basic lists of determiner-noun pairs with each noun occurring only once per list, i.e., with only one of the four determiner types (indefinite, definite, possessive or neutral). The determiner types were counterbalanced across lists, concept types and all targets. Across all four lists, each noun was combined with each determination type. The same set of pseudoword stimuli was mixed into each of the four lists. The

---

[7] http://audacity.sourceforge.net/
[8] http://www.adobe.com/de/products/audition.html

lists were pseudorandomized so that no more than three 'word' or 'pseudoword' answers followed each other. Care was also taken to ensure that no more than three trials using the same concept type or mode of determination followed each other. In total, four randomized versions of each list were created. All lists were preceded by 20 practice trials.

The experiment was run using the experimental software Presentation®[9] on a PC. The stimuli were selected and combined for each trial by the experimental software according to the selected input list. A warning (beep) sound of 260 ms marked the beginning of each trial, after 400 ms it was followed by one of the determiners. The auditory target stimulus followed 400 ms after the offset of the determiner. After the participants' button press (or after a timeout of 5000 ms if no response was made) and a 1000 ms pause the following trial began.

The participants were seated in a soundproof booth. The stimuli were presented aurally via headphones (Sennheiser HD 437, mono signal). The participants were instructed to perform a lexical decision ("word or nonword?") on the nouns as quickly and as accurately as possible by pressing assigned buttons on a response pad that was connected to Presentation® in order to record the reaction times. The reaction times were recorded from noun onset up to the participants' button press.

4.2 Results

Pseudowords, errors and timeouts (RT longer than 5000 ms) were excluded from all analyses (overall error and timeout rate: 1.4 %). Separate analyses of variance (ANOVA) first tested for an effect of the factor congruency (congruent determination, incongruent determination, no determination) on lexical decision times. Congruent determination was defined according to CTD (see table 1 and 3). To determine whether the observed congruency effect was due to congruency with respect to uniqueness, relationality, or both, the data were then tested for effects and interactions of the factors uniqueness (unique, nonunique) and mode of determination (indefinite, definite, none) as well as relationality (relational, nonrelational) and mode of determination (possessive, none).

As reaction time (RT) differences between concept types were irrelevant and, more importantly, the concept types were not equally distributed over conditions (cf. Table 3), a linear normalization ($RT_{norm}=RT*RT$ mean/RT mean per concept

---

[9] http://www.neurobs.com/

type) was applied to minimize mean reaction time differences between the four concept types.

Congruency. The reaction time data showed a significant congruency effect across participants [$F_1(94)=12.387$, p=.000] (cf. Figure 4) and across items [$F_2(78)=22,677$, p=.000]. Post-hoc comparisons (with Bonferroni's α-correction) showed that nouns presented with a preceding congruent determiner yielded faster responses than incongruent determiner-noun combinations (p=.000) or nouns presented with noise (i. e., no determination, p=.001). No significant difference between incongruent vs. no determination was found (p=1.0). Note that, due to the restrictive experimental setup in this experiment, only linguistic congruency (as defined in Section 2) was tested.

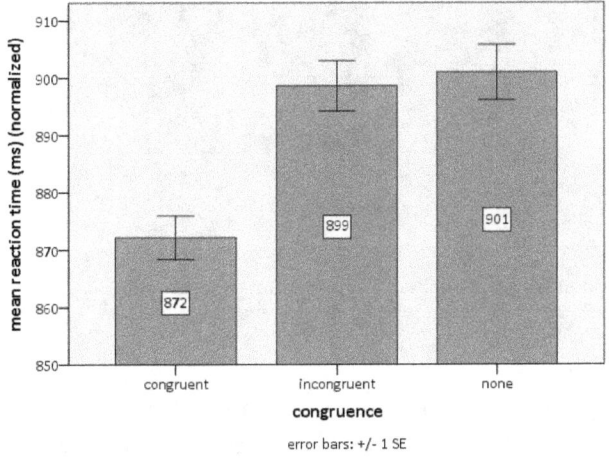

Figure 4: Mean normalized lexical decision times for congruent, incongruent and no determination across participants.

Uniqueness and (in)definite determination. The analysis of the combinations of the factors uniqueness and mode of determination (indefinite, definite, none) yielded a significant interaction effect across participants [$F_1(94)=9.47$, p=.000] (cf. Figure 5) and across items [$F_2(77)=6.373$, p=.003]. Separate analyses for unique (individual, functional) and nonunique (sortal, relational) nouns showed that the reaction to [+U] nouns was faster if combined with a definite article rather than with an indefinite article (p=.001) or the neutral stimulus (p=.006). No reaction time difference between [+U] nouns with a preceding indefinite article could be found in comparison to no determiner (p>.05). For [–U] nouns, the analysis revealed significantly faster reaction times when combined with the indefinite article rather than with no determiner (p=.014). Reaction time differences between the indefinite vs. the definite article and between the definite article and no determiner did not reach significance (p>.05).

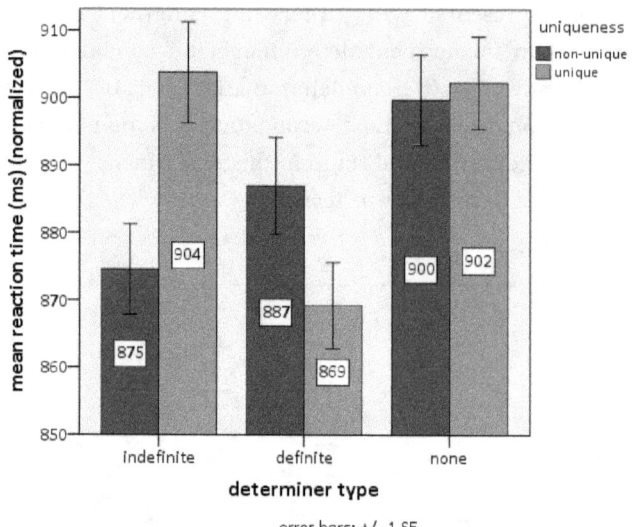

Figure 5: Mean normalized lexical decision times for unique (individual, functional) and nonunique nouns (sortal, relational) following indefinite, definite, or no determiner (across participants).

Relationality and possessive determination. The ANOVA for the relationality feature also yielded a significant interaction effect between determination type and relationality across participants [F1(95)=8.476, p=.004] (cf. Figure 6) and across items [F2(78)=10.741, p=.002]. As a follow-up, separate one-way repeated measures ANOVAs for relational (functional and relational) and nonrelational (sortal, individual) nouns revealed significantly faster reaction times for [+R] nouns following possessive determination in comparison to none (p=.001). For [–R] nouns no reliable difference between the use with possessive vs. no determination was found (p<.05).

Discussion. The lexical decision time data showed a concept type congruency effect with congruent determiner-noun combinations resulting in approximately 30 ms shorter reaction times compared to the no determiner condition. Separate analyses of the factors uniqueness and relationality showed that the congruency

Evidence for four basic noun types

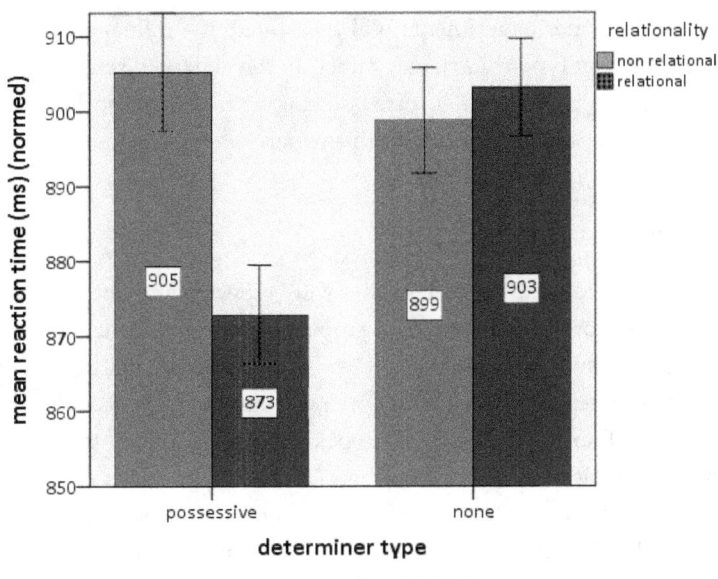

Figure 6: Mean normalized lexical decision times for relational (functional, relational) and non-relational nouns (sortal, individual) following possessive determiner or no determiner.

effect was carried by both factors. For German, at least, this result rules out the possibility that nouns might be lexically unspecified for uniqueness and relationality, as in this case they should combine equally well with all modes of determination to create noun phrases with [±R] and [±U] readings. Instead, the results favor a lexical specification of a noun's uniqueness and relationality as assumed by CTD. Based on this one experiment alone, nothing conclusive can be stated as to whether the observed congruency effect occurs due to faster lexical access to congruently used nouns (favoring ranked lexical specifications of more than one concept type per noun) or due to a delayed response to incongruent nouns undergoing a type shift operation.

Although at first glance these data seem to favor a facilitation for congruent nouns, it should be noted that the reaction times likely include a gender priming effect (Bölte & Connine 2004), because both congruent and incongruent determiners but not the control condition (no determiner) provided correct grammatical gender information. Depending on the size of the gender priming effect, the observed facilitation might be in part or fully explained by gender priming, such that the concept type congruency effect would, to a corresponding degree, be an inhibition by incongruent determination rather than facilitation by congruent determination. Further experiments will investigate the influence of the gender effect on the concept type congruency effect. In the general discussion below, the observed congruency effect will be discussed taking into account the independent corpus-statistical evidence reported in this paper.

5 General discussion

In this article, two corpuslinguistic studies were reported and one new psycholinguistic study were presented to provide empirical evidence about central assumptions of CTD. The corpus-linguistic studies investigated the matter from the perspective of language production based on a German text corpus. The first study investigated whether the four concept types differ with respect to their use with congruent vs. incongruent determination. The results provided evidence for the noun type distinction based on an investigation of the respective referential features [±R] and [±U] and showed that congruent uses were more frequent for three out of four property values. However, [+R] concepts turned out to be used congruently only in roughly one-third of the cases. This finding gave rise to the second study which showed that about half of the linguistically incongruent uses of [+R] concept types were associative anaphors with NP-external nominal anchors (NAAs). These could be accounted for as being pragmatically congruent by virtue of the preceding anchor noun phrase filling the possessor argument slot. From the perspective of language comprehension, the third study used an experimental paradigm investigating lexical decision latencies for nouns preceded by congruent and incongruent determination. The results showed that congruent uses were recognized faster than incongruent determiner-noun combinations and hence provided further evidence for the noun type distinction.

The corpus-linguistic method allows for an analysis of nouns in the natural contexts they occur with. However, the use of natural language can be difficult since there might be numerous other (especially pragmatic) phenomena that might influence the use of the noun (e. g. the use of the definite article in the case of co-referential uses). The researcher cannot control the kinds of nouns she will find nor the contexts in which the nouns occur. This makes such studies also very complex: a prerequisite is to have a procedure that allows to cover all kinds of variation that may show up. From the results found, no direct link to psycholinguistic processes can be drawn: the results might indicate such mental processes but cannot exclude other explanations without any doubt. The psycholinguistic method uses laboratory conditions and hence controls the influence of other phenomena which allows us to gain insights into cognitive processes. On the other hand, the psycholinguistic experiment presented here is limited with respect to the number of nouns tested and focuses on prototypical nouns only. Here the benefit from corpus-linguistic studies comes into play: each noun token is analyzed and thereby each noun has a direct influence on the results, irrespective of the prototypicality of the noun. Taking the advantages of both approaches together, the studies presented here complement each other not only on the basis of their results but also with respect to their method.

Our results support the distinction between "proper" relational *(sister, head)* and nonrelational *(stone, pope)* nouns which has widely been accepted in the literature (cf. Section 1). From the corpus-linguistic perspective, the distinction is supported by the distribution of the [+R] vs. [−R] concepts in the analyzed texts. From the psycholinguistic perspective, the difference in reaction times between [+R] and [−R] nouns in possessive determination contexts also strengthens this distinction. The distinction of nouns into those that are inherently unique *(head, pope)* and those that are inherently nonunique *(sister, stone)* was introduced in CTD (cf. Section 1). Again our investigation provided evidence from two perspectives: the psycholinguistic data presented here mirror this distinction in terms of differences in reaction times. These findings are in line with an electrophysiological study by Burkhardt (2008), who showed that the interpretation of inherently unique nouns in definite NPs requires less cognitive effort than the interpretation of nonunique nouns in definite NPs[10]. In the text corpus, [+U] and [−U] concepts are even more equally distributed than the [±R] concepts are. The proportion of 25.8 % functional concepts (compared to 15.3 % relational concepts) is surprisingly high and also questions their neglected status in the literature, e. g., Partee & Borschev (2012: 445) who assumes that "Among the semantic types that nouns can take on, functional types are the smallest class, and functional nouns are probably not a linguistically distinct subcategory [...]".

A question that arises from these findings is: what consequences can be drawn for theories on definiteness and reference? Several theories have been proposed including the classical approaches on uniqueness (Russell 1905) and inclusiveness (Hawkins 1978), familiarity (Christophersen 1939, Bolinger 1977, Heim 1982, Prince 1992) and identifiability (Birner & Ward 1998, Lyons 1999) and more re-

---

[10] Following Löbner (1985), Burkhardt uses the terms 'semantic definites' for inherently unique nouns and 'pragmatic definites' for inherently nonunique nouns.

cent approaches with an emphasis on the cognitive status of determination (Ariel 1990, Gundel et al. 1993). All of these theories focus on the definite article (and as such on the role of definiteness marking) as the central component of definites and uniquely referring expressions and use it as the starting point of their considerations. Bolinger (1977) proposes to give up the assumption that there is one property that applies to all definite NPs in the same way. He proposes distinguishing between the grammatical marking of definiteness on the one hand and unique reference on the other. In the light of our results, we can go one step further. Our data show that the inherent uniqueness of certain nominal concepts plays a more important role than considered in the theoretical approaches mentioned and rather support the account of CTD. Since roughly half of the annotated nouns in the corpus are inherently unique, their use with definite determination is redundant from a referential perspective (but still necessary with respect to language specific marking on the uniqueness scale).[11]

Since [±R] and [±U] are seen as inherent properties of concepts, they must be stored in the mental lexicon. As a consequence, the assumption that concept type information is not lexicalized can be rejected. However, it is less clear whether exactly one or more than one concept type is lexically specified for each meaning variant of a noun. In order to clarify this point, further investigations of corresponding linguistic phenomena and psycholinguistic experiments are necessary. One additional linguistic explanation for the high proportion of DET_{-R} uses of [+R] concepts (besides NAAs) may be associative anaphors with nonnominal anchors, for example, with the anchor provided by a VP as in (9) where *the door* is interpreted as the door of the house to which the aforementioned man returned from work.

(9) *A man returned from work and opened* ***the door.***

A possible explanation for DET_{+U} uses of [–U] concepts are coreferential cases where a referent that has already been introduced in the preceding discourse of utterance is taken up by a definite NP (*an animal$_i$... the dog$_i$...*). These and other phenomena might also account for a good proportion of incongruent uses for all kinds of nouns and hence would argue in favor of a specification of only one concept type.

---

[11] cf. Gerland & Horn (2010), Löbner (2011), and Ortmann (2014) for the distinction between 'semantic uniqueness' and 'pragmatic uniqueness'. Cf. Löbner (2011) and Ortmann (2014) for considerations on the uniqueness scale.

Further psycholinguistic investigation might clarify whether the differences in reaction times that were found between congruent and incongruent cases are the result of one of the following two factors or a combination of both: (i) a facilitation of noun recognition by congruent determiners due to a higher frequency (and thus higher ranking) of one of the (possibly multiple) stored concept types or (ii) an inhibition by incongruent uses due to additional time-consuming cognitive operations – namely type shifts – to change the respective lexically specified concept type, as assumed by the CTD. So far, the results favor facilitation by congruent determination, but since we are aware of an interacting gender effect (cf. Section 4), further experiments will be conducted to distinguish the influence of gender information from that of the concept type congruency effect. Finally, in order to identify the event-related potential component(s) sensitive to concept type (in)congruency, and electrophysiological paradigms will be employed.

6 Conclusion

In this paper, we reported two corpus-linguistic studies and presented the results of an additionally conducted psycholinguistic experiment investigating the distinction of four basic concept types as proposed by the Theory of Concept Types and Determination. The first study investigated whether the concept types differ with respect to their use with congruent vs. incongruent determination in a collection of German texts. The second study analyzed the extent to which associative anaphors with nominal anchors can account for a large proportion of incongruent uses of functional and relation concepts that occurred in the first study. The psycholinguistic study investigated lexical decision latencies for nouns preceded by congruent and incongruent determination. The results provide evidence both for the (non)relationality distinction and for the (non)uniqueness distinction and consequently for the four basic concept types.

Bibliography

Abendblatt. 2011. (Access: August 2, 2011). http://www.abendblatt.de/vermischt es/article1977661/Taifun-Auslaeufer-erreichen-Manila-noch-mehr-Tote.html.

Anonymous. 2010. Einer den Anderen. (Access: July 10, 2010). http://www.kurz geschichten.de.

Ariel, M. 1990. *Accessing NP antecedents*. London: Routledge.

Baayen, R. H., R. Piepenbrock & L. Gulikers. 1995. The CELEX lexical database. CD-ROM, Linguistic Data Consortium. University of Pennsylvania, Philadelphia.

Barker, C. 1995. *Possessive descriptions*. Stanford: CSLI Publications.

Barker, C. 2004. Possessive weak definites. In J.-Y. Kim, Y. A. Lander & B. H. Partee (eds.), *Possessives and beyond: Semantics and syntax*, 89–113. Amherst, MA: GLSA Publications.

Behaghel, O. 1923. *Deutsche Syntax. Eine geschichtliche Darstellung. Bd. I: Die Wortklassen und Wortformen. A. Nomen. Pronomen.* Heidelberg: Carl Winters Universitätsbuchhandlung.

Berliner Zeitung. 2011. http://www.berliner-zeitung.de/archiv/entwuerdigende-begleiter,10810590,10946740.html.

Birner, B. J. & G. Ward. 1998. *Informational status and noncanonical word order*. Philadelphia: John Benjamins.

Bolinger, D. 1977. There. In *Meaning and form*, 90–123. London: Longman.

Brenner, D. in prep. Why his mother is better than a mother. University of Düsseldorf.

Burkhardt, P. 2008. Two types of definites: Evidence for presupposition cost. In A. Grønn (ed.), *Proceedings of SuB12*, 66–80. Oslo: ILOS 2008.

Bölte, J. & C. M. Connine. 2004. Grammatical gender in spoken word recognition in German. *Perception and Psychophysics* 66. 1018–1032.

Christophersen, P. 1939. *The articles. A study of their theory and use in English*. Copenhagen: Munksgaard.

Clark, H. H. 1975. Bridging. In R.C. Schank & B.L. Nash-Webber (eds.), *Theoretical issues in natural language processing*, 169–174. New York: Association for Computing Machinery.

Cosse, M. 1996. Indefinite associative anaphora in French. Presentation held at the workshop "Indirect Anaphora". Lancaster, UK.

Dobrovie-Sorin, C. 2004. Genitives and determiners. In J.-Y. Kim, Y. A. Lander & B. H. Partee (eds.), *Possessives and beyond: Semantics and syntax*, 115–132. Amherst, MA: GLSA Publications.

Duden. 1997. Duden Universalwörterbuch A–Z. 3rd edition. Mannheim: Bibliographisches Institut und Brockhaus.

Frankfurter Allgemeine Zeitung. 2010. http://www.faz.net/aktuell/technik-motor/computer-internet/defekte-pcs-spione-in-der-werkstatt-1608026.html.

Gerland, D. & C. Horn. 2010. Referential properties of nouns across languages. In Y.-S. Kang, J.-Y. Yoon, J. Hong, J.-S. Wu, S. Rhee, K.-A. Kim, D.-H. Choi,

K.-H. Kim & H.-K. Kang (eds.), *Universal grammar and individual languages. Proceedings of SICOL 2010*, Seoul: University of Korea.

Greber, E. 1993. Zur Neubestimmung von Kontiguitätsanaphern. *Sprachwissenschaft* 18. 361–405.

Grice, H. P. 1975. Logic and conversation. In P. Cole & J. Morgan (eds.), *Speech acts (syntax and semantics 3)*, 41–58. New York: Academic Press.

Gundel, J. K., N. Hedberg & R. Zacharski. 1993. Cognitive status and the form of referring expressions in discourse. *Language* 69–2. 274–307.

Hawkins, J. A. 1978. *Definiteness and indefiniteness: a study in reference and grammaticality prediction*. London: Croom Helm.

Heim, I. 1982. The semantics of definite and indefinite noun phrases. Dissertation. In *Schriftenreihe des Sonderforschungsbereichs 99, Linguistik* 73. Konstanz: Universität Konstanz.

Hirschman, L. 1997. MUC-7 coreference task definition, version 3.0. In *Proceedings of MUC-7*.

Horn, C. & N. Kimm. submitted. Linguistic congruency of concept types in German texts. In C. Bretones Callejas & C. Sinha (ed.), *Construals in language and thought: What shapes what?*. Philadelphia: John Benjamins Publishing.

Kimm, N. & C. Horn. 2011. Nominal associative anaphors – a text-based analysis at the semantics-pragmatics interface. In I. Hendrickx, S. Lalitha Devi, A. Branco & R. Mitkov (eds.), *Anaphora processing and applications*, 108–118. Faro, Portugal. 8th Discourse Anaphora and Anaphor Resolution Colloquium, DAARC 2011.

Lyons, C. 1999. *Definiteness*. Cambridge: Cambridge University Press.

Löbner, S. 1985. Definites. *Journal of Semantics* 4. 279–326.

Löbner, S. 1998. Definite associative anaphora. In S. Botley (ed.), *Approaches to discourse anaphora. proceedings of daarc96 - discourse anaphora and resolution colloquium* UCREL Technical Papers Series, Vol. 8. Lancaster: Lancaster University.

Löbner, S. 2011. Concept types and determination. *Journal of Semantics* 28(3). 279–333.

Ortmann, A. 2014. Definite article asymmetries and concept types: semantic and pragmatic uniqueness. In T. Gamerschlag, D. Gerland, R. Osswald & W. Petersen (eds.), *Frames and concept types. Applications in language and philosophy*, 293–321. Dordrecht: Springer.

Partee, B. H. 1997 (1983). Genitives–a case study. In J. van Benthem & A. ter-Meulen (eds.), *Compositionality. The handbook of logic and language.*, 464–470. Cambridge, MA: Elsevier.

Partee, B. H. & V. Borschev. 2012. Sortal, relational, and functional interpretations of nouns and Russian container constructions. *Journal of Semantics* 29(4). 445–486.

Poesio, M. & R. Vieira. 1998. A corpus-based investigation of definite description use. *Computational Linguistics* 24(2). 183–216.

Prince, E. F. 1981. Toward a taxonomy of given-new information. In P. Cole (ed.), *Radical pragmatics*, 223–256. NY: Academic Press.

Prince, E. F. 1992. The ZPG letter: Subjects, definiteness, and information status. In W. C. Mann & S. A. Thompson (eds.), *Discourse description: Diverse linguistic analyses of a fund-raising text*, 295–326. Philadelphia: John Benjamins.

Russell, B. 1905. On denoting. *Mind* 14. 479–493.

Schwarz, M. 2000. *Indirekte Anaphern in Texten. Studien zur domänengebundenen Kohärenz und Referenz im Deutschen.* Tübingen: Niemeyer.

Vikner, C. & P. A. Jensen. 2002. A semantic analysis of the English genitive. Interaction of lexical and formal semantics. *Studia Linguistica* 56. 191–226.

Authors

Dorothea Brenner
Christian Horn
Nicolas Kimm
Peter Indefrey
Departement of Linguistics and Information Science
Heinrich-Heine-University Düsseldorf
{brennerth,chorn,kimm,indefrey}@phil.hhu.de

Type shifts and noun class changes under determination in Teop

Ulrike Mosel

1 Introduction*

This paper investigates the correlations between the four conceptual types of nouns identified by Löbner (2011) and the three noun classes of the Oceanic language Teop[1] and their subclasses. Both kinds of classification make use of the distinctive binary features [± unique] and [± relational], abbreviated as [±U] and [± R]. But the Teop noun class system does not fully match with the system of conceptual types. Some mismatches can be attributed to the semantic feature [±human] that overrules the features [±U] and [± R]; others may perhaps originate from historical developments of the language.

The conceptual lexical types of nouns, here exemplified by Teop examples, are as follows:

1. individual nouns, i.e. inherently unique non-relational nouns [+U, -R], e.g. *Naphtali, Ruth, iaa* 'Mum', *sivao* 'moon', *Teapu* 'Teop Island';
2. functional nouns, i.e. inherently unique relational noun [+U, +R], e.g. *tama-* 'father', *kahoo* 'head';
3. relational nouns, i.e. inherently relational non-unique nouns [-U, +R], e.g. *kuri-* 'hand', *vavina-* 'sibling of the opposite sex';

---

* I am grateful to Sebastian Löbner and his research team for introducing me to their inspiring semantic theory, the Volkswagenstiftung who funded the Teop Language Documentation project from 2000 to 2007, and the Teop speakers who taught me their language. Many thanks also to the two anonymous reviewers who helped me to avoid shortcomings. The responsibility for all remaining errors rests with me.

[1] For a more detailed classification see Ross (1988: 251–253).

4. sortal nouns, i.e. inherently non-unique non-relational nouns [-U, - R], e.g. *siisia* 'teacher', *moon* 'woman', *naono* 'tree'.

The three Teop noun classes are formally distinguished by three sets of articles in unmarked NP constructions. As the forms of these articles are *e/bene*, *a/bona*, and *o/bono* (see Table 1), the noun classes are simply called the e-, the a- and the o-classes.

In NP constructions, determiners may change the head noun's inherent conceptual type when, for example, a sortal noun is determined by an anaphoric demonstrative and thus unequivocally refers to an individual concept. Modes of determination that lead to a conceptual type shift are classified as incongruent determinations and those that don't as congruent determinations (Löbner 2011: § 5).

In Teop, one congruent mode of determination is, for example, the inalienable possessive construction of a unique body part term (1).

(1) *a   kahoo-na   =e*
    ART2.SG head-3SG.POSS =3SG.PRON
    'its head' (Hel_13RG.009)

In this construction, the body part term belongs to the a-class. But when it is used without the possessive determiner and consequently becomes a non-relational sortal noun, it is assigned to the o-class:

(2) *paa ani bono   kahoo*
    TAM eat OBJ.ART3.SG head
    '(she) ate the head' (Ata_01R.081)

In order to explore the question to what extent the Teop noun classes and noun class changes can be related to conceptual types and type shifts, the subsequent sections of this paper are structured as follows: § 2 describes the Teop article paradigm and compares the three Teop noun classes with the four conceptual types of nouns. § 3 presents a brief overview of the structure of the NP, § 4 deals with the distinction of definite and indefinite noun phrases, § 5 with possessive constructions and § 6 with the expression of plurality. The final section § 7 gives a summary of Teop noun class changes and compares them with conceptual type shifts.

My analysis is based on the consistently growing Teop Language Documentation Corpus (Mosel & Thiesen 2007) that is compiled in ELAN[2] and consists of

---

[2] http://tla.mpi.nl/tools/tla-tools/

spontaneously spoken narratives and descriptions (abbr. R), edited versions of the transcriptions (abbr. E) and written texts that were not derived from previous recordings (abbr. W).

2 Teop articles and the classification of nouns

The Teop articles form a multidimensional asymmetric paradigm that distinguishes three noun classes, singular and plural, objects and non-objects, and three referential categories:

articles	e-articles (ART1) singular	plural	a-articles (ART2) singular	plural	o-article (ART3) singular	plural	abbr.
specific basic article	e	ere	a	o	o	a	
specific object article	bone, bene	bere, benere	bona	bono	bono	bona	OBJ.ART
non-specific article	–	–	ta	to	to	ta	NSPEC.ART
partitive article	–	–			sa		PART.ART

Table 1: The paradigm of Teop articles

The specific object articles are only used with non-topical objects in clauses with a third-person subject. If the subject refers to a speech act participant or if the object is the topic of the clause, it is marked by the basic article (for further information see Mosel 2010b and Mosel 2010a).

The remainder of this section analyses two NP constructions without any articles (§ 2.1), gives an overview of the Teop noun classes and the corresponding conceptual types of nouns (§ 2.2), and briefly describes the structure of the noun phrase (§ 2.3). Due to limitations in space, the use of the partitive article is not analysed in this paper.

2.1 Nominal arguments and adverbials without articles

NPs with an argument function are usually marked by an article, but in fast, spontaneous spoken language the article may be dropped with NPs in clause-initial position. The article is obligatorily absent in vocative phrases with proper names and common nouns, e. g.

(3) O   Taguone! Nomaa a-re   voosu!
    VOC³ PN   come   1PL.IN.PRON-CONSEC go.home
    'Oh Taguone! Come, let's go home! Come quickly!' (Iar_02E(Eno).078)

(4) Si   otei ean   sa antee haa tea   vaa- kuu anaa   …!
    DIM man 2SG.PRON NEG can NEG COMP CAUS- fall 1SG.OBJ.PRON
    'Dear man, you cannot make me fall down (from the tree)!' (Gol_01R.006)

(5) Bua otei, havee to   nao vo=   am?
    two man where REL go   GOAL= 2PL.PRON
    '(You) two boys, where are you going?' (Skae_03W.017)

This absence of an article can be understood as a reflection of the special pragmatic and syntactic status of vocatives. They are forms of address with unique (3, 4) or non-unique definite (5) reference and are syntactically independent linguistic units.

A second nominal construction that obligatorily lacks an article is the locative phrase (LP) that functions as an attribute or an adverbial and refers to a unique place. While in (6) the toponym *Teapu* heads an object NP, *Teapu* without an article is an adverbial LP (7):

(6) Naa   varakaha ni =a   Teapu   …
    1SG.PRON leave   APP =ART2.SG Teop.Island
    'I left Teop Island …' (Mah_01R.039)

(7) Enaa   skul   Teapu   …
    1SG.PRON go.to.school Teop.Island
    'I went to school on Teop Island …' (Mah_01R.029)

In both clauses the reference of the toponym is inherently unique; the adverbial LP *Teapu* in (7) cannot be replaced by a prepositional phrase. Sortal nouns denoting places, however, can be used in LPs as well as in prepositional phrases. When *vaan* 'village', for example, heads an LP, it refers to the particular village where the speaker or the protagonist of the story lives (compare Löbner 2011: 284), whereas the prepositional phrase refers to some other village:

(8) Erau, me=   paa nao vahaa vaan.
    so   and4= TAM go again village
    'And so, (she) went back to the village.' (Nan_03R.137)

---

[3] The vocative particle and the articles *o* ART3.SG and ART2.PL are homonyms.

(9) Enam   na suguna te =a   vaan bona, ...
    1PL.EX.PRON TAM arrive PREP =ART2.SG village ANA
    'When we arrived in that village, ... (and they sent us to Ovovoipa in the area of Aita ...).' (Nan_01E.051)

While in (8) the unique reference of *vaan* 'to the village' is domain-defined, it is established by the anaphoric demonstrative *bona* in (9). Inherently unique LPs like *Teapu* in (7) cannot be specified by the anaphoric demonstrative.

2.2 Noun classes and conceptual types

On the basis of their article selection in simple singular noun phrases, Teop nouns can be classified into three noun classes. The affiliation of nouns to one of the three classes is, to some extent, semantically motivated; the affiliation to the e-class in particular is predictable, whereas there are some idiosyncrasies in the a- and o-classes.

1. The e-class comprises highly individuated human nouns like proper names, inalienably possessed kinship terms, nouns referring to social roles that are unique within certain social institutions such as, for instance, *suunano* 'paramount chief of a clan', but also non-unique social role terms like *siisia* 'teacher' and *subuava* 'old woman', and domestic animal names, e. g. *guu* 'pig', *toa* 'chicken'.
2. The a-class consists of common nouns referring to human beings, e. g. *moon* 'woman', higher animals other than domestic animals, e. g. *keusu* 'rat', landmarks, e. g. *vaan* 'village', food, e. g. *huun* 'soup', and artefacts, e. g. *nahu* 'pot', and part-of-a-whole terms e. g. *kahoo* 'head', *paka* 'leaf'.
3. The o-class comprises common nouns referring to plants and things made of plant materials, e. g. *naono* 'tree', *hoi* 'basket', lower animals *vihivihii* 'jellyfish' and amorphous substances other than water or soup, e. g. *butoo* 'mud', fire and light, e. g. the loanword *raama* 'lamp', and periods of time, e. g. *vinu* 'year'.

Basic noun phrases are introduced by a specific article and function as arguments, complements of prepositions, and predicates. They are singular and not marked by the diminutive particle, a numeral, a plural marker or the indefiniteness marker.

classes	subclasses	example	translation	conceptual type (Löbner 2011)
e-class	person name	e Mark, e Ruth	Mark, Ruth	individual [+U, -R]
	kin name	e iaa, e tetee	Mum, Dad	individual [+U, -R]
	unique social role term	e suunano	the paramount chief	individual [+U, -R]
	relational kinship term	e sinanae	his/her mother	functional [+U,+R]
		e vavinanae	his/her sibling of the opposite sex	relational [-U,+R]
	non-unique social role term	e subuava	an, the old woman	sortal [-U, -R]
		e siisia	a/the teacher	
	domestic animal term	e guu	a/the pig	sortal [-U, -R]
		e toa	a/the chicken	
a-class	place name	a Teapu	Teop Island	individual [+U, -R]
	relational part/whole term	a kahonae	his/her head	functional [+U,+R]
		a kurinae	his/her arm	relational [-U,+R]
		a pakanae	its leaf	
	non-relational common noun	a moon	a/the woman	sortal [-U, -R]
		a iana	a/the fish	
		a vasu	a/the stone	
o-class	relational part/whole term	o naono nae	its wood	relational [-U,+R]
	non-relational common noun	o urita	a/the octopus	sortal [-U, -R]
		o naono	a/the tree/plant	

Table 2: Examples of the three Teop noun classes

Table 3 shows that there is no one-to-one relationship between conceptual types and noun classes in Teop. Individual nouns belong to the e-class if they refer to humans, but to the a-class if they refer to places. Secondly, in contrast to the [+R] types of nouns, the [+R] noun classes are not subclassified by the feature [±U], but by the semantic feature [±human], which does not figure in the system of conceptual types, but plays an important role in the lexical and grammatical structure of Teop. Thirdly, the sortal noun type is found in all Teop noun classes, but in the e-class it is restricted to a few common nouns referring to social roles of humans and to domestic animals.

The distinction between unique and non-unique social roles terms, e. g. *suunano* 'paramount chief' and *subuava* 'old woman' becomes evident in predicative

conceptual type	Teop noun class	
individual [+U,-R]	e-class (names of persons, unique social role terms)	[+human]
	a-class (all place names)	[-human]
functional [+U,+R]	e-class (kinship terms)	[+human]
	a-class (part/whole terms)	[-human]
relational [-U,+R]	e-class (kinship terms)	[+human]
	a-class (part/whole terms)	[-human]
	o-class (only *naono* 'wood' attested)	[-human]
Sortal	a-class (default)	[±human]
	e-class (non-unique social roles)	[+human]
	e-class (domestic animals)	[-human]
	o-class (semantically restricted class)	[-human]

Table 3: Conceptual types and noun classes

constructions[4]. While predicative nouns of the individual type are marked by the article *e* to express identification and the article *a* to express classification (10, 11), e-class nouns of the sortal type only take the article *a* to express classification:

(10) Enaa   e   suunano   ...
      1SG.PRON ART1.SG paramount.chief
      'I am the paramount chief (of the Nao Tahii clan).' (Mah_01R.067)

(11) Enaa   a   suunano.
      1SG.PRON ART2.SG paramount.chief
      'I am a paramount chief.' (Mah_03R.028)

(12) Enaa   a   subuava.
      1SG.PRON ART2.SG old.woman
      'I am an old woman.' (Sii_02R.559)

Although the change from the e-class to the a-class implies a type shift of the individual noun *suunano* 'paramount chief', the non-unique social-role term *subuava* only changes the noun class, but not its conceptual type. This difference corresponds to the fact that only non-unique e-class nouns can enter the indefinite construction and may be determined by an anaphoric demonstrative (see § 4).

---

[4] Note that Löbner (2011) does not deal with predicative NPs.

2.3 Specific vs. non-specific NPs

The distinction between specific and non-specific articles is typical for Oceanic languages (Mosel & Hovdhaugen 1992: 261–264). Specific NPs refer to particular entities and may be definite or indefinite. Thus the protagonist of a legend is often introduced by a specific NP which in English translates as an indefinite NP, and when it is mentioned a second time, it may have exactly the same form. Put differently, the type shift from an indefinite to a definite (pragmatically unique) NP is not overtly expressed.

(13) *Nabunuu vai roho, na tei-tei roho a moon koa,*
long.time.ago DEM before TAM RED-stay before ART2.SG woman only
a moon na tei-tei roho Teapu.
ART2.SG woman TAM RED-stay before Teop.Island
'In former times, there was only one woman, the woman was staying on Teop Island.' (Pur_05E(Eno).002)

In contrast to specific NPs, an NP marked by the non-specific article refers to any item of the category denoted by the NP head. Non-specific NPs are typically found as subjects in negative existential clauses and as objects of the verb *rake* 'want':

(14) *Ae ahiki ta taba ani ta mataa.*
and1 not.exist NSPEC.ART2.SG thing eat NSPEC.ART2.SG good
'And there was not any good food.' (Mor_01R.149)

(15) *Ean na rake nom ta taba?*
2SG.PRON TAM want 2SG.IPFV NSPEC.ART2.SG thing
'Do you want anything?' (Vae_01E(Eno).163)

The negative existential construction is also used with proper names of persons and kinship terms, i.e. inherently unique nouns of the individual and the functional relational type:

(16) *Ahiki ta Gaagin ei!*
not.exist NSPEC.ART2.SG PN here
'Gaagin is not here!' (lit. 'There isn't any Gaagin here!')
(Aro_05E(Eno).059)

(17) *Ahiki he ta sina-ma =nam ...*
not.exist but NSPEC.ART2.SG mother-1PL.EX.POSS =1PL.EX.PRON
'However, none of our mothers (should see us)'

(lit. 'However, there isn't any mother of us') (Bua_01R.119)

The use of the non-specific a-class article *ta* with unique human nouns that inherently belong to the e-class (see Table 1 and 2) clearly signals a noun class change as well as a type shift.

3   The Teop noun phrase

With the exceptions noted above in § 2.1, NPs are introduced by an article and, in addition, may contain a number of pre-head and post-head modifiers (in the widest sense) as summarised in Table 4.

pre-head modifiers	examples	post-head modifiers	examples
articles	all	juxtaposed nouns, verbs, adjectives	14
plural markers	(44,45,48)	demonstratives	(9,13,18)
the diminutive particle	(4,23,49)	adjectival phrases (introduced by an article)	(14,33,34)
the adjectives *rutaa* 'small' and *vahara* 'little.PL'	–	inalienable possessor phrases	(14,19,20)
numerals	3,23,37,38	prepositional phrases	(18,27)
determiners	(21–23,37–40)	relative clauses	(5)

Table 4: Pre-head and post-head modifiers of the Teop NP

Alienable possessor NPs and pronouns are expressed by prepositional phrases introduced by the multipurpose preposition *te* PREP as in (18), whereas inalienable possessor NPs are marked on the possessee NP by a suffixed possessive marker (POSS) that agrees in person and number with the possessor pronoun or NP.

(18)   a   tabaan te   =a   iana   bona
       ART2.SG food   PREP   =ART2.SG   fish   ANA
       'the food of that fish' (Sii_11W.043)[5]

(19)   a   kahoo-n   =e   guu
       ART2.SG head-3SG.POSS   =ART1.SG   pig
       'the head of the pig' (Eno_10E.040)

---

[5] In the Teop orthography the possessive marker and the clitic article or pronoun are often written as a separate word, e.g. *kahoo nae, kahoo rio*.

(20) a   kahoo-ri   =o   aba
    ART2.SG head⁶-3PL.POSS =ART2.PL person
    'the heads of human beings'(Aro_04R.041)

4   Definite and indefinite NPs

As shown in § 2.3, Teop articles do not distinguish between definite and indefinite NPs. But there are two constructions that compensate for this lack of specification. Definiteness may be explicitly indicated by the anaphoric demonstrative *bona* ANA following the NP head and indefiniteness by the use of an indefinite determiner preceding the head of the NP.

(21) *Nabunuu a   peha roosuu na tei-tei   roho. A   roosuu bona*
    long.ago ART2.SG INDEF giant TAM RED-stay before ART2.SG giant ANA
    na   antee nana   tea   taverete oraa   ge ...
    TAM can 3SG.IPFV COMP1 change demon   or
    'Long ago there lived a giant. That giant was able to change into a demon or ...' (Sii_06RG.001-002)

The anaphoric demonstrative *bona* occurs with non-unique nouns of all noun classes and does not change the class affiliation of the noun:

	Translation	Reference
e subuava bona	'this old woman'	Aro_08(Eno).042
e guu bona	'this pig'	Kae_01R.043
a otei bona	'this man'	Tah_05R.035
o naono bona	'this tree'	Val_02R.078

Table 5: The anaphoric demonstrative: type shift without noun class shift

Another means of signalling the type shift of a sortal indefinite noun to a pragmatically unique sortal noun is a change from the a-class to the e-class. After the giant (*a roosuu*) has been introduced in the legend from which the example above (21) is taken, he is later on referred to by *e roosuu* 'the giant' (Sii_06RG.092). This kind of noun class change is common in legends and regularly found with animal names:

In contrast, the indefinite determiner marks a specific NP as indefinite, which yields a noun class change of non-unique e-class nouns:

---

⁶ Note that *kahoo-* is singular, which reflects the fact that it is a functional type of noun [+U,+R].

Type shifts and noun class changes under determination in Teop

sortal		individual		
a bakubaku	Eno_11W.015	*e bakubaku*	Ter_01R.064	'shark'
a manii	Sii_09W.025	*e manii*	Vur_01E(Eno).02	'possum'
a moogee	Val_02R.034	*e moogee*	Val_02R.034	'monkey'

Table 6: Type shift and noun class change with pragmatically unique animal names

(22)　*Na　tei-tei　roho　a　　　peha　subuava,　...*
　　　TAM RED-stay before ART2.SG INDEF old.woman
　　　'There was an old woman, ...' (Aro_07R. 001)

The indefinite determiner *peha/peho* is related to the cardinal numeral *peha/peho* 'one' and inflects for the noun class in the same way. But while the numeral *peha/peho* 'one' logically only occurs in NPs that refer to singular entities, the indefiniteness marker *peha/peho* INDEF is also found in NPs referring to more than one person or thing, which justifies our distinction between the numeral and the indefiniteness marker.

(23)　*a　　　peha　bua　si　beiko*
　　　ART2.SG[7] INDEF two DIM child
　　　'a couple of little children' (Mui_01CE.019)

5 Possessive constructions

There are two kinds of possessor constructions in Teop, the inalienable and the alienable construction. While in inalienable constructions the first person singular possessor is simply formed by a pronominal suffix, all other possessors are indexed on the head noun by a suffix (POSS) that inflects for person and number and agrees with the possessor pronoun or NP.

(24)　*a　　　hena-naa*
　　　ART2.SG name-1SG.PRON
　　　'my name'

(25)　*e　　　sina-na=e*
　　　ART1.SG mother=3SG.POSS-3SG.PRON
　　　'his mother' (Aro_02R.004)

---

[7] NPs determined by cardinal numerals are grammatically singular (see § 6.1).

(26) e   sina-n   =a   beiko
    ART1.SG mother-3SG.POSS =ART2.SG child
    'the child's mother'(Aro_06R.035)

The alienable possessor construction is a prepositional phrase that is introduced by the multipurpose preposition *te* 'in, to, of'. It is typically found with a- and o-class nouns denoting things whose possession is controlled by the possessor referent. The alienable possessor construction does not change the noun class, merely the conceptual type from a sortal concept to a pragmatically unique concept.

(27) o   sinivi te   =an
    ART3.SG canoe PREP =2SG.PRON
    'your canoe' (Sii_06RG.303)

Nouns that obligatorily enter inalienable constructions are grammatically and semantically relational nouns, but not all nouns that are semantically relational are grammatically relational, e. g. *keara* 'sibling of the same sex' (see § 5.1).

5.1 Possessive constructions of e-class nouns and type shifts

Person names differ from all other e-class nouns in that they do not enter any possessive construction, whereas the other e-class nouns enter alienable or inalienable constructions and can be subclassified accordingly.

As shown in Table 2 and Table 7, there are two kinds of expression for kinship: the so-called kin names and the grammatically relational kinship terms. Kin names behave like person names in that they never occur in plural constructions and can be used as vocatives, whereas kinship terms can be pluralised (see § 6.3), but are not used as vocatives.

(28) O   iaa! O   tetee! Sovee rakaha me= am paa mate kahi anaa?
    VOC Mum VOC Dad   why indeed and4= 2PL TAM die from 1SG.OBJ.PRON
    'Mum! Dad! Why indeed did you both die leaving me behind?'
    (Sha_01E(Eno).029)

Secondly, speakers exclusively use the kin name when speaking about their own mother, father or grandparent, though mostly without a possessor, whereas for a third person's mother, father or grandparent the relational kinship term is preferred, which also explains why only kin names are found in the vocative construction (see § 2.1). Thirdly, kin names are grammatically non-relational, but in contrast to person names they may be modified by an alienable possessor construction. Table 8 shows the frequencies of the kin name *iaa* 'Mum' without and with possessors and the corresponding constructions of the kinship term *sina-* 'mother'.

subclass	example	translation	alienable	inalienable
PN			-	-
kin name	iaa	'Mum'	+	-
	tetee	'Dad'	+	-
	bubuu	'Granny'	+	-
sibling of same sex	keara	'sibling of same sex'	+	-
relational kinship term	sina-	'mother'	-	+
	tama-	'father'	-	+
	vavina-	'sibling of opposite sex'	-	+
social role	subuava	'old woman'	-	-
	siisia	'teacher'	+	-
domestic animal name	guu	'pig'	+	-

Table 7: Modification by possessor constructions

The kin name *iaa* 'Mum' is most frequently used by itself (92.8%), in which case it refers to the speaker's mother, whereas the bound kinship term *sina-* 'mother' is never used with a first singular possessor. The distribution of third person singular possessors shows the opposite picture. Only 0.9% of all tokens of *iaa* 'Mum' are modified by a third person singular possessor, whereas with the kinship term *sina-* 'mother' it is 56%.

Since *iaa* 'Mum' is mostly used without a possessor and only occurs in the singular, it can be classified as a noun of the individual type that through the incongruent determination by the alienable possessor construction undergoes a shift to the functional noun type without a change of noun class.

The alienable possessor construction is also found with the kinship term *keara* 'sibling of the same sex'. Grammatically this kinship term is not relational because it does not enter the inalienable possessive construction and may occur without any possessor. But the contexts in which it occurs provide sufficient evidence to affiliate it with the conceptually relational type of nouns. Firstly, it occurs in the special plural constructions of kinship terms which imply relation-

possessor	iaa 'Mum'			sina- 'mother'		
none	iaa	'Mum'	207	–	'mother'	–
1SG	iaa tenaa	'my Mum'	9	–	'my mother'	–
2SG	iaa tean	'your Mum'	2	sina-m-an	'your mother'	20
3SG	iaa teve	'his/her Mum'	2	sina-na-e	'his/her mother'	178
1PL.EX	iaa tenam	'our Mum'	1	sina-ma-nam	'our mothers'	2
1PL.IN	–	'our Mum'	0	sina-ra-ara	'our mothers'	3
2PL	–	'your Mum'	0	sina-me-am	'your mothers'	8
3PL	iaa teori	'their Mum'	1	sina-ri-ori	'their mothers'	32
NP	iaa te =NP	'NP's Mum'	1	sina-n = NP	'NP's mother'	76
	total number of tokens of iaa 'Mum'		223	total number of tokens of sina- 'mother'		319

Table 8: *iaa* 'Mum' and *sina-* 'mother' with possessor attributes

ality (see § 6.3, § 6.4), and secondly, if it is used in the singular without a possessor, it is modified by *beera* 'big' or *rutaa* 'small', which implies a relationship to a small or to a big brother or sister, respectively.

(29) E   keara   beera na   piku-piku nana   bona.
      ART1.SG sibling.of.same.sex big   TAM   RED-lie   3SG.IPFV 4SG.PRON
      'His elder brother lied to him.' (Auv_01R.009)

The grammatical relationality of kinship terms can be cancelled by the derelationalising suffix *-na* and a change of the noun class from the e-class to the o-class. Compare (26) with (30):

(30) o   sina-na   o   beera
      ART3.SG- mother-DEREL ART3.SG big
      'The mother is important.' (Vos_02R(Vos).083)

While in (26) the noun *sina-* 'mother' is a grammatically relational noun of the functional type, it is an abstract absolute term in (30) as it refers to the concept of mother in general or, put differently, to all mothers one can think of.[8]

5.2 Possessive constructions of a-class nouns and type shifts

Similar to the e-class nouns, the a-class nouns can be subclassified on the basis of whether they can be modified by a possessor or not, and those a-class nouns that take possessor attributes can be further divided into (1) those with inalienable, (2)

---

[8] Note that the generic use of nouns is excluded in Löbner 2011.

Type shifts and noun class changes under determination in Teop

those with alienable and (3) those with both inalienable and alienable possessor constructions.

While place names are never used in possessive constructions, e. g. *Teapu* 'Teop Island', nouns denoting a part of a whole, including body parts, have inalienable possessors:

(31)   *a*   *kuri-na*   *=e*
       ART2.SG hand-3SG.POSS =3SG.PRON
       'her hand' (Jan_01W 114)

As with relational e-class nouns, relational a-class nouns shift to the o-class, when they are used without a possessor. This happens, for example, in the context of cutting or eating a body part. Some of these words are bound forms and take the derelational suffix, but others are unbound and used without this suffix, as illustrated by the nouns *kuri-* 'hand' in (32) and *kahoo* 'head' in (2):

(32)   ... *bono*   *meho kuri-na*
       ART3.SG other arm-DEREL
       '(Materua, however, had eaten) the other arm.' (Aro_06E.58)

To conclude, the possessive constructions of a-class nouns show properties similar to those of e-class nouns:

- Names – in this case place names – are semantically unique and do not enter any possessive construction.
- Relational nouns, here typically denoting a part of a whole, may be used in non-relational constructions and then take the article of o-class nouns. But in contrast to the e-class nouns the loss of relationality is not consistently marked by the derelationalising suffix *-na*.
- The shift from the a-class to the o-class construction signifies the separation of a part from its whole, which may be interpreted as a downgrading from a higher to a lower degree of individuality.

5.3   Possessive constructions of o-class nouns

One of the most frequent o-class words is *naono* 1. 'tree, plant', 2. 'wood'. In its second sense 'wood' it is either used by itself or in an inalienable possessive construction:

(33)   *O*   *naono o*   *kikisi*, ...
       ART3.SG wood ART3.SG strong
       'The strong wood (is used for building houses).' (Joy_19W.072)

(34) O   naono-na   =e   o   asi-asi   va-mataa.
     ART3.SG wood-3SG.POSS =3SG.PRON ART3.SG RED-burn ADVR-good
     'Its wood burns well.' (Sha_Aro_01E_trees.018)

In both the absolute and the relational construction it occurs with the same article *o/bono*.

5.4 Summary

All three noun classes contain grammatically relational nouns that occur in inalienable constructions, but may also be derelationalised. With e-class nouns, the loss of relationality is consistently marked by the suffix *-na* DEREL. In the a-class, some inherently relational nouns are marked when used as absolute terms but others are not; whereas in the o-class, inherently relational nouns remain unmarked when used as absolute terms. Derelationalised e- and a-class nouns are affiliated with the o-class, while o-class nouns remain in the o-class.

	semantic class	DEREL	noun class change
e-class nouns	kinship term	+	e-class > o-class
a-class nouns	part-of-a-whole term	+ / -	a-class > o-class
o-class nouns	substance of an object	-	-

Table 9: Derelationalisation

The way relational e-class, a-class and o-class nouns behave differently with respect to possessive and absolute constructions suggests that they form a continuum with e-class nouns showing the highest degree of boundedness and o-class nouns the lowest.

6 The expression of plurality

Plurality in Teop can be expressed by:

1. cardinal numerals (see § 6.1);
2. the associative plural[9] article *ere* ART1.PL (see § 6.2);
3. the kinship plural marker *ba* KIN.PL (see § 6.3);
4. the dyadic plural[10] marker *tom* DYAD (see § 6.4);

---

[9] See Corbett 2000: 101–111.
[10] See Evans 2006.

Type shifts and noun class changes under determination in Teop

5. the specific and non-specific a- and o-articles, which inversely mark the plural of o-class and a-class nouns (see Table 1 and § 6.5);
6. the plural marker *maa* PLM (§ 6.5).

The various kinds of plural marking clearly separate the e-class from the a- and the o-class, since *ere* ART1.PL, *ba* KIN.PL and *tom* DYAD are exclusively used with e-class nouns, while the inverse plural marking by articles and the plural marker *maa* PLM are predominantly used with a- and o-class nouns.

plural marking	e-class	a-class	o-class
associative plural marking	+	-	-
kinship plural marking	+	-	-
dyadic plural marking	+	-	-
plural marking by articles	(+)	+	+
plural marker *maa*	(+)	+	+
cardinal numerals	(+)	+	+

Table 10: The expression of plurality

The e- and a-class nouns can be further subclassified on the basis of their plural marking properties. Apart from one exceptional example, the non-relational non-unique nouns of the e-class behave similarly to the sortal nouns of the a-class (see Table 11).

class	Subclass	ART1.PL ere	KIN.PL ba	DYAD tom	ART2/3.PL o/a	PLM maa
e-class	PN	+	-	-	-	-
	kin name	+	-	-	-	-
	keara 'same sex sibling'	-	+	+	-	-
	kinship term	+	+	+	-	-
	social role term	(+)	-	-	+	+
	domestic animal name	-	-	-	+	+
a-class	toponyms	-	-	-	-	-
	common noun	-	-	-	+	+
o-class	common noun	-	-	-	+	+

Table 11: Subclassification of e-class, a-class and o-class nouns

In the following section, we will first deal with the cardinal numerals and then describe the data for the other ways of marking plurality.

6.1 Cardinal numerals

Nouns of all classes can be modified by a cardinal numeral. With a- or o-class nouns, the cardinal numeral takes the respective singular article and may be modified by the determiner *meha/meho* 'other'. A-class nouns are modified by *meha*, o-class nouns by *meho*. Similar to *meha/meho* 'other', the cardinal numerals *peha/peho* 'one' and *bua/buo* 'two' agree with the head noun with respect to the noun class as illustrated in the following examples:

(35) me =a meha bua otei
 and4 =ART2.SG other two man
 'and two other men' (Mor_01E.165)

(36) o meho buo sinivi
 ART2.SG other two canoe
 'two other canoes' (Eno_12W.013)

When a non-unique e-class noun is modified by a cardinal numeral or *meha/meho* 'other', the NP takes the very same form as a NP headed by an a-class noun:

(37) a meha bua keara te =naa
 ART2.SG other two sibling.of.same.sex PREP =1SG.PRON
 'my two other brothers' (Rum_01E(Joy).010)

(38) A bua vavina-naa ere Maravai bo Unias.
 ART2.SG two sibling.of.different.sex-1SG.PRON ART1.PL Maravai and2 Unias
 'My two sisters are Maravai and Unias.' (Rum_01E(Joy).012)

This shift from the e-class to the a-class obviously correlates with a decrease in individuality, although *keara* 'sibling of the same sex' and *vavina-* 'sibling of the other sex' do not shift to another conceptual type, as they both remain nouns of the relational type with the features [-U,+R].

6.2 The associative plural

The only plural form of person names is the associative plural construction *ere* PN, which refers to a single person and his or her associates:

(39) Ere Rev. Shepherd
 ART1.PL Rev. Shepherd
 'Rev. Shepherd and his people (left Torokina ...)' (Pur_01E(Joy).030)

In addition, the associative plural construction is found with kin names (40), kinship terms (41) and with coordinated constructions that contain a person name (42), a kin name or a kinship term (43). The associative plural construction of *iaa* 'Mum' and *sina-* 'mother' often refers to the mother and the aunts on the mother's side:

(40) ere   iaa
     ART1.PL Mum
     'my Mum and aunties (do not speak like this, ...)' (Aro_14R.049)

(41) ... benere   sina-na   =e   bo   tama-na   =e
         OBJ.ART1.PL mother-3SG.POSS =3SG.PRON and3 father-3SG.POSS =3SG.PRON
         '(and told) her Mum and Dad' (Skae_01W.100)

(42) ere   Gaivaa bo   Vasiri
     ART1.PL PN   and3 PN
     'Gaivaa and Vasiri' (Sha_01E(Eno)G 007)

(43) Ere   sina-na   =e
     ART1.PL mother-3SG.POSS =3SG.PRON
     'Her mother and her aunts (would come now)' (Aro_14R.069)

One thing that all associative plural constructions have in common is that they refer to a group of people, but at the same time either single out a particular person who is accompanied by other unidentified people or refer to a couple of particular people. Searches for constructions of *ere* with the most common human a-class nouns *moon* 'woman' (1030 tokens), *otei* 'man' (857 tokens) and *beiko* 'child' (849 tokens) were unsuccessful.

The associative plural is a characteristic of highly individuated nouns. With the single exception of *ere subuava bo Simura* 'the old woman and Simura' (Sii_07W.099), e-class nouns that are semantically non-unique do not combine with the associative plural article.

6.3 The plural marker *ba*

The kinship plural marker *ba* KIN.PL is used in NPs referring to a group of people who share the same kinship status with respect to some other people as, for instance, the fathers of the children of a village (44) or the brothers of a man (45):

(44) A   ba   tama-ri   =ori   paa koara ri   bari.
    ART2.sg KIN.PL father-3PL.POSS =3PL.PRON TAM scold 3PL.OBJM 4PL.PRON
    'Their fathers scolded them.' (Aro_10E.135)

(45) a   ba   keara   te   =naa
    ART2.sg KIN.PL sibling.of.same.sex PREP =1SG.PRON
    'my brothers' (said by a man) (Mah_13R.587)

Similar to cardinal numerals, the plural marker *ba* KIN.PL requires a change of e-class nouns to the a-class which indicates the loss of individuality and in (44) a shift from the functional conceptual type [+U,+R] to the relational type [-U,+R].

6.4 The dyadic plural construction

Kinship terms can combine with the dyadic marker *tom*. This marker indicates that the NP refers to both sides of a personal relationship. Thus *tom sinana* literally means 'persons in the mother-child relationship':

(46) a   bua tom   sina-na   ...
    ART2.SG two DYAD mother-DEREL
    '(We will let) the mother and her child (go home ...)' (Mat_01R.128)

As illustrated by the preceding example, relational kinship terms are used in their absolute form marked by the derelational suffix *-na* and, similar to the plural marker *ba* take the singular article of the a-class. The grammatically non-relational noun *keara* 'sibling of the same sex' is used in its bare form:

(47) a   bua tom   keara
    ART2.SG two DYAD same.sex.sibling
    'two brothers' (Aro_03R.002)

Dyadic NPs are collective NPs and are always modified by an expression that quantifies the number of people in this dyadic relationship such as, for instance, the numeral *bua* 'two' or the plural marker *maa* (see § 6.5):

(48) a=   maa tom   sina-na
    ART2.SG= PLM DYAD mother-DEREL
    '(Once upon a time there was) a mother with her children.' (Aro_06R.001)

(49) A   bua si   tom   sina-na   te   =ara
    ART two DIM DYAD mother-DEREL PREP =1INC
    'our daughter and her child (lit. 'our two dear mother-child related (people)' (Mat_01E.145)

In the dyadic construction the grammatically and conceptually relational noun [+R] becomes an absolute noun [-R] that can enter the relational alienable possessive construction:

(50) [[a bua tom [sina-]$_{+R}$ -na]$_{-R}$ teara]$_{+R}$

6.5 Plural marking by articles and the plural marker *maa*

Plural marking by articles and the plural marker *maa* signify plurality of discrete entities. Apart from cardinal numerals, they are the only plural form of a- and o-class nouns. The non-unique social role terms and domestic animal names of the e-class are treated like a-class nouns.

class	singular article		plural article		plural marker *maa*	
e	*e siisia*	'the/a teacher'	*o siisia*	'the teachers'	*amaa siisia*	'the teachers'
	e guu	'the/a pig'	*o guu*	'the pigs'	*amaa guu*	'the pigs'
a	*a moon*	'the/a woman'	*o moon*	'the women'	*amaa moon*	'the women'
o	*o naono*	'the/a tree'	*a naono*	'the trees'	*amaa naono*	'the trees'

Table 12: Plural marking by basic articles and the plural marker *maa*

The plural of a-class nouns is marked by the article o (or *bono*) and, inversely, the plural of o-class nouns by the article a (or *bona*).[11]

The plural marker *maa* requires the article *a/bona* irrespective of the noun's inherent class affiliation. With e-class nouns both kinds of plural marking only occur with the sortal type of nouns[12].

Both types of plural marking are also found with a-class nouns of the relational type, but not with the relational o-class word *naono* 'wood'.

(51) ... o-re   paa kosi bono   paka-na   =e.
      3PL-CONSEC TAM cut OBJ.ART2.PL leaf-3SG.POSS =3SG.PRON
      '(They cut the sago palm) and then they cut its leaves.'

(52) me=ori   kisi bona   maa kuri-na   =e
      and4=3PL.PRON tie ART2.SG PLM hand-3SG.POSS =3SG.PRON
      'and they tied his hands' (Viv_01E(Eno).054)

The difference between the two kinds of plural markings are not understood yet.

---

[11] This kind of plural marking is called inverse plural marking; see Corbett (2000: 159–165) who also discusses the case of Teop.

[12] There are two examples of unique kinship terms with *maa* PLM, but since they both occur in spontaneously narrated legends and were corrected by different editors in the edited versions, I consider them not as regular constructions (Aro_12R.134, Aro_12E(Joy).059, Jen_01R.070, Jen_01E(Eno).080).

7 Summary

Teop has three noun classes that are formally distinguished by articles and called the e-, the a- and the o-classes. On the basis of their distribution in various types of possessive and plural constructions, e-class, a-class and o-class nouns can be further divided into subclasses which show some correlations with the conceptual types of individual, functional, relational and sortal nouns (see Table 13). For instance, the individual proper names of persons, kin names, kinship terms all belong to the e-class, whereas there are only a few sortal nouns in the e-class.

class	Subclass	[±U,±R]	inal. poss.	al poss.	plural	type
e	PN	+U, -R	-	-	assoc.	individual
	kin names	+U, -R	-	+	assoc.	individual
	unique kinship terms	+U, +R	+	-	assoc., dyadic, *ba*	functional
	non-unique kinship terms	-U, +R	+	-	assoc., dyadic, *ba*	relational
	keara (same sex sibling)	-U, +R	-	+	assoc., dyadic, *ba*	relational
	social roles terms	-U, -R	-	+	(assoc.), article, *maa*	sortal
	domestic animal names	-U, -R	-	+	article, *maa*	sortal
a	toponyms	+U, -R	-	-	-	individual
	unique part/whole terms	+U, +R	+	-	-	functional
	non-unique part/whole terms	-U, +R	+	-	article, *maa*	relational
	others	-U, -R	-	+	article, *maa*	sortal
o	part/whole terms	-U, +R	+	-	-	relational
	others	-U, -R	-	+	article, *maa*	sortal

Table 13: Noun classes and subclasses

The o-class, on the other hand, contains no individual nouns and only a single relational noun, namely *naono* 'wood'. All other nouns in this class are sortal nouns (mostly plant names) or mass and abstract nouns which, however, have not been dealt with in this paper and are excluded by Löbner (2011).

The a-class is a kind of default class. It contains all nouns referring to human beings other than those of the e-class, all names of vertebrates, insects, spiders and crabs, all landmark terms, all nouns denoting food items, and all part-of-a-whole terms irrespective of whether they belong to the functional or the relational type.

The mismatches between conceptual types and Teop noun classes are mostly due to the semantic feature [± human] which plays a crucial role in the lexical and morphosyntactic structure of the Teop language and overrules the distinction between functional and relational types of nouns.

Type shifts and noun class changes under determination in Teop

The analysis of determination in Teop has shown the following correlations between noun class changes and conceptual type shifts:

1. Individual e-class nouns are regularly moved to the a-class in incongruent determinative constructions yielding a loss of uniqueness as in the constructions of predicative classification (see Table 15), existential negation (Table 16) and dyadic plurals (18).
2. If a sortal animal name of the a-class figures as the protagonist of a story and thus becomes unique, it is moved into the e-class (see Table 16).
3. If the functional and relational types of e-class and a-class nouns are derelationalised, they move from their lexically inherent class to the o-class (see Table 17).

But there are also three cases of type shifts that do not lead to a noun class change:

1. When nouns of the sortal type are determined by the anaphoric pronoun *bona*, they shift from the sortal to the individual, pragmatically unique type of noun, but do not undergo a noun class change (see Table 16).
2. The individual kin names, e. g. *iaa* 'Mum' can be determined by an alienable possessor, e. g. *e iaa tenaa* 'my Mum', without any noun class change, although they shift from the individual to the functional type of noun (see Table 17).
3. Determination by an alienable possessor also does not change the noun class of sortal nouns although it implies a shift from the sortal type to the individual, pragmatically unique type (see Table 17).

Finally, there are two changes of noun class affiliations that do not involve a type shift, although these changes may be interpreted as a decrease of individuality:

1. the marked indefiniteness construction of sortal e-class nouns (see Table 16) and
2. the quantificational determination of non-unique e-class nouns by cardinal numerals, the kinship plural marker *ba* and the plural marker *maa* (see Table 18).

The vocative and locative constructions are characterised by the obligatory absence of an article, i. e. the loss of any noun class distinction (indicated by >0 in Table 14), which in the case of sortal nouns referring to persons and places implies a shift to the individual type of noun.

The conditions and the direction of the Teop noun class changes suggest that the noun classes and their subclasses form a scale of individuation with the proper names of the e-class representing the highest degree of individuality and the sortal o-class nouns the lowest, because a loss of uniqueness or relationality always results in a move from the e-class into the a- or the o-class, whereas a gain of uniqueness can lead to a movement from the a-class into the e-class.

construction	type shift	noun class change	reference
vocative of individual nouns	-	e-class > 0[13]	§2.1 (3)
vocative of sortal nouns	sortal > individual	a-class > 0	§2.1 (4,5)
locative phrase of place names	-	a-class > 0	§2.1 (6,7)
locative of sortal noun	sortal > individual	a-class > 0	§2.1 (8,9)

Table 14: Vocative and locative NPs

construction	type shift	noun class change	reference
identification of individuals	-	-	§2.2 (10)
classification of individuals	individual > sortal	e-class > a-class	§2.2 (11)
classification of sortals	-	-	§2.2 (12)

Table 15: Predicative NPs

construction	type shift	noun class change	reference
existential negation	individual > sortal	e-class > a-class	§2.3 (16, 17)
anaphoric demonstrative	sortal > individual	-	§4, Tab. 5
individuation of the protagonist	sortal > individual	a-class > e-class	§4, Tab. 6
indefiniteness of sortal nouns	-	e-class > a-class	§4 (22)

Table 16: Specific vs. non-specific, indefinite vs. definite anaphoric NPs

construction	type shift	noun class change	reference
alienable possession of kin names	individual > functional	-	§5.1, Table 8
alienable possession of sortal nouns	sortal > individual	-	§5 (27)
derelationalisation of kinship terms	functional > absolute generic	e-class > o-class	§5.1 (26, 30)
derelationalisation of part/whole terms	relational > sortal	a-class > o-class	§5.2 (31, 32)

Table 17: Possessive constructions

---

[13] 0 = loss of noun class distinction because of the absence of any article.

Type shifts and noun class changes under determination in Teop

construction	type shift	noun class change	reference
cardinal numerals with relational and sortal nouns	-	e-class > a-class	§6.1 (35–38)
associative plural	-	-	§6.2. (39–43)
kinship plural	functional > relational	e-class > a-class	§6.3 (44)
	-	e-class > a-class	§6.3 (45)
dyadic plural (derelationalisation)	functional > absolute collective	e-class > a-class	§6.4 (46–49)
	relational > absolute collective	e-class > a class	
article marked plural	-	-	§6.5
plural marker *maa*	-	e-class > a-class	§6.5

Table 18: The expression of plurality

Abbreviations

1PL.EX	1st person plural exclusive
1PL.IN	1st person plural inclusive
1SG	1st person singular
2PL	2nd person plural
2SG	2nd person singular
3PL	3rd person plural
3SG	3rd person singular
4PL	non-topical 4th person plural object pronoun used when the subject is a 3rd person pronoun or NP
4SG	non-topical 4th person singular object pronoun used when the subject is a 3rd person
ADVR	adverbaliser, prefix that derives an adverb from a verb or an adjective
ANA	anaphoric determiner
and1, and2, and3, and4	four distinct coordinating conjunctions
APP	applicative particle *ni*; transitivises intransitive verb complexes
ART1	basic article of the e-class nouns
ART2	basic article of the a-class nouns
ART3	basic article of the o-class nouns
CAUS	causative prefix
COMP	complementiser

CONSEC	consecutive conjunction *re* 'then, so that'
DEM	demonstrative
DEREL	derelationalising suffix
DIM	diminutive particle
DYAD	dyadic quantifier, see § 6.4
GOAL	directional preposition *vo*
INDEF	indefiniteness marker
IPFV	imperfective aspect marker; inflects for person and number
NEG ... NEG	disjunctive negation
NSPEC	non-specific (article)
OBJ.ART	object article
OBJM	object marker
PLM	plural marker
PN	proper name of person
POSS	possessive marker, inflects for person and number, see § 5
PREP	multiple purpose preposition, 'in', 'at', 'from', 'of', etc.
TAM	tense/aspect/mood marker
VOC	vocative particle

Bibliography

Corbett, G. G. 2000. *Number*. Cambridge: Cambridge University Press.

Evans, N. 2006. Dyadic constructions. In K. Brown (ed.), *Encyclopaedia of language and linguistics*, 24–28. Amsterdam: Elsevier 2nd edn.

Löbner, S. 2011. Concept types and determination. *Journal of Semantics* 28(3). 279–333.

Mosel, U. 2010a. Ditransitive constructions and their alternatives in Teop. In A. Malchukov, M. Haspelmath & B. Comrie (eds.), *Studies in ditransitive constructions: a comparative handbook*, 486–509. Berlin, New York: De Gruyter Mouton.

Mosel, U. 2010b. The fourth person in Teop. In J. Bowden, N. P. Himmelmann & M. Ross (eds.), *A journey through Austronesian and Papuan linguistic and cultural space: papers in honour of Andrew K. Pawley*, 391–404. Canberra: The Australian National University: Pacific Linguistics.

Mosel, U. & Even H. 1992. *Samoan reference grammar*. Oslo: Scandinavian Press.

Mosel, U. & Y. Thiesen. 2007. The Teop language corpus. Accessed 2013.09.08. http://www.mpi.nl/DOBES/projects/teop.

Ross, M.. 1988. *Proto-Oceanic and the Austronesian languages of Western Melanesia*. Pacific Linguistics Series C – No. 98. Canberra: The Australian National University: Pacific Linguistics.

Author

Ulrike Mosel
ISFAS, General Linguistics
Kiel University
umosel@isfas.uni-kiel.de

Semantic constraints on multiple case marking in Korean

Byong-Rae Ryu

This paper presents a first attempt to offer a comprehensive typology of the pairs of identical-case marked NPs in Korean. On the basis of such semantic relations between two consecutive NPs like meronymic relation, inclusion relation, quantity-quality relation, spatio-temporal relation, and predication relation, we identify 16 types of these pairs, and propose each type as a licensing condition on double case marking. We argue that the multiple case marking constructions are merely the sequences of double case marking, which are formed by dextrosinistrally sequencing the pairs of the same-case marked NPs of same or different type. Some appealing consequences of this proposal include a new comprehensive classification of the sequences of same-case NPs and a straightforward account of some long standing problems such as how the additional same-case NPs are licensed, and in what respects the multiple nominative marking and the multiple accusative marking are alike and different from each other.

1 Introduction

Despite numerous studies of the so-called multiple case marking constructions (MCCs), there still remain more puzzles unsettled than already solved. There have been only a few scattered attempts to explore the whole range of data in a balanced way. The majority of the previous studies have mainly or exclusively focused on the double nominative constructions (DNCs), missing the crucial points concerning the questions of how DNCs are related to the multiple nominative constructions (MNCs) on the one hand, and to the double accusative constructions (DACs) on the other (see Section 2.2). Furthermore, the question of how DACs are related to the multiple accusative constructions (MACs) still remains to be answered in Korean linguistics.

The latter two questions about double and multiple accusative marking arise out of the observation that multiplication of identical case marking is not confined to the nominative case. It can also be observed in accusative, and dative case marking contexts, as well as in other semantic case marking contexts such as the locative, instrumental, goal, and source cases (see Section 4.2). It has been touched on from time to time that multiple accusative marking is more restrictive than multiple nominative marking (cf. Cho 2003, Cho & Lee 2003, Chae & Kim 2008, among others). However, the question of in what respects the multiple nominative marking and the multiple accusative marking are alike and different from each other has not been explored in detail.

It is well-known that not all the sequences of NPs marked with identical case markers – be it nominative or accusative – are grammatical. This fact drives us to the question of why and how sequences of identical case-marked NPs are licensed. Little attention has been paid so far, however, to this licensing issue (see 2.2 for a critical review). We believe that a satisfactory solution of this licensing issue is a starting point for understanding the exact nature of MCCs better.

The purpose of this paper is twofold. Tackling this licensing issue, we argue that there are at least 16 types of sequences of same-case NPs in Korean on the one hand. On the other, we try to find an answer to the question of in what respects the multiple nominative marking and the multiple accusative marking are alike and different from each other. We explore comprehensive data including some less frequently discussed ones, and identify 16 lexical semantic relations as licensing conditions on identical case marking. After showing that all these types are attested in MCCs, we argue that MCCs are formed by dextrosinistrally sequencing the pairs of the same-case marked NPs of same or different type. We propose a set of licensing conditions from a lexical semantic point of view. We further argue that the two consecutive NPs are identically case-marked via case sharing: More specifically, two NPs share nominative cases if they stand in one of the 16 semantic relations, and they share accusative cases, if they stand in one of the 10 semantic relations. 6 out of 16 relations are not attested in the accusative case marking contexts.

This paper is organized as follows: In Section 2, we first present some key properties of identical case marking phenomena in Korean, and then critically review some previously proposed leading ideas. In Section 3, we argue that at least 16 semantic types of sequences of identical case-marked NPs should be assumed, showing that all these types are attested in MCCs. In Section 4, we propose the 16 semantic relations as licensing conditions for case multiplication, and argue that multiple case marking is simply case sharing between the two consecutive NPs standing in one of the 16 semantic relations. After we show in what respects the multiple nominative and accusative constructions are similar and different from each other, we finally draw a conclusion in Section 5.

2 Data and issues

2.1 Basic properties

Given the common assumption that there is at most one subject per clause, the multiple occurrences of subject-like, nominative-marked NPs are puzzling. This puzzling phenomenon can be noticed in various constructions in Korean, most notably in the so-called Double Nominative Constructions in (1).[1]

(1) [$_{NP_2}$ *ttokki-**ka***] [$_{NP_1}$ *kwi-**ka***] *kil-ta.*
    rabbit-NOM   ear-NOM be.long-DECL
    'The ears of rabbits are long. (lit.)' = 'Rabbits have long ears.'

At first glance, it is tempting to seek a pure representation of the theta structure of (1) in the clause (2), where the first NP is marked with genitive, occurring within the projection of the second NP.

(2) [$_{NP}$ *ttokki-uy kwi-**ka***] *kil-ta.*
    rabbit-GEN ear-NOM be.long-DECL
    'The ears of rabbits are long.'

The sentence (2) shows that the predicate *kilta* (to be long) is intransitive, and that the NP immediately preceding the predicate is the argument of the predicate. It follows from this observation that two nominative case-marked NPs, one of which is not an argument, occur in an intransitive clause in (1).

What makes the things more complicated is the fact that the number of the same-case NPs is not limited to two. Although it may not be indefinite for some – mainly cognitive and/or process-related – reasons, more than two same-case NPs

---

[1] The nominative case markers *-ka* and *-i* and the accusative case markers *-lul* and *-ul* are allomorphs, respectively. The former is post-vowel and the latter post-consonant. The Yale Romanization System is used for the romanization of the Korean words. The abbreviations for the glosses used in this paper are as follows: NOM (nominative), ACC (accusative), GEN (genitive), DAT (dative), PRES (present tense), PAST (past tense), NLZ (nominalizer), REL (relative clause marker), DECL (declarative), QUE (question), LOC (locative), INST (instrumental), CL (classifier), GOAL (goal), TMP (temporal), SRC (source), HON (honorification), SUF (suffix), FOC (focus), and TOP (topic).

may occur in a clause, as shown in (3) (see Choe 1987, Kim 1989, 1990, Maling & Kim 1992, Park 2001, among many others).

(3) a. [$_{NP_3}$ ttokki-**ka**] [$_{NP_2}$ kwi-**ka**] [$_{NP_1}$ kkuth-**i**] ppyocokha-ta.
 rabbit-NOM ear-NOM top-NOM be.pointed-DECL
 'The tops of the ears of the rabbit are pointed.'

b. [$_{NP_4}$ ttokki-**ka**] [$_{NP_3}$ kwi-**ka**] [$_{NP_2}$ kkuth-**i**] [$_{NP_1}$ thel-**i**]
 rabbit-NOM ear-NOM top-NOM fur-NOM
 kil-ta.
 be.long-DECL
 'The fur of the top of the ears of the rabbit is long.'

The sequences of same-case NPs can be observed not only in nominative case marking contexts like in (1) and (3), but also in accusative case marking contexts, as in (4).

(4) Hans-ka [$_{NP_3}$ ttokki-**lul**] [$_{NP_2}$ kwi-**lul**] [$_{NP_1}$ kkuth-**ul**] cap-ass-ta.
 Hans-NOM rabbit-ACC ear-ACC top-ACC grab-PAST-DECL
 'Hans grabbed the top of the ears of rabbits.'

Multiple case marking is observed in the clauses formed with various predicate types including intransitive stative verbs shown in (1) and (3), transitive verbs (4), ditransitive verbs (5), and activity verbs (6). The examples (1) and (3)–(6) clearly show that, contrary to the previous claims (e. g., in Kim, Sells & Yang 2007 among others, see also Kim 2000 for a similar claim), multiple case marking is not confined to the stative verbs.

(5) Hans-ka na-eykey [$_{NP_2}$ haksayng-**ul**] [$_{NP_1}$ yehaksayng-**ul**]
 Hans-NOM I-DAT student-ACC girl student-ACC
 ponay-ess-ta.
 send-PAST-DECL
 'Hans sent me girl students of students.'

(6) [$_{NP_2}$ haksayng-**i**] [$_{NP_1}$ yehaksayng-**i**] o-ass-ta.
 student-NOM girl student-NOM come-PAST-DECL
 'Girl students of students came.'

More than one nominative case-marked NP and more than one accusative case-marked NP can occur in a single transitive clause, as shown in (7).

(7) [$_{NP_{12}}$ haksayng-**i**] [$_{NP_{11}}$ yehaksayng-**i**] [$_{NP_{23}}$ ttokki-**lul**] [$_{NP_{22}}$
    student-NOM   girl student-NOM   rabbit-ACC

kwi-**lul**] [$_{NP_{21}}$ kkuth-**ul**] cap-ass-ta.
ear-ACC   top-ACC   grab-PAST-DECL
'Girl students of students grabbed the top of the ears of rabbits.'

Multiple case marking is noticed not only in an active clause, but also in a passive clause. The sentence (8) is a passive counterpart of the active sentence (7).[2]

(8) [$_{NP_{23}}$ thokki-**ka**/*-**lul**] [$_{NP_{22}}$ kwi-**ka**/-**lul**] [$_{NP_{21}}$ kkuth-**i**/-**ul**] [$_{NP_{12}}$
    rabbit-NOM/*-ACC   ear-NOM/-NOM   top-NOM/-ACC

haksayng-**eykey**] [$_{NP_{11}}$ yehaksayng-**eykey**] cap-hi-ess-ta.
student-by   girl student-by   grab-PASS-PAST-DECL
'The top of the ears of rabbits were grabbed by girl students of students.'

It is important to note that not all sequences of the same-case marked NPs are grammatical. The occurrence of the same-case marked NPs is not arbitrary, and the order of the same-case marked NPs is not random in many subtypes of the multiple case marking constructions. Scrambling of the same-case marked NPs is highly restricted, and generally results in ungrammaticality of the clause, as shown in (9).

(9) a. [$_{NP_3}$ Mary-**ka**] [$_{NP_2}$ chinkwu-**ka**] [$_{NP_1}$ sanguy-**ka**] khu-ta.
       Mary-NOM   friend-NOM   jacket-NOM be.big-DECL
       'The jacket of (a) friend of Mary is big.'

    b. *[$_{NP_3}$ Mary-**ka**] [$_{NP_1}$ sanguy-**ka**] [$_{NP_2}$ chinkwu-**ka**] khu-ta.
        Mary-NOM   jacket-NOM   friend-NOM be.big-DECL

So far, we have illustrated some core properties of the data we are dealing with. They are summarized as follows:

P1 Nonargument: Only one of the nominative case-marked NPs is the argument of the predicate, occurring in the subject position, and only one of the accusative case-marked NPs is the argument of the transitive predicate, occurring in the direct object position. All the other additional same-case NPs are nonargument.

---

[2] There are some claims that Korean has no passive constructions, unlike English or German. But it is clear in (8) that there is a construction in which a direct object argument is promoted to subject in the relevant nonactive sentences and the subject argument is demoted to the so-called agentive PP.

P2 Multiplicity: The number of the consecutive same-case NPs are not confined to two, but may be basically infinite.

P3 Nominative/Accusative marking: Multiple occurrences of the same-case NPs are not restricted to nominative case marking contexts (i.e., in subject position), but observed also in accusative case marking contexts (i.e., in direct object position).

P4 Semantic Regularity: In many subtypes of MCCs, the semantic relations between the two consecutive NPs turn out to be identical in the nominative case marking contexts and in the accusative case marking contexts.

P5 Predicate-independence: Multiple case marking is observed in the clauses formed with various predicate types including intransitive stative verbs, transitive verbs, ditransitive verbs, and activity verbs.

P6 Voice alternation: The semantic relations between the two consecutive NPs remain unchanged in the active and passive voice.

P7 Licensing condition: The multiple occurrences of the same-case marked NPs are not arbitrary or random, but systematic.

The core property **P1** is one of the most important criteria for distinguishing MCCs from some other constructions in which two consecutive NPs happen to be marked with the same-case marker. While additional same-case marked NPs do not saturate the valency of a predicate in MCCs, there are some constructions in which two identically case-marked NPs are subcategorized by a predicate, as can be seen in the psych-verb constructions in (10) and the copulative constructions in (11).

(10) *(John-i)   *(holangi-**ka**) silh-/musep-/cikyep-ta.
John-NOM tiger-NOM   dislike-/fear-/be.tired.of-DECL
'*(John) dislikes/fears/is tired of tigers.'   (psych-verb constructions)

(11) *(mul-i)   *(elum-i) toy-ess-ta.
water-NOM ice-NOM become-DECL
'*(Water) became ice.'   (copulative constructions)

Such examples as in (10) and (11) have been regarded as a type of MCCs in some studies (e.g., Rhee 1999, Park 2001, and Cha 2008, among others). It is clear, however, that they do not share the core property **P1**, since deletion of one NP results in ungrammaticality. They do not show the core properties **P3**, **P4**, **P5**,

P6 and **P7**, either. For these reasons, we are not concerned here with psych-verb constructions or copulative constructions containing two same-case NPs, and propose that they be excluded from MCCs.³ The only property they share with MCCs is **P2**, which is not a sufficient condition for being MCCs.

In the same vein, it is worth noting that the applicative formation as shown in (12b) should be distinguished from MCCs, in that the promoted argument – *Maria* in (12b) – is an argument of the predicate.

(12)   a. *Hans-ka   Maria-eykey kkoch-ul   cwu-ess-ta.*
           Hans-NOM Maria-DAT   flower-ACC give-PAST-DECL
           'Hans gave Maria flowers.'

       b. *Hans-ka   Maria-lul   kkoch-ul   cwu-ess-ta.*
           Hans-NOM Maria-ACC flower-ACC give-PAST-DECL
           'Hans gave Maria flowers.'

For this reason, we suggest that examples like in (12b) are not MCCs.⁴

2.2 A critical review of some previous main ideas

2.2.1 Double nominative/subject constructions

Sentences like (1) have been received much attention in Korean linguistics, as the long list of references of this paper already suggests. They have been examined under various terms such as Double Nominative Constructions (Cho 1999, Cha 2008, Choi 2012, Kang 1987), and Double Subject Constructions (Yoon 1987, 2007). Whatever term one may choose, it should be pointed out that the studies exclusively focusing on the clauses with two nominative case-marked NPs have difficulties in explaining the core properties **P2**, **P3**, and **P5**.

Examples like (1), (3), (6), (7), and (8) drive us to one of the key questions whether all nominative-marked NPs are subjects, and if not, what is the grammatical status of the nominative-marked nonsubject NPs. Regarding this question, two main streams of proposals are basically discernible.

---

[3] This is not to say that these two constructions may not involve sequences of identical case marked NPs. Since they show the core property **P2**, it is possible to add additional nominative NPs to the position preceding the first or the second NP. In other words, the two constructions can be MCCs, if more than three identical case-marked NPs occur. See Section 4 for further discussions.

[4] One might ask whether or not there is any case where MACs have no counterpart in MNCs. The example set (12) might be regarded as one of the cases. But it is not an example of MCCs, as discussed above. So we may draw a conclusion that there is no case where MACs have no counterpart in MNCs. I thank Yong-hun Lee (p.c.) for pointing out this aspect of MCCs.

One stream maintained that both NP_1 and NP_2 are subject, trying to define various notions of subject: e. g., Yu (1909) called them big and small subject, Yoon (2004, 2007) major and grammatical subject, and Lee (2007) subject [Spec, RefP] and subject [Spec, TP], respectively.[5] The other stream posited that only the right-most NP is subject, proposing that the left-most NP is topic or focus: e. g., Hong (1991) topic vs. subject; Rhee (1999) topic/focus vs. subject; Schütze (2001), Kim (2000, 2001), and Kim, Sells & Yang (2007) focus vs. subject; Park (2001) focused subject vs. subject; Choi (2012) sentential specifier vs. subject.

But there remain many essential problems unsolved in the first stream of thought, as partly pointed out by Chae & Kim (2008) among others.

First of all, a clause with more than one subject is highly odd from a perspective of theory of grammar.

Second, there is no straightforward answer to the question of what the logical structure of the clause looks like. In other words, there are clear difficulties in answering the question as to how the clauses can be interpreted in this view.

Third, there is no convincing independent evidence for assuming the various notions of subject – be it 'big' or 'small,' or 'major' or 'grammatical' – cross-linguistically as well as just in this language. Additionally, it is pointed out that the relationship between the various notions of subject is extremely vague (See Yoon 2004, 2007 for a series of efforts to define these two notions of subject).[6]

Fourth, the multiple subject view has difficulties in finding any clear answer to the status of the third and fourth NP. For example, the grammatical status of NP_3 and NP_4 in (3) remains unclear in the first main stream of thought. In other words, they have difficulties in explaining the core property **P2**.

Fifth, unduly evaluated in the first main stream of thought is the observation that multiple case marking is possible in the accusative case marking contexts as well as in the nominative case marking contexts, as pointed out in **P3**, **P4**, **P5**, and **P6**. For the multiple accusative case marked NPs, as observed in (4), (5), and (7), further notions such as 'major object' and 'grammatical object' would be needed.

For these reasons, any attempt to wrestle with the various notions of subject or exclusively with the clauses only with two nominative case-marked NPs may result in confusion of the issue at point.

---

[5] Choi (2008) differentiated two types of DNCs. In one type, the first nominative nominal is a grammatical subject, while the second one is a complement. In the other, both nominals are subjects, as a specifier of an IP or an AgrP.

[6] Yoon (2004, 2007) proposed subject-to-object raising and nominative case marking as diagnostics for 'major subjects,' and subject honorification and equi-controller in obligatory control as diagnostics for 'grammatical subjects.'

2.2.2 Focus/Topic

There are many unsettled problems also in the second main stream of thought. Kim (2001) claims that the sentence-initial nominative is the realization of information focus, as speculated in previous literature (Yoon 1997, 1989, O'Grady 1991, Lee 1994, Schütze 1996, among others). One of the main arguments he presented is the observation that only the first nominative case *-i/-ka* marked phrase can be *wh*-questioned, as shown in (13a). It is not allowed to *wh*-question the second one as shown in (13).

(13) a. *Nwu-ka apeci-ka kyoswu-i-si-ni?*
   who-NOM father-NOM professor-COP-HON-QUES
   '(lit.) Who is it whose father is a professor?'

   b. **John-i nwu-ka kyoswu-i-si-ni?*
   John-NOM who-NOM professor-COP-HON-QUES
   '(lit.) John's 'who' is a professor?'

However, it is highly questionable how the notion of focus/topic can be extended to the non-sentence-initial, non-preverbal nominative NPs (i. e., NP_2 in (3a), and NP_2 and NP_3 (3b)). The contrast in grammaticality between (14a) and (14b) suggests that these notions be applied only to the first NP among the sequences of the same-case NPs. In sum, the second main stream of thought faces difficulties in explaining the core property **P2**, too.

(14) a. $[_{NP_3}$ *mues-i*$]$ $[_{NP_2}$ *kwi-ka*$]$ $[_{NP_1}$ *kkuth-i*$]$ *ppyocokha-ni?*
   what-NOM   ear-NOM   top-NOM be.pointed-QUES
   '(lit.) What is it whose top of the ears is pointed?'

   b. *$[_{NP_3}$ *mues-i*$]$ $[_{NP_2}$ *mues-i*$]$ $[_{NP_1}$ *kkuth-i*$]$ *ppyocokha-ni?*
   what-NOM   what-NOM   top-NOM be.pointed-QUES

Furthermore, it is highly unclear how the notion of focus/topic can be applied to the accusative case-marked NPs (i. e., NP_2 and NP_3 in (4), and NP_2 in (5)), simply because the proponents of this view exclusively examined the double nominative/subject constructions. We can speculate that such notions may be applied only to the first NP among the sequences of the accusative-case marked NPs, as the contrast in grammaticality between (15a) and (15b) suggests.

(15) a. Hans-ka [$_{NP_3}$ *mues*-**lul**] [$_{NP_2}$ *kwi*-**lul**] [$_{NP_1}$ *kkuth*-**ul**]
Hans-NOM   what-ACC   ears-ACC   top-ACC
cap-ass-ni?
grab-PAST-QUES
'(lit.) The top of the ears of what did Hans grab?'

b. *Hans-ka [$_{NP_3}$ *mues*-**lul**] [$_{NP_2}$ *mues*-**lul**] [$_{NP_1}$ *kkuth*-**ul**]
Hans-NOM   what-ACC   what-ACC   top-ACC
cap-ass-ni?
grab-PAST-QUES

Based on the discussion above, it is safe to draw the conclusion that the second main stream of thought faces difficulties in explaining the core properties **P2, P3, P4, P5,** and **P6.** This gives us enough reason to believe that one might miss the point if one were to exclusively deal with the double nominative constructions. At the same time, this allows us to assume that double nominative constructions should be examined in more general contexts of multiple identical case marking in Korean linguistics. Therefore, a promising approach to this topic should cope not only with double nominative constructions, but also with clauses with more than two same-case NPs – MNCs and MCCs – in a balanced way.

2.2.3 Double vs. multiple and nominative vs. accusative

It is interesting to note that the majority of the previous works with the terms of multiple nominative/subject constructions and multiple accusative/object constructions have mainly, if not exclusively, focused on the double nominative/subject constructions and double accusative/object constructions (for MNCs see Yim 1984, Choe 1987, Choi 1988, Youn 1990, Gerdts 1991/2000, Kim 1996, Jang 1998, Koh 1999, Moon 2000, Park 2001, Kim 2001, Hong 2001, Suh 2003, Kim, Sells & Yang 2007, Choi 2008, and Lee 2008; see Bak 1992 and Kim 2006 for MACs). It is undeniable that the question of how MCCs and DMCs are related with each other remains blurred in the majority of the previous works with the exception of only a few, e. g., Yang (1972), Park (2001), and Kim (2001) among others.

There are, however, many pieces of evidence for the insight that multiple case marking is systematically possible in the object as well as in the subject position. This shows that, contrary to the prevailing views, multiple case marking is restricted neither to stative verbs nor to the sentence-initial position. It has been touched on from time to time but not explored in detail that the multiple accusative marking is a little more constrained than the multiple nominative marking (e. g., in Bak 1992, Lee 1994, Choi 2008 among others).

2.2.4 Possession as generative source

Sentences like (1) and (3) have been examined under terms like inalienable possession constructions (Choi 2007, Yoon 1997), possessor ascension constructions (Choi 1988), and possessor agreement constructions (Cho 2003, Lee & Cho 2003). These terms reflect the insight that the referent of the first NP inalienably possesses the referent of the second NP in (1). It has been tacitly assumed that there are some semantic relations between the referents of the same-case marked NPs. Some researchers advanced this insight and tried to classify the sequences of the same-case marked NPs into several subtypes. The studies mentioned above in this paragraph can be regarded as attempts to find an answer to the question related to the core properties **P4** and **P7**.

As suggested above, it could be tempting to try and find a licensing condition for the sequences of same-case NPs (e. g., (1)) in the corresponding NP with a genitive-marked NP (e. g., (2)). The most widespread approach claims that the sequences of same-case NPs may be formed if the two consecutive same-case NPs are in a *possessor-possessed* relation. The approach advanced along this line of thinking is highly common in the derivational grammar framework. According to this approach, generally known as the genitive approach, additional nominative NP occurs via cyclic NP movement out of the subject NP with genitive specifiers. Since this approach is the most influential, it deserves detailed discussions in a separate Section 2.2.4.

While there can be no doubt that there exists a certain similarity between the multiple nominative constructions and the corresponding sentence with subject with a genitive NP, there are many other conceptual or distributional differences between the two sentences (see Na & Huck 1993 and Kim 2000, among others).

First, the two sentences manifest meaning differences, as Na & Huck (1993: 190) pointed out. If this is true, in terms of the transformational grammar, the MNCs and the genitive constructions may not share the same D-structure, whatever it may be. This is the first and the most fundamental problem which the genitive approach faces.

Second, MNCs in which more than two nominative NPs occur do not have corresponding genitive sources, where the second NP is realized in genitive, as shown in (16).

(16) *John-i   chinkwu-**ka**/*-uy apeci-**ka**   pwuca-i-ta.*
John-NOM friend-NOM/*-GEN father-NOM be.rich-PRES-DECL
'The father of John's friend is rich.'

Third, while the genitive approach might seem to be plausible at least for some MNCs, there are other MNCs which have no acceptable genitive source (Na & Huck 1993: 190). As the examples in (17) show, all the MNCs, where the two consecutive NPs stand in a class-membership, an object-quantity, a space-object, or a conventional relation, are systematically ungrammatical.

(17)   a. *pihayngki-**ka**/*-uy   777-**i**   khu-ta.*
          airplane-NOM/*-GEN 777-NOM be.big-DECL
          'It is as for airplanes that 777 is big.'   (class-membership relation)

       b. *mal-**i**/*-uy   twu mali-**ka**   talli-n-ta.*
          horse-NOM/*-GEN two head-NOM run-PRES-DECL
          'Two heads of horses are running.'   (object-quantity relation)

       c. *thomatho-**ka**/*-uy pelley-**ka**   tulkkulh-nun-ta.*
          tomato-NOM/*-GEN worm-NOM be.infested-PRES-DECL
          'Tomatos are infested with worms.'   (space-object relation)

       d. *catongcha-**ka**/*-uy [isangha-n   naymsay]-**ka** na-n-ta.*
          car-NOM/*-GEN   be.strange-REL smell-NOM   be.emitted-PRES-DECL
          'A strange smell is emitted from the car.'
                                                  (conventional relation)

Fourth, in a variety of cases a genitive is not readily convertible into a nominative NP (cf. Na & Huck 1993: 191).

Fifth, some multiple nominative constructions have a proper noun NP in the position immediately preceding the main predicate. The last two points can be seen in example (18), which shows that the first NP in (18) may not be a possessor occurring in the specifier position of the corresponding NP structure.

(18) *san-**i**/*-uy   selaksan-**i**   alumtap-ta.*
     mountain-NOM/-GEN Mt. Seorak-NOM be.beautiful-DECL
     'As for mountains, Mt. Seorak is beautiful.'

To sum up, it is safe to draw the conclusion that, based on the semantic and distributional differences, multiple nominative constructions are constructions which may not be derived from the corresponding genitive sources.

3 A typology of multiple case marking constructions

It goes back to Yang (1972), to my knowledge, to try to find the generative source of the sequences of same-case NPs in some semantic relationships between two consecutive nominative NPs. He argues that the 'macro-micro relation' is one of the generative sources, refuting the genitive view.[7] This relation refers to a relation where an NP is conceptually divided into the whole NP itself and a subpart of it. The NP which corresponds to the former is referred to as a macro-NP, while that corresponding to the latter is referred to as a micro-NP. Yang (1972: 42ff.) classifies this macro-micro relation into 5 subtypes on the basis of their semantic contents: (i) whole-part, (ii) class-member, (ii) type-token, (iii) total-quantity, and finally (v) affected-affector.[8]

The licensing issue has been tackled again by Na & Huck (1993). They proposed that two consecutive nominative case-marked NPs need to be in a certain semantic relation, called 'thematic subordination': X is 'thematically subordinate' to an entity Y iff Y's having the properties that it does entails that X has the properties that it does. The view in Na & Huck (1993) has been adopted in many subsequent works in Korean linguistics (see Kim 2000, 2001, and Kim, Sells & Yang 2007, among others). Na & Huck (1993: 195) classify these thematic subordination relations into five subtypes: (i) part-whole relation (e. g., *cover-book, morning-day, eye-person*, etc.), (ii) qualitative relation (e. g., *use-tool, length-pants, height-woman*, etc.), (iii) conventional relation (e. g., *car-man, picture-woman, dog-girl*, etc.), (iv) conversive relation (e. g., *parent-child, master-servant, employer-employee*, etc.), and (v) taxonomic relation (e. g., *apple-fruit, oak-tree, chair-furniture*, etc.).

The part-whole relation and the taxonomic relation in Na & Huck (1993) roughly correspond to the whole-part and the class-member relation in Yang (1972), respectively. The other three relations – qualitative, conventional, and conversive – are newly proposed.

---

[7] For other generative sources of the multiplication of case markers, Yang (1972: 159 & 195) added two groups of verbs. One group includes verbs of self-judgment (e. g., *siphta* (to be desirous of), *cohta* (to be fond of), *kipputa* (to be glad), *masissta* (to be tasty), etc.) and verbs of semi-self-judgment (e. g. *philyohata* (to be necessary), *chwungpunhata* (to be enough), *kanunghata* (to be possible), *swipta* (to be easy), etc.). The other group Yang (1972: 175) adds is verbs of existence (*issta* (to exist), *epsta* (not to exist), *manhta* (to exist a lot), and *cekta* (to barely exist)). The first group may well be regarded as psych-verbs.

[8] According to Yang (1972: 45), the affected-affector macro-micro relation is a 'solidarity' relation and some sort of natural pairing, e. g., kinship, teacher-student, society-individual, etc. We do not assume this relation as an independent class, but regard it as an instance of conversive relation.

Such terms as whole-part, (inalienable/alienable) possessor-possessum, kinship, thing-property, locative-theme, etc. have sometimes been adopted in the literature (e.g., Choe 1987, Choi 1988, Youn 1990, Gerdts 1991/2000, Whitman 1991/2000, Kim 1996, Yoon 1997, Koh 1999, Moon 2000, Hong 2001, Lee 2008, etc.), and used to name the whole constructions at the same time (see Koh 1999, Hong 2001, Lee 2008, Choi 2008: 902 for a critical survey). At least three pieces of desiderata of this tradition may be alluded to.

First of all, the definitions of each term are not clear at all. For example, the whole-part relation is interchangeably used with the inalienable possessor-possessum relation in many works. As will be discussed below in detail, however, the inalienable possessor-possessum relation is only a subtype of six subtypes of the meronymic relation, and not all subtypes of the whole-part relation share the same properties with the inalienable possessor-possessum relation. This is one of the major sources of confusion found in many of the previous studies.

Another point of desiderata can be found in the sentences like (19), which Yang (1972: 43) regarded as an example of a part-whole relation. Such examples are problematic simply because of the fact that *sayk* (color) is not a part of *mucikay* (rainbow).

(19) ce   mucikay-ka   sayk-i   kop-ta.
      that rainbow-NOM color-NOM be.pretty-DECL
      'That rainbow's color is pretty.'   (= (2b), Yang 1972: 43)

A third piece of desiderata of the previous works is their incompleteness of classification. As will be clear soon, there are many other semantic relations which are responsible for multiplication of same-case NPs in Korean, but have unduly received little attention.

To remedy these desiderata, we start our discussion by advancing some important achievements of mereology and taking into consideration some data, which have, relatively speaking, been less frequently discussed in the literature.

3.1 Meronymic relations

Whole-part relations or meronomies gave rise to a wide range of studies in linguistics, psychology, philosophy and artificial intelligence (Cruse 1986, Iris et al. 1988 and Winston et al. 1987). Based on psycholinguistic experiments and the way in which the parts contribute to the structure of the wholes, Winston et al. (1987) determined six types of part-whole relations: (i) component-integral object, (ii) member-collection, (iii) portion-mass, (iv) stuff-object, (v) feature-activity, and (vi) place-area. Only the first relation has been previously discussed in the context of MCCs. We adopt the definition of the six types of meronymic relations in Winston et al. (1987), as summarized in Table 1. We argue that all six types should be assumed for licensing of the sequences of same-case NPs.

Relation	Examples	Functional	Homeomerous	Separable
integral-obj.-component	cup-handle / punchline-joke	−	−	+
collection-member	forest-tree / deck-card	−	−	+
mass-portion	pie-slice / salt-grain	−	+	+
object-stuff	martini-gin / bike-steel	−	−	−
activity-feature	shopping-paying / adolescence-dating	+	−	−
area-place	Florida-Everglades / desert-oasis	−	+	−

1. Functional (+)/Nonfunctional (−): Parts are/are not in a specific spatial/temporal position with respect to each other, which supports their functional role with respect to the whole.
2. Homeomerous (+)/Nonhomeomerous (−): Parts are similar/dissimilar to each other and to the whole to which they belong.
3. Separable (+)/Inseparable (−): Parts can/cannot be physically disconnected, in principle, from the whole to which they are connected.

Table 1: Six types of meronymic relations: Winston et al. (1987: 421)

TYPE 1: INTEGRAL OBJECT-COMPONENT. The integral object-component relation is a relation between components and the objects to which they belong. Integral objects have a structure; their components are separable and have a functional relation with their wholes (e.g., *elephant-nose, person-leg, bike-pedal, tree-bark, opera-aria, cup-handle, car-wheel, person-hand, person-hair*, etc.). This relation roughly corresponds to the whole-part relation in Yang (1972), the part-whole relation in Na & Huck (1993), and the inalienable possessive specifier relation of Park (2001). This relation is attested in the pairs of two consecutive NPs found in MNCs (20a) and MACs (20b).

(20) a. *thokki-**ka** kwi-**ka** kil-ta.*
rabbit-NOM ear-NOM be.long-DECL
'The ears of rabbits are long.'

b. *Hans-ka   thokki-**lul** kwi-**lul** cap-ass-ta.*
      Hans-NOM rabbit-ACC ear-ACC grab-PAST-DECL
      'Hans grabbed the ears of rabbits.'

As Winston et al. (1987) notes, pieces of objects are distinct from their components, and pieces belong to a different family of meronymic relations that we call mass-portion relation (see Type 3: Mass-portion below). Unlike components, pieces lack a determinate functional relation to their wholes, and typically have arbitrary boundaries, as Cruse (1986: 157ff.) notes.

TYPE 2: COLLECTION-MEMBER. The collection-member relation represents membership in a collection. Members are parts, but they cannot be separated from their collections and do not play any functional role with respect to their whole (e. g., *fleet-ship, army-soldier, faculty-professor, forest-tree, deck-card,* etc.). Membership in a collection is determined on the basis of spatial proximity (e. g., to be part of a forest, a tree must be spatially close to the other trees) or by social connection (e. g., groups). This relation is also attested in the pairs of two consecutive NPs found in MNCs (21a) and MACs (21b).

(21) a. *i   hamtay-**ka** camswuham-i   manh-ta.*
         this fleet-NOM   submarine-NOM be.plenty-DECL
         'There are plenty of submarines in this fleet.'

      b. *cekkwun-i   i   hamtay-**lul** camswuham-**ul** paksalnay-ass-ta.*
         enemy-NOM the fleet-ACC   submarine-ACC destroy-PAST-DECL
         'The enemy destroyed the submarines of this fleet.'

Collection must be distinguished from classes. The class-membership relation (see Type 7: Class-membership below) is not a meronymic relation, because it is not expressed by 'part,' but by 'is.'

TYPE 3: MASS-PORTION. The mass-portion relation captures the relations between portions and masses, extensive objects, and physical dimensions. The parts are separable and similar to each other and to the wholes which they comprise, and do not play any functional role with respect to their whole (e. g., *pie-slice, kilometer-meter, salt-grain of salt, cake-piece,* etc.). This relation is also attested in the pairs of two consecutive NPs found in MNCs (22a) and MACs (22b).

(22) a. *sokum-**i** alkayngi-**ka** kwulk-ta.*
         salt-NOM grain-NOM   be.thick-DECL
         'The grains of (this) salt are thick.'

b. *Hans-***ka** *sokum-***ul** *alkayngi-***lul** *noki-ess-ta.*
Hans-NOM salt-ACC grain-ACC melt-PAST-DECL
'Hans melted the grains of (this) salt.'

TYPE 4: OBJECT-STUFF. The object-stuff category encodes the relations between an object and the stuff of which it is partly or entirely made. The parts are not similar to the wholes that they comprise, cannot be separated from the whole, and have no functional role (e. g., *car-steel sheet, desk-wood, bike-steel*, etc.). This relation is also attested in the pairs of two consecutive NPs found in MNCs (23a) and MACs (23b).

(23) a. *KIA cha-***ka** *kangphan-***i** *twukkep-ta.*
KIA car-NOM steel sheet-NOM be.thick-DECL
'The steel sheet of KIA cars is thick.'

b. *Hans-***ka** *KIA cha-***lul** *kangphan-***ul** *cohaha-n-ta.*
Hans-NOM KIA car-ACC steel sheet-ACC like-PRES-DECL
'Hans likes the steel sheet of KIA cars.'

TYPE 5: FEATURE-ACTIVITY. The feature-activity relation captures the semantic links within features or phases of various activities or processes. The parts have a functional role, but they are not similar or separable from the whole (e. g., *golf-putting, eating-swallowing, shopping-paying* and *eating-chewing*, etc.). This relation is also attested in the pairs of two consecutive NPs found in MNCs (24a) and MACs (24b).

(24) a. *kolphu-***ka** *phething-***i** *elyep-ta.*
golf-NOM putting-NOM be.difficult-DECL
'As as as the game of golf is concerned, the putting is difficult.'

b. *Hans-***ka** *kolphu-***lul** *phething-***ul** *cohaha-n-ta.*
Hans-NOM golf-ACC putting-ACC like-PRES-DECL
'What Hans likes about golf is the putting.'

TYPE 6: AREA-PLACE. The area-place relation captures the relation between areas and special places and locations within them. The parts are similar to their wholes, but they are not separable from them (e. g., *Korea-Seoul, Florida-Everglades, desert-oasis*, etc.). This relation is also attested in the pairs of two consecutive NPs found in MNCs (25a) and MACs (25b).

(25) a. *California-***ka** *Silicon Valley-***ka** *ttattusha-ta.*
California-NOM Silicon Valley-NOM be.warm-PAST-DECL
'It is warm in California's Silicon Valley.'

b. *Hans-ka California-lul Silicon Valley-lul pangmunha-ess-ta.*
   Hans-NOM California-ACC Silicon Valley-ACC visit-PAST-DECL
   'Hans visited Silicon Valley in California.'

So far, we have introduced 6 types of whole-part relations. We have argued that each type functions as a licensing condition for multiplication of same-case NPs, showing that each type can be attested in the pairs of two consecutive NPs found in MNCs and MACs. It amounts to the claim that the meromymic relations are syntactically visible in MCCs in Korean. We will show 10 more nonmeronymic relations which are responsible for multiple case marking in Korean.

3.2 Inclusion relations

TYPE 7: CLASS-MEMBERSHIP. Class-membership or hyponymy is not a part-whole relation, and is usually expressed in the frames, 'Xs are type of Y,' 'Xs are Ys,' 'X is a kind of Y,' and 'X is a Y' (Cruse 1986: 89, Lyons 1977: 292, Miller & Johnson-Laird 1976: 241). Class inclusion and meronymy (especially, collection-membership) are clearly distinguished when expressed by 'kind of' and 'part of.' (e. g., *flower-rose, airplane-777, dog-German shepherd, fruit-apple, tree-oak, furniture-chair, tool-saw, bird-sparrow, clothes-shirt, games-soccer*, etc.).[9]

This relation corresponds to the class-member relation in Yang (1972) and Park (2001), and the taxonomic relation in Na & Huck (1993). This relation is one of the major sources of the pairs of two consecutive NPs found in MNCs (26a) and MACs (26b).

(26) a. *pihayngki-ka eyepesu-ka khu-ta.*
       airplane-NOM Airbus-NOM be.big-DECL
       'The Airbus airplane is big.'

   b. *Hans-ka pihayngki-lul eyepesu-lul tha-ass-ta.*
      Hans-NOM airplane-ACC Airbus-ACC take-PAST-DECL
      'John took the Airbus airplane.'

---

[9] They are sometimes difficult to distinguish in the case of activities and abstract nouns. They can be ambiguous as to whether they are to be taken as expressing class inclusion or meronymy (Lyons 1977: 314–316), as can be seen in (i).

   (i) a. *Frying is part of/a type of cooking.*
       b. *Honesty is part of/a type of virtue.*

This relation properly includes the type-token relation in Yang (1972), since 'rising sun' is a kind of 'sun' in (27).

(27) *hay*-**ka** [*ttu-nun hay*]-**ka** *mesiss-ta*.
  sun-NOM rise-REL sun-NOM be.spectacular-DECL
  'As for the sun, the rising sun is spectacular.'

Free relatives with bound nouns like *kos* (place) and *pun* (honored person) may be regarded as an example of class-membership, as can be seen in (28). Given that the relative pronoun must be co-indexed with the preceding noun, 'the restaurant whose foods are delicious' is a kind of 'restaurant' in (28).

(28) a. *siktang*-**i**   *(*masiss-nun*) *kos*-**i**   *cek-ta*.
    restaurant-NOM be.delicious-REL place-NOM be.rare-DECL
    'Restaurants whose foods are delicious are rare.'

  b. *kyoswu*-**ka**   *(*yumyengha-n*) *pun*-**i**   *manh-ta*.
    professor-NOM be.famous-REL person-NOM be.many-DECL
    'There are many professors who are famous.'

TYPE 8: OBJECT-ATTACHMENT. Pairs such as *ear-earring, chimney-TV antenna*, and *fishing line-hook* do not express a part-whole relation, since the latter may be attached to, but not parts of, the former. This relation, which we call object-attachment relation, might be confused with meronymy since the relation paraphrased by 'to be attached to' can be also observed in whole-part relations: for example, *earrings are attached to ears* and *fingers are attached to hands*. Fingers are attached to hands, but they are also parts of hands; while earrings are attached to ears, but are not parts of ears (cf. Cruse 1979).

This relation is also attested in the pairs of two consecutive NPs found in MNCs (29a) and MACs (29b).

(29) a. *kwi*-**ka** *kwikoli*-**ka**   *nemu khu-ta*.
    ear-NOM earring-NOM too be.big-DECL
    'The earrings of the ears are too big.'

  b. *Hans*-**ka** *kwi*-**lul** *kwikoli*-**lul** *cap-ass-ta*.
    Hans-NOM ear-ACC earring-ACC grasp-PAST-DECL
    'John grasped the earrings of the ears.'

3.3 Quality-quantity relations

TYPE 9: OBJECT-QUALITY. The object-quality relation captures a relation between an object and its typical property. The objects may or may not form a structure, their properties have a characterizing function (e. g., *tool-use, pants-length, person-height, eyes-color, skin-texture, room-temperature, food-taste, hair-shine*, etc.). The object-quality relation is frequently attested in the sequences of the two consecutive same-case NPs, as shown in (30).

(30) a. *paci-**ka**   kili-**ka**   ccalp-ta.*
pants-NOM length-NOM be.short-DECL
'The length of the pants is short.'

b. *Hans-ka   paci-**lul**   kili-**lul**   calu-ess-ta.*
Hans-NOM pants-ACC length-ACC cut-PAST-DECL
'Hans cut the length of the pants.'

TYPE 10: OBJECT-QUANTITY. The object-quantity relation captures a relation between an object and its floated quantifiers (e. g., *student-number CL, horses-number CL, water-number CL, car-number CL, apple-number CL*, etc.). The sentences in (31) are sometimes called floating quantifier constructions (FQCs). They clearly show that they are formed on the basis of this object-quantity relation, and contain consecutive NPs sharing nominative case ((31)a) or accusative case ((31)b).

(31) a. *haksayng-i   twu myeng-i   o-ass-ta.*
student-NOM two person-NOM come-PAST-DECL
'Two of the students came.'

b. *John-i   haksayng-**ul** twu myeng-**ul**   ponay-ess-ta.*
John-NOM student-ACC two person-ACC send-PAST-DECL
'John sent two of the students.'

In Sections 3.2 and 3.3, we introduced 4 more types of semantic relations which are different from meronymic relations. Type 7 (class-membership relation) and Type 8 (object-attachment relation) are grouped into inclusion relation, and Type 9 (object-quality relation) and Type 10 (object-quantity relation) are grouped into quality-quantity relation. We argued that each of these 4 types functions as a licensing condition for multiplication of same-case NPs, showing that each type can be attested in the pairs of two consecutive NPs found in MNCs and MACs. We will show 6 more relations which are responsible for multiple case marking in Korean.

3.4 Spatio-temporal relations

TYPE 11: SPACE-OBJECT. The space-object relation represents a relation between an object and the space in which it is placed (e. g., *container-crack, tomato-worm, beach-girl; city-weather, kids-illness*, etc.). This relation captures the relationship between two NPs found in the locative type of Park (2001). This relation, however, is not attested in MACs as shown in (32b), but only in the sequences of the two consecutive nominative NPs, as can be seen in (32a).

(32) a. *ku haypyen-i miin-tul-i katukha-ta.*
 that beach-NOM sexy girl-PL-NOM be.crowed-DECL
 'The beach is crowded with sexy girls.'

 b. **na-nun ku haypyen-ul miin-tul-ul cohaha-n-ta.*
 I-TOP that beach-ACC sexy girl-PL-ACC like-PRES-DECL

TYPE 12: TIME-OBJECT. The time-object relation captures a relation between an object and the time in which it occurs (e. g., *summer-beer, autumn-weather, nowadays-camera, spring-flowers, yesterday-body, tomorrow-kids, that time-cinema,* etc.). Sentences like (32a) are sometimes called adjunct type DNCs (cf. Kim, Sells & Yang 2007 among others). Interestingly enough, this relation is not attested in MACs as shown in (33b), but only in MNCs, as can be seen in (33a).

(33) a. *yelum-i maykcwu-ka masiss-ta.*
 summer-NOM beer-PL-NOM be.tasty-DECL
 'Beers of summer are tasty.'

 b. **na-nun yelum-ul maykcwu-lul cohaha-n-ta.*
 I-TOP summer-ACC beer-PL-ACC like-PRES-DECL

3.5 Predication relations

TYPE 13: POSSESSOR-OBJECT. The possessor-object relation, in general, is an asymmetric relationship between two constituents, the referent of one of which (= the possessor) possesses the referent of the other (= the object). X and Y may enter into a possessor-object relation, if their relations may be characterized by such predicates as *have, own,* and *rules over*. This relation is not attested in MACs, but only in MNCs, as can be seen in (34).

(34) a. *ku yeca-ka kapang-i mesiss-ta.*
 that lady-NOM bag-PL-NOM be.fashionable-DECL
 'The bag of that lady is fashionable.'

b. *na-nun ku yeca-**lul** kapang-**ul** cohaha-n-ta.
      I-TOP   that lady-ACC bag-PL-ACC like-PRES-DECL

Alienable and inalienable possession are commonly distinguished. We understand only the alienable possession under Type 13 (possessor-object relation). The inalienable possession is a proper portion of Type 1 (integral object-component relation).

TYPE 14: CONVENTIONAL RELATION. The conventional relation captures relations in which some entity X is related to some individual Y by virtue of convention, rather than as a consequence of their inherent properties. Following Cruse (1986) and Na & Huck (1993), we'll call these relationships conventional (e.g., *man-car, woman-picture, car-smell, tiger-area of movement, girl-dog, boy-hat, bird-nest, animal-territory, person-clothes*, etc.). There are in principle a variety of conventional relations into which X and Y may enter if a conventional relation holds between X and Y, and these relations may be more accurately characterized by a variety of predicates other than *have* (cf. Na & Huck 1993: 197).[10]

(35) a. *the car that the man drives*

   b. *the clothes that the boy is modeling*

   c. *the house that the architect designed*

This relation is not attested in MACs, but only in MNCs, as can be seen in (36).

(36) a. tokil-**i**   catongcha-**ka** thunthunha-ta.
         Germany-NOM car-NOM   be.solid-PRES-DECL
         'The cars manufactured in Germany are solid.'

   b. *na-nun tokil-**lul**   catongcha-**lul** cohaha-n-ta.
      I-TOP   Germany-ACC car-ACC   like-PRES-DECL

TYPE 15: OBJECT-PREDICATION. The object-predication relation captures an asymmetric relation between two consecutive NPs; the referent of the one is construed to be agent or theme argument of the other (e.g., *person-complaint, father-love, bomb-explosion, car-acceleration, ship-voyage*, etc.). The NPs expressing predication are typically Sino-Korean verbal nouns as *pulphyeng* (complaint) in (37), but

---

[10] According to Na & Huck (1993), conventional relations differ from meronomic and qualitative relations in at least one respect which has important linguistic consequences. If X is thematically subordinate to Y, and if X and Y are in a meronomic relation (similarly for qualitative relations), then there is only one possible relation into which X and Y can enter. In English, this relation is characterized by the predicate *have*, so that a complex NP may be formed such that 'X which (a, the) Y has' is grammatical.

they can be gerunds formed by attaching a derivational suffix -*ki* or -*um* as *ilk-ki* (reading) in (38).[11] The two NPs involved in an object-predication relation cannot occur in the context of MACs (37b), but only in MNCs, as shown in (37a).

(37) a. *ttal-i   pulphyeng-i   taytanha-ta.*
       daughter-NOM complaint-NOM be.plenty-DECL
       'The complaints of (my) daughter are plenty.'

   b. **na-nun ttal-**ul**   pulphyeng-**ul**   miwuyha-n-ta.*
       I-TOP   daughter-ACC complaint-ACC hate-PRES-DECL

When a gerund is a predication noun, the case marking pattern is somewhat different from that of the sentences in which a Sino-Korean verbal noun is used as a predication noun. While the left-most NP may be marked either by nominative or by accusative case in the context of MNCs, only accusative marking is allowed in the context of MACs, as can be seen in (38).

(38) a. *i   chayk-i/-**ul**   ilk-ki-**ka**   elyep-ta.*
       this book-NOM/-ACC read-NMZ-NOM be.difficult-DECL
       'This book is difficult to read.'

   b. *Hans-ka   i   chayk-*i/**ul**   ilk-ki-**lul**   silheha-n-ta.*
       Hans-NOM this book-*NOM/-ACC read-NMZ-ACC hate-PRES-DECL
       'Hans hates to read this book.'

Nominative marking in (38a) and accusative marking in (38b) are not surprising, but accusative marking in (38a) needs an explanation. Given that a gerund like *ilk-ki* (reading) has both a nominal and a verbal property at the same time, it is reasonable to assume that the accusative-marked [$_{NP}$ *i chayk-ul*] (this book) is in the complement position inside the VP headed by *ilk-* (to read): [$_{NP}$ [$_{VP}$ [$_{NP}$ *i chayk-ul*] [$_V$ *ilk-*]] [$_N$ *-ki*]].

TYPE 16: CONVERSIVE RELATION. Following Na & Huck (1993), we define the conversive relation as a (roughly symmetric) relation in which the entities denoted by the first nouns are in the relevant cases construed to be in institutional hierarchies to the entities denoted by the second nouns with which they are paired (e. g., *parent-child, master-servant, employer-employee, husband-wife, doctor-patient, host-parasite,* etc.). The kinship relations, the social relations, and the so-called affector-

---

[11] The object-predication relation is a major source of multiple same-case marking in verbal noun constructions, in which the functional verbs *hata* (to do) and *toyta* (to become) are used to form active and passive sentences, respectively (see Ryu 1993 for details).

affected relation in Yang (1972) are subsumed by the conversive relation. This relation is not attested in MACs, but only in MNCs, as can be seen in (39).

(39) a. *ku uysa-**ka**   hwanca-**ka**   manh-ta.*
       that doctor-NOM patient-NOM be.plenty-DECL
       'The patients of that doctor are plenty.'

   b. **na-nun ku uysa-**lul**   hwanca-**lul**   cohaha-n-ta.*
       I-TOP   that doctor-ACC patient-ACC like-PRES-DECL

So far, we have introduced 6 semantic relations which can be observed in the context of MNCs, but not in MACs. As a whole, we have identified 16 types of the sequences of same-case NPs in Korean, as summarized in Table 2.

Proposed type of MCCs	Yang (1972)	Na & Huck (1993)	Other terms used elsewhere in the literature
Type 1: integral obj.-component	whole-part	meronomic rel.	inalienable possession con.
Type 2: collection-member	×	×	×
Type 3: mass-portion	×	×	×
Type 4: object-stuff	×	×	×
Type 5: activity-feature	×	×	×
Type 6: area-place	×	×	×
Type 7: class-membership	class-member type-token	taxonomic rel.	NP-split con. type-token
Type 8: object-attachment	×	×	×
Type 9: object-quality	×	qualitative	thing-property
Type 10: object-quantity	total-quantity	×	floating quantifier con.
Type 11: space-object	×	×	locative-theme
Type 12: time-object	×	×	adjunct focus con.
Type 13: possessor-object	×	×	alienable possession
Type 14: conventional relation	×	conventional	×
Type 15: object-predication	×	×	*tough* con. light verb con.
Type 16: conversive relation	affected-affector	conversive	kinship, solidarity, or social relation

1. rel. and con. is an abbreviation for 'relation' and 'constructions', respectively.
2. The symbol × refers to 'not mentioned.'

Table 2: A comparison of types of multiple case marking constructions

4 The formation of multiple case marking constructions

4.1 The 16 semantic relations as licensing conditions

We have identified 16 semantic relations which may hold between the two consecutive identical case marked NPs in MCCs. We have shown that 10 out of 16 semantic relations (Type 1 to Type 10) are attested in both MNCs and MACs. The other 6 semantic relations (Type 11 to Type 16) are attested in MNCs, but not in MACs. It follows from what has been discussed that at least the 16 semantic relations constitute the backbone of the formation of a pair of the same-case marked NPs.

In Section 1, we showed that the NP immediately preceding the intransitive predicate is an argument. This argument is the right-most NP of the sequences of the identical case-marked NPs, regardless of the number of the NPs occurring in the sequence. All additional NPs preceding the argument NP are nonargument.

DCCs are exactly the constructions in which two consecutive same-case marked NPs occur, one of which is not subcategorized for by the predicate. We argue that MCCs are formed by dextrosinistrally sequencing the pairs of the same-case marked NPs of same or different type. In other words, the 16 semantic relations constitute a licensing condition for forming a pair of the same-case marked NPs, and consequently a licensing condition for forming MCCs.

Let me illustrate the process of formation of MCCs step by step. We made it clear that the most basic clause of MCCs is DCCs in which only two consecutive same-case marked NPs occur. For example, the MCCs in (40b)–(40d) are formed on the basis of the clause (40a).

(40) a. [$_{NP_1}$ *thel-i*]   *kil-ta.*
      fur-NOM be.long-DECL
      'The fur is long.'

   b. [$_{NP_2}$ *kkuth-i*] [$_{NP_1}$ *thel-i*]   *kil-ta.*
      top-NOM   fur-NOM be.long-DECL
      'The fur of the top is long.'

   c. [$_{NP_3}$ *kwi-ka*] [$_{NP_2}$ *kkuth-i*] [$_{NP_1}$ *thel-i*]   *kil-ta.*
      ear-NOM   top-NOM   fur-NOM be.long-DECL
      'The fur of the top of the ears is long.'

d. [$_{NP_4}$ *ttokki-***ka**] [$_{NP_3}$ *kwi-***ka**] [$_{NP_2}$ *kkuth-***i**] [$_{NP_1}$ *thel-***i**]
   rabbit-NOM   ear-NOM   top-NOM   fur-NOM
   kil-ta.
   be.long-DECL
   'The fur of the top of the ears of the rabbit is long.'

The NP_2 is licensed in (40b), since it stands in an object-attachment relation (Type 8) to NP_1. The NP_3 is licensed in (40b), since it stands in an area-place relation (Type 6) to NP_2. The NP_4 is licensed in (40b), since it stands in an integral object-component relation (Type 1) to NP_3.

More complicated clauses can be explained according to our proposal. Let us examine the sentence (7), repeated here in (41b) for ease of presentation.

(41) a. [$_{NP_{11}}$ *twu myeng-***i**]   [$_{NP_{21}}$ *kkuth-***ul**] *cap-ass-ta.*
       two person-NOM   top-ACC   grab-PAST-DECL
       'Two persons grabbed the top.'

   b. [$_{NP_{12}}$ *haksayng-***i**] [$_{NP_{11}}$ *twu myeng-***i**]   [$_{NP_{23}}$ *ttokki-***lul**] [$_{NP_{22}}$
       student-NOM   two person-NOM   rabbit-ACC
       *kuy-***lul**] [$_{NP_{21}}$ *kkuth-***ul**] *cap-ass-ta.*
       ear-ACC   top-ACC   grab-PAST-DECL
       'Two students grabbed the top of the ears of rabbits.'

In (41), the predicate *cap-* (to grab) is a transitive verb, subcategorizing NP_{11} and NP_{21}. The clause (41b) is formed on the basis of the simplest clause (41a). NP_{12} is licensed in (41b), since it stands in an object-quantity relation (Type 10) to NP_{11}. NP_{22} is licensed in (41b), since it stands in an area-place relation (Type 6) to NP_{21}. NP_{23} is licensed in (41b), since it stands in an integral object-component relation (Type 1) to NP_{22}.

The licensing condition proposed here can explain the formation of MCCs like (9a), but also the ungrammaticality of sequences like (9b). For the purpose of presentation, we repeat the relevant examples in (42).

(42) a. [$_{NP_5}$ *Mary-***ka**] [$_{NP_4}$ *chinkwu-***ka**] [$_{NP_3}$ *os-***i**]   [$_{NP_2}$ *baci-***ka**]
       Mary-NOM   friend-NOM   clothes-NOM   pants-NOM
       [$_{NP_1}$ *thong-***i**]   *khu-ta.*
       pant legs-NOM be.wide-DECL
       'The pant legs of pants of clothes of friends of Mary are wide.'

b. *[$_{NP_5}$ Mary-ka] [$_{NP_1}$ thong-i] [$_{NP_2}$ baci-ka] [$_{NP_3}$
   Mary-NOM   pant legs-NOM   pants-NOM
   os-i]   [$_{NP_4}$ chinkwu-ka] khu-ta.
   clothes-NOM   friend-NOM   be.wide-DECL

In (42a), [$_{NP_5}$ Mary-ka] stands in a conversive relation (Type 16) to [$_{NP_4}$ chinkwu-ka], which in turn stands in a possession-object relation (Type 13) to [$_{NP_3}$ os-i], which in turn in a class-membership relation (Type 7) to [$_{NP_2}$ baci-ka], which in turn stands in an object-quality relation (Type 9) to [$_{NP_1}$ thong-i]. The NP$_1$ is subcategorized for by the predicate *khu-* (to be big) and all other NPs are licensed by the licensing condition proposed here.

However, the example (42b) is ungrammatical, although the same NPs occur as in the grammatical counterpart (42a). It should be noted that, unlike in (42a), [$_{NP_4}$ chinkwu-ka] – i.e., not [$_{NP_1}$ thong-i] – is subcategorized for by the predicate in (42b). The ungrammaticality of (42b) can be explained in various ways: first of all, the second right-most NP [$_{NP_3}$ os-i] may not be licensed by any semantic relations. Second, although [$_{NP_5}$ Mary-ka] stands in a conversive relation (Type 16) to [$_{NP_4}$ chinkwu-ka], there are many other NPs between them, which do not stand in a semantic relation to the latter. In other words, the example (42b) is ungrammatical, since NP$_5$ and NP$_1$ are not consecutive.

4.2 Multiple case marking as case sharing

The main idea being put forward in this paper is that the sequences of same-case NPs can be cyclically formed, if the immediately preceding NP stands in one of the 16 semantic relations to the right-most NP of the sequence. Therefore, the right-most NP of the sequence of same-case NPs is the starting point of the formation of the sequences of same-case NPs in Korean.

There are some pieces of evidence for the assumption that the right-most NP of an NP sequences functions as "conceptual head" and argument of the predicate. Let us examine the example (43) from Cho & Lee (2003):

(43) a. *Mary-ka   John-ul   elkwul-ul ttayly-ess-ta.*
       Mary-NOM John-ACC face-ACC hit-PAST-DECL
       'Mary hit John's face.'

   b. **Mary-ka   John-ul   elkwul-ul salanghay-ss-ta.*
       Mary-NOM John-ACC face-ACC love-PAST-DECL
       'Mary loved John's face.'

The sentence (43b) is ungrammatical, since the NP *elkwul* (face) violates the selectional requirement of the verb *salanghata* (to love). This example shows that the the right-most NP of an NP sequences is argument of the predicate.

The contrast between (44a) and (44b) further supports the view that the right-most NP of an NP sequence is the argument selected by the predicate.

(44) a. *Vampire-ka   John-ul   phi-lul   ppal-ass-ta*
Vampire-NOM John-ACC blood-ACC suck-PAST-DECL
'A vampire sucked John's blood.'   (Type 1: Integrated object-component)

b. **Vampire-ka   John-ul   phi-lul   masi-ess-ta*
Vampire-NOM John-ACC blood-ACC drink-PAST-DECL
'A vampire drank John's blood.'   (Type 13: possessor-object)

The sentence (44b) is ungrammatical, since the verb *masita* (to drink) requires an NP having the feature [-integrated], whereas the verb *ppalta* (suck) selects an NP [+integrated] (examples from Cho & Lee 2003). The NPs standing in a possessor-object relation cannot occur in multiple accusative marking contexts. So, (44b) is ungrammatical.

We argue in this section that the two consecutive NPs are identically case-marked via case sharing, if they stand in one of the 16 semantic relations. In this sense, licensing of NPs is morphosyntactically visible by the identical case. We can illustrate the mechanism of multiple case marking as follows:

(45) Multiple case marking as case sharing
   a. Double case marking

   ... NP_2[CASE $\boxed{1}$] NP_1[CASE $\boxed{1}$] ... V

   b. Multiple case marking

   ... NP_3[CASE $\boxed{1}$] NP_2[CASE $\boxed{1}$] NP_1[CASE $\boxed{1}$] ... V

There are many pieces of evidence showing that the licensing of NPs is accompanied by the identical case. First of all, the active-passive alternation shows that the identical case should be shared between the NPs within the sequence. We have already illustrated this point in (7) and (8), which we repeat here in (46a) and (46b).

Semantic constraints on multiple case marking in Korean

(46) a. [$_{NP_{12}}$ *haksayng*-**i**] [$_{NP_{11}}$ *yehaksayng*-**i**] [$_{NP_{23}}$ *ttokki*-**lul**] [$_{NP_{22}}$
　　　　student-NOM　　　　girl student-NOM　　　　rabbit-ACC

kwi-**lul**] [$_{NP_{21}}$ *kkuth*-**ul**] *cap-ass-ta.*
ear-ACC　　　　top-ACC　grab-PAST-DECL
'Girl students of students grabbed the top of the ears of rabbits.'

b. [$_{NP_{23}}$ *thokki*-**ka**] [$_{NP_{22}}$ *kwi*-**ka**] [$_{NP_{21}}$ *kkuth*-**i**] [$_{NP_{12}}$
　　rabbit-NOM　　　　ear-NOM　　　　top-NOM

haksayng-**eykey**] [$_{NP_{11}}$ *yehaksayng*-**eykey**] *cap-hi-ess-ta.*
student-by　　　　　　girl student-by　　grab-PASS-PAST-DECL
'The top of the ears of rabbits were grabbed by girl students of students.'

There are two sets of sequences of NPs marked with the same case in (46a); one set in the context of nominative case marking, and the other in the context of accusative case marking. By contrast, the former occurs in the context of agentive postposition marking *-eykey* in (46b), and the latter in the context of nominative case marking.[12] The point to be noted here is that all the NPs in each sequence can be marked with the same-case marker.

---

[12] In Korean, the case markers on the case-agreeing nominal in some highly restricted set of MCCs alternate between nominative and accusative depending on voice. In addition to the passive sentence (46b), a more complicated passive sentence is possible in Korean, where the second and the third NP are alternatively marked with accusative case, as shown in (i). I thank Ik-Soo Kwon (p.c.) for drawing my attention to this phenomenon. Maling & Kim (1992) and Cho & Lee (2003) assume that the lexical passives of Korean do not always absorb accusative case. In particular, they assume that an indirect 'adversity' passive adds a benefactive/malefactive subject and assigns accusative case to its complements.

(i) [$_{NP_{23}}$ *thokki*-**ka**] [$_{NP_{22}}$ *kwi*-**lul**] [$_{NP_{21}}$ *kkuth*-**ul**] [$_{NP_{12}}$ *haksayng*-**eykey**] [$_{NP_{11}}$
　　rabbit-NOM　　　　ear-ACC　　　top-ACC　　　　student-by

yehaksayng-**eykey**] *cap-hi-ess-ta.*
girl student-by　　grab-PASS-PAST-DECL
'The top of the ears of rabbits were grabbed by girl students of students.'

Some technical details aside, Maling & Kim (1992) and Cho & Lee (2003) do not account for such sentences as in (i) in the same way as they do for passive sentences in general. Many researcher seem to agree that these sentences should be regarded as a special case, and they may not be seen as a counter-example against the general case-sharing proposal.

The peculiarity of such sentences as in (i) can be found in several points: First, this case marking pattern is not observed in the so-called phrasal passive, but only in the lexical passive. Second, some additional selectional restrictions such as [+animateness] are required for the left-most NP. Third, a transitive relation should hold between the NPs occurring within the sequence of NPs. We speculate that some sort of theta-transfer (cf. Lee & Cho 2003) is involved in the process of passivization. We further speculate that this peculiar case marking pattern occur only in the subtypes of meronymic relations (Type 1 to Type 6). Other types of MCCs do not show this peculiarity. The generalization would be as follows: Only the left-most NP of the sequence of NPs entering the 6 meronymic relations (Type 1 to Type 6) can be marked with nominative in passive voice, leaving all other NPs marked with accusative case, if a transitive relation holds between the NPs within the sequence.

A second set of evidence comes from Yang's (1972) observation. Yang (1972: 51 ff.) observed that the macro-micro relations are not confined only to the nominative marker. This relation also holds true with other case markers. In our terms, NPs may be marked with the same case – be it with nominative, accusative or other semantic case markers – if they are licensed by the semantic relations.

(47) a. *John-ka   ai-**eykey** chakha-n   ai-**eykey** Bible-ul   kaluchi-ess-ta.*
      John-NOM child-DAT be.good-REL child-DAT Bible-ACC teach-PAST-DECL
      'John taught the Bible to a child, a good child.'   (class-membership)

   b. *Mary-ka   cha-**lo**   pemphe-**lo**   cencwu-lul pat-ass-ta.*
      Mary-NOM car-INST bumper-INST pole-ACC hit-PAST-DECL
      'Mary hit an electric pole with her car's bumper.' (integral object-component)

   c. *i   kangaroo-ka   nampankwu-**eyse**   Australia-**eyse***
      this kangaroo-NOM Southern Hemisphere-SRC Australia-SRC
      o-ass-ta.
      come-PAST-DECL
      'This kangaroo came from the Southern Hemisphere, from Australia.'
      (area-place)

   d. *Mary-ka   caknyen-**ey**   kaul-**ey**   sicipka-ass-ta.*
      Mary-NOM last year-TMP autumn-TMP marry-PAST-DECL
      'Mary married last fall.'   (mass-portion)

   e. *saca-ka   holangi-**hanthey** twu mali-**hanthey** ka-ass-ta.*
      lion-NOM tiger-GOAL   two heads-GOAL   go-PAST-DECL
      'A lion went to two heads of tigers.'   (object-quantity)

   f. *Mary-ka   cip-**eyse**   pang-**eyse** kongpwuha-ess-ta.*
      Mary-NOM home-LOC room-LOC study-PAST-DECL
      'Mary studied at home, in the room.'   (integral object-component)

The examples in (47) show that the two consecutive NPs which enter into one of the 16 semantic relations are identically marked with semantic case markers such as dative, instrumental, source, temporal, goal, and locative case marker.

Concerning the core property **P1**, we argued in Section 1 that the simplest form of the psych-verb constructions in (10) and the copulative constructions in (11) is not an instance of MNCs, consequently not an instance of MCCs. This is not to say that these two constructions may not involve sequences of identical case-marked NPs, since it is possible to add an additional nominative NP to the position preceding to the first or the second NP. The examples in (48) are MCCs formed on the basis of these two constructions.

(48) a. [$_{NP_3}$ *John-i*]   [$_{NP_2}$ *holangi*-**ka**] [$_{NP_1}$ *ippal-i*]   *silh-/musep-ta.*
       John-NOM   tiger-NOM   teeth-NOM dislike-/fear-DECL
       'John dislikes/fears the teeth of tigers.'

   b. [$_{NP_3}$ *mul-i*]   [$_{NP_2}$ [*matang-uy*] *mul-i*]   [$_{NP_1}$ *elum-i*]
       water-NOM   backyard-GEN water-NOM   ice-NOM
       toy-ess-ta.
       become-DECL
       'Water, water in the backyard, became ice.'

It should be noted that, while NP_3 and NP_1 are subcategorized for in (48a), NP_2 and NP_1 are subcategorized for by the predicate in (48b). The only nonargument NP in (48a) is NP_2, which is licensed by Type 1 integral object-component relation holding between NP_2 and NP_1. In the same vein, the only nonargument NP in (48b) is NP_3, which is licensed by Type 7 class-membership relation holding between NP_1 and NP_2. Thus, our proposal predicts that the two constructions can be MCCs, if more than three identical case-marked NPs occur.

4.3 Multiple nominative vs. accusative marking

It has been touched on from time to time but not explored in detail that multiple accusative marking is a little more constrained than multiple nominative marking (e. g., in Bak 1992, Lee 1994, Choi 2008 among others). In Section 3, we have shown that 10 out of 16 semantic relations (Type 1 to Type 10) are attested in both MNCs and MACs. The other 6 semantic relations (Type 11 to Type 16) are attested in MNCs, but not in MACs. The discussion in Section 3 enables us to answer the long-standing question as to in what respects the multiple nominative marking and the multiple accusative marking are alike and different from each other. If our discussion is correct, the answer is the generalization of the discussion in Section 3 which can be stated as follows:

(49) Multiple nominative vs. accusative marking

   a. The nominative case of the right-most NP may be shared with an additional preceding consecutive NP, if the latter stands in one of the 16 semantic relations to the former (Type 1 to Type 16).

b. The accusative case of the right-most NP may be shared with an additional preceding consecutive NP, if the latter stands in one of the first 10 semantic relations to the former (Type 1 to Type 10).

The semantic relations which do not license the sequence of accusative NPs are Type 11 (space-object), Type 12 (time-object), Type 13 (possessor-object), Type 14 (conventional relation), Type 15 (object-predication), and Type 16 (conversive relation). The set of the semantic relations in MACs is a proper subset of the semantic relations in MNCs. It turns out that there is no relation which occur in MACs, but not in MNCs.

5 Conclusion

The purpose of this paper was twofold. The first purpose was to argue that there are at least 16 types of sequences of same-case NPs in Korean. The second purpose was to answer the question of in what respects the multiple nominative marking and the multiple accusative marking are alike and different from each other.

We examined comprehensive data including some less frequently discussed examples, and identify 16 semantic relations found in the pairs of identical case-marked NPs. After showing that all these types are attested in MCCs, we argue that MCCs are formed by dextrosinistrally sequencing the pairs of the same-case marked NPs of same or different type. We further show that, while the nominative case marker is shared between two consecutive NPs standing in one of the 16 semantic relations, multiplication of the accusative case marker is possible between two consecutive NPs standing in only one of the 10 semantic relations.

Some appealing consequences of this proposal include a new comprehensive classification of the sequences of identical case-marked NPs and a straightforward account of some long standing problems such as how an additional same-case NPs are licensed, in what respects the multiple nominative marking and the multiple accusative marking are alike and different from each other, how only some subsets of sequences of same-case NPs are possible, and why the order of the NPs in the sequences of same-case NPs should be strictly preserved.

Bibliography

Bak, Jung-Sup. 1992. Multiple subjects and multiple objects. In *Studies in Generative Grammar 2*. 293–334. Written in Korean.

Cha, Jong-Yul. 2008. A typology of double nominative constructions in Korean. Ms., Paper presented at the 18th International Congress of Linguists (SIL XIII), Seoul, Korea.

Chae, Hee-Rahk & Ilkyu Kim. 2008. A clausal predicate analysis of Korean multiple nominative constructions. *Korean Journal of Linguistics* 33. 869–900.

Cho, Sae-Youn. 1999. The syntactic structure of some double nominative constructions in Korean. *Linguistics* 7. 335–348.

Cho, Sungeun. 2003. A conditioning factor in possessor agreement constructions. In Patricia M. Clancy (ed.), *Japanese/Korean linguistics*, vol. 11, 343–351. Stanford: CSLI Publications.

Cho, Wonbin & Sungeun; Lee. 2003. Possessor agreement as Theta feature sharing. *Language and Information* 7. 163–178.

Choe, Hyun-Sook. 1987. Syntactic adjunction, A-chains, and multiple identical case constructions. In Joyce McDonough & Bernadette Plunkett (eds.). *Proceedings of North Eastern Linguistic Society (NELS)*, vol. 17, 100–121.

Choi, Incheol. 2007. A constraint-based approach to Korean inalienable possession constructions. *Studies in Modern Grammar* 47. 95–115. Stanford: CSLI Publishing.

Choi, Incheol. 2012. Sentential specifiers in the Korean clause structure. In Stefan Müller (ed.), *Proceedings of the 19th international conference on head-driven phrase structure grammar*, 75–85.

Choi, Kiyong. 2008. Two types of double nominative constructions in Korean: A case of GEN/NOM alternation. *Korean Journal of Linguistics* 33, 901–928.

Choi, Young-Seok. 1988. *A study of possessor ascensions construction in Korean*, Doctoral dissertation. University of Hawaii dissertation.

Cruse, D. A. 1979. On the transitivity of the part-whole relation. *Journal of Linguistics* 15, 29–38.

Cruse, D. A. 1986. *Lexical semantics*. Cambridge: Cambridge University Press.

Gerdts, D. 1991/2000. The syntax of case-marked possessors in Korean. In John Whitman & Chungmin Lee (eds.), *Korean syntax and semantics LSA institute workshop, Santa Cruz 1991*, 19–34. Seoul: Taehaksa.

Hong, Ki-Sun. 1991. *Argument selection and case-marking in Korean*: Stanford University dissertation. Doctoral dissertation.

Hong, Yong-Tcheol. 2001. Structure des constructions à sujet multiple. *Enseignement de Langue et Littérature Françaises* 11, 159–183. Written in Korean.

Iris, M. A., B. E. Litowitz & M. Evens. 1988. Problems of the part-whole relation. In M. Evens (ed.), *Relational models of the lexicon*, 261–288. Cambridge: Cambridge University Press.

Jang, Youngjun. 1998. Multiple subjects and characterization. *Discourse and Cognition* 5, 99–116.

Kang, Myung-Yoon. 1987. Possessor raising in Korean. In Susumu Kuno et al. (eds.), *Harvard studies in Korean linguistics*, vol. II, 80–88. Seoul: Hanshin Publishing Company.

Kim, Jong-Bok. 2000. A constraint-based approach to some multiple nominative constructions in Korean. In Akira Ikeya & Masahito Kawamori (eds.), *Proceedings of the 14th pacific asia conference on language, information, and computation*, 165–176. Toyko: Logico-Linguistic Society of Japan.

Kim, Jong-Bok. 2001. A constraint-based and head-driven analysis of multiple nominative constructions. In D. Flickinger & A. Kathol (eds.), *Proceedings of the 7th international conference on head-driven phrase structure grammar*, 166–181. Stanford: CSLI Publishing.

Kim, Jong-Bok, P. Sells & Jaehyung Yang. 2007. Parsing two types of multiple nominative construction: A constructional approach. *Language and Information* 11, 25–37.

Kim, Kwang-sup. 1996. Multiple subject constructions in Korean and English. In Hee-Don Ahn et al. (eds.), *Morphosyntax in generative grammar*, 235–249. Seoul: Hanguk Publishing Company.

Kim, Yong-Ha. 2006. A case for ellipsis in Korean: The non-movement multiple object construction. In *Studies in generative grammar* 16, 707–742.

Kim, Young-joo. 1989. Inalienable possession as a semantic relationship underlying predication: The case of multiple-accusative constructions. In Susumu Kuno et al. (eds.), *Harvard studies in Korean linguistics*, vol. III, 445–467. Seoul: Hanshin Publishing Company.

Kim, Young-joo. 1990. *The syntax and semantics of Korean case: The interaction between lexical and syntactic levels of representation*. Doctoral dissertation. Harvard University.

Koh, Jae-Sol. 1999. Multiple nominative constructions and the inner subjects of adjectives. *Korean Journal of Linguistics* 24, 531–556. Written in Korean.

Lee, Chungmin. 1994. Definite/specific and case marking in Korean. In Young-Key Kim-Renaud (ed.), *Theoretical issues in Korean linguistics*, 345–361. Stanford: CSLI Publications.

Lee, Hyeran. 2008. Criterial effects and multiple nominative constructions. In *Studies in generative grammar* 18. 477–508.

Lee, Seong-yong. 2007. Two subject positions in multiple nominative constructions. *Journal of Language Sciences* 14, 239–262.

Lee, Wonbin & Sungeun Cho. 2003. Case agreement in possessive constructions. In *Studies in generative grammar*, vol. 13, 633–655. Walter de Gruyter.

Lyons, J. 1977. *Semantics*, vol. 1. Cambridge: Cambridge University Press.

Maling, J. & Soowon Kim. 1992. Case assignment in the inalienable possession construction in Korean. *Journal of East Asian Linguistics* 1, 37–68.

Miller, G. A. & P. N. Johnson-Laird. 1976. *Language and perception*. Cambridge, MA: Harvard University Press.

Moon, Gui-Sun. 2000. The predication operation and multiple subject constructions in Korean. In *Studies in generative grammar* 10. 239–263.

Na, Younghee & G. J. Huck. 1993. On the status of certain island violations in Korean. *Linguistics and Philosophy* 16, 181–229.

O'Grady, W. 1991. *Categories and case*. Amsterdam: John Benjamins Publishing.

Park, Byung-Soo. 2001. Constraints on multiple nominative constructions in Korean: A constraint-based lexicalist approach. *The Journal of Linguistic Science* 20, 147–190.

Rhee, Seongha. 1999. On the multiple nominative constructions in Korean. In Young-Wha Kim, Il-Kon Kim & Jeong-Woon Park (eds.), *Linguistic investigations: In honor of professor In-Seok Yang*, 198–430. Seoul: Hankuk Publisher.

Ryu, Byong-Rae. 1993. Structure sharing and argument transfer: An HPSG approach to verbal noun constructions. SfS-Report 04-93. Seminar für Sprachwissenschaft, University of Tübingen.

Schütze, C. 1996. Korean case stacking isn't: Non-case uses of case particles. In Kiyomi Kusumoto (ed.), *Proceedings of the North East Linguistic Society*, vol. 26, 351–365.

Schütze, C. T. 2001. On Korean 'case stacking': the varied functions of the particles ka and lul. *The Linguistic Review* 18, 193–232.

Suh, Sangki. 2003. The distribution of multiple subject constructions in Korean. *Language Research* 39, 839–857.

Whitman, J. 1991/2000. Adjunct major subjects in Korean. In J. Whitman & Chungmin Lee (eds.), *Korean syntax and semantics LSA institute workshop*, Santa Cruz 1991. 1–8. Seoul: Taehaksa.

Winston, M., R. Chaffin & D. Hermann. 1987. A taxonomy of part-whole relations. *Cognitive Science* 11, 417–444.

Yang, In-Seok. 1972. *Korean syntax: Case markers, delimiters, complementation and relativization*. Doctoral Dissertation. The University of Hawaii.

Yim, Young-Jae. 1984. The syntactic nature of the multiple subject construction. *Language Research* 20, 321–330.

Yoon, J. H. 1987. Some queries concerning the syntax of multiple subject constructions in Korean. In Susumu Kuno et al. (eds.), *Harvard studies in Korean linguistics*, vol. II, 138–162. Seoul: Hanshin Publishing Company.

Yoon, J. H. 1989. The grammar of inalienable possession construction in Korean, Mandarin and French. In Susumu Kuno et al. (eds.), *Harvard studies in Korean linguistics*, vol. III, 357–368. Seoul: Hanshin Publishing Company.

Yoon, J. H. 2004. Non-nominative (major) subjects and case-stacking in Korean. In P. Bhaskararao & K. V. Subbarao (eds.), *Non-nominative subjects*, vol. 2, 265–314. Berlin: Mouton de Gruyter.

Yoon, J. H. 2007. The distribution of subject properties in multiple subject constructions. In Y. Takubo (ed.), *Japanese/Korean linguistics*, vol. 16, 64–83. Stanford: CSLI Publications.

Yoon, Jeong-Me. 1997. The argument structure of relational nouns and inalienable possessor constructions in Korean. *Language Research* 33, 231–265.

Youn, Cheong. 1990. *A relational analysis of Korean multiple nominative constructions*. Seoul: Hanshin Publishing Company.

Yu, Kil-chun. 1909. *Tayhanmuncen (Korean Grammar, written in Korean)*. Yungmunkwan.

Author

Byong-Rae Ryu
Department of Linguistics
Chungnam National University, South Korea
ryu@cnu.ac.kr

Semantic and grammatical aspects of verbs and sentences

Glück auf, der Steiger kommt: a frame account of extensional and intensional *steigen*

Thomas Gamerschlag, Wilhelm Geuder & Wiebke Petersen

Abstract[*]

The paper investigates the meaning variation of the German movement verb *steigen* ('climb'/'rise'). Three major uses are contrasted within a frame-based analysis: *steigen* as a verb of manner of motion, as a verb of directed movement and as an intensional verb. The modeling in terms of Barsalou frames, i. e., in terms of functional attributes and their values, allows an explicit account of the correlations that hold among subevents, manner, positions and the overall path traversed by the theme argument, and yields a representation of the event structure and the argument structure with flexible granularity. By investigating the variation in the attribute structure of the verb *steigen* in the extensional and intensional uses we give an analysis that captures the relation between the uses as a transfer of the relevant attributes from verb-frame-internal attributes in the extensional use to verb frame-external attributes which are realized by functional nouns such as *Temperatur* 'temperature' in the intensional use. Thereby, we offer an account of the polysemy of *steigen* which goes beyond the usual picture of a metaphor.

---

[*] The research presented in this paper was supported by the CRC 991, funded by the German Research Foundation (DFG). Moreover, we are grateful to three anonymous reviewers for their insightful questions and valuable suggestions.

Thomas Gamerschlag, Wilhelm Geuder & Wiebke Petersen

1 Introduction[1]

The empirical domain addressed in the present paper is the meaning variation found in spatial and abstract senses of movement verbs, specifically the German verb *steigen*. On the whole, this verb belongs to the same lexical field as English *climb*, which has generated some amount of discussion in the literature on verb semantics (from Fillmore 1982b and Jackendoff 1985 up to Levin & Rappaport Hovav 2013). However, the case of *steigen* is somewhat more complex because the meaning spectrum is richer: *steigen* encompasses meanings that can variously be translated into English as *climb*, *rise*, and to some extent *step*. The four major uses illustrated in (1) can be distinguished.

(1) *steigen*

    a. as a verb of manner of motion
        Sebastian stieg   auf einen Berg.
        S.   climbed on a   mountain
        'Sebastian climbed a mountain.'

    b. as a verb of directed motion
        Der Ballon stieg.
        the balloon climbed
        'The balloon was climbing.'

    c. as a static verb of "fictive motion"
        Die Straße steigt   langsam (an).
        the road   climbs slowly   PART
        'The road climbs slowly upwards.'

    d. as an intensional verb of change along a property scale
        Die Temperatur der   Flüssigkeit steigt.
        the temperature of.the liquid   is rising
        'The temperature of the liquid is rising.'

Here, our main objective is to elucidate the relationship between the uses as a movement verb, especially as a verb of directed movement, and the intensional variant. A frequently cited example of the intensional use is *The temperature is*

---

[1] In the wake of the first version of this paper, numerous requests have been voiced that we should translate or explain the obscure German line in its title. However, given that it is a cultural item that largely eludes translation, and given that Sebastian may have immediately noticed the most important conceptual relations between *Glück auf* and *Glückwunsch*, we feel we may refrain from addressing this issue in depth. The following may be helpful, though: http://www.youtube.com/watch?v=lwz_dfxpeKo.

ninety and rising (in the German version of this, *rise* would translate as *steigen*) — and the classic puzzle arising from it is that the temperature may be said to be '90°', but '90°' cannot be said to be rising (cf. Montague 1973, Jackendoff 1979, Löbner 1981). While in most of the literature authors have capitalized on the intensionality effect associated with the subject of the construction, we want to focus here on the conditions in the lexical semantic representation of the verb that enable such uses. In doing this, we will also point out the connections that relate this use to the other variants of *steigen* which do not translate as *rise*. (Although interesting in itself, the third variant is outside the scope of the present paper).

As for the theoretical domain of investigation, it turns out that the analysis of extensional and intensional *steigen* is at the intersection of a whole number of issues that have been central concerns throughout Sebastian Löbner's work: it touches on the topic of intensional verbs and functional concepts, both of which are already keywords of his 1979 dissertation, as well as on his recent endeavors at advancing frame theory as a tool for semantics (Löbner 2014). Beginning with the earlier strand of work, it is to be noted that the subject in an intensional use of *steigen* is precisely a functional noun in the sense of Löbner (1985), i. e., a noun that refers to a function which relates an explicitly or contextually given carrier of an attribute to a unique value (at each point of time). In *Die Temperatur des Wassers steigt* ('The temperature of the water is rising'), 'water' is assigned the attribute TEMPERATURE whose value is increasing during the event time of rising.

In the latter strand of work mentioned above, Sebastian Löbner has put forward two fundamental hypotheses about cognition and conceptual representations: (1) "The human cognitive system operates with a single general format of representations [and (2)] ... this format is essentially Barsalou [1992] frames", (Löbner 2014: 23 f.). Frames represent concepts in terms of a network of functional attributes and their values (instead of, say, feature sets or sets of entailments). Hence, one can say that "[f]unctional concepts constitute the representational 'vocabulary' of categorization" (Löbner 2011b: 14). One task that we are facing now is to represent event categories, e. g., the lexical meanings of our movement verbs, in terms of such frame structures. What is more, however: with intensional *steigen/rise*, we begin to see an interplay of the use of functional concepts in the architecture of the verb's representation and the appearance of a functional concept as the subject argument of this verb (as in *The temperature (of the water) is rising*). This double appearance of functional concepts, both as the denotation of argument expressions and as components inside the frame representation of verbs, has been emphasized in Löbner (2011b: 18) as being of general significance:

> "If Barsalou is correct in assuming that the basic structure of all concepts in human cognition is frames, then functional nouns represent the type of concepts which our entire cognition is based on. Attribute concepts, i.e., instances of functional concepts, form the structure of the mental representations in our cognitive system: we categorize whatever we categorize in terms of functional concepts."

What we would like to offer, therefore, in an attempt to add to this general program laid out in the quotations, is an investigation of the variation in the attribute structure of the verb *steigen* in its different uses, in connection with an investigation of the shift between functional concepts occurring either in the verb's meaning or in the verb's arguments, depending on the lexical variant at hand.

We will proceed as follows: in Section 2 we set out the differences in the uses of *steigen* as a manner of motion verb and as a verb of directed motion. A frame-based analysis of these uses is provided in Section 3, which also contains a brief general introduction to this representation format. The intensional variant of *steigen* is the topic of Section 4 where it will be analyzed as based on the directed motion reading. Finally, Section 5 provides a brief summary and outlook.

2 Manner of motion and direction of motion in the semantics of *steigen*

Diachronically, the underlying sense of *steigen* seems to have been something like 'step'/'walk'/'stride'. According to Grimm's dictionary (Grimm 1971, s.v. *steigen*), the verb is related to Greek στείχω ('stride, climb') [Grimm's translation: 'schreiten, steigen'], Sanskrit *stighnōmi* ('stride') and Old Irish *tíagaim* ('walk'). It can thus be assumed that the other readings have historically developed out of a manner of movement sense. However, in present-day German a semantic connection between the manner use and the other uses is no longer obvious, and this is already one of the main problems in the analysis of its lexical meaning.

As a first step in the analysis, we want to separate a variant in which *steigen* denotes a directed movement from a variant which denotes manner of movement. In the classification of Levin (1993), the English verb *climb* already occurs with a double classification of this kind; and in more recent work, Levin & Rappaport Hovav (2013) have elaborated on the idea that *climb* has these two lexical senses. We do not want to defend an alternative analysis for *climb* here, but nevertheless would like to point out that it is especially German *steigen* which shows signs of such a polysemy, which *climb* at least does not exhibit as clearly. One argument for a polysemy of *steigen* emerges from an observation pointed out in Geuder & Weisgerber (2008) according to which the manner component of *steigen* is much more specific than that of the English verb *climb*. Consider the following paradigm:

(2) a. √ *Die Ziegen stiegen aufs Dach.*
         the goats climbed onto.the roof
         √ The goats climbed onto the roof.

     b. ?? *Die Schnecke stieg auf die Pflanze.*
         the snail climbed onto the plant
         √ The snail climbed onto the plant.

     c. ?? *Der Zug stieg auf den Berg.*
         the train climbed onto the mountain
         √ The train climbed the mountain.

     d. √ *Das U-Boot stieg an die Oberfläche.*
         the submarine climbed to the surface
         √ The submarine climbed towards the surface.

     e. √ *Der Ballon stieg höher und höher.*
         the balloon climbed higher and higher
         √ The balloon climbed higher and higher.

The examples are arranged in terms of a gradient that runs from a very palpable manner component in terms of the use of limbs in (a), to interpretations involving more indistinct movements of the whole moving entity as in (b) and (c), and further to uses involving a freely suspended object without extremities in the last examples. In all cases, English *climb* may be used. In view of this dense distribution of variants along the gradient just sketched, Geuder & Weisgerber conclude that the underlying lexical meaning of *climb* merely specifies force exertion in upward direction while everything else comes in via inferences about additional properties of the manner component according to specific contexts (cf. also the discussion in Levin & Rappaport Hovav 2013: 59ff.). In our view, it is not clear whether a cut-off point could be found, marking the distinction envisaged by Levin & Rappaport Hovav between a manner sense and a direction sense of *climb*: would the disappearance of a manner feature be seen as happening between (c) and (d), or between (d) and (e)? Be this as it may, German *steigen* does show a disruption in the distribution, and hence gives evidence of two lexical variants. We interpret the last two uses of *steigen* as involving a pure verb of directed movement, in line with the fact that the English examples in (d) and (e) are the variants in which the meaning of *climb* is especially hard to tell apart from the purely directional verb *rise;* Levin & Rappaport Hovav (2013: 65) therefore assume both to be directional verbs (however, Geuder & Weisgerber 2008 argue that a manner-direction distinction can be maintained).

What is important for the analysis of the manner variant is that the attempts to use *steigen* in (b) and (c) are unacceptable. The reason seems to be that the manner variant which is called for contains a restriction that an entity is moving on its legs. Example (b) is not merely unacceptable but ridiculous, precisely because it is felt to presuppose that snails have legs. By and large, *steigen* can be predicated of all moving entities that could be said, in a stative snapshot, to be "standing" on their legs. This condition holds for those uses which imply ground contact; however, as soon as there is reference to a freely suspended entity, as in (d) and (e), usage of *steigen* is no longer constrained in the same way, and hence we conclude that we are dealing with a different lexical variant. Another observation on the manner features associated with *steigen* mentioned in Geuder & Weisgerber (2008) points in the same direction: in some uses it is translated by English *step* as in (3) below.

(3) a. *Er stieg über die Pfütze.* | He stepped over the puddle.
 he stepped over the puddle

 b. *Er stieg auf die Leiter.* | 1. He climbed the ladder.
 he stepped/climbed onto the ladder   2. He stepped onto the ladder.

These examples show that *steigen* can be instantiated by one single step, provided that there is some remarkable vertical movement of the legs associated with that step (for the example 'stepping over a puddle' we would imagine people lifting their leg to some extent). Here again, we see a manner component that is sufficiently similar to the one that produced a deviance with (2b) and (c) above: *steigen* is about movement supported by legs, with a feature of upward force exertion associated to it (although the walk-type uses of *steigen* in (3) might be considered as involving some amount of polysemy).

A second argument for the existence of an independent directional variant of *steigen* comes from the interaction with directional modifiers. It is typically expected of manner verbs that they should be neutral with respect to a direction feature and therefore, they should be able to stand on their own in order to express just the manner feature, or optionally to allow combination with all kinds of directionals, even downward directionality, as in *Die Ziegen stiegen vom Dach (herunter)* 'The goats climbed (down) from the roof'. Examples (2d) and (e), in contrast, cannot be used to refer to downward direction. These latter examples occur in uses without directional complement, but this time they imply a direction even in isolation, hence display a different lexical sense. This is the main criterion used by Levin & Rappaport Hovav (2013) to distinguish a manner variant and a direction variant.

With respect to German *steigen,* we find the somewhat unexpected restriction that a directional complement is actually necessary in the manner reading. (There are only a few unproductive agent nominalizations that use *steigen* in the direction-independent way expected from a manner verb, such as *Bergsteiger* 'hill-climber' and the strongly lexicalized *Steiger* 'foreman of miners'). However, the putative directional variant behaves as expected, and so, eventually, the distinction between two meaning types is confirmed in the sense that the complementation behavior differs as shown in (4):

(4) a. *Sebastian stieg auf den Berg.*
           S.   climbed onto the mountain
           Sebastian climbed the mountain.

    b. ? *Sebastian stieg den ganzen Tag.*
           S.   climbed the whole day
           Sebastian was climbing the whole day long.

    c. *Der Ballon stieg.*
           the balloon climbed
           The balloon was climbing.

    d. *Der Ballon stieg höher und höher*
           the balloon climbed higher and higher
           The balloon was climbing higher and higher.

Example (4d) shows a modifier applying to directional *steigen*. This case reminds us of an observation in Rappaport Hovav (2008: 22f.), according to which verbs which lexically incorporate a scale are only able to combine with complements modifying that scale, rather than with complements introducing any new scale; hence, (4d) can be seen as an indication that a scale of vertical position is part and parcel of the verb meaning in this use (see Fleischhauer & Gamerschlag, in press, for a tentative treatment of *steigen* in this use). Apparently the scalarity of *steigen* in this variant leads to difficulties in using it with a goal PP. We see a minimal contrast in the following set of examples, in that, for instance, the addition of *bis* ('until/up to'), which contributes an extended portion of a vertical path to the goal description, saves the otherwise awkward example in (5a) below.

(5) a. ? *Der Ballon stieg unter die Decke / ... neben die Laterne.*
the balloon climbed under the ceiling next.to the lantern
intended: 'The balloon climbed up to the ceiling / next to the lantern.'

b. √ *Der Ballon stieg bis unter die Decke / ... bis neben die*
the balloon climbed until under the ceiling until next.to the
Laterne.
lantern
'The balloon climbed up as far as the ceiling / until it was next to the lantern.'

This contrast could be explained by positing that directional *steigen* refers to paths in terms of an orientational feature (namely an absolute "upward" direction indicated by the direction of gravity), and that it does not, in contrast to the manner reading, involve a positioning of an object in terms of a reference object (which would be given for the manner variant of *steigen* by the entity that supports the 'standing' configuration required by the manner feature).

To conclude this section, we have pointed out the existence of two polysemic variants of *steigen*: a manner variant can be clearly singled out due to its very specific meaning of 'making steps (with some vertical component)' — which is actually still fairly close to its etymological origins mentioned at the outset — and also due to its inability to occur without a directional complement. We are then left with a separate variant denoting directed movement without manner, i. e., movement in upward direction.

3 Components in the frame representation of *steigen*: manner, path, and event structure

In the following, we will confront the manner of motion and the directed motion variants of *steigen* by discussing their frame representations, starting with a brief introduction into the representational format. Then, by means of these variants, we will demonstrate the flexibility of the frame format which accounts for the power of frame theory. Frames allow one to zoom into conceptual structures to any desired degree and to unify lexical and general conceptual representations.

Additionally, it is possible to represent interrelations between fundamentally different domains like time and space in an adequate fashion.

3.1 Frames: some basics

In Petersen (2007), a formal account of frames for nominal concepts is given which represents them by graphs built up from attributes as transition functions between nodes. In this way, the central role of functional concepts which was mentioned in the introduction is captured. Nodes represent objects and their respective attribute values.

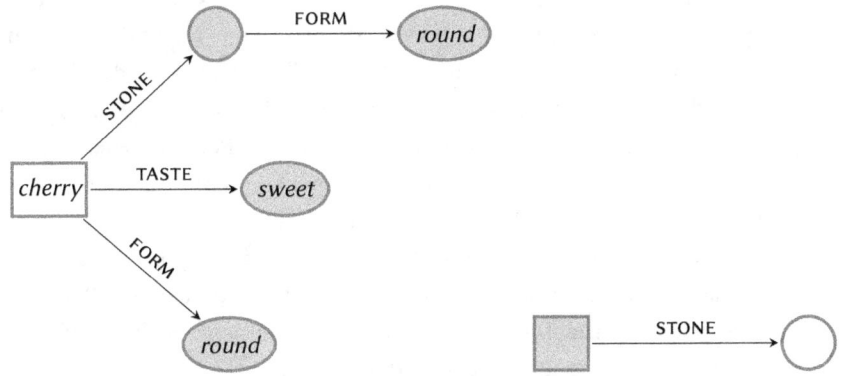

Figure 1: Frames for nominal concepts: sortal concept *cherry* (left), functional concept *stone* (right).

Figure 1 gives two examples of nominal frame graphs. The graph on the left represents the frame for the sortal concept *cherry*. Here a cherry is characterized by its sweet taste, its round form and the round form of its stone. The graph on the right represents the frame of the functional concept *stone of something*. A stone (in this sense) is an object for which something must exist of which it is the stone. The arcs in the frame graphs are labeled by attributes, i.e., by partial functions denoted by functional concepts, and the graph nodes are labeled by types.[2] The latter are often left unspecified if they are determined by the context. For example, the nonlabeled node in the left frame graph could be typed by *stone* since values of the attribute STONE must be stones. In a logical notation, types correspond to one-place predicates and attributes to unary functions. Rectangular nodes represent open frame arguments and the central node which represents the

---

[2] We assume that types are ordered in a type hierarchy which specifies for each type its admissible attributes.

referent of the frame is marked by not being shaded grey. The two frame graphs in Figure 1 can be translated into the following lambda expressions (predicate constants are written in italics and function constants in small capitals; open argument nodes introduce lambda-bounded variables; for more details on this translation see Petersen & Osswald 2014):

(6)   a. (cherry, sortal)
$\lambda x.cherry(x) \wedge round(\text{FORM}(\text{STONE}(x))) \wedge sweet(\text{TASTE}(x)) \wedge round(\text{FORM}(x))$ [logical type: $<e,t>$]

    b. (stone, functional) $\lambda x \iota y. y = \text{STONE}(x)$ [logical type: $<e,e>$]

Comparing the graph-based frame representations in Figure 1 with their translations into lambda expressions in (6), we would like to point to the following advantages of the former representation format: first, Löbner's fundamental idea that attribute concepts constitute the basic components of cognitive concept formation is explicitly built into the graph-based representations, as it are the arcs which connect nodes and thereby span the frames. Second, the graph-based representation is variable-free and thereby better suited as a cognitive representation. We believe that 'thinking' is more about drawing connections than about building a register of variables. A further related advantage of the graph-based representation is that it is more flexible than the logical one since it does not presuppose a language of predicates of fixed arity with a fixed argument order but rather allows for addressing arguments by attributes.

So far the frame account, sketched above, has been proven useful in representing concepts belonging to different static concept types and in modeling their compositional semantics. In a recent study, Naumann (2013) extends this approach to capture dynamic concepts of actions and events. We will now apply his ideas in the modeling of the meaning of *steigen*.

3.2 Frames for events

To represent the different variants of *steigen*, it is first of all necessary to clarify the issues that arise with respect to the representation of manner. In the recent literature, there has been a lively discussion of "manner-result complementarity", i.e. the hypothesis that verbs specifying manner features and verbs specifying direction features should form a dichotomy, excluding hybrid verbs that contain both specifications simultaneously (cf. Levin & Rappaport Hovav 2013 and earlier related work). It is important to note that this discussion concerns a level of lexical representation which, in the context of the frame model we are employing, can be seen as the starting configuration for a process of constructing a full-fledged cognitive representation of a situation. Hence, in a frame model, lexical entries and conceptual representations do not appear as qualitatively different things. We tentatively assume here that manner-result complementarity indeed holds for the division of *steigen* into different lexical senses, i.e., a pure manner sense and a pure directional sense. However, the frame model allows for dynamic elaboration of its attribute structure in the course of interpretation, i.e., enrichment with more fine-grained specifications. Therefore, the frame model forces us to decide on whether certain attributes should count as admissible in principle even if they do not figure in the "lexical" configuration. Resolution of this issue ultimately has to await a general theory of (adverbial) modification in the frame format. For the specific case at hand, we can state the following: the manner use of *steigen* has already been found to select for a directional complement, and it is well-known that manner verbs can be elaborated into manner + direction descriptions in the syntax in certain (especially the Germanic) languages. From the fact that this process obeys restrictions that are part of the syntactic and/or semantic composition rules of a specific language, we tentatively conclude that the frames of manner verbs and directional verbs cannot unconditionally be augmented by attributes of the opposite sort but that representations exempt from manner-result complementarity have to be constructed from special rules of frame composition. With *steigen* the case is unproblematic, since a directional complement is selected as an argument anyway. In the same vein, we believe that any elaboration of the frame in the directional variant by way of manner features will have to be licensed by special construction rules, which we do not seek to develop here. This is why, in the lexical representation, we do not provide attributes of directional *steigen* that foreshadow the appearance of any manner components (and it is also evident that "manner" never occurs as an argument selected by a verb, which would give rise to the mirror image of manner *steigen*).

Let us now turn to the task of constructing a frame representation specifically for *steigen*. In the tradition of "frame semantics" in the sense of Fillmore, frames are used to model the static dimensions of events (Fillmore 1982a), i.e., their relations to objects participating in the event. The frame in Figure 2 shows the static dimensions of *steigen* as a manner of motion verb (henceforth *steigen*$_{mm}$). As explained above, two objects participate in a *steigen*$_{mm}$ event: the moving object which is linked to the central frame node by the THEME attribute and the path along which the object moves i.e., the value of the PATH attribute. The value specifications of both attributes correspond to arguments at the level of semantic composition and hence must be provided by linguistic composition. This is indicated by the rectangular shape of their nodes in the frame graph. Such nodes will be called *argument nodes*. Two further attributes of *steigen*$_{mm}$ are MANNER and EVENT STRUCTURE; they differ from the former in that their values are part and parcel of the verb meaning and neither can be nor need to be provided by the context. (As stated above, adverbial modification is still an option for elaborating a frame but will not be treated here). In a first approximation, these two attributes appear as global properties of the event in the representation in Figure 2:

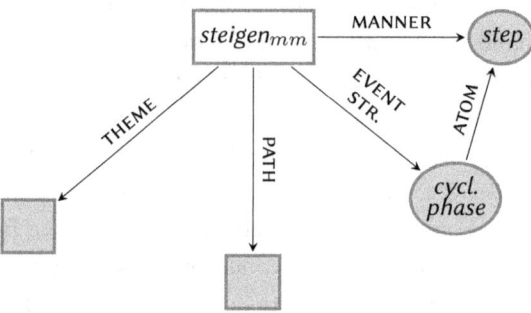

Figure 2: Static event frame of *steigen*$_{mm}$.

By zooming into the values of MANNER and EVENT STRUCTURE, however, the dynamic aspects of *steigen*$_{mm}$ events are revealed.[3] Events have a temporal structure, that is, they evolve over a time period. Events with *cyclic phase structure* are cumulative and have an event structure that is made up of atoms (cf. Rothstein 2004, chapter 8, on the role of atoms in the constitution of activities). An event e is of a cumulative event type if it does not change its type when a repetition is added (type(e) = type(ee*)). It is made up of atoms if it can be decomposed into a series of proper subevents $e_1 \ldots e_n$ of one type such that: type(e_i) = type(e_j) for all i, j ∈

---

[3] For simplicity we use the term *zooming* here for two different operations: (1) for 'refinements' in which attribute values are further specified by attribute value pairs, and (2) for 'temporalizations' which assign event decompositions to static event frames (see Naumann 2013 for more details). Possible refinements are determined by the type of the attribute value and by the constraints attached to it in the type signature. Temporalizations are determined by the type of the event which is as well given by its position in the type signature. Thus, it would be more adequate to type the central node of the *steigen*$_{mm}$ frame with a subtype of cyclic phase structure, but in order to keep our frame graphs simple and to improve readability we do not discuss type signatures here and store the information about the type of the event structure as a separate attribute value pair.

1,...,n and type(e_i) ≠ type(e) and none of the subevents e_i has a proper subevent e' of the same type, type(e_i) ≠ type(e'). An event has a *continuous phase structure* if it is cumulative and its event structure is not made up of atoms.

Figure 3 shows the details of the event structure of *steigen*$_{mm}$. Given that the manner description we have argued for in Section 2 contained "steps", these function as atoms of the activity which will be iterated over the course of the event. This relation between the event structure of *steigen*$_{mm}$ and its manner component is modeled in Figure 2 by the ATOM attribute of the EVENT STRUCTURE value.

On the event decomposition (ED) level the event is decomposed into single *step* subevents. This level represents the temporal structure of the event and links it to the level of the described situation, the participating objects, and their roles in the event. The linking between the ontologically different levels is given by a zoom function (Z) or bridge in the sense of Blackburn & De Rijke (1997). Each temporally extended event *e* on the ED level is bounded by two boundary events α(e) (left boundary) and β(e) (right boundary) whose runtimes are singletons (cf. Piñón 1997). Nonboundary events are linked to global properties of the event, termed "static event frames" (SEF) in Naumann (2013). In this case, the SEFs represent single *step* events (cf. the SEF level in Figure 2). Boundary events, in turn, are linked to situation frames (SF) which are built up from the frames for the objects involved in the event. In the given example, the only involved object is the one who steps, hence the value of the THEME of *step*. The SFs specify the relevant information about the moving object, namely its position.[4] The SF level in the figure below provides snapshots of the moving object at different time points of the event.

After having analyzed the temporal event structure of *steigen*$_{mm}$, we will now zoom into the manner component of the SEF in Figure 1. A *steigen*$_{mm}$ event *consists* of a series of *step* events. A *step* event contributes its own SEF with one theme argument. Additionally, steps can be characterized by a specific FORCE CONSTELLATION leading to a special step MOVEMENT (see Figure 4, top).

The value of the FORCE CONSTELLATION of *step* is depicted in Figure 4 (bottom). It is a noticeable, upwards-directed force (STRENGTH : ≫ 0, DIRECTION : *upwards*)

---

[4] Events may involve more complex SFs. For example, the SFs for *Mary gives John the book* are composed of three object frames (one for Mary, one for John, and one for the book). The first and the last SF differ in that in the first SF *Mary* is the value of an attribute POSSESSOR attached to *book*, while in the last SF this value is *John*.

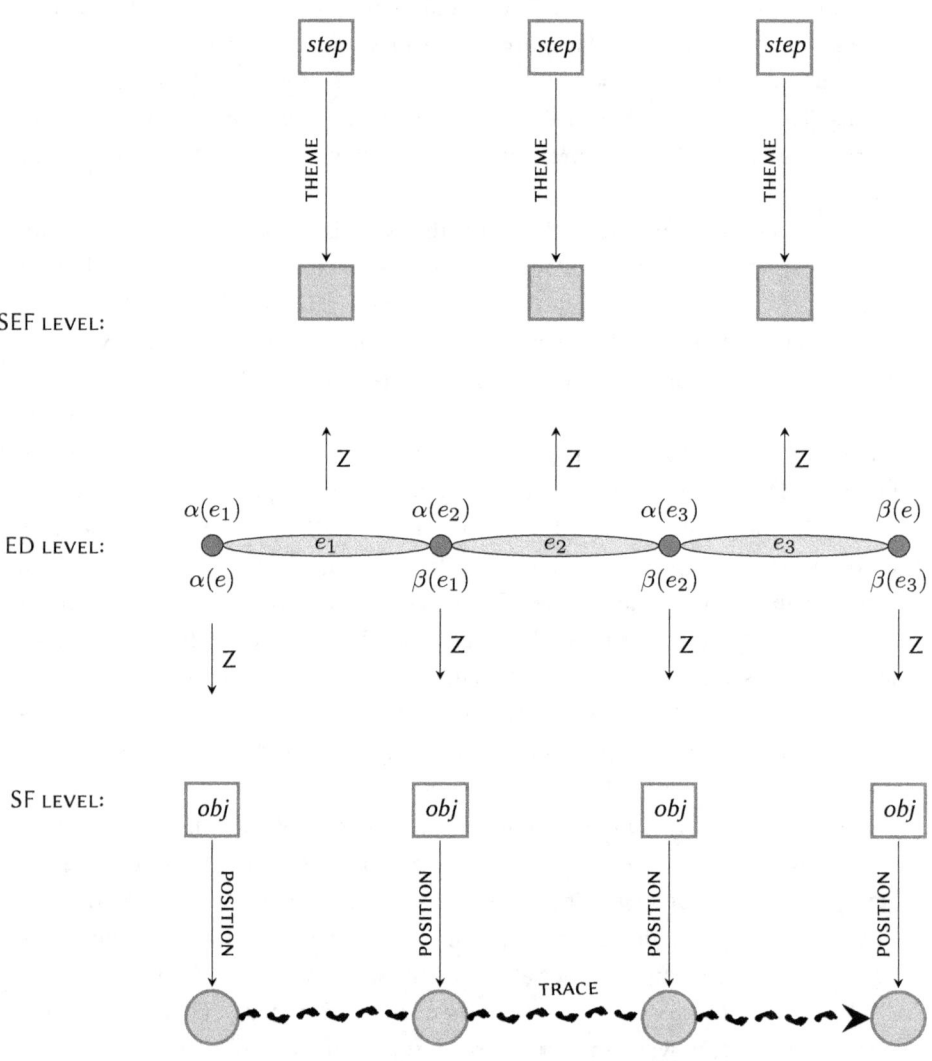

Figure 3: Event structure of *steigen*$_{mm}$.

Glück auf, der Steiger kommt: a frame account of extensional and intensional steigen

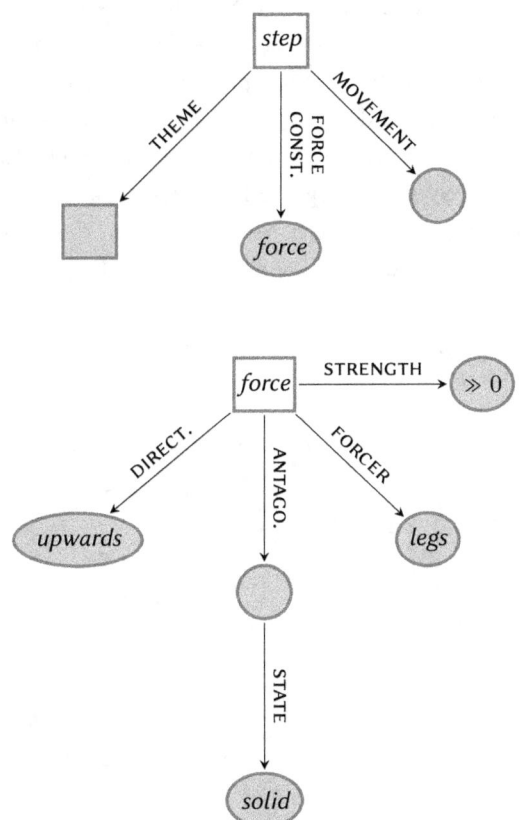

Figure 4: Zooming into the manner component of *steigen*$_{mm}$.

that is exerted by legs against a solid antagonist (FORCER : *legs*, ANTAGONIST : STATE : *solid*).

The frames from the preceding figures can be composed into a single *steigen*$_{mm}$ frame, exhibiting the correlations between the attribute values (Figure 5). The composition is controlled by constraints like "the theme of an event with a cyclic event structure is coreferential with the theme of the atoms of the event structure", which are not subject of this paper. Note that there is now a LEGS attribute linking the theme of *step* and *steigen*$_{mm}$ to the *legs* node coming from the *force* frame.[5] Since LEGS is a functional concept, the *legs* node needs to be the value node of a LEGS attribute. And given that the only possible node in the frame which could carry a LEGS attribute is the THEME value node, the attribute is attached to this. Thus, by specifying the force constellation of a *step* event, the theme value of *steigen*$_{mm}$ events gets restricted to entities with legs, excluding manner of motion readings of *Der Ballon steigt in die Höhe*.

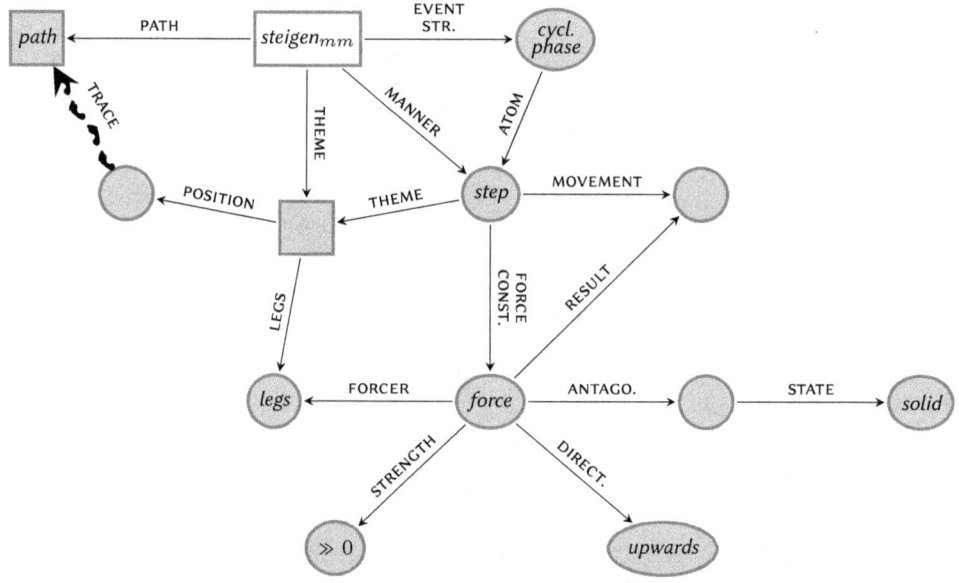

Figure 5: Detailed frame of *steigen*$_{mm}$.

A special case is the TRACE attribute linking the position of the THEME of *steigen*$_{mm}$ to its PATH specification. Here, TRACE is a dynamic attribute that is projected into

---

[5] The problem of intermixing entity-valued with pair-valued attributes lies outside the scope of this paper.

this frame from the event decomposition frame in Figure 3 and maps the POSITION of the THEME value to the record of its trace in the time span of the event. Note that although paths are static objects, traces are not. Paths are directed spatial entities that can be modeled as "continuous functions from the real unit interval to positions in some model of space" (Zwarts 2005: 748); thus, they are non-temporal structures. In contrast, a trace is a function from the time span of an event into the value space of an attribute of one of the participants of the event (here, the POSITION of the THEME participant) (cf. also Eschenbach et al. 2000). Hence, spatial traces like traces of object positions are temporal in the sense that each position point is indexed by a time stamp. Only the image of the function trace restricted to the full time span of the $steigen_{mm}$ event gives the path of the event.

This architecture also instantiates a basic distinction between two independent tiers: "translational movement", i. e., change of location in space, and, to be kept separately from it, potential "internal movements", i. e., movements that entirely pertain to the manner domain. In our case, the stepping movement, as it occurs in the manner description of *steigen*, will be classified as an object-internal movement rather than a translational movement. It is the result of a special force constellation exerted by the legs. The translational movement proceeds along the PATH, specified, for example, by the PP in *Die Ziegen stiegen aufs Dach* 'The goats climbed onto the roof'. Given that paths as directed spatial entities have no temporal dimension, it is the POSITION TRACE of the THEME of *steigen* that denotes the translational movement.[6] Although the force has to have an upward component in *steigen* situations, the path need not: a movement that opposes itself to gravity may still result in horizontal or even downward movement.

In contrast to a manner of motion verb, the use of *steigen* as a verb of directed movement ($steigen_{dir}$) appears without a manner component and hence with a pure theme argument that changes its position in space. We get the following simplified frame decomposition in Figure 6 (left).

The PATH attribute now has a fixed value, which can perhaps be motivated from a stereotype of upward movement associated with the manner use of *steigen* (cf. Levin & Rappaport Hovav 2013). Since the semantic distance between directional and manner variants is fairly large anyway, due to the complete absence of the

---

[6] This difference becomes important if one investigates the use of *steigen* as a static verb, as in *Das Gelände steigt an* 'The terrain rises'. Here, a state is described which does not evolve over time and thus no trace of an object is given and no translational movement occurs. However, we still have a path component which is now embedded as a spatial entity into the spatial entity *Gelände* 'terrain, land'.

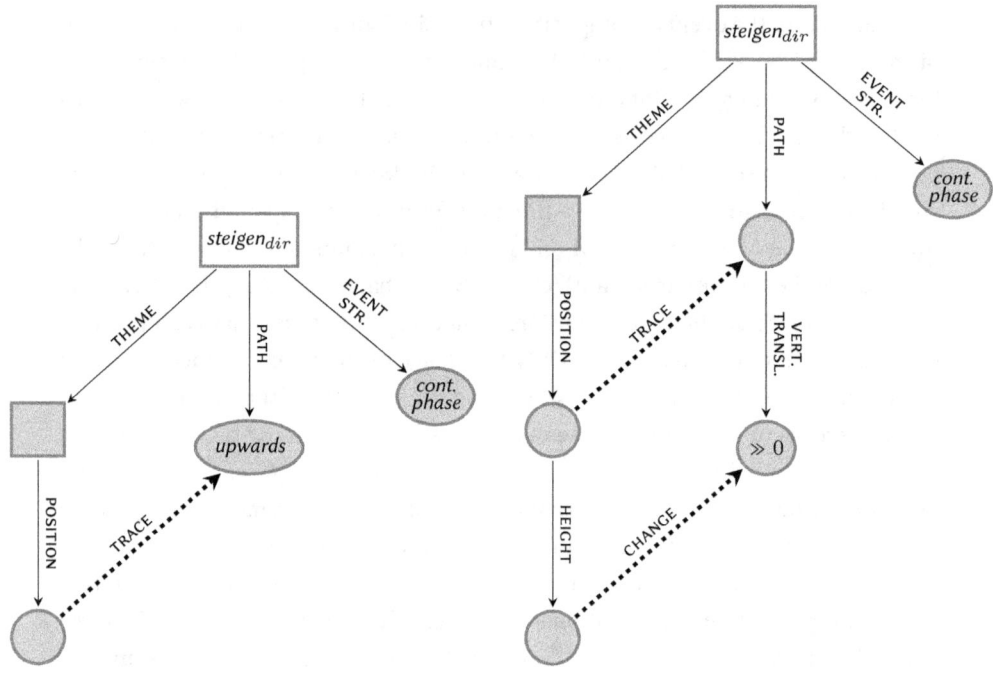

Figure 6: Simplified frame of the directed motion use of *steigen*.

very richly specified manner component, we do not attempt to sketch any mechanism that claims a regular meaning extension. However, note that the same direction specification – "upwards" – has occurred in the frame of the manner of motion use of *steigen* as the specification of the force direction (cf. Figure 5).

With regard to the upwards component of *steigen*$_{dir}$, we can also be more detailed: the frame in Figure 6 (right) results from zooming into the "upwards" node. As can be seen, an UPWARDS path means that the VERTICAL TRANSLATION of the movement is greater than zero. This in turn implies that the HEIGHT of the POSITION of the moving entity changes accordingly over the running time of the *steigen* event. Formally, this is captured by the dynamic attribute CHANGE which requires that the difference in HEIGHT at the beginning and the end of *steigen*$_{dir}$ is greater than zero.

However, note what now happens to the relationship between event structure, theme, and path. With the absence of the manner component, we also lose the atoms that yielded a cyclic event structure. Therefore, this time the event structure must be dense (unless information that comes in via semantic composition indicates otherwise, e. g., by means of a modifier like *stepwise*). The path component can still be modified by directional PPs that provide reference objects, these then could provide localizations of the theme during certain stretches of the event structure as illustrated in (7).

(7) Der Ballon stieg über die Baumwipfel (hinaus).
the balloon rose above the treetops (beyond)
'The balloon rose above (and beyond) the treetops.'

The meaning here is that there is a nonfinal portion of the path (presumably also noninitial) on which the balloon is localized at the same absolute height as the treetops. In the absence of such modifiers, we retain a bare linear ordering which says that with increasing progression of the event we get positions at least as high as the previous ones. In the manner variant, a directional PP would also provide a reference object, and points of the path would have to be localized in a way relative to this object that needs to be determined by contextual inference. For instance, in (8) the reference object *Zaun* 'fence' triggers a construal according to which an initial portion of the path has upward direction, a medial portion is on top of the fence, and a final portion has downward direction. This construal is driven by our world knowledge of how we would interact with this type of obstacle (given the constraints imposed by the preposition).

(8) Sebastian stieg über den Zaun.
S. climbed over the fence
'Sebastian climbed over the fence.'

So, to sum up, we find that with the manner variant, properties of the reference object influence the directionality of the path (interacting with the prepositional meaning). With the directional variant, it is rather the other way round: path PPs merely act as modifiers of a path whose primary description has already been established.

4 Intensional *steigen*

The readings of *steigen* illustrated so far all refer to vertical motion in space while they differ primarily with respect to the presence of a manner component. As illustrated by the examples in (9), there is also a figurative use of *steigen* which abstracts away from spatial motion. In this use the movement along a vertical path originally expressed by *steigen* is related to abstract "motion" along a scale.

(9) a. *Die Temperatur der Flüssigkeit steigt.*
the temperature of.the Liquid rises
'The temperature of the liquid is rising.'

b. *Der Preis des Apartments steigt.*
the price of.the apartment rises
'The price of the apartment is rising.'

c. *Der Druck in der Kabine steigt.*
the pressure in the cabin rises
'The pressure in the cabin is rising.'
(examples taken from Fleischhauer & Gamerschlag, in press)

In all of the examples above, the subject noun, instead of simply denoting a moved object (a theme), introduces a scale. For instance, *Temperatur (der Flüssigkeit)* 'temperature (of the liquid)' in (9a) refers to the temperature of the liquid which can be specified by a particular degree on the temperature scale. Likewise, *Preis* 'price' and *Druck* 'pressure' in (9b) and (c) denote the price and pressure of an entity which can be explicated by a degree on the price and pressure scales, respectively. If *steigen* 'rise' is combined with a scale-denoting noun like *Temperatur* 'temperature', we assume that the noun contributes a new scale. *Steigen* then indicates that there is some abstract movement along this scale such that the degree or "position" on the scale at the end of the *steigen* event is greater or "higher" than at the beginning.

As already stated at the beginning of the paper, the figurative use of *steigen* in (9) can be characterized as an *intensional use* (Montague 1973, Löbner 1979, 1981) since it involves a total change of the subject referent over time. As a result, replacing the subject with an expression which refers to the denotation of the subject at a specific point of time yields an awkward sentence such as #*90 Grad Celsius steigen* lit. '90 degrees Celsius are rising'. This is opposed to the partial change characteristic of the *extensional use* in which case the reference of the subject does not change. Thus, the uses of *steigen* introduced in the preceding sections can all be regarded as extensional since the subject referent only changes with respect to a single dimension, namely its spatial location. As a contrast to the intensional use, the subject can be replaced by an expression with the same reference as in the sentence *Das Luftfahrzeug steigt* 'The aircraft is rising' in which *Ballon* 'balloon' has been replaced by the coreferring expression *Luftfahrzeug* 'aircraft'.

The figurative relation between upward movement and increasing scale values is well recognized in the literature on metaphor and reflected, for example, in Lakoff & Johnson's (1980) conceptual metaphor formula 'up is more/down is less.' The use of the metaphor is not restricted to verbs but also systematically exploited by nouns (e. g., *die Höhe der Temperatur* lit. 'height of the temperature'), adjectives (e. g., *die Temperatur ist hoch* 'the temperature is high'), and prepositions (e. g., *Temperaturen über dem Gefrierpunkt* 'temperatures above freezing point'). In spite of their intuitive correctness, metaphor approaches in the tradition of Lakoff & Johnson are usually vague when it comes to structural and representational issues. By contrast, our approach is based on frame representations with a focus on structural differences between the extensional and intensional uses of *steigen*.

If the origin of *steigen*$_{ins}$ lies in a verb of vertical movement, we can now see how this restricts its combination with nouns in the subject position, to the effect that the noun must introduce a scale. More precisely, it must express a function which maps a given argument (realized as a genitive possessor of the noun or understood from the context) onto the value of a particular scale. For instance, the head of the noun phrase *Temperatur der Flüssigkeit* 'temperature of the liquid' in (9a) denotes a function which maps the referent of the genitive possessor *der Flüssigkeit* 'of the liquid' to a degree on the temperature scale. Scale-denoting nouns like *Temperatur* are natural language expressions of functional concepts in the sense of Löbner (2011a). Functional nouns are characterized by unique reference, i. e., for a given argument (at a given time) they single out a unique value. Scalar nouns form a subclass of functional nouns, but there are also functional nouns which express concepts whose values are not ordered scalarly. For instance, *Vater* 'father' and *Geburtsort* 'place of birth' also refer to functional concepts which, however, do not have a scalar value range. By consequence, these nouns cannot combine with *steigen* in the intensional use.

As shown in (10), there are also some scalar nouns which cannot combine with *steigen*. All of the nouns in (10) make reference to spatial properties which are clearly of a scalar nature such as the circumference and the width of an object. However, the combination of concrete spatial meaning contributed by the respective nouns and abstract spatial meaning introduced by the intensional verb seems to be excluded. In spite of the origin of *steigen*$_{ins}$ in *steigen*$_{dir}$, even the combination of *Höhe* 'height' and *steigen*$_{ins}$ is ruled out.

(10) *Der Umfang   / die Fläche / die Breite / die Höhe steigt.
     the circumference the area   the width   the height rises
     lit.: 'The circumference/area/width/volume/height is rising.'

If *steigen* is substituted by *zunehmen* 'increase', a verb which does not derive metaphorically from vertical movement, the sentence becomes fine as shown in (11).

(11) Der Umfang   / die Fläche / die Breite / die Höhe nimmt zu.
     the circumference the area   the width   the height increases
     'The circumference/area/width/volume is increasing.'

In addition, the use of intensional *steigen* is restricted with respect to the direction of change. As illustrated by (12), it can only express an increase along the respective scale as in (a) but never a decrease as intended in (b).

(12) a. *Die Temperatur steigt   von 3 auf 10 Grad.*
        the temperature is.rising from   to   degrees
        'The temperature is rising from 3 to 10 degrees.'
     b. **Die Temperatur steigt   von 10 auf 3 Grad.*
        the temperature is.rising from   to   degrees
        intended: 'The temperature is rising from 10 to 3 degrees.'

The restriction to change in an "upward direction" groups intensional *steigen* together with the use of *steigen* as a verb of directed motion, which is also confined to upward movement, and sets these two uses apart from the manner of motion use, which also allows for reference to downward motion. The three uses can be ordered according to the degree of abstractness with the use as a manner of motion verb as the most concrete one, the use as a verb of directed motion as a use which abstracts away from manner but still denotes motion in space, and the intensional use which makes reference to abstract motion along a scale. Since both directional and intensional *steigen* lack manner information while at the same time being restricted to upward movement, it seems plausible to consider directional *steigen* as the source concept underlying the metaphor resulting in intensional *steigen*.

The frame for intensional *steigen* as in *die Temperatur steigt* 'the temperature is rising' is given in Figure 7 below. As can be seen, the frame is almost identical to the frame for *steigen* in the directed motion use in Figure 6 above: it retains much of the structure of the source concept.

Glück auf, der Steiger kommt: a frame account of extensional and intensional steigen

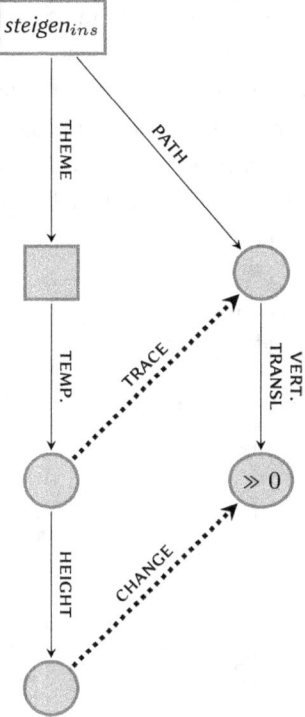

Figure 7: Frame representation of *die Temperatur steigt* 'the temperature is rising'.

In Figure 7, the position attribute of directional *steigen* has been replaced by the scalar attribute TEMPERATURE contributed by the functional noun *Temperatur*. As with the preceding uses of *steigen*, we assume that the value change which takes place during the *steigen* event is summed up in the form of a trace defined in terms of values with a temporal ordering. This trace is an abstract object which can be conceived as a path through the value space determined by the dimension that comes with the particular attribute (e. g., TEMPERATURE, PRICE, PRESSURE). As a consequence, the frame shown in Figure 7 still exhibits a PATH attribute whose value is identical to the value of the dynamic attribute TRACE. Moreover, the change in height literally expressed by the directional use of *steigen* is reflected in the presence of the HEIGHT attribute which maps the value of TEMPERATURE, PRICE, PRESSURE, etc. on its respective (abstract) HEIGHT on the corresponding scale. Note that this conception of the HEIGHT attribute entails that the attribute is not restricted to the spatial position of an object as in the directional use. By contrast, we conceive of HEIGHT as a more abstract function which returns scale degrees in dependence of the entity it applies to. As in the preceding use, the total change in HEIGHT during the course of the event is restricted to a value greater than zero in order to ensure an increase. Again, the total change of HEIGHT over the event time is identified with the vertical translation of the value trace. The frame representation of intensional *steigen* before combining it with an adequate functional noun is given in Figure 8, in which FC is a placeholder for the attribute introduced by the functional noun.

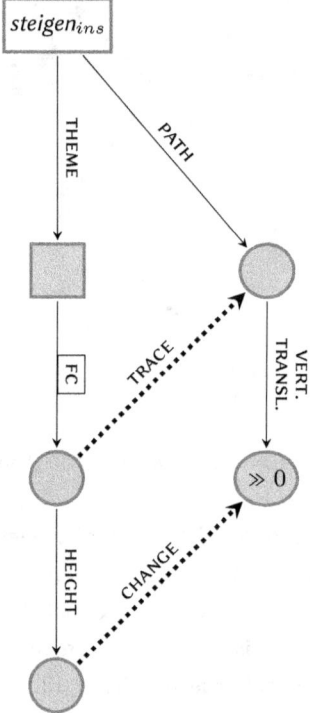

Figure 8: Frame representation of intensional *steigen* 'rise'.

In the frame in Figure 8, neither the theme argument nor the particular attribute whose values change during the *steigen* event are stated. Consequently, the frame has two open parameters: one open argument node and one open arc argument.[7] When *steigen* combines with a functional noun, the missing attribute is specified by the noun. Simultaneously, the theme argument of *steigen* is identified with

---

[7] These different types of arguments would correspond to an individual argument and a higher-order argument in a predicate logic representation of $steigen_{ins}$.

the genitive possessor argument of the noun. Consider, for instance, the complex noun phrase *Temperatur der Flüssigkeit* 'temperature of the liquid' which is represented by the frame in Figure 9.

Figure 9: Frame representation of *Temperatur der Flüssigkeit* 'temperature of the liquid'.

As a functional concept 'temperature' has an open argument node for the entity which is mapped onto its unique temperature value. From the argument node, the arc labeled with the attribute encoded by the functional noun leads to the central node which specifies what the frame is above (see Petersen & Osswald 2014, for a detailed frame analysis of genitive constructions). As stated above, intensional *steigen* has an open argument node as well as an open arc argument which need to be specified by the subject taken by the verb. Because of their property of encoding a single attribute for an open argument, functional nouns are suited for contributing the information required in the frame of intensional *steigen* shown above. Thus, when the complex noun phrase *Temperatur der Flüssigkeit* 'temperature of the liquid' combines with *steigen*, it contributes both the attribute TEMPERATURE and the theme argument *Flüssigkeit* 'liquid' which undergoes a change with respect to temperature. Note that by identifying the DP-internal possessor argument with the theme argument of the verb, it becomes an argument of the complex verb consisting of intensional verb and functional noun (for further discussion of the combination of different types of functional nouns and intensional verbs see Fleischhauer & Gamerschlag, in press).

The fact that *steigen* only selects functional nouns with a scalar value range is achieved by the HEIGHT attribute which requires that the function it is applied to exhibits a scalar order of values. However, as shown by the examples in (10) above, functional nouns denoting spatial dimensions such as *Breite* 'width' and *Fläche* 'area' are ruled out as well, even though they have scalar value ranges. Functional nouns of this type can be excluded by assuming a type hierarchy for the types denoted by the functional nouns that occur as subjects of *steigen*$_{ins}$. In principle, this type hierarchy would distinguish between scales that allow for making reference to their (abstract) height and those that do not. For the sake of simplicity, we will not elaborate on that issue here.

The frame analysis of *steigen* + *Temperatur* can also be applied to the change of state verb *(sich) erwärmen* 'warm' illustrated in (13).

(13) Die Flüssigkeit erwärmt sich.
   the liquid   warms REFL
   'The liquid is warming up.'

The verb *erwärmen*, which is represented by the frame in Figure 10, also refers to a positive value change along the temperature scale.[8]

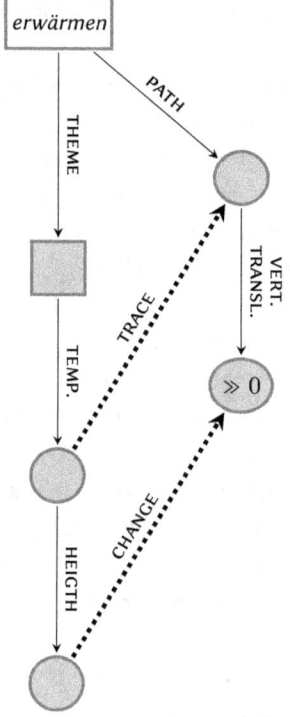

Figure 10: Frame representation of *erwärmen* 'warm'.

As can be seen, the frame for *erwärmen* is identical to the frame for *die Temperatur steigt* in Figure 7 above. Yet, in contrast to *steigen* + *Temperatur*, the attribute TEMPERATURE is already part of the verb meaning and does not need to be contributed by a functional noun. Consequently, the theme is not introduced as a

---

[8] Although the frame in Figure 10 does not make explicit reference to the deadjectival origin of *erwärmen*, the derivation of *erwärmen* from the adjectival base *warm* 'warm' is reflected by the fact that both are represented by frames containing TEMPERATURE as a core attribute with the difference that the frame for the adjective does not address a value change. Likewise, we assume that the frames for the antonyms *abkühlen* 'cool (down)' and *kalt* 'cool' also build on the central attribute TEMPERATURE (cf. Kennedy & McNally 2005 for the assumption that antonymous adjectives involve the same dimension/attribute).

DP-internal possessor either, but rather realized as the subject of the verb. Since the frame above is a conceptual representation, it does not reflect the different grammatical realization of the theme argument. We do not aim here at a theory of how the mapping of natural language to conceptual frames is accomplished. Since this would require embedding frame representations as a conceptual level into a full-fledged grammatical model with an elaborate linking module, it would surely go beyond the scope of this paper. In principle, however, models such as HPSG (Pollard & Sag 1994), which also apply recursive attribute-value structures, are particularly well-suited for combining with conceptual frame representations due to their structural affinity.

5 Conclusions and outlook

In this paper, we have offered a first attempt at a frame analysis of a climb-type movement verb, German *steigen*. The modeling in terms of Barsalou frames allowed us to delineate the event structure and the argument structure in every detail, especially the correlations that hold among subevents, manner, positions and the overall path traversed by the theme argument. Based on this representation, we have explored the ways in which intensional uses of *steigen* come about. The crucial point was to show the interplay of the lexical representation of the verb and the semantic type of the nominal argument, which denotes a functional concept. Going beyond received ideas that *steigen* in this use involves a metaphorical transfer from movement in space to a value scale, we were able to show how functional concepts internal to the event frame in the concrete readings are delegated to the nominal argument in the scalar use. Among other things, this makes it possible to explain the role of genitive arguments of the theme of *steigen* as well as the selection restriction imposed by this variant of the verb. Clearly, a number of questions surrounding this case remain to be addressed, among them the question of possible differences between directional verbs (like *rise*) and manner verbs (like, perhaps, *climb*) with respect to polysemic extensions such as the intensional use. We proposed tracing back the intensional use to a purely directional verb meaning, hence it remains to be clarified to which extent intensional uses of manner verbs are possible.

Bibliography

Barsalou, L. 1992. Frames, concepts, and conceptual fields. In A. Lehrer & E. Feder Kittay (eds.), *Frames, fields, and contrasts: New essays in semantic and lexical organization*, 21–74. Hillsdale, NJ: Lawrence Erlbaum Associates Publishers.

Blackburn, P. & M. De Rijke. 1997. Zooming in, zooming out. *Journal of Logic, Language and Information* 6 (1). 5–31.

Eschenbach, C., L. Tschander, C. Habel & Lars Kulik. 2000. Lexical specification of paths. In C. Freksa, W. Brauer, C. Habel & K. F. Wender (eds.), *Spatial cognition*, vol. II, 127–145. Berlin: Springer.

Fillmore, C. 1982a. Frame semantics. In *Linguistics in the morning calm*, 111–137. Seoul: Hanshin Publishing Co. The Linguistic Society of Korea.

Fillmore, Charles. 1982b. Toward a descriptive framework of spatial deixis. In Robert Jarvella & Wolfgang Klein (eds.), *Speech, place and action: Studies in deixis and related topics*, 31–59. London: John Wiley.

Fleischhauer, J. & T. Gamerschlag. in press. We're going through changes: How change of state verbs and arguments combine in scale composition. Lingua special issue 'Argument realization in morphology and syntax'.

Geuder, W. & M. Weisgerber. 2008. Manner of movement and the conceptualization of force. Talk presented at the workshop Il y a manière et manière, Université d'Artois, Arras, France. http://semanticsarchive.net/Archive/Tk5Ym EwN/MannerMovement_slidescompact.pdf.

Grimm. 1971. Deutsches Wörterbuch von Jacob und Wilhelm Grimm. 16 Bände in 32 Teilbänden. 16 Bände in 32 Teilbänden. (1854–1961). Leipzig edition, 1971. Available online: http://woerterbuchnetz.de/DWB/.

Jackendoff, R. 1979. How to keep ninety from rising. *Linguistic Inquiry* 10. 172–176.

Jackendoff, R. 1985. Multiple subcategorization and the θ-criterion: The case of climb. *Natural Language and Linguistic Theory* 3. 271–295.

Kennedy, C. & L. McNally. 2005. Scale structure and the semantic typology of gradable predicates. *Language* 81 (2). 345–381.

Lakoff, G. & M. Johnson. 1980. *Metaphors we live by*. Chicago: Chicago University Press.

Levin, B. 1993. *English verb classes and alternations*. Cambridge MA: MIT Press.

Levin, B. & M. Rappaport Hovav. 2013. Lexicalized meaning and manner/result complementarity. In B. Arsenijević, B. Gehrke & R. Marín (eds.), *Studies in the composition and decomposition of event predicates*, 49–70. Dordrecht: Springer.

Löbner, S. 1979. *Intensionale Verben und Funktionalbegriffe. Zur Syntax und Semantik von 'wechseln' und den vergleichbaren Verben des Deutschen.* Tübingen: Narr.

Löbner, S. 1981. Intensional verbs and functional concepts: More on the "rising temperature" problem. *Linguistic Inquiry* 12 (3). 471–477.

Löbner, S. 1985. Definites. *Journal of Semantics* 4. 279–326.

Löbner, S. 2011a. Concept types and determination. *Journal of Semantics* 28(3). 279–333.

Löbner, S. 2011b. Functional concepts and frames. http://semanticsarchive.net/Archive/\\jl1NGEwO/.

Löbner, S. 2014. Evidence for frames from human language. In T. Gamerschlag, D. Gerland, R. Osswald & W. Petersen (eds.), *Frames and concept types: Applications in language and philosophy*. Studies in Linguistics and Philosophy 94, 23–67. Dordrecht: Springer.

Montague, R. 1973. The proper treatment of quantification in ordinary English. In J. Hintikka, J. Moravcsik & P. Suppes (eds.), *Approaches to natural language. proceedings of the 1970 stanford workshop on grammar and semantics*, 221–242. Dordrecht: Reidel.

Naumann, R. 2013. Outline of a dynamic theory of frames. In G. Bezhanishvili, S. Löbner, V. Marra & F. Richter (eds.), *Logic, language, and computation*, vol. 7758 Lecture Notes in Computer Science (LNCS), 115–137. Berlin, Heidelberg: Springer.

Petersen, W. 2007. Decomposing concepts with frames. *Baltic International Yearbook of Cognition, Logic and Communication* 2. 151–170.

Petersen, W. & T. Osswald. 2014. Concept composition in frames – focusing on genitive constructions. In T. Gamerschlag, D. Gerland, R. Osswald & W. Petersen (eds.), *Frames and concept types: Applications in language and philosophy*. Studies in Linguistics and Philosophy 94, 243-266. Dordrecht: Springer.

Piñón, C. 1997. Achievements in an event semantics. *Proceedings of semantics and linguistic theory* 7. 276–292.

Pollard, C. & I. Sag. 1994. *Head-driven phrase structure grammar.* Chicago: University of Chicago Press.

Rappaport Hovav, M. 2008. Lexicalized meaning and the internal temporal structure of events. In S. Rothstein (ed.), *Theoretical and crosslinguistic approaches to the semantics of aspect*, 13–42. Amsterdam: John Benjamins.

Rothstein, S. 2004. *Structuring events: A study in the semantics of lexical aspect.* Oxford: Blackwell Publishing.

Zwarts, J. 2005. Prepositional aspect and the algebra of paths. *Linguistics and Philosophy* 28 (6). 739–779.

Authors

Thomas Gamerschlag
Wilhelm Geuder
Wiebke Petersen
Departement of Linguistics and Information Science
Heinrich-Heine-University Düsseldorf
{gamer,geuder,petersen}@phil.hhu.de

Comparative lexicology and the typology of event descriptions: a programmatic study

Volker Gast, Ekkehard König & Claire Moyse-Faurie

1 Introduction*

It is a well-known fact that the vocabularies of individual languages are structured very differently. Even if it is always possible to translate a certain utterance from one language into another, it is rarely, if ever, possible to say that all or even some lexemes making up an utterance in one language correspond perfectly and completely to the lexemes rendering that utterance in another. In most cases the content cut out from the amorphous mass of notions and ideas by one lexeme A may be similar to the content identified by some translational counterpart in another, but there is hardly ever complete identity and what we find is partial overlap at best. The consequence of this basic observation for structuralists was that semantic analysis in one language amounts to describing the structural relations between the lexemes of a language in terms of oppositions (antonymy, complementarity, converseness, etc.), super- and subordination, meronymy, etc. (cf. Lyons 1972, Cruse 1986, Löbner 2002, etc.), and that comparative semantics or comparative lexicology is nothing more than a comparison between these networks of structural relations.

More recent theorizing about semantics, specifically the idea of semantic decomposition in terms of hierarchical structures ("decompositional event seman-

---

* In the publications of Sebastian Löbner, to whom we dedicate this article on the occasion of his 65th birthday, comparative studies on lexicology and meaning have played a considerable role (see for instance Löbner 2002: 153, ff. or Löbner 2011). We would like to thank two anonymous reviewers for their critical comments and valuable suggestions.

tics"), typically associated with the generative paradigm, or the ideas associated with the basic assumptions of Cognitive Linguistics, is less agnostic about the semantic or propositional substance underlying the vocabularies of individual languages and has led to a wide variety of comparative studies in semantics or lexicology,[1] and even to attempts at formulating lexical typologies. These studies agree with the structuralist view that each language carves up conceptual space in a different manner, but – in clear analogy to morpho-syntactic typology – the cuts are assumed not to be completely random and not to differ without limits. What we find, then, are two extreme views and several shades of grey in between. On the one extreme, there is the view that there are innate lexical concepts and constraints arising from the structure of the mind or the world. The other extreme is the view that languages differ arbitrarily in their semantic organization of conceptual domains. The middle ground is held by positions which accord some role to biases in perception and cognition as well as to communicative constraints and cultural practices, still underlining the importance and necessity of arbitrary linguistic conventions (cf. Narasinhan et al. 2012).

A closer look at the lexical typologies currently available reveals the difficulties and limits of such cross-linguistic lexical studies. Combining onomasiological and semasiological perspectives, they are typically based on ontological domains easily identifiable across languages (e. g. body parts, colors, temperatures, possession, kinship terminology, motion, perception, eating, placing and displacing, etc.), on comparatively small samples of languages, or on both. There is a bias towards nominal or adjectival denotations, a bias which can also be observed in fieldwork on lesser described languages (cf. Evans 2011a on the neglect of verbs in elicitation, as well as some reasons for it). Moreover, the typological distinctions are not really analogous to those developed for morpho-syntactic properties. In most cases, gradual rather than clear-cut distinctions, e. g. more or fewer lexical differentiations found for kinship relations or for hair on humans vs. animals, on heads vs. bodies, etc. (cf. Koch 2001), are described for comparable lexical subsystems of different languages, and only very rarely do we find implicational generalizations (such as the well-known hierarchy of basic color terms from Berlin & Kay 1969), and even more rarely connections between different variant properties.

How can the search for cross-linguistic generalizations in the lexicons overcome these difficulties and limitations and go beyond contrastive or comparative

---

[1] Cf. the special issue of *Linguistics*, 50.3, 2012, edited by M. Koptjevskaya-Tamm and M. Vanhove for a recent survey, especially the introduction (Koptjevskaya-Tamm 2012).

studies of a few lexical subsystems? In the current state of the art we can see two promising approaches in pursuit of this goal. The first one, clearly delineated in a recent handbook article by N. Evans (Evans 2011b), abstracts from specific notional domains and their encoding in lexical subsystems, for the benefit of generalizations of a higher order. The major generalizations made in Evans (2011b) are formulated not so much in terms of lexical subsystems but in terms of four general properties of nominal denotations or event descriptions: We find differences in the GRANULARITY of lexical distinctions, in the BOUNDARIES between lexical categories, in the GROUPING and the DISSECTION of semantic components.

The parameter of 'granularity' concerns the degree of 'ramification' in a meronymical tree. For example, English makes a distinction between *branch* and *twig*, which is not made in other languages (e. g. Georgian, which only has *t'ot'i* for both 'branch, twig'). With respect to the location of boundaries between subcomponents of an object, Evans (2011b: 512) points out that "the Savosavo 'leg' category begins at the hip joint (and encompasses the foot), whereas Tidore *yohu* – roughly, 'leg' – cuts off three-quarters of the way up to the thigh".

In addition to different organizations of meronymical systems (part-whole relations), cross-linguistic differences can also be observed in the level of generality at which a given category is located ('grouping', in terms of Evans 2011b). As an example of 'grouping' in the domain of body-parts, Evans (2011b) considers terms for 'finger' and 'toe'. English does not have a cover term for these body parts. Other languages, by contrast, do not distinguish lexically between them. For instance, Serbo-Croatian uses the same term for fingers and toes (*prst*), as does Spanish (*dedo*). While being located at different parts of the body as far as meronymical organization is concerned, these languages 'group' them together because of their similarities with respect to their position, form, function, etc. Evans's parameter of 'dissection', finally, concerns the ways in which "complex phenomena are decomposed into parts" (Evans 2011b: 514). One of the most frequently cited examples of using dissection for typological distinctions is the well-known typology for verbs of motion developed by Talmy (1985, 2000).

Based on the inspiration of such work, which has only been characterized here in its basic outlines, lexical typology can now ask very ambitious questions such as: What aspects or components of verbal meanings are typically lexicalized across languages? What differentiations are found, and what types of generalizations can we make? What are possible and impossible verbal meanings? For instance, can the hypothesis of Manner/Result complementarity made by Levin &

Rappaport Hovav (e. g. Levin & Rappaport Hovav 1991, 2006, 2013, Rappaport Hovav & Levin 2010) be defended against recent criticism, brought forward *inter alia* by Beavers & Koontz-Garboden (2012) and Husband (2011)?[2] Do new data from lesser described languages confirm or falsify such hypotheses? These are the questions guiding our investigation, which we carry out with the objective of identifying cross-linguistic tendencies and generalizations over the ways in which languages lexicalize event descriptions.

Our generalizations will be formulated in terms of hierarchies,[3] the format typically used by typologists. The study is exploratory insofar as it is also limited in its empirical scope and programmatic as it points out possible avenues for future typological research, rather than presenting well-founded cross-linguistic generalizations.

As far as the empirical basis of our study is concerned, we have partly selected domains known to manifest differential degrees of generality at least in two languages on the basis of previous work. As far as languages are concerned, we have primarily selected our native tongues as well as languages one of us has studied in detail. The starting point is invariably provided by observations on clear distinctions in the lexical organization of certain conceptual domains. Attempts to find the counterpart of certain verbs like *eat, cut, kill, beat*, for instance, reveal that some languages have a wide variety of possible translations depending on event parameters (like properties of Agents and/or Patients) which play no role in English and these languages may even lack a general term such as we find in English.

We start with some theoretical background assumptions that are needed for a lexical typology of verb meanings (Section 2). In Sections 3 and 4, we present some case studies, i.e., comparisons of verbal inventories for the domains of eating and drinking (Section 3), and for verbs of physical impact (Section 4), i.e., verbs of killing, beating and cutting. Section 5 contains some thoughts on possible explanations for the patterns and limits of variation that we can observe. Section 6 provides a summary and the conclusions.

---

[2] For a recent publication supporting the Manner/Result complementarity hypothesis, see Alexiadou & Anagnostopoulou (2013).

[3] Since only two features will be ranked at a time, the term 'hierarchy' is strictly speaking unjustified. The predictions associated with more extended scales would be far too strong and too easily falsifiable at the current state of our knowledge.

2 Aspects of event descriptions

In keeping with basic assumptions of Davidsonian event semantics, we regard events as entities with the same ontological status as objects. Like objects, events can thus be predicated over, i.e., they can have properties. We can distinguish different types of properties of events. The most 'essential' property is the one that makes an event what it is. Consider the example in (1).

(1) *The Tacoma Narrows Bridge collapsed slowly in 1940.*

The property of being a 'collapse' – more specifically, the collapse of the Tacoma Narrows Bridge – is the 'most essential' property of the event described in (1). It is a matter of debate to what extent event predicates are conceivable without participants. Can a 'collapsing event' be imagined without having information about the (type of) entity that collapses, e.g. a bridge, a house or a man? We would not like to take a stance in this matter, but we will make a terminological distinction between 'bare' and 'saturated' event descriptions. We adopt the term 'lexicalized meaning' from Levin & Rappaport Hovav (2013), which is "taken to comprise a verb's core meaning", and which is defined on the basis of "constancy of entailment across all uses of verbs" (Levin & Rappaport Hovav 2013: 1). In the case of the verb *collapse*, the lexicalized meaning could be described as 'to fall together ... by external pressure or withdrawal of the contents' or 'by loss of rigidity or support ...' (OED, s.v. *collapse*). Unsaturated verbs, accordingly, are taken to denote 'lexical predicates'.

More specific event types emerge when the participants of a given event are specified. The collapse of a bridge or house is more easily imaginable than an event of collapsing that abstracts away from the participants involved. Event predicates together with their core arguments will be called 'saturated'.

In the case of (1), the saturated predicate (describing the collapsing of a bridge) is modified by the adverb *slowly*, which can be regarded as an additional attribute of the event in question (the type of modification is intersective). Moreover, this event is attributed the property of having taken place in 1940. Another type of property that can be predicated of an event is, obviously, the place at which it takes place.

In Davidsonian event semantics, the referential argument of a verbal predicate – the events – is represented with a variable e. The lexical predicate of an event is simply represented as a predicate which is said to be true of the relevant event (e.g. COLLAPSE(e)). Additional specifications like *slowly* are represented in the same way (SLOW(e)). In a Neo-Davidsonian framework (cf. Parsons 1990), participants are regarded as entities that stand in a thematic relation to the event argument e. For example, in (1) there is one argument/participant, i.e., the Tacoma Narrows Bridge. This bridge can be regarded as a Patient of the event in question (participant roles are capitalized). Moreover, the event is said to have taken place in 1940 (i.e., the time of the event t_e is fully included in the time span corresponding to the year 1940, t_{1940}). The meaning of (1) can thus be represented as shown in (2).

(2) ∃e [COLLAPSE(e) ∧ PATIENT(TNB,e) ∧ SLOW(e) ∧ $t_e \subset t_{1940}$]
'There is an event e such that e is a collapsing event, the Tacoma Narrows Bridge (TNB) is the Patient of e, e is slow and the temporal extension of e is fully included in the temporal extension of the year 1940.'

Event predicates furthermore differ in terms of parameters relating to matters of *aktionsart* or actionality. In particular, event descriptions often differentiate in accordance with the Result of the event in question. Such specifications mostly concern properties of either the Theme or Patient as in (3) (more generally speaking, of the Undergoer of an event; cf. Van Valin & LaPolla 1997), or the Agent (or 'Actor', in terms of Van Valin & LaPolla 1997), as in (4).

(3) *The thief was shot dead.*

(4) *John overate.*

We can thus distinguish between Agent-related and Patient-related Results, and we will make that distinction whenever necessary. Agent-related Results will be abbreviated as 'Result$_{Ag}$', Patient-related results as 'Result$_{Pat}$'. Another distinction that is important to make is the one between 'category-level' and 'verb-specific' Results. Category-level results are lexical entailments associated with major classes of verbs. For example, verbs of killing lexically imply the death of a protagonist, verbs of eating imply that food is consumed and verbs of cutting imply an "incision with clean edges" (Levin & Rappaport Hovav 2013:5). In addition to such category-level Results, verb-specific ones may be encoded as well. For instance, *slice*, in addition to entailing an incision with clean edges (by virtue of being a verb of cutting) implies that the Patient is divided into parts with a specific shape (slices). In the following, we will only be concerned with verb-specific Results.

Just as (dynamic) events are often characterized by a Result (or 'post-state'), some predicates inherently come with an event type preceding the event in question (a 'pre-state'). In particular, verbs of action (such as intentional killing) are by definition preceded by a decision or, more generally speaking, a Motivation (a specific type of Cause). Such events can thus often (minimally) be regarded as sequences of a Motivation, a sub-event which is characteristic of the entire class and a Result.

Neo-Davidsonian semantics does not distinguish 'layers' of meaning (as, for instance, in Functional Grammar, cf. Dik 1997), but represents the various aspects of event descriptions simply as conjunctions. For our study it will be useful, however, to distinguish between 'more intrinsic' and 'more extrinsic' properties of events. The lexical predicate is the most intrinsic property, as it provides the basic unit of categorization at a rather abstract level. The core participants (Agent and Patient) are required by the lexical predicate, i. e., an event is not conceivable without them and they render it 'imagineable'. The Motivation and the Result are closely associated with the core participants and are therefore located at the same level as the latter. Manners and Instruments provide additional, more peripheral specifications. The Time and Place at which an event takes place, finally, is 'extrinsic' insofar as (in most cases) the same type of event can be thought of as taking place at another Time or Place. The 'layered' structure of a predication emerging from these considerations is shown in (5).

(5)
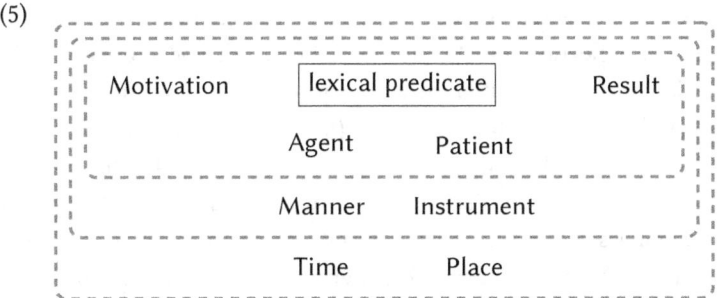

Among the parameters of event descriptions summarized in (5), two have played a very prominent role in recent theoretical discussion of verb semantics. Among the many authors contributing to this topic we will only single out Levin & Rappaport Hovav, who in a large number of publications (e. g. Levin & Rappaport Hovav 1991, 2006, 2013, Rappaport Hovav & Levin 2010) have formulated, discussed and defended a constraint on possible verb meanings, which will also provide an important point of orientation for our study. They make the following claim of Manner/Result complementarity:

(i) MANNER/RESULT COMPLEMENTARITY: Manner and result meaning components are in complementary distribution: A verb may lexicalize only one.

This generalization and constraint draws a distinction between two broad classes of verbs: (a) Manner verbs (e. g. *hit, run, sweep, bite, caress, cook*), and (b) Result verbs (e. g. *cut, arrive, clean, swallow, open*). More recent work on verbs of motion (Beavers et al. 2010) has shown that the distinction identified by Talmy (1985, 2000) is one specific manifestation of this more general distinction. Given that the hypothesis of Manner/Result complementarity has played a prominent role in the recent discussion, we will refer to it whenever relevant observations can be made.

3 Verbs of eating and drinking

3.1 The basic parameters of variation

We will begin our comparison with the English verbs *eat* and *drink*, since it has been pointed out that these verbs and their counterparts in other languages often manifest remarkable properties and do not behave like ordinary transitive verbs (cf. Naess 2011). Our data shows that all of the properties of events shown in (5) above may be lexicalized in verbs of eating and drinking in specific languages and that languages may differ with respect to these lexical components. A first type of variation concerns selectional restrictions on the Agent and the Patient. For the Agent, some languages have different verbs for humans and animals. German is of this type, as it distinguishes between *essen* (human) and *fressen* (animals) for eating, and between *trinken* (humans) and *saufen* (specific animals[4]) for drinking. English does not make any such distinction and uses *eat* and *drink* for animals alike. In an extended sense, Germ. *fressen* and *saufen* can also be used with human subjects if the Manner of food consumption (quantity, noise produced, etc.) is more like that associated with animals (*Karl frisst wie ein Schwein* 'Karl eats like a pig').

Much more variation can be found when we consider selectional restrictions on the Patient. Note first that the basic verbs of English – *eat* and *drink* – already exhibit selectional restrictions insofar as they can only be used with (more or less solid) food and liquids, respectively. Some languages (e. g. Kalam, Walpiri) have only one verb for both activities (cf. Wierzbicka 2009, Naess 2011: 415), roughly

---

[4] An anonymous reviewer pointed out to us that *saufen* would not be used with *mice, birds* and other types of (smaller) animals.

corresponding to the English expression 'take in/consume food/liquid'. In East Uvean, there is a honorific term (when one speaks to/of the king) for both types of activity, i. e. *taumafa,* but there are two different terms in the ordinary language (*inu* 'drink' and *kai* 'eat').

It is sometimes difficult to determine whether it is primarily the Manner of consumption or the type of food consumed that is lexicalized. For example, Japanese uses *taberu/tabemasu* for solid food and *nomu* for liquid food (e. g. soups), but Löbner (2002:232) has pointed out that *nomu* also combines with all kinds of medicine, including pills. Accordingly, *nomu* seems to be associated with events of ingestion that do not imply chewing.[5]

In many languages differentiation of verbs according to the substance of what is consumed is taken much further, and there are even languages that have no generic eating verb of the type commonly found in European languages. Navajo has different verb stems for eating hard, compact things, leafy things, meat, marrow and mushy things, among others (cf. Rice 2009). A particularly rich inventory of lexical differentiations depending on the type of food taken in is found in East Futunan (cf. Moyse-Faurie 1993). Some examples of highly specific root meanings are given in (6). A remarkable phenomenon in this language is also the differentiations drawn between eating certain food alone or in combination with other dishes, as in (6b). We will return to such differentiations in Section 3.2, where some particularly interesting differentiations found in Melanesian and Polynesian languages are discussed.

(6) East Futunan
    a. *fono'i*   'to practice cannibalism'
    b. *kina*   'eat two things together (starchy food and side dishes)'
    c. *kītaki*   'eat starchy food or ripe bananas with coco'
    d. *'ota*   'eat raw things, Tahitian salad'
    e. *otai*   'eat certain fruit (grated guava mixed with grated coconut)'
    f. *mafana*   'drink the juice of the dish *su* before eating it'

So far we have focused on the core participants (Agent and Patient) for the description of cross-linguistic differentiation of lexical inventories. Let us now turn to the other parameters of variation. The Manner of eating is clearly expressed

---

[5] This was pointed out to us by an anonymous reviewer. Note that if liquid food or medication is given to babies or elderly people one can also use *boire* 'drink' in French (*boire le médicament à la cuillère,* lit. 'drink the medicine with a spoon').

in verbs like *wolf down, devour, slurp* in English and *chipoter* 'pick/nibble at the food' , *picorer* 'eat very little/selectively', *dévorer* 'devour, wolf down', *engloutir* 'wolf down' in French or *schlingen* 'wolf down', *herunterwürgen* 'gulp down' in German. More often than not these expressions seem to be based on Manners of eating observable in the behavior of animals. As mentioned above, in German the verbs used with animal subjects may also be used with human subjects to describe immoderate eating and drinking.

Instruments are rare lexical components of verbs of eating, and if they are lexicalized, they are often morphologically complex or the result of conversion. Examples that come to mind are *aus-löffeln* 'spoon out', *auf-gabeln* 'pick/dig up' in German, verbs that are primarily used in metaphorical extensions (e. g. *aus-löffeln* with the meaning 'face the music', *auf-gabeln* as 'accidentally pick up a person').

The Time of eating is expressed in such lexemes as *déjeuner* 'have breakfast', *goûter* 'have an afternoon snack', *dîner* 'have dinner', *souper* 'have supper' in French, as *zaftrakat'* 'have breakfast', *obedat'* 'have lunch', *uzhinat'* 'have dinner', etc. in Russian, and as *dine* and *sup* in English. The Place of eating is rarely expressed, except for cases like *piqueniquer* 'eating outside' in French.

Some languages make lexical differentiations concerning the Result of eating, i. e. the effect either on the Patient (Germ. *auf-essen* 'eat up', *aus-trinken* 'drink up') or the Agent (*sich voll-essen, sich satt-essen* 'eat one's fill', *sich über-essen* 'overeat').[6] As these examples illustrate, the relevant verbs are typically morphologically complex and contain an independent morpheme indicating results.

Having pointed out some general parameters in the lexicalization patterns of eating verbs, we will now turn to a group of languages that exhibit particularly rich inventories of verbs of eating, i. e. selected Melanesian and Polynesian languages.

3.2 More fine-grained distinctions in Melanesian and Polynesian languages

Some of the parameters discussed in the preceding section can be illustrated with examples from East Futunan (cf. Moyse-Faurie 1993). In this language a generic verb (*kai*) corresponding to *eat* is available and is used both transitively and intransitively. This verb is often used with modifiers indicating, for instance, Manners and Results of eating. Consider the following examples:

---

[6] Cf. Putnam & Gast (2012) for a semantic analysis of 'excess predicates' like *overeat*.

(7) a. *kai fakavale* 'to overeat' (Result$_{Ag}$)
    b. *kai mākona* 'eat one's fill' (Result$_{Ag}$)
    c. *kai okooko* 'eat moderately' (Manner)
    d. *kai vasuvasu* 'eat in accordance with what is customary' (Manner)

The examples given so far suggest that East Futunan uses simple verbs for specific types of food (cf. (6) above) and complex constructions to indicate the Manner or Result of eating, but there is actually no complete complementarity between the generic verb *kai* and specialized verbs like those in (6). There are also cases of specialized verbs referring to the Manner of eating (cf. (8)) and we find *kai* with objects indicating the type of food (cf. (9)).

(8) a. *ma'ama'aga* 'eat excessively' (Result$_{Ag}$)
    b. *pakalamu* 'chew well; eat noisily (of people)' (Manner)

(9) a. *kai samukō* 'eat only fish and meat/proteins'
    b. *kai koko* 'eat all kinds of things'
    c. *kai tauvalo* 'eat constantly good things'

If we broaden out our perspective from the case of East Futunan to Melanesian languages of New Caledonia and Polynesian languages in general, we get a more or less uniform general picture, in spite of some differences between New Caledonian Mainland languages (several specific terms), the languages of the Loyalty Islands (general eating term versus meat/fish distinction) and Polynesian languages (raw versus cooked, only one sort of food or different sorts). Before looking at the more fine-grained and, from the perspective of European languages, remarkable examples, let us briefly consider the higher-level eating terms that are available. As pointed out in Section 3.1, East Uvean has a (honorific) verb which is used for both eating and drinking (*taumafa*). A more or less general term for 'eat' (*kai*), which is used both intransitively ('have a meal') and transitively, is found in East Uvean and Tongan, in addition to East Futunan. On the Loyalty Islands there are terms used intransitively and for eating starch food, fruits, vegetables (but not for meat): *kaka/kakan* in Nengone, and *xen* in Drehu. The New Caledonian Mainland languages have a term for 'eat' which is used intransitively and for most fruits and salad (but not for bread, coconut, banana or meat), i.e. Xârâcùù *da* and Ajië *ara*.

We can use examples from East Uvean to illustrate some eating verbs relating to the Manner of food consumption. There is a verb for 'stuffing oneself', i.e.

fa'apuku/ha'apuku. If food is swallowed without chewing (ripe bananas), or if an eater has no teeth, *momi* is used. Noisy eating habits, compared to those of animals, are implied by the verb *pakalamu*. Finally, there is a verb for enjoying food, i. e. *'unani*.

More specialized verbs of eating are typically differentiated into those requiring starch food (yam, taro, sweet potato, rice, banana, manioc, bread) and those requiring meat, fish or related types of food (e. g. animal products). The first class is found in the New Caledonian Mainland languages Xârâcùù (*kê*) and Ajië (*kâi*). All New Caledonian languages have verbs that are used with meat, fish, coconut (perhaps as a metaphorical extension of flesh), as well as egg and milk products (Nengone *ia/ian*, Drehu *öni*, Xârâcùù *xwè*, Ajië *oi*). New Caledonian and Polynesian languages have verbs of eating that are restricted to the consumption of sugarcane, orange and all other fruits that are sucked (Xârâcùù *xwii*, Ajië *wa*, East Uvean/East Futunan/Tuvaluan *gau*). Polynesian languages have verbs for raw food (fish, meat, shells), i. e. *'ota* (East Futunan, East Uvean) and *ota* (Tuvaluan), deriving from PPn **'ota*.

While such degrees of specificity are surprising from the perspective of European languages, it is probably even more uncommon to find specific verbs which relate not to the type of food, but to the number of types of food consumed. In Polynesian languages there are verbs that are used when only one thing is eaten, i. e., either starch food or bread without any meat or fish, or vice versa. These verbs are also used for leftovers (non-protein food): *hamu/hamuko* (East Uvean), (*kai*) *samukō* (East Futunan), and *samusamu* (Tuvaluan), all deriving from PPn **hamu*.

Finally, there are also verbs of eating that are used when both starch food and fish or meat is consumed. Xârâgurè *haakéi/xaakéi* means (roughly) 'eat as accompaniment to protein food', and the meanings 'food eaten with another food as relish' or 'meat or fish provided to eat with vegetable food, relish' are expressed by the verbs *kīnaki* (Māori), *kīkī* (East Uvean), *kiki* (Tuvaluan), and (*kai*)*kina* (East Uvean, West Uvean), all deriving from PPn **kina*. Even more specifically, the verb *kītaki* (East Futunan, East Uvean) denotes an event of eating both starch food and coconut flesh or ripe bananas.

Obviously, food can also be combined with beverages, and given the highly specific verb meanings mentioned above it is perhaps not surprising to see that there are also verbs for food-beverage combinations. The East Uvean verb *omaki*

(< PPn *omaki) and the Tuvaluan verb *peke* mean 'dunk food into water before eating it'. East Uvean *fono* (< PPn *fono) is used when food is eaten with kava.

We will conclude this overview of the rich inventories of verbs of eating found in Melanesian and Polynesian languages with examples of verbs that do not denote eating actions, but the desire to eat specific things, i. e. terms meaning 'feel like eating specific kinds of food'. East Futunan *gā* and Haméa *treu* mean 'crave for proteins (i. e. fish or meat)', and East Uvean as well as Tongan *'umisi* (< Proto-Fijian *kusima) means 'crave for fish/seafood'.

3.3 Towards cross-linguistic generalizations

Obviously, it is very difficult to make generalizations in lexical typology in general, and even more so in the (highly) abstract domain of verbal meanings. We will propose hierarchies which rank properties of event descriptions in terms of the (hypothesized) likelihood that these properties will be lexicalized in specific verbs. The hierarchies will rank pairs of parameters that make similar contributions to the predication in question. Before formulating such hierarchies, we will consider the various parameters individually, however.

In the languages that we have looked at, the most important property that is lexicalized in eating verbs seems to be the type of food or beverage consumed (the Patient). In Europe (as well as probably in most other parts of the world), there are consistent differentiations between eating and drinking, and languages that do not make a distinction here at all seem to be rare. As the Melanesian and Polynesian languages discussed in Section 3.2 have shown, there are hardly any limits on the level of specificity found in differentiations according to the type of food consumed.

The Agent has been found to be relevant in German. We have not investigated whether there are distinctions according to age, but it seems likely to us that cross-linguistic studies will reveal that at least some languages use specific eating verbs for children. Still, distinctions according to properties of the Agent are clearly less prominent than distinctions according to properties of the Patient, in terms of both the number of languages which make such distinctions, and the number of distinctions made in the languages that do (basically, human vs. non-human).

A property of eating verbs that has been found to be relatively prominent concerns the Manner of consumption. Note that this parameter is obviously not totally independent of the type of food consumed or of selectional restrictions on the Agent. It makes a difference who eats what. As has been pointed out, in many cases it is probably difficult to tell apart whether it is primarily the Manner of eating or the type of food that is lexicalized in a given case. Soups are liquid but they are 'eaten' in English, perhaps because they are consumed with a spoon and with specific portion sizes. As was pointed out in Section 3.1, Japanese treats soups in the same way as beverages and thus seems to distinguish more clearly on the basis of substance rather than the Manner of eating; but then, medicine (including pills and powders) patterns with beverages, suggesting that it is the absence of chewing which characterizes actions denoted by *taberu/tabemasu*.

The Instrument of eating, by contrast, seems to be less commonly encoded, and we have noticed that the relevant verbs are often interpreted metaphorically in German. Few lexical distinctions have also been found with respect to the Result of eating or drinking events. The examples that we have considered were all Agent-related, e. g. *overeat*. Such predicates typically appear to be morphologically complex.

Verbs of eating which lexicalize the Time of eating are widespread in Europe, perhaps because different types of meals are consumed at specific times of the day (cf. Section 5 on explanations). A verb like Germ. *frühstücken* 'have breakfast' is thus quite informative, as it conveys information not only about the Time of eating but also about the food that is typically consumed. In Polynesian and Melanesian communities the same type of food is eaten at all times of the day and this could be the reason that Oceanic languages do not have differentiations of this kind. The Place of eating, by contrast, is hardly ever lexicalized, and given that there is not much variation possible, it is not surprising to find that this parameter is of minor importance in the present context.

On the basis of the considerations made above, we propose the following hierarchies of properties associated with eating and drinking events:

(10) Hierarchies for eating and drinking verbs
  a. Patient > Agent
  b. Manner > Instrument
  c. Time > Place

Given that the relationship between Manner and Result has played an important role in recent discussion of lexical semantics, we will also consider the relationship between these two properties. Their lexical encoding seems to be largely complementary. Our data thus lends support to the Manner/Result complementarity hypothesis. In eating verbs, the encoding of Manner is clearly more prominent than the Result, abstracting away from the category-level entailment that food is consumed. We can thus postulate the hierarchy in (11).

(11) Manner and Result in verbs of eating and drinking
Manner > Result

The hierarchies in (10) and (11) are, obviously, intended as hypotheses about the tendencies for specific properties of events to be lexicalized in the world's languages. Such hierarchies can of course only be probabilistic, as they are certainly, at least partially, culture-specific. Those properties located to the left are (hypothesized to be) more likely to be lexicalized in verbs of eating or drinking than those further on the right.

4 Verbs of physical impact

We will now turn to an entirely different group of verbs, which call for different generalizations and explanations, i.e. verbs of physical impact. We have chosen the three groups 'verbs of killing', 'verbs of beating' and 'verbs of cutting' because the relevant verbs seemed to exhibit interesting differentiations in the languages investigated by us. Needless to say, there are certainly many more interesting verbs belonging to this group, and the discussion in this section is far from exhaustive.

4.1 Verbs of killing

The concept of 'killing' is expressed by prototypical transitive verbs like Engl. *kill*, Germ. *töten*, Fr. *tuer*, etc. (cf. Beavers & Koontz-Garboden 2012 for a recent study of killing verbs). Taking again the selection of Agents as a point of departure, we can see that in many European languages there is a neutral verb, such as the three verbs mentioned above, that can be used irrespective of the exact nature of the Agent, i.e., for human and non-human Agents alike. Moreover, there are verbs of killing that require premeditation and, hence, a human Agent (e.g. *assassinate, murder*), and certain verbs like *shoot* require a human Agent for non-linguistic reasons, as shooting implies an intentional Agent with certain fine motor skills (and it is questionable if we would use the verb *erschießen* 'shoot dead' if an animal – say, a cat – accidentally shot a person by playing with a gun). In more specialized registers, there are also verbs that are used specifically for animals, e.g. German *reißen* (of lions, tigers, wolfs, etc.) and *schlagen* (of predator birds).

If we consider the selectional restrictions concerning the Patient, we find, again, some interesting cases of differentiation, like Engl. *slaughter* or Germ. *schlachten*, Fr. *abattre*, etc., which are used for killing animals (for food production), and this seems to be the only restriction found in that domain, unsurprisingly so, since only animals and human beings can be killed.[7]

An interesting and subtle difference in the lexical inventories of English and German, however, is described by Plank (1984). There are as many as five possible translations for the English verb *shoot* in German, depending on the Patient and the Motivation of the activity. The (intransitive) German root *schieß-* is similar to Engl. (transitive or intransitive) *shoot* insofar as it does not carry any resultative implications. This root is also used transitively in a highly specialized meaning, however, i.e. when referring to the shooting of game animals (cf. 12a). In most cases, the root *schieß-* is used transitively only with some resultative prefix of the type illustrated in (12b) to (12e).

(12) a. *schießen*
   Karl hat in der letzten Jagdsaison 10 Wildscheine geschossen.
   'Charles shot 5 wild boars during the last hunting season.'

   b. *ab-schießen*
   Jäger sollen noch mehr Wild abschießen.
   'Hunters are urged to shoot more game.'

   c. *er-schießen*
   Die Terroristen haben vier Zivilisten erschossen.
   'The terrorists shot 4 ordinary civilians.'

   d. *tot-schießen*
   Wir mussten den entlaufenen Löwen totschießen.
   'We had to shoot the escaped lion.'

   e. *nieder-schießen*
   Der Polizist wurde auf offener Straße niedergeschossen.
   'The police man was shot in the street.'

Ab-schießen focuses on 'successful completion' – typically used with flying objects like birds (and also airplanes) – and does not convey any specific Motivation – unlike (transitive) *schießen*, which is clearly associated with hunting, and thus either the reduction of game population or the supply of meat. *Er-schießen* is

---

[7] Of course there are metaphorical extensions, such as *to kill time*, Fr. *tuer le temps*, Germ. *die Zeit totschlagen*.

only used with human objects and perhaps higher animals. *Tot-schießen*, which carries a connotation of child language, could be used if danger is to be avoided, or if a person or an animal is killed *ad hoc*, i. e. if there is no specific Motivation. *Nieder-schießen*, finally, which is restricted to human Patients, is not a verb of killing, and the survival of the object would even be assumed by implicature. The English verb *shoot* is completely neutral with regard to all these facets of meaning.

Let us consider the parameter of Motivation in more detail. For the killing of persons, three major Motivations can be distinguished: persons may be killed for criminal reasons (e. g. *murder*), for political or ideological reasons (e. g. *assassinate*), and they may be killed 'legally' (e. g. *execute*). Note that the two cognate verbs *assassiner* in French and *assassinate* in English have different implications with respect to both the Patient and the Motivation of a killing event. While the former permits any kind of human object, the latter is restricted to public figures.

Given that killing is an ethically highly sensitive action, it is not surprising to find that languages indicate *why* someone is killed. This distinguishes verbs of killing from verbs of eating. As we will see below, the Motivation is also rarely encoded in verbs of beating or cutting (cf. also Section 5 on explanations).

The examples in (12) above also illustrate a further parameter of variation, i. e. the Instrument of killing. The English verb *shoot* and the stem appearing in all its German counterparts, viz. *schießen*, denote actions in which a rifle, gun or pistol is used. Consider now the examples given in (13) (from German and French) as well as their English translations. These verbs imply the use of some specific Instrument:

(13)   a.   *er-stechen*   'stab' ('killing with a knife', Fr. *poignarder*)
         b.   *er-würgen*   'strangle' ('killing with the hands', Fr. *étrangler*)

(14)   a.   *er-schlagen*   'slay' ('kill with a club/blunt object', Fr. *assommer*)
         b.   *er-schießen*   'shoot dead' ('kill with a gun', Fr. *fusiller*)

In the case of killing verbs, it is sometimes difficult to tell whether it is an Instrument or a Manner that is encoded. More broadly speaking, we could also use the term 'method'. Levin (1993) distinguishes between '*murder* verbs' – which imply no specific Manner (or method) (cf. (15)), and '*poison* verbs', which do provide a Manner, but which do not entail the death of the Patient (cf. (16)).

(15)   Levin's (1993) *murder* verbs
        assassinate, butcher, dispatch,
        eliminate, execute, immolate, kill, liquidate, massacre, murder, slaughter, slay

(16) Levin's (1993) *poison* verbs
asphyxiate, crucify, drown, electrocute, garrotte, hang, knife, poison, shoot, smother, stab, strangle, suffocate

Beavers & Koontz-Garboden (2012) have argued for distinguishing a third class, i. e. 'manner-of-killing verbs' (cf. (17)). Some of these verbs are categorized as *poison* verbs by Levin (1993).

(17) Beavers and Koontz-Garboden's (2012) manner-of-killing verbs
crucify, drown, electrocute, guillotine, hang

We will return to the (controversial) question of whether verbs like those in (16) encode Manner and Result (death) at the same time below. For the time being, let us consider some German and French verbs of killing which do appear to encode both a manner of killing and the Patient's death in (18). Note that most of these verbs are not morphologically simple – the German verbs carry a resultative prefix – and therefore do not represent a challenge to the claim of Manner/Result complementarity made by Levin & Rappaport Hovav (2006).

(18) a. *er-tränken*   'killing by putting someone under water', (Fr. *noyer*)
     b. *ver-giften*   'poison' 'killing with poison', (Fr. *empoisonner*)
     c. *ver-brennen* 'burn' 'killing by fire', (Fr. *brûler*)
     d. *er-hängen*   'hang', (Fr. *pendre*)

Note that German also has a couple of non-prefixed stems describing the Manner of killing, though it uses the suffix *-ig* in some cases to form denominal verbs:

(19) a. *köpf-en*   'behead', (Fr. *décapiter*)
     b. *stein-ig-en* 'stone to death', (Fr. *lapider*)
     c. *kreuz-ig-en* 'crucify', (Fr. *crucifier*)

Systematic inventories of verbs of killing providing information about the Instrument used are found in Melanesian languages of New Caledonia. In Xârâcùù, for example, verbs translating the action 'to kill' are compounds which are made up of an element indicating the Manner or Instrument, and a second element indicating the Result (cf. Moyse-Faurie & Néchérö-Jorédié 1986, Moyse-Faurie 1995). The first component is often a bound form (with CV- syllable structure) derived from a verb through a reduction of all but the first syllable (Ozanne-Rivierre & Rivierre 2004). The second, recurrent component *-amè/-èmè/-ömè* 'completely, definitive, lethal' could be identified with the stative verbs *amè* 'to be paralyzed', or perhaps -*mè* 'to be extinguished', and thus provides the resultative component. Here are some examples:

(20) a. *bo-èmè*   'kill by hitting with a stick'
         bo   'hit with a stick or a bludgeon'
    b. *cha-amè*   'kill s.o. with an axe'
         cha   'cut with an axe or a saber'
    c. *chuu-amè* 'kill with a fist'
         chuu   'hit, pound (with a downward motion, with fist)'
    d. *fi-èmè*   'kill with a stick'
         fi- < fida 'hit with an instrument'
    e. *kwi-amè*   'kill with a downward movement'
         kwi-   'kill with an instrument and a downward movement'
    f. *pwâ-âmè* 'kill, beat unconscious with a stick'
         pwâ-   'action of throwing a war club'
    g. *sö-amè (~ söömè)* 'kill, beat unconscious with your hand'
         sö   'hit, make a circular movement with your hands'
    h. *ta-amè*   'kill with gun, arrow'
         ta   'shoot, throw a long object'
    i. *tè-èmè*   'kill with hands, or with a long object'
         tè-   'action with hands'

The most remarkable fact is perhaps that there is no cover term for all these verbs, i.e. no hyperonym that is unmarked for the Manner of killing (though a euphemism may be used, i.e. *sa* 'hit'; see also Section 4.2).

A comparison of the specific (related) pairs of parameters that may be encoded lexically, as provided in the discussion of verbs of eating and drinking in Section 3, is more difficult to carry out in the case of killing verbs. Note first that, again, the Patient seems to be more prominently encoded than the Agent. For Agents, we basically have a binary distinction between verbs restricted to human Agents (*murder*) and generic verbs (*kill*). Moreover, we have seen that there are many ways of encoding an Instrument or Manner of killing, even though such verbs are often morphologically complex or derived via conversion. Given that it is often difficult to determine whether it is primarily a Manner or an Instrument that is encoded, we have not differentiated between these aspects of meaning.

Results beyond the category-level implication of death – verb-specific Results concerning either the Agent or the Patient – do not seem to figure prominently in the class of killing verbs. By contrast, the Motivation has been shown to be an important parameter, at least in the European languages that we have looked at. Assuming that Instrument and Manner are ranked more or less equally, we can thus postulate the following hierarchies:

(21)   a. Patient > Agent
       b. Instrument ~ Manner
       c. Motivation > Result

Considering the encoding of Manner and Result, it is clear that Manner is more prominent, at least if we focus on verb-specific Results. Agent-related Results do not seem to be encoded at all. We have not found a single verb of the type *The soldier overkilled*, in the sense of 'he killed too many persons and therefore felt bad'. Patient-related Results appear more likely, but verbs like Germ. *zer-stückeln* 'hack to pieces' should probably not be categorized as verbs of killing, as one can also hack a computer to pieces. Accordingly, we propose the following hierarchy:

(22)   Manner and Result in verbs of killing
       Manner > Result

On the basis of these comparative observations we can now return to the recent controversies concerning specific groups of verbs as counterexamples to the hypothesis on Manner/Result complementarity. In two recent papers, Beavers & Koontz-Garboden (2012) and Husband (2011) have argued that counterexamples can be found in three groups of English verbs: (a) in verbs of ballistic motion (*fling, flip, toss, kick, flip*), which express displacement and manner of motion, (b) in verbs of cooking (*sauté, poach, braise*) and (c) in some verbs of killing, the only case that will be discussed here. It is argued in these studies that verbs like those in (17) (*crucify, drown, hang, guillotine, electrocute*) entail both a Manner and a Result (death), thus taking issue with Levin & Rappaport Hovav's complementarity hypothesis.[8] Both the complementarity hypothesis and its critical discussion throw some interesting light on our comparison. Note first of all that our data from German (as well as other Germanic languages) and Xârâcùù confirm the complementarity hypothesis. Whenever both a Manner and the Result of the violent action are encoded in a verb, the verb is bi-morphemic encoding these two

---

[8] Other possible counterexamples are perhaps provided by *slay* 'kill in a violent way' and *slaughter* 'kill large numbers in a way that is cruel and unnecessary'.

components in separate parts. In German the verbal root encodes Manner and an inseparable prefix (*er-, ver-, zer-*) the result (death), in contrast to English, where a corresponding form with a prefix is not available and where complex tests are required to determine whether a result is entailed in addition to the manner encoded by a root:

(23)   German   English
   a. *stechen – er-stechen*   'stab'
   b. *schießen – er-schießen*   'shoot'
   c. *würgen – er-würgen*   'strangle'
   d. *schlagen – er-schlagen*   'slay'

This contrast between English and German ties up nicely with the fact that German has almost no simple roots expressing Direction of motion, whereas English may encode both Manner and Direction in simple roots. The complementarity hypothesis is thus confirmed for some Germanic and some Oceanic languages. Moreover, there is another problem that needs to be solved in any attempt at validating or attacking the complementarity hypothesis: The problematic cases are largely denominal verbs borrowed from other languages (*guillotine, crucify, electrocute*) in one list and/or morphologically complex (*be-head, de-capitate*) in the other. In other cases, it is not clear whether a verb does or does not entail the death of the Patient. The fourth stanza of Friedrich Nietzsche's poem *Unter Feinden* ('Among enemies') opposes 'hanging' to 'dying' (there is obviously some 'poetic license' involved):

(24)   *Auch nach hundert Todesgängen*   Even after a hundred walks to deaths
       bin ich Atem, Dunst und Licht.   I am breath, mist and light.
       Unnütz, unnütz, mich zu hängen!   Useless, useless, hanging me!
       Sterben? Sterben kann ich nicht! Die? Die, I cannot.

Our tentative conclusion of the preceding discussion is (a) that generalizations across lexicons about possible and impossible word meanings should be based on broad samples of languages, and (b) that it would not be completely surprising if some generalizations have to be relativized to certain historical layers of the vocabulary. Moreover it is hard to separate purely lexical entailments from matters of world knowledge, as shown by the example from Nietzsche's poem.

4.2 Verbs of beating

Our next semantic domain and the relevant subsets of basic vocabulary also have to do with more or less unfriendly interactions between man and his fellow human beings or with his environment. The cover term 'verbs of beating' subsumes verbs which denote actions in which force is exerted manually, with fast movements on another object, typically with a body part or blunt Instrument. It is probably not surprising that the aspects of meaning that we find encoded in the relevant verbs are similar – though not identical – to those that we found in the domain of killing. Again we will use English, German and French as starting points and turn to Oceanic languages for examples of more extensive differentiations.

The domain of 'verbs of beating' includes at least the following expressions in English: *hit, beat* as the most general expressions; *crash, smash, trash, smite, slay, knock*, which incorporate an element of great force and characterize the Result as devastating; *kick* (foot), *punch* (hand), *slap* (hand), *smack* (hand), *cane, whip, flog, lash, flail*, which incorporate a reference to the Instrument of the action. The last five of these are de-nominal verbs indicating the Instrument explicitly and are typically found in contexts of punishment.

In German we also have de-nominal verbs expressing the Instrument directly (*prügeln* 'beat with a club',[9] *aus-peitschen* 'whip'), but such lexical differentiation as we find is mainly based on formal modifications of the basic general verbs *schlagen* and *hauen* through separable and inseparable prefixes, the most common strategy of lexical differentiation in typical Germanic languages. Many of these formations (*an-schlagen* 'strike against, post', *ab-schlagen* 'knock off, deny', *vor-schlagen* 'propose', *auf-schlagen* 'knock open, serve [in tennis], pitch [a tent]', *unter-schlagen* 'embezzle', *über-schlagen* 'flip over, estimate', *um-schlagen* 'knock over, transact', etc.) are nowadays mainly restricted to metaphorical or idiomatic usage. The set of semantic aspects expressed by the verbs that are normally used with a literal meaning includes only two: the Result$_{Pat}$ (*zer-schlagen* 'smash, disintegrate', *er-schlagen* 'slay', *be-schlagen* 'stud', *zusammen-schlagen* 'beat up', *ab-schlagen* 'knock off'), and the Direction of the hitting action (*ein-schlagen* 'in-beat/bang in', *aus-schlagen* 'out-beat/knock out', *zu-schlagen* 'to-beat/strike', *an-schlagen* 'on-beat/butt'). The two parameters are hard to keep apart, however, as the Direction of a hitting action – for instance, *ein-* 'in(to)', *aus-* 'out' – has

---

[9] The verb *prügeln*, while being a derivate of the noun *Prügel* historically speaking, is also used generically today, i. e., as a common verb of beating. It implies a high degree of force, however.

primarily implications on the Result$_{Pat}$, e.g. insofar as hitting 'into' a window implies that the window breaks. *Ein Fenster einschlagen* thus means 'break a window', and *einen Zahn ausschlagen* implies that a tooth was lost. The originally directional prefixes have thus assumed basically aspectual functions and German verbs of beating thus seem to focus on the Result$_{Pat}$. What we find here then is a further confirmation of the generalization stated in Beavers et al. (2010).

In French, *frapper, taper, battre* are the more general terms for actions of beating, but there are also several specific terms, such as *gifler* 'slap' (with hand, in the face) or *claquer* 'beat lightly (with hand)', *cogner* 'punch', 'bang', 'knock' (hit with fist or instrument in fist), *fouetter* 'whip', *rosser* 'thrash (beat in a violent manner)'.

Turning to Melanesian languages, we find that in Xârâcùù, the relevant subset of the vocabulary manifests a higher degree of differentiation than in the two European languages just discussed. As far as the formal expression is concerned, we find an interesting similarity with processes of derivation in Germanic. The verbs to be discussed are compounds where the first element is a prefix derived from a verb of exercising force by reducing all but the first syllable. In addition to the basic general verb *sa* 'hit, beat', there is a wide variety of verbs exhibiting this basic structure, all expressing variations in the semantic domain of hitting and beating. Interestingly enough, all of these verbs express the semantic dimension of Instrument in addition to the fact of hitting or beating and the Result of this activity. The examples in (25) are based on the verb *dù-* 'hit with the fist, punch':

(25) a. *dù-kari*   'punch gently'
     b. *dù-kè*   'box, punch'
     c. *dù-chëe*   'fail to hit with a punch'

In (26), some examples are provided of verbs based on the root *fi-* 'hit with an Instrument' (<*fida*). Some of these examples provide information about the Instrument and/or the Result.

(26) a. *fi-akè*   'hammer in' (Instrument)
     b. *fi-atapö*   'hitting on sth. to explode it' (Result)
     c. *fi-buru*   'break s.th. by hitting' (Result)
     d. *fi-èmè*   'kill by hitting with a stick' (Instrument, Result)
     e. *fi-wi*   'hit on s.th. so that it falls' (Result)

Finally, a number of verbs can be derived from the roots *sö-* 'hit with a circular movement of the hand or arm'. There is, thus, a Manner component encoded in all these verbs. In addition, there are often aspects of Result expressed, and some verbs are used for specific types of Patients:

(27) a. *sö-chèpwîrî* 'turn over by hitting' (Result)
 b. *sö-chö* 'bend sth. by hitting with hand' (Result)
 c. *sö-kai* 'wipe out with hand (a mosquito)' (Patient, Result)
 d. *sö-paari* 'remove weeds' (Patient, Result)
 e. *sö-pisii* 'wipe away' (Result)

A major difference to the verbs of killing seems to be that the Motivations for an action of beating do not seem to be encoded in verbs of beating. Using the same pairs of parameters that we compared for verbs of eating and drinking and verbs of killing, we can thus postulate the following hierarchies:

(28) a. Patient > Agent
 b. Instrument > Manner
 c. Result > Motivation

The Patient is, again, more prominently encoded than the Agent. Unlike in the case of verbs of killing, it seems to us that on the whole, the Instrument is more prominent in verbs of beating than the Manner. Another difference to verbs of killing is that languages seem to put more emphasis on the Result than on the Motivation of beating.

As far as the relation between Manner and Result is concerned, their exact interaction is hard to determine. As has already been pointed out, verbs like *crash*, *smash*, *trash*, etc. imply a certain degree of force – which could be regarded as an aspect of Manner – and it is unlikely that an object will remain undamaged if it is smashed, for instance, so some Result seems to be implied as well (cf. the denial-of-result test applied by Beavers & Koontz-Garboden 2012: 336 ff.). Some of the verbs discussed in this section are thus potential counterexamples to the Manner/Result complementarity hypothesis. However, it seems to us that – in monomorphemic words at least – both Manner and Result are only sparingly encoded, insofar as the only prominent Manner specification that we have found is that of 'force', and implications concerning the Result hardly go beyond attributing a high degree to the (category-level) entailment of 'damage' done to the Patient.

4.3 Verbs of cutting

The action of cutting, i.e., of using a of sharp Instrument to change the physical integrity of an object or, to use Levin & Rappaport Hovav's (2013: 5) words, "the production of an incision with clean edges", is just as dramatic an act of interference into the existence and shape of living organisms or objects as the actions discussed before, but in contrast to the preceding two domains this action is typically associated with creative activities such as preparing food, constructing, repairing s.th., etc. (for a comparative study, cf. the special issue of *Cognitive Linguistics* edited by Majid & Bowerman 2007, in particular Majid et al. 2007). If we look at our three European languages again which provide the starting point for our investigation, we note that there is not much differentiation in the basic vocabulary of English. In addition to the most general and most versatile verb *cut*, and its combinations with particles (*across, off, out, up, through, lengthwise*) there are verbs like *chop, clip, prune, hew, carve, trim, slit, slice*, nearly all of them incorporating some characterization of the Result$_{Pat}$ of the action, as well as a few very specialized 'synonyms' such as *mow* (grass) and *amputate* (leg or arm) exhibiting specific collocational distinctions. Examples of more specific verb meanings are provided by the verb *hew*, which typically implies an axe as Instrument and stone or wood as Patients, and the verb *slice*, which exclusively expresses the Result of an action.

In French the major distinctions in the corresponding basic vocabulary are the ones between *couper* 'cut', *hacher* 'chop', *fendre* 'split', *émonder* 'prune', *tailler* 'cut, prune' and *découper* 'cut up, carve'. The first verb is the most general and versatile one and implies neither the use of specific Instruments, nor any specific Results. *Découper*, by contrast, is associated with a specific purpose or goal (i.e., Motivation) and expresses the process of cutting according to a specific plan (*découper une étoffe, du carton* 'cut up the fabric, cardboard') in order to create something. *Découper un article* means to rearrange the sections of the article, *couper un article* means to cut or drop the article. In the remaining verbs the Result is lexicalized: *fendre* 'separate, create two parts', *tailler* 'cut with a specific shape in mind', *hacher* 'cut into small pieces', *émonder* 'prune (a tree)'.

In German, differentiation between certain subtypes of the general action is, again, achieved through the use of separable or inseparable prefixes. The resultant distinctions mostly relate to the Result of an action (*be-schneiden* 'clip', *zer-schneiden* 'cut (into pieces)', *ab-schneiden* 'cut off', *an-schneiden* 'cut (a cake)', *auf-schneiden* 'cut open', *aus-schneiden* 'cut out'). The verb most closely corresponding to *découper* in French is *zuschneiden*.

In Oceanic languages we find a wide variety of verbs of cutting whose choice depends primarily on the Instrument (including body parts) used, on the Result and the Manner of the action, as well as on the Patient of the activity. The following list is a first attempt to systematize the factors relevant for the choice of a verb.

(i) Choice depends primarily on the Instrument and the Result

In Xârâcùù (New Caledonia), the first part of the verbal compound indicates the Instrument or the body part involved in the cutting event. The following expressions are examples of such first parts: *ki-* < *kiri* 'saw', *kwi-* 'cut with a tool in the hand, from top to bottom', *pwâ-* cut or split with a warclub', *cha* 'cut with an axe or a saber held in the fist'. The second part of a compound typically refers to the Result of the cutting. The examples in (29) – (33) provide illustration for this Instrument+Result-pattern:

(29) Xârâcùù
    cha- 'cut with an axe or a saber held in the fist'
    a. *cha-cöö*   'cut the bark vertically' (*cöö* 'break into fibers')
    b. *cha-chëe*   'miss a cut, cut across' (*-chëe* 'miss')
    c. *cha-gwéré*   'succeed in cutting with an axe' (*-gwéré* 'succeed')
    d. *cha-körö*   'cut into pieces' (*-körö/-görö* 'break into pieces')
    e. *cha-nyûû*   'pierce' (*-nyûû* 'pierce')
    f. *cha-pèrè*   'cut efficiently' (*-pèrè/-bèrè* 'efficiently')
    g. *cha-pöru*   'cut the bark from every part of the stem' (*pöru/-böru* 'peel')
    h. *cha-puru*   'cut in two' (*-puru/-buru* 'cut in two vertically')

(30) *ki-* < *kiri*   'saw'
      ki-caa   'saw away the slit of wood' (*-caa* 'move away')

(31) *kwi-*   'cut with a tool in the hand, from top to bottom'
      kwi-puru   'cut in two with a tool' (*-puru/-buru* 'cut in two vertically')

(32) *pwâ-*   'cut or split with a warclub'
      pwâ-dia   'split with a warclub' (*tia/-dia*, 'split')

(33) *sö-*   'make a circular movement with the hand or arm'
      sö-puru   'cut in two with the hand' (*-puru/-buru* 'cut in two vertically')

(ii) Choice depends primarily on the Patient

In the following (monomorphemic) examples from East Futunan the choice of the verb depends primarily on the Patient, i.e. on the material to be cut (e.g. hair, grass, wood, etc.):

(34) East Futunan
- a. *moli'i*   'cut off a small piece of something'
- b. *mutusi*   'amputate, cut off the tail of a pig'
- c. *paki*   'cut off leaves or bananas'
- d. *tā'i*   'cut off, harvest (bananas)'

The verbs in (35) encode some additional aspect of meaning together with the Patient, e.g. the Instrument, the Result, the Place and the Motivation:

(35) East Futunan
- a. *autalu*   'to cut the weeds with a knife, to weed' (Patient, Instrument)
- b. *fakainati*   'to cut meat into portions' (*inati* 'parts, portions of meat') (Patient, Result)
- c. *fakasāfuni*   'cut and adorn the hair of the bride' (Patient, Manner)
- d. *kati'i*   'cut (sugar cane, coconut) with teeth' (Patient, Instrument)
- e. *koto*   'cut off leaves (of the taro) from their stem by hand' (Patient, Instrument/Manner)
- f. *lovao*   'cut plants alongside roads' (Patient, Place)
- g. *tā*   'cut wood for construction' (Patient, Motivation)

(iii) Choice depends primarily on the Result

The Result of cutting is encoded by some prefixes of Xârâcùù like, for instance, *ji-*, which combines with other predicates yielding rather specific meanings (cf. (36)). There are also monomorphemic words lexicalizing the Result of an action (cf. (37a)) and the reduplicated form in (37b)).

(36) *ji-* 'shorten, cut to a specific shape'
- a. *ji-kai*   'cut up'
- b. *ji-kakai*   'cut up in pieces'(*-kai* 'reduce to crumbs')
- c. *ji-mîîdö*   'sharpen' (*mîîdö* 'pointed')

	d. *ji-pöru*	'cut off bark, skin, to peel'
	e. *ji-puru*	'slice', 'cut in two'
	f. *ji-tia*	'cut lengthwise'
(37)	a. *sërù*	'cut into small pieces'
	b. *sësërù*	'cut into very small pieces' (reduplicated)

Once again these examples seem to confirm the Manner/Result comlementarity hypothesis. Whenever both Manner and Result components are encoded in a verb, they are expressed by different parts of a polymorphemic verb. As the examples given above show, languages may vary considerably in the extent to which they lexicalize parameters of variation in the domain of cutting verbs. The European languages that we have looked at have rather poor vocabularies in the domain of cutting verbs and basically distinguish between different Results achieved by a cutting action. Other distinctions, in particular distinctions relating to the nature of the Agent, the Patient or the Instrument, are rare. The Manner of cutting is of course closely related to the Result, but otherwise not prominently encoded in verbal meanings.

A completely different picture emerges when we look at Oceanic languages. As has been demonstrated with examples from Xârâcùù, these languages make numerous and highly specific distinctions according to the parameters Patient, Instrument and Result, and the Manner of cutting is also often implied or even explicitly expressed. Even though this diversity renders any generalization in the domain of cutting verbs difficult, we will, again, rank the pairs of dimensions that we also used for the other types of verbs.

First, it is obvious that the Patient plays a more prominent role than the Agent. With respect to the relation between Instrument and Manner, we can note that there seems to be hardly any difference between the two parameters in the languages investigated by us. European languages care little about either of them, and the Oceanic languages that we have considered make distinctions according to both parameters. In lack of further comparative evidence, we will therefore assume that both parameters are ranked equally. The Result, finally, is clearly a very prominent aspect of meaning and is certainly more important than the Motivation of an action, since manipulation of and interference with the integrity of an object is usually goal-directed. The hierarchies characterizing the domain of cutting verbs can thus be represented as in (38):

(38) a. Patient > Agent

b. Instrument ~ Manner

c. Result > Motivation

As has been mentioned, these hierarchies are basically identical to those characterizing verbs of beating, with the exception that there does not seem to be any noticeable difference between Instrument and Manner in the class of cutting verbs.

Comparing the Manner and the Result of a cutting action, it is probably not surprising to find that the (Patient-related) Result is more important than the Manner of cutting. There are not so many manners available in which an object can be cut. We will thus assume that Manner and Result are ranked as shown in (39). Interestingly, there seem to be hardly any examples that combine the encoding of Manner with that of Result, which seems to lend support to Levin & Rappaport Hovav's claim of Manner/Result complementarity.

(39) Manner and Result in verbs of cutting
Result > Manner

4.4 Some generalizations

We have been rather cautious in formulating our generalizations and have only opposed pairs of parameters to each other which make a similar contribution to the predication – Agent vs. Patient, Instrument vs. Manner, Motivation vs. Result. One generalization that emerged from all verb classes – quite unsurprisingly – is that the Patient is encoded more prominently than the Agent. The following hierarchy can thus be assumed to be more or less universal (cf. also Kratzer 1996, among others, on the different statuses of Agents and Patients in predications):

(40) Patient > Agent

Distinctions according to the Patient have been found in all classes of verbs under consideration, and given that the nature of the Patient has a considerable impact on the type of event that is encoded, this is not surprising. We can make the following generalization:

(41) THE PATIENT-PROMINENCE GENERALIZATION
Restrictions on, or implications about, the nature of the Patient are more commonly lexicalized than restrictions on, or implications about, the Agent.

If we move on to the more 'peripheral' parameters of variation, we notice that Instrument and Manner are more prominently encoded than Time and Place. This is, again, not unexpected, as the Time and Place at which an event takes place are (genuinely) extrinsic, while the Manner and Instrument have a stronger impact on the lexical predicate. It is likely that Time and Place will only be encoded in verbs denoting activities that are habitually carried out by a considerable number of individuals in a speech community. Eating is such an activity, and we have pointed out that there are in fact lexical distinctions according to the Place and Time of eating in European languages.

Making an internal differentiation between the Instrument and the Manner of an event is tricky, as the two aspects of interpretation often overlap – the use of different Instruments implies differences in the Manner in which an action is carried out. The difference is that an Instrument is a 'genuine' participant of an event, while a Manner is a property of (some aspect of) the event in question. It thus basically subsumes all those properties of events which are not related to the use of a specific Instrument, e.g. the type of movement made (e.g. straight vs. circular, upward vs. downward, cf. the Xârâcùù examples in (19)), the 'speed' of movement, etc. We have proposed the following hierarchies for the classes of verbs investigated by us:

(42) a. verbs of eating/drinking
 Manner > Instrument

 b. verbs of killing and cutting
 Instrument ~ Manner

 c. verb of beating
 Instrument > Manner

While all of the activities have in common that they imply the use of some Instrument, they differ in their internal event structures. Eating and drinking are complex events, with specific sub-events, e.g. biting, chewing and swallowing in the case of eating. Beating events, by contrast, are basically punctual and 'monolithic', i.e., they do not comprise sub-events but are typically carried out with a single movement (with the arm). Killing events are also basically punctual, or are at least conceived as such – as a matter of fact, intrinsically so, because by their very nature they focus on the endpoint of the action. Cutting events are located in between eating events and beating events with respect to the internal complexity of their event structure. For example, cutting often implies repeated movements in opposite directions and can thus also been broken down into sub-events.

The generalization that emerges from the considerations made above is the following:

(43) THE MANNER-MODIFICATION GENERALIZATION
The Manner of an event is lexicalized more commonly in verbs denoting internally complex events, i. e., events comprising clearly distinguishable sub-events.

Let us now turn to the parameters Motivation and Result. These parameters are considered together because they correspond to the initial and the final stage of an event, respectively. We have found the following hierarchies:

(44) a. verbs of eating, beating, cutting
         Result > Motivation
      b. verbs of killing
         Motivation > Result

As has been mentioned, verbs of killing carry category-level implications about the Result, i. e., the Patient is dead after the event has taken place. Differentiations with respect to the 'physical appearance' of the Patient are conceivable, but not prominently encoded in the languages that we have looked at. The Motivation of a killing event, by contrast, is an important factor. This is different in the other verb classes considered in the present study. Verbs of eating, beating and cutting focus more on the Result of the action than on the Motivation, which is hardly encoded at all. The difference seems to be that killing is an action which, by its very nature, can be assumed to carry ethical implications. One cannot kill just like that, and any killing event needs to be motivated in some way. This is obviously different for eating and cutting, though beating, too, may require some ethical justification at times.

What we can conclude from the preceding discussion is that – varying a famous quotation from historical linguistics[10] – we can make the following generalization:

(45) THE RELEVANCE-LEXICALIZATION PRINCIPLE
Languages lexicalize best what matters most to speakers.

---

[10] "[G]rammars code best what speakers do most" (Du Bois 1985: 363).

5 Towards explanations

We have discussed some dimensions of variation along which specific verb classes differ, and we have made some generalizations on the basis of examples from a small sample of languages. We will now consider possible explanations for the patterns and limits of variation that can be observed in the domain of event descriptions under discussion. The generalizations made in the preceding section lend themselves to three types of explanations. First, we can assume that there is a general tendency for verbs to encode 'more intrinsic' properties to a greater extent than 'more extrinsic' ones. In other words, the stronger the impact of a parameter on the internal make-up of a given event, the more likely the relevant parameter will be encoded lexically. This principle accounts for the fact that Patients are more prone to be encoded lexically than Agents, and that Instruments and Manner specifications are more likely to be encoded than Time and Place. The explanatory principle of this tendency is perhaps one of 'encoding economy': Intrinsic properties of events lead to more homogeneous ('natural') classes of events, and homogeneous or natural classes of events will occur more often in conversation than highly specific ones. The degree of homogeneity of an event description can thus be assumed to be reflected in lexicalization patterns, and we propose the following explanation:

(46) THE INTRINSICNESS-LEXICALIZATION HYPOTHESIS
The more closely a parameter of event description interacts with the intrinsic properties of the event in question, the more often it will be encoded lexically, because lexical items tend to correspond to natural classes recurring in natural discourse, and events form natural classes on the basis of more intrinsic, rather than extrinsic, properties.

The second principle concerns the compatibility of events or event descriptions with specific types of modification. Manner predicates specify the internal organization of a given event. In order to be susceptible to such modification, there must be a certain flexibility for ways in which an event can take place. For example, a punctual event like an explosion does not lend itself to 'internal' modification; only the 'force' of the explosion provides some room for variability. An eating event, by contrast, implies a specific way of putting food into one's mouth, with or without biting, a specific way of chewing as well as relations between such sub-events (e.g. simultanety vs. sequences). This type of 'internal complexity' leaves room for modification; one can eat noisily or quietly (in the chewing phase), one can chew with an open or closed mouth, one can eat fast or slowly (predicated of the chewing sub-events and the succession of swallowing sub-events), etc. This observation provides the basis of the explanation in (47):

(47) THE PRINCIPLE OF MANNER-MODIFICATION
Descriptions of complex events, i.e., descriptions of events comprising several (more or less clearly distinguishable) sub-events, lend themselves more to Manner modification because a higher number of sub-events (and relations between sub-events) implies a higher number of aspects of an event description to which Manner predicates can apply.

Finally, we have seen that there is at least one explanatory factor that is 'system-external', in the sense that it does not concern the relationship between form and meaning, but the relation between the speech community and the linguistic system. As has been pointed out, languages tend to encode the Motivation of a killing event to a greater extent than they encode the Motivation of any other event type that we have considered. This is intuitively plausible, as the Motivation of a killing event is an important piece of information, certainly much more important than the Motivation for cutting an onion or a piece of meat. As was stated in the 'Relevance-lexicalization principle', we assume that there is a tendency for languages to lexicalize those aspects of event descriptions that 'matter most' to a given speech community. This is perhaps a trivial finding; at the same time, however, it leads over to matters of linguistic relativity, a highly controversial and certainly non-trivial topic. The following formulation is an attempt to find a balance between a more or less trivial observation and a strong – linguistically relative – claim. It makes reference to Grice's (1975) Cooperative Principle:

(48) THE PRINCIPLE OF RELEVANT LEXICALIZATION
Languages tend to lexicalize those aspects of event descriptions which affect the social life of the relevant speech communities, because important information is frequently provided, in accordance with the Cooperative Principle, and thus tends to be conventionalized and lexicalized to a greater extent than unimportant information.

While the three explanations given above emerged more or less directly from the generalizations made in Section 4.4, we would finally like to discuss an additional factor which has not been mentioned so far. It seems to us that the amount of information conveyed by a given parameter plays an important role in the probability of that parameter being lexicalized in a given language. A parameter can be assumed to be informative to the extent that it allows the hearer to make inferences about other parameters. Languages can be expected to lexicalize those parameters that allow speakers to make as many inferences as possible.

Let us illustrate this point with eating verbs. Given that eating is a rather heterogeneous activity, the (more) intrinsic properties of eating events are, to a considerable extent, a function of the (more) extrinsic properties. The type of food consumed (the Patient) is the most informative parameter, because it conveys information about the Manner of eating as well as the Agent, e.g. insofar as meat is consumed in a different way than soup, and insofar as humans tend to eat different things than animals (e. g. schnitzel with salad vs. raw meat). Depending on cultural differences, we can also expect specific types of food to be consumed at specific times of the day. It is thus not surprising to find that there is such enormous variation in the domain of eating verbs depending on the properties of the Patient.

While the fact that Patients are encoded prominently in eating events is not specific to that class of verbs, we have noticed that eating verbs, unlike all of the other classes considered in this study, sometimes also encode the Time of eating. This observation might be related to the fact that the Time of eating is also a relatively good predictor of other parameters, at least in European speech communities. Depending on the country or region, one can more or less safely predict what is eaten (the Patient) at specific times of the day. Note that the relevant verbs are also restricted to human Agents. The amount of information contained in a sentence like *Bill is having breakfast* is thus considerable – it tells us that Bill is a man (rather than a dog), that he is probably having coffee or tea with his meal, and – assuming that he lives in France – he is likely to have a baguette on his table.

6 Summary and conclusion

Building on earlier contrastive and cross-linguistic work (e. g. Leisi 1971, Plank 1984) and more recent theoretical studies, especially those by Rappaport Hovav & Levin (2010), we hope to have made some new observations on differences in the lexical inventories of different languages for the notional domains under investigation, i. e., descriptions of events of eating and drinking, and of physical impact (killing, beating, cutting). What are the general conclusions we can draw from the preceding comparative observations?

The first conclusion is that the semantic parameters differentiating between similar lexical items and similar lexical inventories differ in many more and much more subtle ways than we find in comparing grammatical items. It is for this reason that lexical typology is so much more difficult than morpho-syntactic typology. Still, we have noted that specific dimensions of variation – those relating to restrictions on, or the encoding of, participant relations, temporal and locative specifications as well as the Manner and Result of an action – allow for certain generalizations. In particular, we have proposed hierarchies ranking pairs of event parameters which make similar contributions to the meaning of a sentence. Thus we found that all types of verbs considered in our study tend to encode aspects of the Patient to a greater extent than those of the Agent, that the lexicalization of the Manner and Instrument seems to be more common than that of Time and Place (in the event types investigated by us), and that there are differences, in particular, between the relative rankings of Manner and Instrument, depending on the specific verb class investigated.

A second and probably not totally unexpected finding is that languages may differ strikingly in the differentiations they manifest. There are only few verbs of eating and drinking in most European languages, but there seem to be many such verbs in Polynesian languages. A similar contrast is found with respect to verbs of cutting; there are few such verbs in the European languages considered, but a wide variety of them is found in Oceanic languages. We have not discussed any explanations for these differences, and we have refrained from making a point for linguistic relativity in this context. While it is tempting to assume that speech communities with a broader range of dishes will make more relevant distinctions in the verbal lexicon, we are fully aware that such claims are easily falsified, e. g. when speech communities with similar eating and dressing habits differ considerably in their lexical inventories. As has been shown by Plank (1984), English uses only two very general terms for putting on or taking off clothes and accessories, while German has a wide variety of very specific terms depending on the garment or accessory and their contact with the body. Does that mean that Germans pay more attention to their clothes than Englishmen do? It certainly does not.

Even so, we have proposed one explanation that makes reference to habits of a speech community, i. e., the special status of verbs of killing. Killing is such a dramatic action for any speech community, and it is likely to be evaluated in such different ways depending on the Motivations of that action – killing can make one a hero (in war), or result in the loss of one's live (in the case of murder) – that we can expect the Motivation of a killing event to figure prominently in descriptions of the relevant actions.

In addition to that 'system-external', perhaps partly relativistic, explanation, we have proposed three 'system-internal' explanations, all of which could be regarded as boiling down to matters of economy in the relationship between form and function. First, we have argued that the degree of 'intrinsicness' of an event parameter correlates positively with the probability of that property being encoded lexically, as intrinsic aspects of event descriptions can be assumed to lead to natural classes more easily than extrinsic ones (for instance, it is more likely to find a specialized lexical item for 'raining heavily' than for 'raining in Spain'). Second, we have pointed out that the internal organization of an event – its degree of complexity – has implications for the likelihood with which that event will be modified by a Manner specification. The more 'sub-aspects' there are of a given event, the more Manner specifications are conceivable. Finally, we have argued that 'informativeness' may play a role, and that languages tend to encode those parameters lexically that allow hearers to make inferences about other parameters.

We are fully aware that the observations and suggestions made in this study are tentative, which is why we have added the hedge 'programmatic' to the title of this contribution. We have proposed a framework allowing for the formulation of generalizations by ranking pairs of event parameters, based on a Neo-Davidsonian event semantics, hoping that this method will prove useful for further, more comprehensive, typologies of event descriptions.

Bibliography

Alexiadou, A. & E. Anagnostopoulou. 2013. Manner vs. result complementarity in verbal alternations: A view from the clear alternation. In *NELS*, vol. 42, 39–52.

Beavers, J. & A. Koontz-Garboden. 2012. Manner and result in the roots of verbal meaning. *Linguistic Inquiry* 43. 331–369.

Beavers, J., B. Levin & Shiao Wei Tham. 2010. The typology of motion events revisited. *Journal of Linguistics* 46. 331–377.

Berlin, B. & P. Kay. 1969. *Basic color terms. Their universality and evolution.* Berkeley, California: University of California Press.

Cruse, D. A. 1986. *Lexical semantics.* Cambridge: Cambridge University Press.

Dik, S. 1997. *The theory of functional grammar*. Berlin/New York: Mouton de Gruyter.
Du Bois, J. 1985. Competing motivations. In J. Haiman (ed.), *Iconicity in syntax*, 343–365. John Benjamins.
Evans, N. 2011a. Anything can happen. In N. Thieberger (ed.), *The Oxford handbook of linguistic fieldwork*, 183–208. Oxford: Oxford University Press.
Evans, N. 2011b. Semantic typology. In J. J. Song (ed.), *The Oxford handbook of linguistic typology*, 504–533. Oxford: Oxford University Press.
Grice, H. P. 1975. Logic and conversation. In P. Cole & J. Morgan (eds.), *Speech acts (syntax and semantics 3)*, 41–58. New York: Academic Press.
Husband, E. M. 2011. Rescuing manner/result complementarity from certain death. In *Proceedings of CLS 47*.
Koch, P. 2001. Lexical typology. In M. Haspelmath, E. König, W. Oesterreicher & W. Raible (eds.), *Language typology and language universals: An international handbook*, 1142–1178. Berlin: Mouton de Gruyter.
Kratzer, A. 1996. Severing the external argument from the verb. In J. Rooryck & L. Zaring (eds.), *Phrase structure and the lexicon*, 109–137. Dordrecht: Kluwer.
Leisi, E. 1971. *Der Wortinhalt. Seine Struktur im Deutschen und Englischen*. Heidelberg: UTB.
Levin, B. 1993. *English verb classes and alternations: A preliminary investigation*. Chicago: University of Chicago Press.
Levin, B. & M. Rappaport Hovav. 1991. Wiping the slate clean: A lexical semantic exploration. *Cognition* 41. 123–151.
Levin, B. & M. Rappaport Hovav. 2006. Constraints on the complexity of verb meaning and VP structure. In H.-M. Gärtner, R. Eckardt, R. Musan & B. Stiebels (eds.), *Between 40 and 60 puzzles for Krifka*, ZAS Berlin.
Levin, B. & M. Rappaport Hovav. 2013. Lexicalized meaning and manner/result complementarity. In B. Arsenijević, B. Gehrke & R. Marín (eds.), *Studies in the composition and decomposition of event predicates*, 49–70. Dordrecht: Springer.
Lyons, J. 1972. *Structural semantics: An analysis of part of the vocabulary of Plato*. London: Basil Blackwell.
Löbner, S. 2002. *Understanding semantics*. London: Arnold.
Löbner, S. 2011. Concept types and determination. *Journal of Semantics* 28 (3). 279–333.
Majid, A. & M. Bowerman (eds.). 2007. *Cutting and breaking events: A cross-linguistic perspective*. Special issue of Cognitive Linguistics 18.2.

Majid, A., M. Bowerman, M. van Staden & J. S. Boster. 2007. The semantic categories of cutting and breaking events: A cross-linguistic perspective. *Cognitive Linguistics* 18.2. 133–152.

Moyse-Faurie, C. 1993. *Dictionnaire futunien-français*. Langues et cultures du Pacifique 8. Leuven: Peeters-Selaf.

Moyse-Faurie, C. 1995. *Le xârâcùù, langue de Thio-Canala (Nouvelle-Calédonie). Éléments de syntaxe*. Langues et Cultures du Pacifique 10. Leuven: Peeters-Selaf.

Moyse-Faurie, C. & M.-A. Néchérö-Jorédié. 1986. *Dictionnaire xârâcùù-français, (Nouvelle-Calédonie)*. Nouméa: Édipop. (1989: 2ème éd.).

Naess, Å. 2011. The grammar of eating and drinking verbs. *Language and Linguistics Compass* 5/6. 413–423.

Narasinhan, B., A. Kopecka, M. F. Bowerman, M. Gullberg & Asifa M. 2012. Putting and taking events: A cross-linguistic perspective. In B. Narasinhan & A. Kopecka (eds.), *Events of 'putting' and 'taking': A cross-linguistic perspective*, 1–18. Amsterdam: Benjamins.

Ozanne-Rivierre, F. & J.-C. Rivierre. 2004. Verbal compounds and lexical prefixes in the languages of New Caledonia. In I. Bril & F. Ozanne-Rivierre (eds.), *Complex predicates in Oceanic languages: Studies in the dynamics of binding and boundedness*, 347–371. Berlin: Mouton de Gruyter.

Parsons, T. 1990. *Events in the semantics of English. A study in subatomic semantics*. Cambridge/Mass.: MIT Press.

Plank, F. 1984. Verbs and objects in semantic agreement: Minor differences between English and German that might suggest a major one. *Journal of Semantics* 3. 305–360.

Putnam, M. & V. Gast. 2012. The syntax and semantics of excess: over-predicates in Germanic. In J. Choi, E. A. Hogue, J. Punske, D. Tat, J. Schertz & A. Trueman (eds.), *Proceedings of WCCFL 29*, 223–231. Somerville, MA: Cascadilla Press.

Rappaport Hovav, M. & B. Levin. 2010. Reflections on manner/result complementarity. In E. Doron, M. Rappaport Hovav & I. Sichel (eds.), *Syntax, lexical semantics, and event structure*, 21–38. Oxford: Oxford University Press.

Rice, S. 2009. Athabascan eating and drinking verbs and constructions. the linguistics of eating and drinking. In J. Newman (ed.), *The linguistics of eating and drinking*, 109–52. Amsterdam: Benjamins.

Talmy, L. 1985. Lexicalization patterns: Semantic structure in lexical forms. In T. Shopen (ed.), *Language typology and description, vol. 3: Categorization and the lexicon*, 57–149. Cambridge: Cambridge University Press.

Talmy, L. 2000. *Toward a cognitive semantics*. Cambridge, MA: MIT Press.

Van Valin, R. D. Jr & R. LaPolla. 1997. *Syntax: structure, meaning and function.* Cambridge: Cambridge University Press.
Wierzbicka, A. 2009. All people eat and drink. Does this mean that 'eating' and 'drinking' are universal human concepts? In J. Newman (ed.), *The linguistics of eating and drinking,* 65–89. Amsterdam: Benjamins.

Authors

Volker Gast
Department of English and American Studies
Friedrich-Schiller-Universität Jena
Volker.Gast@uni-jena.de

Ekkehard Koenig
Freie Universität Berlin & Albert-Ludwigs-Universität Freiburg
koenig@zedat.fu-berlin.de

Claire Moyse
CNRS, LACITO (Langues et Cultures à Tradition Orale)
Villejuif, France
moyse@vjf.cnrs.fr

Spatio-temporal modification and the determination of aspect: a phase-theoretical account

Michael Herweg

Introduction*

This paper examines how directional prepositional phrases, in conjunction with adverbials of temporal measurement, determine the aspectual type of sentences with verbs of dynamic localization in German, i. e., with the German equivalents of verbs such as *run, push, throw,* and *put.* In order to represent the aspectual properties of lexical items and phrases, the concept of a phase array (PA) is introduced, which receives its theoretical fundament in phase-theoretical semantics as established in Löbner (1988) and refined in subsequent work. PAs are characteristic arrangements of phases of states and can, for different types of predicates, be grounded in different conceptual domains, such as space and time. In the approach presented here, the aspectual type of a sentence is determined by its PA, which in turn is composed of the PAs of its constituents. A crucial feature of this account is the notion of aspectual underspecification. For both verbs and PPs, as well as for combinations thereof, aspectual properties may remain undetermined between the basic dichotomy 'bounded' and 'unbounded.' Various elements of the context may contribute to determining the aspect of simple and complex expressions whose semantics is underspecified in this regard.

1 Scope and orientation of the study

This paper examines how directional prepositional phrases, in conjunction with different types of temporal modifiers, determine the aspectual type of sentences

---

* I wish to thank two anonymous reviewers for their valuable advice and Nick Quaintmere for correcting my English.

which contain verbs of dynamic localization. I will use examples from German, i. e., the German equivalents of verbs such as *run, push, throw* and *put,* and prepositions such as *into, out of, through, along,* and *around*. The verbs under consideration describe a change of position of the referents of their theme arguments on a path whose properties are further specified by the directional PPs.[1] The temporal modifiers under consideration are different types of measurement phrases which indicate the temporal extent of the represented situations. The objective is to describe the semantic properties of verbs, prepositions and temporal measurement phrases which account for the differences in constructions like the following:[2]

(1) *Er schob sein Rad*
   a. * *zwei Minuten lang/in zwei Minuten in die Wechselzone.*
   b. *zwei Minuten lang/in zwei Minuten durch die Wechselzone.*
   c. *zwei Minuten lang/*in zwei Minuten längs der Wechselzone.*

   'He pushed his bike for/in two minutes into/through/along(side) the transition area.'

In (1), I use the classic diagnostics for aspectual type, namely the combination with time-span adverbials (TSA) such as *in 2 Minuten* '(with)in 2 minutes' and with adverbials of duration (TDA) such as *2 Minuten lang* 'for 2 minutes' (literally '2 minutes long').[3] Applying these two basic types of temporal measurement phrases as criterial contexts reveals that a sentence with a transitive/causative motion verb and a directional PP receives a bounded (or more specifically: a telic) interpretation if the PP is headed by *in* 'into' and an unbounded (or atelic) interpretation if the PP is headed by *längs* 'along(side)'. The preposition *durch* 'through' licenses both a bounded and an unbounded interpretation and lets the temporal measurement adverbial set the aspectual type of the sentence.

---

[1] Note that I focus exclusively on direction-related uses of these prepositions. More generalized uses as discussed in the literature are left out of consideration.

[2] Expressions which are semantically ill-formed are marked by '*.' Expressions which deviate from basic semantic assumptions but can be used under specific conditions that involve a semantic adjustment (which I call a 'reinterpretation'; see also Egg 2002) of some of their components are marked by '+.' This flag complements the prevalent '?,' which has a strong bias towards marking an expression as questionable, rather than as an expression whose interpretation involves some additional semantic adjustment, i. e., a reinterpretation, as assumed in the account on hand.

[3] It is crucial to note that the German TDA *zwei Minuten lang* (literally: 'two minutes long') differs in some important respects from the English *for two minutes*. I will therefore include the literal translations whenever I want to make sure that semantic judgments of the German examples will not be based on the English renderings of the TDA in terms of a *for*-adverbial alone.

Spatio-temporal modification and the determination of aspect

The classification of verbs of dynamic localization in (2), which I will take as a basis in the following, stays close to the classification in Kaufmann (1995), a comprehensive and in-depth study of German spatial verbs and prepositions:[4]

(2) Classes of dynamic localization verbs
1. Intransitive verbs of motion (IMV) such as *gehen* 'go', *laufen* 'walk', *kommen* 'come', *schwimmen* 'swim'
2. Transitive/causative verbs of motion (CMV) describing
   (a) causation of a motion by a continuous impulse (CMVC): *schieben* 'push', *ziehen* 'pull', ...
   (b) causation of a motion by an instantaneous impulse (CMVI): *werfen* 'throw', *schießen* 'shoot', ...
3. Transitive/causative verbs of positioning (CPV) describing
   (a) causation of a change of position: *stellen, setzen, legen* 'put'/'lay'

For directional spatial prepositions I will use the traditional classification in (3) as a starting point:

(3) German directional prepositions:
1. Source: *aus* 'out of', *von* 'from'
2. Goal: *in* 'into', *auf* 'onto', *an* 'on(to)', *vor* 'in front of', *hinter* 'behind', *neben* 'beside', *unter* 'under';[5] *zu* 'to'
3. Route/path: *um* 'around', *längs/entlang* 'along(side)'; *durch* 'through', *über* 'over/across'

Note, however, that this classification is partly pre-theoretical and mainly used for ease of reference. We will see later that in particular the prepositions in the

---

[4] Note that Kaufmann (1995) gives a more fine-grained classification of both verbs and prepositions which distinguishes several semantic sub-classes of the general classes listed here. I use (translations of) Kaufmann's terminology in the present paper by virtue of its systematic perspicuity. There are of course other notable and influential nomenclatures: Rappaport Hovav & Levin (1998) use 'verbs of change of location' for the entire class of verbs under consideration here. Gropen et al. (1989) introduced 'verbs of continuous causation of accompanied motion in some manner' for *push, pull, ...* (cf. class CMVC above) and 'verbs of instantaneous causation of ballistic motion' for *throw, kick, ...* (cf. class CMVI). Levin (1993) calls the former class 'verbs of exerting force' and refers to the Gropen et al. term for the latter in the comments to her class 'verbs of throwing,' subclass 'throw verbs,' which Rappaport Hovav (2008) briefly calls 'verbs of ballistic motion.'

[5] These prepositions all come with a static/local variant with an NP complement in dative case and a directional variant with an NP complement in accusative case.

third category form quite heterogeneous classes with regard to their aspectual properties.

The theoretical framework for this study is the phase-theoretical semantics of tense, aspect and temporal modification which was established in Löbner (1988, 1989) and expanded in Herweg (1990, 1991b,c,a), Egg (1994, 1995), Egg & Herweg (1994), among others.[6] In this approach, various semantic properties of expressions of different categories[7] are described in terms of characteristic arrangements of phases and operations on these. Phases in this sense are segments of a scale, i.e., convex partitions of any set with a linear ordering, which are characterized by the fact that a certain predicate holds for them. As an illustration, take the role of the goal PP *in die Wechselzone* 'into the transition area' in (1.a): the PP states that there is a transition from a time when the bike is not located in a specific region to a time when the bike is in fact located in this region. The underlying scalar structure to which the localization predicate in question is applied in this case is a set of times.

I consider phases to be static (or 'frozen') perspectives on potentially complex abstract structures which themselves may be inherently dynamic. The underlying structures can originate from a manifold of conceptual domains, such as times, paths, events and other scales of different provenance, as well as the theoretically preeminent complex "Krifka-style" constructs which integrate structures from different conceptual domains by a bundle of mappings between them.[8] I see one of the representational and conceptual benefits of phase theory in the fact that it makes it possible to abstract away from different underlying structures;

---

[6] The first application of phase-theoretical semantics to spatial prepositions that I am aware of was Kaufmann (1989), who focused on the opposition between *in* 'in'/'into' and *außerhalb/aus* 'outside'/'out of'. Kaufmann (1995) incorporates phase-theoretical considerations quite frequently. Egg (1994) gives a detailed analysis of *in* and Egg (1995) examines *through*. The phase-theoretical idea was revived more recently by Zwarts (2008), who repeatedly points to a kinship of elements of his approach with phase theory but only touches upon details of semantic composition.

[7] In addition to the references cited above, see Löbner (2011) for an overview of linguistic phenomena to which he applies his phase-theoretical notion of 'phase quantification.'

[8] Relevant ontologies of times are set out in van Benthem (1983). Paths, modeled as sequences of regions, are described, among others, in Wunderlich & Herweg (1991). Habel (1989) defines richer spatial structures, including abstractions of paths such as traces (Habel 1989). For vector spaces as alternative spatial ontologies see Zwarts & Winter (2000). An elaborate theory of event structures has been developed in Krifka (1989b) and subsequent work; see also Rothstein (2004). Scales are used as a fundamental semantic concept, *inter alia*, by Rappaport Hovav (2008), Beavers (2008) and Filip (2008). A source for what I call complex "Krifka-style" structures is Krifka (1998). Elements of Krifka's theory are, in different degrees, employed in most of the more recent approaches listed above.

a phase-theoretical construct can by design be simultaneously instantiated by structures that represent diverse conceptual domains, yielding a unified perspective on them.

A crucial feature of my phase-theoretical account is the notion of aspectual underspecification. For both verbs of dynamic localization and their directional PP modifiers, as well as for combinations thereof, I will allow that their aspectual properties remain undetermined between bounded and unbounded. This serves to account for the difference between (1.b) above, on the one hand, and (1.a) and (1.c), on the other hand. In (1.b) the combination of verb and PP alone is open with regard to a bounded or unbounded meaning; it is rather the temporal measurement phrase which pushes the interpretation in one direction or the other.

An important point of reference for my analyses is Filip's (2008) claim that, in Germanic languages, all underived (i.e., stem) verbs and many VPs are inherently unmarked with respect to boundedness ('telicity/maximality' in Filip's theory) and obtain bounded interpretations only in specific linguistic contexts or through pragmatic inferences. I will review this claim in the domain of dynamic localization, looking not only at the relevant verbs but also at directional prepositions (which were of course not in the scope of Filip's study).

2 Theoretical foundations[9]

2.1 Bounded and unbounded predicates

I specify the distinction between bounded and unbounded predicates in terms of cumulativity (cf. Zwarts 2005, 2008, Csirmaz 2012). Unbounded predicates apply to the seamless concatenation – the sum – of any two entities in their extension. By contrast, bounded predicates are noncumulative. As regards the domain of situations, I subscribe to Egg's (1994, 1995) position that the property of boundedness does not coincide with the property of telicity; rather, the latter is a subcategory of the former, which in addition comprises nontelic but bounded predicates, the so-called intergressives such as *cough* and *play a sonata*.[10]

---

[9] I can only give a short and high-level overview of the theoretical background in the present context, which focuses on a specific application of phase-theoretical semantics. For details of the framework itself the reader is referred to the phase-theoretical literature listed in § 1. I will also set aside any formal definitions of well-established logical properties as well as of specific (phase-)theoretical notions that have been introduced in previous work. Unless otherwise stated, the reader is referred to Herweg (1991c) for explicit formal definitions.

[10] The category of intergressive predicates was introduced in Löbner (1988) and characterized as interruptions of an unmarked state, i.e. preceding and subsequent state are identical. The category was

In the domain of situations, the distinction between bounded and unbounded predicates – which in this domain are composed of the semantics of verbs, their arguments and specific modifiers – corresponds to different perspectives on situations. A bounded predicate describes a situation as an event, i. e., as an abstract individual occurrence which takes place in time. Since this kind of predicate characterizes the types of the events in their extension, I call them 'event-type predicates.' An unbounded predicate characterizes a situation as a state or process – 'states of no change' vs. 'states of change' in Galton's (1984) terms – and is represented in the theory on hand as a predicate about times, *viz.* the times at which the state holds or the process takes place (see Löbner 1988). A state of no change involves no development of a parameter other than the progress of time. Being conceived of as a state of change, a process in addition involves the homogeneous development of a parameter on an underlying structure other than just time, such as on specific scales that model the advancement of creating (*build*), destroying (*dismantle*) or consuming (*eat*) an object, the progressing coverage of an object (*read*), or a motion (*walk*).[11]

2.2 Temporal measurement and count adverbials

The two types of adverbials of temporal measurement witnessed in (1) are sensitive to the bounded/unbounded distinction: a TSA like *(with)in two minutes* operates on bounded predicates only and sets an upper limit to the duration of the noninstantaneous event which the predicate describes; whereas a TDA like *for*

---

elaborated in Herweg (1990, 1991b) and most notably in Egg (1994, 1995). A subset of intergressives are semelfactives, a category which usually (e. g., Comrie 1976, Smith 1991) is confined to predicates about instantaneous situations, like *cough*, as opposed to *say (something), greet* (Löbner's original examples, in addition to the classic semelfactives) and *play a sonata, run a mile* (Egg's examples).

[11] One reviewer demands a more elaborate classification of what I subsume under the category of state expressions. I wish to argue, however, that for the objectives of the present study it is sufficient to employ the general category of state expressions as introduced in this section, which comprises all unbounded predicates. I would nevertheless like to point out that the framework of phase-theoretical semantics allows the definition of much more fine-grained differentiations. For instance, Egg (1994, 1995) and Egg & Herweg (1994) show how process predicates – Galton's 'state of change' expressions - can be distinguished from state predicates in the narrow sense, i. e., Galton's 'state of no change' expressions. In addition, Egg & Herweg (1994) define eight linguistically significant subtypes of the latter. This classification goes beyond Carlson's (1977) influential twofold distinction between individual level and stage level predicates (ILP vs. SLP), which appear only as the terminal points in this more fine-grained classification. The eight subtypes are beneficial in order to account for a whole variety of linguistic phenomena over and above the ILP/SLP distinction, such as semantic compatibility of predicates and temporal connectives (*as soon as he was old/*young* vs. *as long as he was *old/young*), constraints on the progressive, specific effects of interpretation, etc.

two minutes operates on unbounded predicates only and specifies the minimum duration of a homogeneous state or process.

One note of caution is necessary when we use TSAs and TDAs as criterial contexts for determining the aspectual type of an expression. Quite often, semantically inconsistent combinations of event/state/process predicates and temporal measurement adverbials do not lead to strictly unacceptable constructions. Rather, they trigger a reinterpretation in order to accommodate the aspectual properties of the predicate to the requirements of the adverbial. The reinterpretation can be that of a 'state of iteration' for an event-type predicate, as in *cough for 10 minutes*; or it can lead to the result state of an event, like in *open the door for 10 minutes*; and it can also be one in which an instantaneous event is supplemented with a process that culminates in the event described by the overt predicate, like in *reach the finish line in 30 minutes*. Similarly, a state predicate can undergo an ingressive reinterpretation, as in *be in Düsseldorf in 30 minutes*, where the TSA is understood as indicating the temporal distance between a contextually given reference point and the onset of the state.[12]

In order to cope with these phenomena, the classic test for compatibility with TSAs and TDAs is often supplemented by a test that uses temporal count adverbials (TCA) such as *twice* (see Herweg 1991c and the references cited therein). Since they are noncumulative, bounded predicates treat their arguments as logical individuals, i.e., as entities which can be counted. By contrast, unbounded predicates, being cumulative, cannot provide a criterion of individuation and counting for the entities to which they are applied. These different logical properties are responsible for the fact that bounded predicates can be combined with TCAs without any restriction (*cough twice*), whereas unbounded predicates do not accept

---

[12] One reviewer disputes my claim that *reach the finish line in 30 minutes* requires a reinterpretation and refers me to the classic insight that *reach* entails a preparatory phase which is followed by a point-like transition and which can be picked up by the progressive, by *for*-adverbials (TDA) and apparently by *in*-adverbials (TSA). I am familiar with this position and the cited phenomena but do not draw the same conclusions as the reviewer. Verbs like *reach* (achievement verbs, in the terms of Vendler 1957) differ from accomplishments in the extent to which the preparatory phase/process that leads to a transition/culmination is accessible to further linguistic qualification. As an example, the temporal adverbial in *He started to reach the finish line at 10 a.m.* cannot refer to the time of the onset of the (preparatory) process, in contrast to accomplishments such as *He started to run to the finish line at 10 a.m.* or *He started to write a letter at 10 a.m.* Differences like these lead me to assume for the contested class of examples a reinterpretation in which the full situation or time frame which the TSA picks up is not provided by the semantic representation of the verb per se but is rather inferred from conceptual knowledge about specific types of events such as 'reaching' events. Why this works better for TSAs (and I conjecture that the same holds for the progressive) than for verbs like *start* plus time specification must be left open in the present context.

TCAs or again call for an adequate reinterpretation, as in *be in Düsseldorf twice*, which typically receives a "chunking" reinterpretation in which we package temporally separate states into individual chunks which can be counted (cf. the 'PO' operator in Herweg 1991b,c). So, since more often than not we will be able to accommodate the aspectual interpretation of an expression to the demands of its context, we are well advised to always use a combination of all applicable tests in cases of doubt.

2.3 Periods, phases and paths

The basic temporal ontology which I subscribe to is a classical mereological period structure in the style of van Benthem (1983) with a precedence relation, a part-of relation, and a sum operator which forms a complex period out of two less complex periods that have no temporal gap between them. A period that is conceptualized as a point in time is one which we conceive of as not being further divided into proper subperiods. And finally, two periods are adjacent if they are separated at most by such a point-like period. For the domain of events, we also assume a mereological structure, plus an operator that maps events to their runtimes (cf. Krifka 1989b).

On the basis of mereological structures like the ones outlined here, the notions of bounded and unbounded predicates can be defined in the obvious way in terms of (non)cumulativity, as sketched in § 2.1. Since state and process predicates are treated as predicates over times, their aspectual property of unboundedness/cumulativity is defined in period structures, whereas the boundedness/noncumulativity of event-type predicates is defined in event structures (see § 2.1). Both domains are related by a set of operators (see Herweg 1991b for details). In order to (again informally) explicate the role of these operators, two features of state (including process) predicates are crucial:

First, a phase of a state S is a period of time for which the state predicate S continuously holds. Second, states come in pairs of positive and negative instantiations, i. e., for every state predicate S there is a contrary counterpart ~S which has the same formal properties, especially the property of unboundedness, as its positive counterpart. Since '~' transforms a predicate S into its contrary predicate (not into its logical, i.e., contradictory, complement), we only require that there are no times for which both S and ~S hold (principle of contrary). This does allow, however, for times in which neither S nor ~S apply.

Spatio-temporal modification and the determination of aspect

Based on this notion of phases of a state and its contrary, we can now define fundamental subclasses of event-type predicates such as ingressive, egressive and intergressive predicates (whose logico-semantic properties, including their boundedness, are technically represented by operators on state predicates, as mentioned above; see Herweg 1991b). Ingressive and egressive predicates describe events which mark single changes of state, modeled as instantaneous (i. e., point-like) transitions from a phase to its adjacent contrary: Ingressive event-type predicates like *switch on the light* and *enter the room* mark the transition from a phase of a negative state ~S to an adjacent phase of its positive counterpart S; egressive event-type predicates such as *turn off the light* and *leave the room* mark the reverse transition from a phase of S to an adjacent phase of ~S. Finally, intergressive event-type predicates like *flash, cough,* etc. involve a dual transition from phases of a negative state ~S to its positive counterpart S and back to ~S.

Turning now to the spatial domain, a simple definition of a path will do for the purpose of this paper. I will thus use the definition in Zwarts (2008), who describes a path informally as a directed curve, corresponding to a sequence of positions in space. Formally, Zwarts defines a path in the proven way as a continuous function p from the real interval [0,1] to a domain of places. Within this framework, the starting point of a path can be indicated by p_0, the endpoint by p_1, and for any i such that $0 < i < 1$, p_i is an intermediary position on the path.

2.4 Phase arrays

In my subsequent analyses, I will use what I call *phase arrays* (PA) as the basic structure for aspectual composition. A PA is a sequence of adjacent phases of states (in the broad sense of § 2.1) $S_1, S_2, ..., S_n$, written as $\langle [S_1], [S_2], ..., [S_n] \rangle$, where $S_1, S_2, ..., S_n$ can be logically related in different ways. PAs are abstract constellations of phases defined over underlying ordered structures which can be grounded in different conceptual domains. The following examples shall serve as illustrations.

The aspectual properties of the different kinds of event-type predicates introduced above are represented by the following PAs:

(4) Phase arrays for event-type predicates:
   a. ingressive (*switch on the light*): $\langle [\sim S], [S] \rangle$
   b. egressive (*turn off the light*): $\langle [S], [\sim S] \rangle$
   c. intergressive (*flash*): $\langle [\sim S], [S], [\sim S] \rangle$

The associated PAs represent these event-type predicates as transitions between adjacent phases of opposite states of the theme argument of the action (leaving aside here any explicit representation of the agent's activity). The PA (4.a) should be read as a sequence of adjacent states of the light being off and the light being on. (4.b) shows the reverse sequence of states and (4.c) represents a dual transition from the light being off to the light being on and then back to the original state.

We can refrain from an explicit representation of events in PAs because these can be inferred from the specific constellation of phases by invoking the phase-theoretical definitions of the respective event-type predicates.[13] Note that the event-type predicates generated by the above PAs have the semantic property of boundedness.

(5) shows the PA for a state predicate:

(5) Phase array for state predicates (e. g., *be in Düsseldorf*): $\langle [S] \rangle$

The PA for a state predicate is monadic and specifies only the element S itself – in (5) the state of some object being located at a particular place – so the corresponding predicate is correctly represented as unbounded, since no state of change is expressed. The PA for a state predicate carries no reference whatsoever to what happens prior to or after a phase of the state.

One important enhancement of the PA representation, of which I will make ample use in subsequent paragraphs, is to enrich PAs with a notion of underspecification. To this end, I define an operator '|' on state predicates S, which serves as a compact representation of a set of semantic alternatives: |S indicates that it is left open, until further information becomes available, whether S is positive or negative. So, upon availability of additional information, in a PA like $\langle [S], [|S] \rangle$, |S will turn out to be either a seamless continuation of S (if |S is specified to S) or the contrary state adjacent to S (if |S is specified to ~S).

In the following discussion of how directional prepositions and different types of verbs of dynamic localization contribute to the composition of aspect, the representational device of PAs will play a crucial role. I will capitalize on the fact

---

[13] Herweg (1990, 1991b) defines a system of axioms which make it possible to infer, given a particular constellation of phases, that there is an event with the appropriate temporal properties. So, from the PAs (4.a) and (4.b) it can be derived that there is an ingressive or egressive event of a particular type, resp., that separates the two contrasting phases, and from the PA (4.c) it can be derived that there is an intergressive event, again of a particular type, which temporally coincides with the middle phase. We can thus omit the explicit representation of events here and rather keep our representations simple for the purpose of this specific study.

that PAs are inherently underspecified representations of aspectual properties which can be instantiated by linguistic items in several ways:

1. The aspectual type of a sentence is determined by its PA, which is composed of the PAs of its constituents.
2. The verb introduces a basic PA which may or may not already predefine parts of the final PA; parts of the verb's PA may be left underspecified by the verb itself.
3. Arguments and modifiers of the verb contribute to the specification of the PA on all projection levels of the verb; however, these elements themselves can also preserve some level of underspecification.

In order to link verbs of dynamic localization and directional PPs into the shared format of PAs, I make the following assumptions:

- The relevant verbs carry a motion component in their semantics that links the changing positions of their theme argument to positions on an abstract path which they introduce into the semantic representation. Information about the motion of the theme is thus represented as sequences of states of localization which are related to the segments of a path.
- Directional PPs specify positions of what I call the localized object (LO) – which is the external argument of the preposition and the theme argument of the verb – on the path provided by the verb. They do this in the form of a sequence of states of localization of the LO/theme. The positions of the LO on the path are determined by the semantics of the preposition as specific regions – such as the interior in the case of *in* – relative to what I call the reference object (RO), which is the internal argument of the preposition (cf. Herweg 1989).
- The basic elements of a path – its initial, intermediary and final segments p_0, p_i and p_1 – are linked to a basic tripartite PA as in (6); this holds both for the verbs and the prepositions under consideration here:

(6) $\langle\, [_{p_0}\, S_1]\, ,\, [_{p_i}\, S_2]\, ,\, [_{p_1}\, S_3]\, \rangle$

This PA expresses that the states S_1 and S_3 hold at the marginal path segments p_0 and p_1, resp., and that the state S_2 holds at the intermediate path segments p_i. Different types of verbs and prepositions link their PA information to specific elements of this structure. The verbs under consideration here relate the motion of their theme arguments – which is represented in terms of the changing positions that the objects in question assume over the course of the described situations –

to segments of the abstract path that the verbs introduce. A directional PP adds more specific information about the positions of the theme in regard to this path: it contributes through its associated series of state predicates particular spatial properties of the theme/LO, namely that it is – or is not, in the case of negative state predicates – located in a region defined relative to some RO.

Note that the PAs for verbs employed here provide information about motion of their theme arguments only in terms of sequences of states of localization. Information about specific manners of motion (*walk, run*), as well as specific activities of the initiator of a motion (*push, throw*), for example, would have to be reflected in additional elements of the semantic representations of the verbs in question; these are, however, not relevant in the present context.

While for nonmotion verbs like those in (4) and (5) I assume just one underlying conceptual structure to which the elements of their PAs apply, namely periods of time (there may be more, but these would be out of the scope of the present considerations), I assume that the PAs of verbs of dynamic localization are related to two underlying structures, namely periods of time and paths. A simple way to link times and paths would be to make times the indices of the path function p. This would yield temporally parameterized paths in the sense of Habel (1989) and Wunderlich & Herweg (1991). I prefer, however, to keep the two structures independent from each other on principle – cf. Habel's generalized path concept which abstracts away from time (but retains orientation) – and stipulate a separate mapping between periods of time and segments of paths which is employed when necessary. This makes it possible to clearly differentiate between verbal and prepositional predicates. The former relate to times and – in the case of verbs of dynamic localization – to paths, whereas the latter relate to paths only. This distinction takes into account the fact that PP predicates cannot be temporally modified independently from their host verbs. Therefore, a construct like **He walked out of his house at 6:30 into the village at 7:30* is excluded. The state of affairs in question would need to be described by a coordination structure like *He walked out of his house at 6:30 and into the village at 7:30*, which provides two instantiations of the verbal predicate and thus two anchor points for the different temporal modifiers. The PP predicates will, of course, be integrated through semantic composition into the semantic representation induced by the verb and will thereby eventually receive a temporal interpretation. They will, however, do so only mediated by the semantics of the verb which they accompany.

For ease of exposition, the temporal dimension of PAs will not be represented explicitly in what follows but can be derived, if necessary, from the sequence of states associated with verbal predicates. I will rather focus in my representations on how verbal and prepositional PAs relate to the paths which are provided by the semantics of the verbs and to which the PP predicates refer.

With this basic inventory we can now turn to the different types of directional prepositions. I will use as evidence mostly combinations of directional PPs with simple and quite general intransitive verbs of motion such as *gehen* 'go/walk' and *laufen* 'walk/run'. As a working hypothesis I will assume that these verbs do not introduce any constraints on the aspect of their projections on their own but that specifications of aspect come from the PPs they combine with. That is, I assume that these intransitive motion verbs are underspecified with regard to the bounded/unbounded contrast and thus carry a PA of the form $\langle$ [$_{p0}$ |S], [$_{pi}$ S], [$_{p1}$ |S] $\rangle$. I will revisit this hypothesis in § 4.

3 Aspectual properties of directional prepositions

3.1 Ingressive and egressive prepositions: *in, aus* etc.

Source and goal prepositions introduce single changes of states in two variants:

- Source prepositions introduce a transition from the LO being located in a particular region at the initial segment of a path (p_0) to the LO no longer being located in this region at the middle section of the path (p_i).
- Goal prepositions introduce, for the middle and final segment of a path, the reverse transition: the LO is initially, at p_i, not located in the specific region where it is located later, at p_1.

The PAs for PPs involving these prepositions thus follow the egressive and ingressive scheme, resp.:

(7)   a. *aus dem Park* 'out of the park' $\langle$ [$_{p0}$ IN(x, p)] , [$_{pi}$ ~IN(x, p)] $\rangle$

   b. *in den Park* 'into the park' $\langle$ [$_{pi}$ ~IN(x, p)] , [$_{p1}$ IN(x, p)] $\rangle$

In these simplified representations, x is a variable for the LO and p represents the denotation of the NP complement of the preposition (i. e., the RO). IN is a relation of localization which places its LO in a specific region that it assigns to the RO (simplified: the interior space of the park in question). The path indices show in which segment of the PA of a dynamic verb the PAs of the directional PPs fit.

Applying the standard test criteria to combinations of motion verbs with source/goal prepositions yields the following results:

(8) a. ⁺ *Er ging zwei Minuten lang in das Haus/aus dem Haus.*
'He went into/out of the house for two minutes (two minutes long).'

b. ⁺ *Er ging in zwei Minuten in das Haus/aus dem Haus.*
'He went into/out of the house in two minutes.'

c. *Er ging zwei Mal in das Haus/aus dem Haus.*
'He went into/out of the house twice.'

The combination with a TDA as in (8.a) triggers a mandatory reinterpretation in German: the adverbial cannot measure the duration of the situation of walking into or out of the house – which confirms that we are indeed dealing with descriptions of events and not processes or states – but rather gives the duration of the result states of the events, *viz* the states of being located inside or outside of the house. We may marginally also obtain an iterative reinterpretation in the sense that the subject repeatedly entered the house over a period of 2 minutes. Note that these reinterpretations are actually blocked if we replace *zwei Minuten lang* with another kind of duration adverbial, such as *seit zwei Minuten* (literally: 'since two minutes'): **Er ging seit zwei Minuten in das Haus/aus dem Haus* (literally: 'he went since two minutes into/out of the house').

TSAs as in (8.b) are difficult to combine with the prepositions in question because the change of state is preferably understood as instantaneous. TSAs require, however, events with a real (non-point-like) duration. As a consequence, the adverbial in (8.b) is preferably understood as measuring the time span from a contextually given point in time to the time of the change of state ('he set out for the house/to leave the house within the next 2 minutes'); i.e., they obtain what we can call a distance reading. I will come back to this type of construction below.

TCAs as in (8.c) yield the clear-cut result that we are indeed dealing with bounded expressions; there is no need at all for any kind of reinterpretation in order to accommodate the combined verbal and prepositional predicate to the aspectual requirements of the adverbial.

Coming back to examples like (8.b), we can observe that combinations of TSAs with egressive and ingressive prepositions become much better, and do not call for any kind of reinterpretation, if the motion or the path are either explicitly accentuated by linguistic means such as more specific verbs of motion (9.a), additional adverbs of manner (9.b) or additional directional PPs (9.c), or if extra-linguistic knowledge leads us to assume an extended motion on an elongated path; see the contrast between (10.a) and (10.b).

(9) a. *Er kroch in zwei Minuten in das Kellerverlies.*
'He crawled into the dungeon in two minutes.'

b. *Er ging zielstrebig/hastig/langsam in fünf Minuten ins Dorf.*
'He went determinedly/hastily/slowly into the village in five minutes.'

c. *Er ging in einer Minute vom Haus über den Hof in die Garage.*
'He went in 1 minute from the house over/across the yard into the garage.'

(10) a. $^+$ *Er lief in zwei Sekunden (aus dem Wohnzimmer) in den Flur.*
'He walked (out of the living room) into the corridor in two seconds.'

b. *Er lief in zwei Tagen (vom Schwarzwald) in die Vogesen.*
'He walked (from the Black Forest) into the Vosges Mountains in two days.'

We can conclude that, even if the path is further qualified only by an ingressive PP, which by itself introduces an instantaneous transition from one state to the opposite state, the motion that leads to this change of state is, in principle, nevertheless accessible to temporal measurement by a TSA. Acceptability of TSAs in conjunction with egressive/ingressive prepositions is very much a question of the extent to which the motion and its manner are explicitly described or what world knowledge tells us.

Other source and goal prepositions, such as *von* 'from' and *auf* 'onto' and the dimensional prepositions *hinter* 'behind', *unter* 'under', ..., exhibit the same aspectual behaviour as the ones explicitly discussed in this paragraph. However, *zu* 'to' is sometimes claimed to differ from the other goal prepositions in important respects. According to Kaufmann (1995), *zu* often only indicates the orientation of a motion. As evidence, Kaufmann cites examples of the sort (11.b), where the motion can be called off before the goal area has been reached, although (11.a) shows that *zu* is nevertheless a bounded preposition:

(11) a. *Er lief in einer Stunde/*stundenlang zum Bahnhof.*
'He walked in one hour/for hours (literally: hours long) to the train station.'

b. *Er lief heute früh wie immer zum Bahnhof, kam aber nie dort an.*

'He walked this morning as always to the train station but never got there.'

In her analysis of *zu*, in which she employs the notion of a supremum of a path, Kaufmann models the default interpretation, according to which the path ends in the vicinity of the RO, in terms of the supremum being part of both the path and the proximal region of the RO. If, however, the context endorses the interpretation that the path ended before the goal area was reached, the supremum is still within the proximal region of the RO but external to the path under consideration. In this vein Kaufmann captures the idea that with *zu* the path can be understood as the intended path, rather than the real path, without giving in the assumption that *zu* is in fact bounded.

Looking this proposal over we observe that we can find examples of the sort (11.b) for other goal (i. e., bounded) prepositions as well, if we choose an appropriate context of interpretation:

(12) *Er wanderte heute früh auf den Feldberg/in die Vogesen, als er wegen des aufkommenden Unwetters beschloss umzukehren.*
'He hiked onto the Feldberg mountain/into the Vosges Mountains this morning, when he decided to return because of the upcoming thunderstorm.'

Thus, rather than hardwire observations like in (11.b) into the semantics of *zu*, as opposed to other goal prepositions, I'd rather confer their explanation – in contrast to Kaufmann's account – upon a general (albeit yet to be elaborated) account of 'intentional dilution' – or the 'imperfective paradox', to use the classic notion (Dowty 1979) – of telic constructions.

One final remark: We must concede that, more often than not, *zu* appears to be more open to 'intentionally diluted' readings than the other goal prepositions. This may be due to the fact that German does not have a simple counterpart of *towards* which would supplement the *to*-like semantics of *zu*. German actually has a PP which can function like a P that expresses orientation only, namely *in Richtung* 'in direction'. This P in the guise of a PP forms expressions of unbounded aspect:

(13) *Er ging stundenlang in Richtung Colmar.*
'He walked for hours (literally: hours long) in the direction of Colmar.'

We might hypothesize that *zu* is quite open to the sort of 'intentional dilution' outlined above because by this *zu* partly fills a gap in the German prepositional

Spatio-temporal modification and the determination of aspect

system (cf. French *vers*, Italian *verso*), at least in quite specific contexts, however, without adopting an unbounded reading.

3.2 The intergressive preposition *um*

Um 'around' is traditionally often classified as a route PP, together with *längs/entlang* 'alongside/along'. We will see shortly, however, that *um* and *längs/entlang* differ considerably in their aspectual properties.

The combination with the standard test contexts reveals that PPs headed by *um* are bounded predicates:

(14) a. *Er lief in einer Stunde um den See.*
'He ran around the lake in one hour.'

b. ⁺ *Er lief eine Stunde lang um den See.*
'He ran around the lake for one hour.'

c. *Er lief drei Mal um den See.*
'He ran three times around the lake.'

TSAs and TCAs combine well with *um*-PPs without triggering any reinterpretation. By contrast, the TDA in (14.b) triggers an iterative reinterpretation: the TDA measures the time it takes to circle around the lake an indefinite number of times. Zwarts (2005, 2008) calls this a plural reading, which he models with an explicit plural operator on a basically bounded PP.

I represent the aspectual properties of *um*, as it is used in examples like (14), by an intergressive PA which reflects the fact that in PPs like *um den See* the initial position is reestablished when the LO has completed a round of running around the RO:

(15) Phase array for *um* + *NP*: $\langle$ [$_{p0}$ S], [$_{pi}$ ~S], [$_{p1}$ S] $\rangle$

Intergressive predicates lend themselves perfectly to iterative uses in unbounded contexts, as combinations of semelfactives with TDAs show: *cough/blink/knock for hours*. This is due to the fact that, since the state that holds before the event is the same as the state that holds after the event (cf. Egg 1995), the event can easily be started over and over again. This is different for egressive and ingressive predicates, for which iterative readings require much more interpretational effort (compare (14.b) above with (8a.); see also *switch on/turn off the light for hours* vs. *flash for hours*). These characteristics of intergressive predicates account for the ease with which *um* can be used with an iterative reinterpretation in unbounded contexts (see (14.b)).

The above representation is likely to be somewhat simplistic in that it does not palpably capture the full bandwidth of usage of this preposition. As an example (there are many more; see, e. g., Wunderlich & Herweg 1991), consider the use of *um/around* as in *Er lief um die Ecke* and *He ran around the corner*, where the start and end positions of the motion are different. There is clearly a need for a more detailed analysis of the characteristics of the path associated with this preposition (see, e. g., Zwarts 2005 and 2008). We could accommodate PPs like the above in our PA-based approach by way of relaxing the condition on the phases that surround the middle phase, demanding only that this phase is surrounded by contrasting phases which may or may not be locally identical. The PA (15) would then be a special instantiation of this more general PA. Note that this would not alter the aspectual properties which we ascribe to this preposition. A more comprehensive account of *um* has, however, to be deferred to subsequent research.[14]

3.3 Process-like pre-/postpositions: *längs, entlang*

The second type of what is traditionally classified as route prepositions is *längs* 'alongside', together with the postposition *entlang* 'along'. As Klein (1991) points out, these pre-/postpositions are not full synonyms: *längs der Straße* means 'roughly in parallel alongside the road', whereas *die Straße entlang* allows the LO to move alongside (like *längs*) or on the road.

Based on the observations about the behaviour of the preposition in the well-known test contexts in (16), I assign to *längs* the unbounded monadic PA of a state/process predicate, as in (17):

(16) a. * *Er lief in einer Stunde längs der Straße.*
'He walked alongside the street in one hour.'

b. *Er lief eine Stunde lang längs der Straße.*
'He walked alongside the street for one hour.'

c. * *Er lief drei Mal längs der Straße.*
'He walked alongside the street three times.'

---

[14] Note that German *um* does not have the 'crisscross' reading of English *around* (cf. Zwarts 2005) as in *He drove around the city center for hours*. In German this needs to be expressed by the adverbial *umher* in conjunction with a static local PP like *im Stadtzentrum* 'in the city center'.

(17)   Phase array for *längs + NP*: ⟨ [pi S] ⟩

In contrast to the other prepositions which we have examined so far, *längs* quite strongly defies any aspectual reinterpretation. If at all, the typical reinterpretations of state expressions described in § 2.2 – ingressive and "chunking" – may be marginally possible. This would, however, not impact the above aspectual classification, which assigns to a PP like *längs der Straße* a state of localization on a path that extends in its middle segment (p_i) alongside the street and whose initial and final course are blanked out in terms of localizing the LO. This PA does not at all refer to what happens with regard to S at the left and right context of the path segment which it singles out. Any bounding of the path and the associated state of localization needs to come from other PPs, like in *Er lief von der U-Bahn-Station längs des Botanischen Gartens zum Heinrich-Heine-Saal* 'He walked from the metro station alongside the Botanic Garden to the Heinrich Heine Hall'.

Although *längs* und *entlang* are nearly synonyms, the subtle difference between them that Klein points out may not be the only one. Substituting *entlang* for *längs* in our test contexts shows a much less pronounced concord with the stative constellation for *entlang* than for *längs*:

(18)   a.   ⁺ *Er lief in einer Stunde die Straße entlang.*
            'He walked along the street in one hour.'
       b.   *Er lief eine Stunde lang die Straße entlang.*
            'He walked along the street for one hour.'
       c.   ⁺ *Er lief drei Mal die Straße entlang.*
            'He walked three times along the street.'

I see two courses of explanation for this difference in aspectual behaviour. First, we can speculate from Klein's observation that, with *längs*, the RO (in the present case, a street) provides little more than a general orientation for the motion of the LO/theme, whereas with *entlang*, the LO/theme can enter into a much more direct, functional relationship with the RO (if this is of an adequate sort). This may allow one to figure a situation in which the LO/theme paces out or perambulates the street in its entirety, for some surmised purpose. And this kind of adaptive conceptual reasoning might in turn make it much easier to accommodate the basically unbounded predicate to a bounded context than in the case of *längs*.

A second line of explanation – and I'd rather leave the decision open here – would be to clearly contrast the aspectual properties of *entlang* with those of *längs* and abandon for the former the claim that this preposition unequivocally heads unbounded PPs (*pace* Kaufmann 1995: 75). This would mean moving *entlang* into the class of prepositions which I am going to discuss in the next section, namely those prepositions which are semantically underspecified with regard to the property of boundedness vs. unboundedness.

3.4 Aspectually underspecified prepositions: *durch, über*

The semantics of *durch* 'through' and *über* 'over/across' is quite intricate and has, particularly in the case of *durch* and its English equivalent *through*, been subject to a number of deep and insightful studies.[15] I take it that *durch* and *through* are selected as a path preposition when the RO is conceptualized as a three-dimensional object, like in *durch den Tunnel* 'through the tunnel'. In contrast, *über*, which overlaps with English *across* and *over*, is typically selected as a path preposition with ROs that are conceptualized as two-dimensional surfaces, as in *über den Platz* 'across the square'.

As regards their aspectual properties, these prepositions are usually considered to have a basic bounded meaning. This position is based on the assumption that the middle segment of the path to which the prepositions relate usually completely traverses the interior (for *durch/through*) or the surface (for *über/*across) of the RO, and that the path both starts and ends outside of the RO. This would indeed yield a twofold change of state, which of course would render the respective PPs bounded.

In this vein, Zwarts (2005) posits a primary bounded meaning for *through* and *across* on the basis of examples of the kind shown in (19.a). Unbounded uses of these prepositions are derived by the operations of grinding and pluralization on the basic bounded meaning. Prepositional grinding, in analogy to cases such as *There is apple in the salad* in the nominal domain, effectively blanks out all parts of a path that are outside the relevant region of the RO. Grinding thus yields the unbounded readings of sentences like (19.b), in their non-goal-directed 'seesaw' sense which gives the impression that someone is strolling around in the park or on the green. Pluralization (which accords with my notion of iteration; see § 3.2) would be used to derive the unbounded readings of sentences like (19.c), in their 'back and forth' sense:

---

[15] Kaufmann (1993) is the most detailed study of this preposition that I am aware of. See also Zwarts (2005) and Krifka (2012) for many interesting considerations about possible path shapes for *through*. As regards *über*, note that I'm dealing with motion-related uses of this preposition only.

(19) a. *He walked through the tunnel/across the bridge in two minutes.*
b. *He walked through the park/across the green for one hour.*
c. *He walked through the tunnel/across the bridge for hours.*

Similarly, Kaufmann (1993, 1995) assumes the bounded uses as basic and derives unbounded uses by way of conceptually suppressing any borders that the RO may in fact have. Egg (1995) treats *through* as the main exemplar of an intergressive (i. e., bounded) predicate in the spatial domain. However, Csirmaz (2012) argues just the other way around: The unbounded meaning of *through* is basic; bounded readings arise because a change-of-state interpretation is imposed upon the basic meaning.

My position is that neither the bounded nor the unbounded meanings can be taken as basic without reservation (at least for the German versions, although I conjecture the same for English). Rather, both prepositions are underspecified with regard to their aspectual properties. This means that their PA looks like (20) and that aspectual properties of the sentences they appear in are determined not by the prepositions themselves but by other elements in their context.

(20) Phase array for *durch/über* + NP: ⟨ [$_{p0}$ |S], [$_{pi}$ S], [$_{p1}$ |S] ⟩

This position is based on two major observations: First, as we already saw in (19), and as is also demonstrated by (21), more often than not *durch* and *über* are equally fine in both bounded and unbounded contexts, with no traceable demand for reinterpretation.

(21) *Er lief in einer Stunde/eine Stunde lang/drei Mal durch den Park/über die Wiese.*
'He walked through the park/over|across the lawn in one hour/for one hour/three times.'

Secondly, and in disagreement with the claims cited above, in many cases no complete traversal of the relevant regions of the RO is required for *durch/through* or *über/across*. What is more, a complete traversal can even be explicitly excluded. Take the examples in (22). Here, the moving object does not leave the respective region of the internal arguments of *durch* and *über* (the office and the pitch, resp.) at all; the full path, including start and end, stays within these regions (at least on standard interpretations):

(22) a. *Er ging vom Schreibtisch durch sein Arbeitszimmer zum Regal.*
'He walked from his desk through his office to the bookshelf.'

b. *Er lief von seinem Tor über das Spielfeld zum gegnerischen Strafraum.*
'He ran from his goal across the pitch to the opposing penalty area.'

I conclude from examples like these that the meanings of the prepositions on their own do not imply any demarcation of the path, especially not in terms of the borders of the RO. The task of delimiting the motion and its path is rather delegated to other elements in the sentence. In (22), this task is performed by the accompanying egressive (source) and ingressive (goal) PPs. In (19.a) and (21) the bounded reading is imposed upon the sentence by the TSA or TCA. In cases like *Er kam durch den Park/über die Wiese* 'he came through the park/across the lawn' it is the meaning of the verb that determines a bounded reading (more on *kommen/come* below, § 4.2). In other cases, it may even be conceptual knowledge or assumptions about functional properties and shape of objects which decide on preferred interpretations. So, barring contradicting evidence from other elements in the sentence, unbounded interpretations are most likely preferred – albeit by no means mandatory – for objects such as cities, forests, parks in the case of *durch/through*, and places, squares, fields, etc. in the case of *über/over/across*, where motion can easily be taken as being not primarily goal-directed. However, if properties of the RO suggest a goal-directed path function (tunnels, passages, etc. for *durch*; bridges, streets, etc. for *über*), the preference for a bounded interpretation clearly increases. And the extreme cases are doors, windows, etc. in combination with *durch*, and lines, borders, etc. in combination with *über*, i. e., ROs for which one factual dimension is conceptually downgraded. In these cases, bounded interpretations are vastly preferred and unbounded interpretations can almost exclusively be obtained only via iterative reinterpretations (⁺*He walked through the door/over the border for hours*).

I'd like to stress at this point that the impact of conceptual knowledge about object shape and function on semantic interpretation and compatibility is not specific for the prepositions under consideration here, but is a pervasive phenomenon especially in the spatial domain. It is conceptual knowledge about object shape that distinguishes the way in which dimensional adjectives can be applied to objects of similar orientation, as in *high/+long tower* vs. ⁺*high/long pole*; or that makes the depth of a room a different dimension of the object than the depth of a hole – in the former case, the depth is a horizontal dimension, whereas in the latter case it is a vertical dimension. What is more, conceptual knowledge about typical functions of objects, such as their use as means of public transportation, may account for distinctions such as *bus/taxi/riksha into town* vs. +*car/+bicycle into town*. In our present area of interest, we can point to examples like *Ich bin eine Stunde zum Schwimmbad/zu Ikea gegangen* 'I went to the swimming pool/to Ikea for one hour (literally: one hour)'. Only the latter object licenses the interpretation that the speaker's stay in the goal region lasted one hour (for swimming pools this interpretation is only available in combination with the preposition *in(s)*).[16]

As an alternative to the present approach, we could assume an intergressive PA ⟨ [$_{p0}$ ~S], [$_{pi}$ S], [$_{p1}$ ~S] ⟩ as representation of the basic aspectual meaning of *durch* and *über* and allow particular RO properties (the ones that parks and lawns exhibit, as opposed to tunnels and bridges or even doors and borders) to "despecify" this PA to the underspecified representation ⟨ [$_{p0}$ |S], [$_{pi}$ S], [$_{p1}$ |S] ⟩. This "despecification" would still be different from Zwart's grinding approach or any other "unbounding" mechanism in that it would allow the aspect of expressions like *He walked through the park/over the green* to go either way (see (19) and (21)). However, in the light of the examples plus the observations in (22), I prefer to assign to these prepositions an underspecified PA which can be made more specific by a plethora of contextual features, which comprise not only explicit linguistic indicators such as other spatial and temporal modifiers but also typical object properties. I thus assume that conceptual knowledge about objects such as doors and borders can narrow down the space of interpretation of an aspectually underspecified preposition like *durch* and *über* to eventually one preferred specific aspect.

As a consequence, considering the shape of the paths which *durch* and *über* characterize, traversal of only a significant portion of the characteristic region of the RO is required, rather than a full traversal.

Are there aspectually underspecified directional pre-/postpositions other than *durch* and *über*? One candidate might be *entlang*, as discussed in §3.3. Other candidates are *hinauf* 'up(wards)' and *hinab* 'down(wards)':[17]

(23) *Er lief in einer Stunde/eine Stunde lang/drei Mal den Berg hinauf/hinab.*
 'He walked up/down the mountain in one hour/for one hour/three times.'

---

[16] I assume that many of the relevant parameters in the interpretation of *durch* and *über* could be explained in terms of Lang's (1989) theory of object schemata. I do, however, subscribe to Kaufmann's (1993) position that object schemata have to be enriched with functional information in order to account for the *bus/taxi/car/... into town* example.

[17] Zwarts (2005) treats the English prepositions *up* and *down* as ambiguous between an unbounded "comparative" and a bounded "superlative" reading.

The syntactic and semantic category of these words is not clear; they can be treated as postpositions or as directional adverbs (a category which Kaufmann 1995 also considers for *entlang* and even *längs*). Anyway, the examples in (23) show that in the present framework their aspectual contribution as directional postpositions would be captured by the underspecified PA scheme (20).

4 Aspectual properties of verbs of dynamic localization

4.1 Phase arrays for motion verbs

In the following paragraphs, I will discuss the aspectual properties of verbs of dynamic localization according to the classification set out in § 1. As for dynamic prepositions, I will represent the aspectual properties of these verbs in terms of the constraints they impose on the PA that is associated with the path they introduce into the semantic representation. These constraints are represented by predicates over the theme argument of the verb, i. e., the LO which is subject to the dynamic localization (see § 2.4). The predicates are again linked to the specific sections of the PA that we already used in order to represent the aspectual contributions of prepositions. The aspectual properties of V-PP combinations will thus be computed from the combined constraints which verbs and PPs impose on the different sections of the underlying PA, in the form of conjoined predications.

4.2 Intransitive verbs of motion (IMV)

The analysis of directional prepositions in combination with intransitive motion verbs showed that these verbs (disregarding *kommen* 'come' for the moment) indeed do not contribute any aspectual constraints on their own to semantic composition. In fact, they combine freely with all sorts of directional prepositions, which in turn determine the aspectual properties of the resulting phrases. We can thus gather from the discussion in § 3 that verbs like *laufen* 'walk', *gehen* 'go', *rennen* 'run', etc. are indeed underspecified with regard to aspect, as I hypothesized at the outset of the examination of prepositions. The PA for the verbs in question therefore looks as follows:

(24) Phase array for IMVs *laufen, gehen, rennen*, etc.: $\langle\, [_{p0}\, |S_V\,],\, [_{pi}\, S_V\,],\, [_{p1}\, |S_V\,]\, \rangle$

The findings for *kommen* 'come' are different: (25.a) shows that the combination with an underspecified preposition leads to a bounded predicate. (25.b) shows that directional PPs in combination with *kommen* can refer to all segments of a

Spatio-temporal modification and the determination of aspect

path. We can therefore posit the PA (26) for *kommen*, which factors in a change of state concerning the position of the LO (which is determined by the *origo*; see Kaufmann 1995) at the end of the path, and leaves all further details to the directional modifiers.

(25)   a.   *Er kam *eine Stunde lang/in einer Stunde durch den Park.*
              'He came through the park for/in one hour.'
         b.   *Er kam in einer Stunde aus der Stadt durch den Park in das Dorf.*
              'He came out of the town through the park into the village in one hour.'

(26)   Phase array for the bounded IMV *kommen*: $\langle\ [_{pi}\ \sim S_V\ ],\ [_{p1}\ S_V\ ]\ \rangle$

In order to illustrate how the PA of a complex predicate is composed of the constraints coming from the PAs of its components, let us look at two (simplified) examples with an aspectually underspecified verb of motion. (27) shows the composition of the PA of the bounded VP-predicate *aus dem Haus in das Dorf gehen* 'go/walk out of the house into the village'. I use S_{GO}, S_{IH} and S_{ID} as abbreviations for the predicates contributed by the verb and the two PPs; the subscripts of the PP-predicates indicate the states of being in the house and in the village, resp. (28) shows how the PA of the aspectually underspecified VP-predicate *durch den Park gehen* 'walk through the park' is composed. The meaning of *durch den Park* 'through the park' is represented in a rather simplistic form using the predicate of being located on a pathway in the park, S_{DP}, just for the purpose of illustration.

(27)   PAs for
         a.   *gehen*: $\langle\ [_{p0}\ |S_{GO}\ ],\ [_{pi}\ S_{GO}\ ],\ [_{p1}\ |S_{GO}\ ]\ \rangle$
         b.   *aus dem Haus*: $\langle\ [_{p0}\ S_{IH}\ ],\ [_{pi}\ \sim S_{IH}\ ]\ \rangle$
         c.   *in das Dorf*: $\langle\ [_{pi}\ \sim S_{ID}\ ],\ [_{p1}\ S_{ID}\ ]\ \rangle$
         d.   *aus dem Haus in das Dorf gehen*: $\langle\ [_{p0}\ |S_{GO}\ \&\ S_{IH}\ ],\ [_{pi}\ S_{GO}\ \&\ \sim S_{IH}\ \&\ \sim S_{ID}\ ],\ [_{p1}\ |S_{GO}\ \&\ S_{ID}\ ]\ \rangle$

(28)   PAs for
         a.   *gehen*: $\langle\ [_{p0}\ |S_{GO}\ ],\ [_{pi}\ S_{GO}\ ],\ [_{p1}\ |S_{GO}\ ]\ \rangle$
         b.   *durch den Park*: $\langle\ [_{p0}\ |S_{DP}\ ],\ [_{pi}\ S_{DP}\ ],\ [_{p1}\ |S_{DP}\ ]\ \rangle$
         c.   *durch den Park gehen*: $\langle\ [_{p0}\ |S_{GO}\ \&\ |S_{DP}\ ],\ [_{pi}\ S_{GO}\ \&\ S_{DP}\ ],\ [_{p1}\ |S_{GO}\ \&\ |S_{DP}\ ]\ \rangle$

(27.d) is bounded, due to the involved changes of state, whereas (28.c) remains aspectually underspecified, as desired. It can easily be verified that adding the PA for an egressive or ingressive PP like (27.b) or (27.c) to (28.c) would render the predicates *aus dem Haus durch den Park gehen* and *durch den Park in das Dorf gehen* bounded. Adding an underspecified PA like (28.b) to a bounded PA like (27.d) would, of course, not change the aspect.

How can we account for the fact that VP predicates like *längs des Bachs laufen* 'walk alongside the brook' are unbounded? The PA for this predicate has to be computed from one underspecified PA for the verb – $\langle$ [$_{p0}$ |S$_V$], [$_{pi}$ S$_V$], [$_{p1}$ |S$_V$] $\rangle$ – and one decidedly unbounded PA for the PP: $\langle$ [$_{pi}$ S$_{AB}$] $\rangle$ (where S$_{AB}$ is a simplified representation of being located on a pathway alongside the brook). We have to make sure on the one hand that, if no further information is added by a bounded PP, the resulting predicate (29.a) will be unbounded – cf. (29.b-c). On the other hand, the aspect must not be specified to 'unbounded' before all other constraints of the sentence have been evaluated, because additional PPs could indeed make the construction bounded, like in (29.d).

(29) a. *längs des Bachs laufen*
         'walk alongside the brook'

     b. *stundenlang längs des Bachs laufen*
         'walk alongside the brook for hours'

     c. * *in einer Stunde längs des Bachs laufen*
         'walk alongside the brook in one hour'

     d. *in einer Stunde längs des Bachs in das Dorf laufen*
         'walk alongside the brook into the village in one hour'

In (29.d), the constraints of the PA for the goal preposition are integrated with the PAs of the other elements in the normal way, which yields a bounded structure, due to the change of state with regard to the location of the LO in the final section of the path. In order to account for (29.a-c) I assume some principle of informational completeness. When all conditions are evaluated, the resulting combination of predicates is assumed to be complete for this discourse segment in focus. In the above example (29.a), there is just one single PP which blanks out what happens before and after the relevant phase. In this case, where no change-of-state information is provided, the stative PP determines the aspectual type of the sentence by way of concealing all phases other than its own. This is characteristic of the unbounded aspect, a fact that is indeed borne out by (29.b-c).

Now what happens if there is no directional PP modifier at all, i.e., if the path remains unspecified, like in (30)?

(30) a. *Er lief zwei Stunden lang im Park.*
        'He walked in the park for 2 hours.'

   b. */⁺ *Er lief in zwei Stunden im Park.*
        'He walked in the park in 2 hours.'

(30.a) shows that *im Park laufen* 'walk/run in the park', where the PP *im Park* is locative, i.e., nondirectional, is unbounded. Combining this predicate with a TSA as in (30.b) yields deficient results or may, in a quite marginal reading, induce the ingressive reinterpretation typical for unbounded predicates. Here I assume that the path predicate is defaulted to the unbounded aspect whenever the path component is left unspecified. If there is no directional modifier at all, this triggers the impression of a non-goal-directed 'seesaw' or 'to-and-fro' motion, which we could capture by a nonovert but unbounded path specification of type $\langle [_{pi} S_{\emptyset}] \rangle$. This presumed default specification equates to an existential closure on path arguments, assigning to *he was running* the reading *he was running some place*, just like we understand *he was sitting* as *he was sitting somewhere* and *he was eating* as *he was eating something*.

4.3 Transitive verbs of motion

As noted in § 1, transitive verbs of motion come in two variants: those that express a continuous impulse which the agent exerts on the theme/LO, such as *schieben* 'push' and *ziehen* 'pull' (CMVC), and those where the impulse is instantaneous or punctual, such as *werfen* 'throw' and *schießen* 'shoot' (CMVI).

The aspectual properties of verbs of type CMVC are underspecified, as the examples in (31) show: In combination with underspecified PPs they accept both bounded and unbounded contexts, as in (31.a), whereas decidedly bounded or unbounded contexts enforce the corresponding interpretation (see (31.b–c)):

(31) a. *Er zog den Schlitten eine Stunde lang/in einer Stunde/drei Mal über das Feld.*
        'He pulled the sleigh across/over the field for one hour/in one hour/three times.'

   b. *Er zog den Schlitten *eine Stunde lang/in einer Stunde/drei Mal auf den Hügel.*

'He pulled the sleigh onto the hill for one hour (one hour long)/in one hour/three times.'

c. *Er zog den Schlitten eine Stunde lang/*in einer Stunde/*drei Mal längs der Loipe.*
'He pulled the sleigh along the ski trail for one hour/in one hour/three times.'

We can thus conclude that the PA of a verb of type CMVC has the following aspectually underspecified structure:

(32) Phase array for verbs of type CMVC: $\langle\ [_{p0}\ |S_V\ ],\ [_{pi}\ S_V\ ],\ [_{p1}\ |S_V\ ]\ \rangle$

By contrast, verbs of type CMVI are bounded, independently from the aspectual properties of their directional modifiers (more on the combination with TSAs below):

(33) a. *Er warf den Ball *fünf Sekunden lang/$^?$in fünf Sekunden/drei Mal über das Spielfeld.*
'He threw the ball over/across the field/pitch for five seconds/in five seconds/three times.'

b. *Er warf den Ball *fünf Sekunden lang/$^?$in fünf Sekunden/drei Mal ins Tor.*
'He threw the ball into the goal for five seconds/in five seconds/three times.'

c. *Er warf den Ball *fünf Sekunden lang/$^?$in fünf Sekunden/drei Mal längs der Seitenlinie.*
'He threw the ball along(side) the touch line for five seconds/in five seconds/three times.'

Verbs of type CMVI express an instantaneous release of contact and/or control by the agent with regard to the theme (which is the LO). I represent their aspectual properties with the PA structure in (34):

(34) Phase array for verbs of type CMVI: $\langle\ [_{p0}\ S_V\ ],\ [_{pi}\ {\sim}S_V\ ],\ [_{p1}\ \varnothing_V\ ]\ \rangle$

The change of state from S_V to ${\sim}S_V$ makes these verbs bounded. Their PA is similar to an egressive PA, but the tripartite structure shows that the described situation is more complex than a simple bipartite egressive constellation (cf. (4.b)). The third element of the PA, $\varnothing_V$, makes use of a notational device that serves to indicate that, although the situation is explicitly acknowledged to be more complex and, in fact, to involve a full path, the verb itself decidedly excludes any reference to the final section of the path. As an example, a verb like *werfen/throw* contributes to the temporal properties of the events in its denotation only the fact that there is an instantaneous change of state, determined by the release of an object, through which the object is set in motion. On its own, the verb does not aggregate the initial, middle and final part of the path into a cohesive and continuous unit by means of a predicate that expressly does or does not (S_V or $\sim S_V$, or the underspecified $|S_V$) hold for all segments of the path.

This conception of their PA serves to account for the fact that quite often verbs of type CMVI do not go together easily with TSAs, as is typical for predicates which describe an instantaneous change of state (this is why I put a question mark on these adverbials in (33); cf. the discussion in § 2.2 and § 3.1).[18] We can observe, however, that acceptability of these constructions comes in degrees. If the PP only puts an additional constraint on the punctual state of change from $[_{p0}\ S_V\ ]$ to $[_{pi}\ \sim S_V\ ]$ and nothing is said about $[_{p1}\ \varnothing_V\ ]$, the application of a TSA (as describing the duration of the theme's motion, not in a reinterpretation to something like *it took him two seconds to finally get the ball out of the restricted area*) is close to being impossible; see (35.a). Adding information on p_1 to $[_{p1}\ \varnothing_V\ ]$, as the goal PP does in (35.b), improves the situation. And if we give a full-fledged description of all components of the motion and its path, as in (35.c), the result is quite impeccable. (36) sketches the PAs associated with the combinations of V and PP for (35) in a rather simplified form (S_V, S_{IZ}, S_{UF} and S_{IK} are the predicates associated with the verb, the source, the path and the goal PP, resp.).

(35) a. */⁺ *Er warf den Ball in zwei Sekunden aus der eigenen Zone.*
'He threw the ball in two seconds out of his own restricted area.'

b. ? *Er warf den Ball in zwei Sekunden aus der eigenen Zone in den gegnerischen Korb.*

---

[18] This observation is given quite some consideration in Kaufmann (1995) and Rappaport Hovav (2008). Kaufmann considers as one possible explanation that the verbs in question do not introduce any information about the motion of the object and its associated continuous path into the semantic representation (in terms of Kaufmann's decompositional approach: these verbs do not involve a MOVE component). She concedes, however, and rightly so I believe, that this assumption makes it hard to explain how route or path prepositions can at all be linked into the semantic representation. Rappaport Hovav, by contrast, claims that the two subevents involved in a throwing event, *viz* the instantaneous release of an object and its traversing a path, are both lexicalized in the verb. However, the times of the two subevents do not coincide and the second subevent – the traversal – does not structure the first subevent – the release – by way of imposing on it an incremental process. I consider my account to be closer to Rappaport Hovav's line of thought than to Kaufmann's (*nota bene* explicitly tentative) idea.

'He threw the ball in two seconds out of his own restricted area into the opponent team's basket.'

c. *Er warf den Ball in zwei Sekunden aus der eigenen Zone über das gesamte Spielfeld in den gegnerischen Korb.*
'He threw the ball in two seconds out of his own restricted area over/across the entire court into the opponent team's basket.'

(36) a. $\langle\ [_{p0}\ S_V\ \&\ S_{IZ}\ ],\ [_{pi}\ {\sim}S_V\ \&\ {\sim}S_{IZ}\ ],\ [_{p1}\ \varnothing_V\ ]\ \rangle$
b. $\langle\ [_{p0}\ S_V\ \&\ S_{IZ}\ ],\ [_{pi}\ {\sim}S_V\ \&\ {\sim}S_{IZ}\ \&\ {\sim}S_{IK}\ ],\ [_{p1}\ \varnothing_V\ \&\ S_{IK}\ ]\ \rangle$
c. $\langle\ [_{p0}\ S_V\ \&\ S_{IZ}\ \&\ |S_{UF}\ ],\ [_{pi}\ {\sim}S_V\ \&\ {\sim}S_{IZ}\ \&\ S_{UF}\ \&\ {\sim}S_{IK}\ ],$
     $[_{p1}\ \varnothing_V\ \&\ |S_{UF}\ \&\ S_{IK}\ ]\ \rangle$

To sum up, we can claim that verbs of type CMVI in fact do allow of temporal measurement via TSAs, though under specific conditions only. As a minimum, the final segment of the involved path, about which the verb itself does not say anything, needs some qualification by an appropriate PP. Providing even more information about the course of the path apparently accentuates the fact that there is indeed an event taking place that has some duration which can reasonably be measured. The structure of the PA assigned to the verbs in question gives at least some clue of what is happening here.

4.4 Transitive position verbs

Transitive/causative position verbs (CPV) exhibit the characteristics of single-change-of-state verbs. They combine well with TCAs and reject both TSAs and TDAs as direct specifications of the events they describe. If TSAs and TDAs are accepted at all, then only marginally so and only with the appropriate reinterpretations in terms of temporal distance or iteration, resp.:

(37) *Er stellte das Buch *$^{*/+}$*in drei Sekunden/*$^{*/+}$*drei Sekunden lang/drei Mal ins Regal.*
'He put the book onto the bookshelf in three seconds/for three seconds (three seconds long)/three times.'

This observation suggests representing their aspectual properties with the PA structure in (38), which is in line with Kaufmann's (1995) claim that causative position verbs do not introduce a full path but rather describe simple transitions into a specific state of localization of the LO.

(38)   Phase array for verbs of type CPV: $\langle$ [$_{p0}$ ~S_V], [$_{p1}$ S_V] $\rangle$

Simple egressive and ingressive PPs like in (39.a) combine with CPVs without any qualification.[19] Route/path PPs cannot be added because they do not find a landing point in the verb's PA, since there is no middle section [$_{p0}$ _] – see (39.b):

(39)   a.   *Er legte das Buch vom Regal auf den Schreibtisch.*
            (literally) 'He put the book from the bookshelf onto the desk.'

     b.   * *Er legte das Buch vom Regal durch sein Arbeitszimmer auf den Schreibtisch.*
            (literally) 'He put the book from the bookshelf through his office onto the desk.'

The PA in (38) will account for the vast majority of constructions with causative position verbs. Nevertheless there are some very special situations in which at least *legen* and *hängen*, and possibly also *stellen*, allow of prepositions which are applied to the middle segment of a path. As a consequence, temporal measurement in the form of TSAs is also accepted in these sentences:

(40)   a.   *Er legte (in einer Minute) das Kabel vom Flur durch das Wohnzimmer in den Garten.*
            'He laid the cable from the corridor through the living room into the garden (in one minute).'

     b.   *Er hängte (in einer Minute) die Leine vom Wohnzimmer über den Balkon in den Garten.*
            'He hung the rope from the living room over/across the balcony into the garden (in one minute).'

     c.   *Er stellte (in einer Stunde) die Verstärkeranlage über die Rampe auf die Bühne.*
            'He put the amplification system over/across the ramp onto the stage (in one hour).'

---

[19] With their definitions in § 3.1 in terms of the PAs $\langle$ [$_{p0}$ S], [$_{pi}$ ~S] $\rangle$ for egressive PPs and $\langle$ [$_{pi}$ ~S], [$_{p1}$ S] $\rangle$ for ingressive PPs, which include reference to the middle section of a path (p_i), these PPs would not immediately fit into the PA for verbs of type CPV, which does not even include this section. We can, however, accommodate the PAs for these PPs if we align only the phase of their positive state (S) with a specific path segment (for egressive PPs: p_0; for ingressive PPs: p_1) and require that their negative state (~S) is linked to the subsequent (p_i or p_1 in the egressive case) or previous (p_i or p_0 in the ingressive case) PA segment, which varies depending on the type of verb (CPV vs. the other verb-classes).

These cases are very specific in that they all call for objects of a specific shape and constitution. Sentences like (40.a–c) would not work with a single book. In fact, adequate objects have to have a considerable length, since combinations like in (40) require objects whose position on a path can unfold over time. The status of these uses of causative position verbs is not fully clear. On the one hand, with the exception of (40.c), there is no real change of position of an object from a source location across a path to a goal location, but rather the unfolding of a wide-stretched location. On the other hand, even these sentences are not static, but describe extended events, as is shown by the fact that they accept TSAs (and refuse TDAs, barring reinterpretations).

Since the conditions for this use of causative position verbs are highly specific, it is not reasonable to reflect at the same time core uses, as in (37), and marginal uses, as in (40), in one underspecified representation. I'd rather assume that, under the specific circumstances sketched above, the ingressive PA for verbs of type CPV can be relaxed to something like $\langle\ [_{p0}\ \sim S_V\ ],\ [_{pi}\ \varnothing\ ]\ ,\ [_{p1}\ S_V\ ]\ \rangle$, which acknowledges that there is a middle phase to which a PP can be applied, but on its own does not put any constraints on it. As a general representation of the aspectual properties of causative position verbs, this structure would, however, be much too loose.

4.5 The aspectual impact of the theme argument

In addition to their own PA and those of their directional PP modifiers, the aspectual properties of transitive motion and position verbs depend on (at least) one more dimension, namely the way in which the theme/LO of the dynamic localization is subject to the phasal development along a path. Just like in nonspatial domains (*eat an apple* vs. *eat apples/applesauce*), a complex predicate of a dynamic spatial localization can be applied in a holistic way to the denotations of bounded NPs, i.e., to individuals, or in a distributed way to the denotations of unbounded NPs, i.e., masses or plural objects.[20]

In the spatial domain, we can observe this phenomenon already with the aspectually underspecified causative motion verbs of type CMVC when these are combined with a bounded PP: Although the PP yields a bounded change-of-state predicate, the combination of the resulting V-PP predicate with the unbounded

---

[20] Cf. the seminal work of Krifka (1989a,b,c). These studies put a particular emphasis on verbs of creation and consumption (*write, eat*) and on verbs with gradual patient arguments (*read*). Krifka (1998) shows how the approach can be expanded to selected spatial prepositions.

theme NP in (41.a) is unbounded. The same holds for similar constructions with causative motion verbs of type CMVP (41.b), for constructions with causative position verbs (41.c), as well as for *kommen* (41.d), which are all bounded from the outset, as we saw in the previous paragraphs:[21]

(41) a. *Er schob (eine Stunde lang/*in einer Stunde) Schnee vom Gehweg.*
 'He pushed snow from the sidewalk (for one hour/in one hour).'

 b. *Er warf (eine Stunde lang/*in einer Stunde) Schnee auf den LKW.*
 'He threw snow onto the truck (for one hour/in one hour).'

 c. *Er stellte (eine Stunde lang/* in einer Stunde) Bücher ins Regal.*
 'He put books into the bookshelf (for one hour/in one hour).'

 d. *(Eine Stunde lang/*in einer Stunden) kam (nur) schmutziges Wasser aus der Leitung.*
 '(For/in one hour) (only) muddy water came out of the tap.'

This means that when we embed our semantic analyses of the aspectual properties of verbs of dynamic localization and their directional modifiers into a full-fledged theory of grammar with an appropriate formalism, this would need to allow the representation and calculation of the aspectual type on the basis of information from all relevant sources, i. e., from the phasal characteristics of verbs and directional PPs, as well as from the referential properties of the verb's arguments. A suitable formalism would ideally supply a rich representational inventory from which the aspectually relevant properties of verbs and their arguments and modifiers could be directly calculated. This would require a means for representing the internal structure of events, processes and states with both their parts and participants, as well as properties of and a manifold of relations between these elements. In addition, fine-grained distinctions would be needed among types of actions that can be executed on objects with different effects (such as pushing, throwing, putting, etc., in the domain under investigation here). Furthermore, there is a need to represent the different ways in which entities of different types (like simple and complex individuals, plural entities and masses – cf. a ball, a

---

[21] Looking beyond the theme argument, it is not surprising that for all of the transitive verbs of dynamic localization we also find examples where it is the referential properties of the subject or agent which determines the aspect, rather than the object or theme, similar to Dowty's (1979) famous example *Tourists discovered that quaint little village for years.* In the following examples, the object/theme NPs are all bounded, while the subject/agent NPs are unbounded and render the aspect of the entire construction unbounded: *Touristen trugen/warfen/stellten (jahrelang) den Maibaum auf den Dorfplatz* 'Tourists carried/threw/put (for years) the maypole onto the village square'.

team, soccer players and snow) can be subject to change in various dimensions. I have to leave it at this here and defer further considerations about a suitable grammar formalism to future investigation.

5 Summary

In order to describe and represent the aspectual properties of verbs of dynamic localization and their directional PP modifiers, I introduced the concept of a phase array (PA), which receives its theoretical fundament in a "Löbner-style" phase-theoretical semantics. In this approach, the aspectual type of a predicate is determined by its PA, which in turn is composed of the PAs of its constituents. The verbal head of a sentence introduces a basic PA which may or may not predefine parts of the final PA. The verbs under consideration include in their semantics a motion component which links the changing positions of their theme argument to positions on an abstract path which they introduce into the semantic representation. Directional PPs in turn specify positions of their localized object (LO) – which is the verb's theme argument – on the path provided by the verb. They do this in the form of a sequence of states of localization of the LO/theme which are defined in terms of specific regions in relation to the reference object (RO), i.e., the internal argument of the preposition. Like PAs for verbs, PAs for prepositions/PP can be of the type bounded, unbounded, or underspecified.

To conclude this study I would like to relate the results of the present study to Filip's (2008) claim that, in Germanic languages, all stem verbs and many VPs are inherently unmarked with respect to boundedness ('telicity/maximality' in Filip's theory) and obtain bounded interpretations only in specific linguistic contexts or through pragmatic inferences. The picture I obtained from my analyses is multifaceted: firstly, I found clear cases of decidedly unbounded expressions among both verbs and prepositions. State/process verbs like *schlafen* and *sitzen* and their English counterparts *sleep* and *sit*, as well as a state/process-like preposition like *längs* (and Engl. *towards*), can be accommodated to contexts which select bounded predicates only with some level of reinterpretation with varied degrees of intelligibility and acceptability. If we want to enforce a bounded reading of these verbs, we have to apply specific reinterpretations, which are felicitous only under rather specific circumstances.

Secondly, quite a few verbal and prepositional predicates fit without any restraint into both bounded and unbounded constellations. In the spatial domain, these are intransitive motion verbs (except *kommen* 'come') and transitive motion verbs that express a continuous impact on the theme (*schieben* 'push' etc.), as well as the prepositions *durch* and *über*, plus *hinauf/hinab* and possibly even *entlang*. I consider the verbs in question (plus the prepositions, which were not in the scope of Filip's claim) to be the cases that most directly conform to Filip's notion about aspectual unmarkedness.

Thirdly, I found both verbs and prepositions with a strong bias towards the bounded aspect. Among them are causative position verbs (*stellen* 'put', *legen* 'lay'), causative motion verbs that express an instantaneous impact (*werfen* 'throw'), the intransitive motion verb *kommen* 'come', plus ingressive, egressive and intergressive prepositions. These verb classes seem to contradict Filip's strong claim about category V. However, although the verbs and prepositions in question form bounded predicates in V-PP combinations, they nevertheless all exhibit a systematic dependency on the referential properties of their theme arguments (*throw balls, push snow from the sidewalk*, and the German equivalents), just like verbs such as *read, write* and *eat* do. Thus, if we build the dependency on properties of the theme directly into the semantic representations of the dynamic spatial verbs in question, from which we compute their aspectual properties, we would retain in their semantics a strong element of underspecification of aspect.

To close, I would like to point out that, although aspectually underspecified verbs can equally well enter into bounded or unbounded constructions, we could nevertheless observe a certain primacy of the unbounded interpretation in the domain of dynamic spatial expressions. Whenever, in the case of aspectually underspecified verbs, there is no information, like that coming from a bounded directional PP, which moves the aspect in a definite direction, the aspect is always defaulted to unbounded; cf. *Lola rennt (im Park)* 'Lola runs (in the park)'. We observed no case where an underspecified aspect is specialized by default to bounded in an indeterminate context; bounding appears to always require a specific context.

Bibliography

Beavers, J. 2008. Scalar complexity and the structure of events. In J. Dölling et al. (ed.), *Event structures in linguistic form and interpretation*, 245–265. Berlin/New York: de Gruyter.

van Benthem, J. F. A. K. 1983. *The logic of time. A model-theoretic investigation into the varieties of temporal ontology and temporal discourse.* Dordrecht: Reidel.

Carlson, G. N. 1977. A unified analysis of the English bare plural. *Linguistics and Philosophy* 1. 413–458.

Comrie, B. 1976. *Aspect: An introduction to the study of verbal aspect and related problems.* Cambridge Textbooks in Linguistics. Cambridge: Cambridge University Press.

Csirmaz, A. 2012. Durative adverbials and homogeneity requirements. *Lingua* 122. 1112–1133.

Dowty, D. 1979. *Word meaning and Montague grammar.* Dordrecht: Reidel.

Egg, M. 1994. *Aktionsart und Kompositionalität. Zur kompositionellen Ableitung der Aktionsart komplexer Kategorien.* Berlin: Akademie-Verlag (studia grammatica 37).

Egg, M. 1995. The intergressive as a new category of verbal aktionsart. *Journal of Semantics* 12. 311–356.

Egg, M. 2002. Semantic construction for reinterpretation phenomena. *Linguistics* 40.3. 579–606.

Egg, M. & M. Herweg. 1994. A type hierarchy for aspectual classification. In H. Trost (ed.), *Konvens 94. Verarbeitung natürlicher Sprache. Tagungsband.* Informatik Xpress 6, 92–101. Wien.

Filip, H. 2008. Events and maximalization: The case of telicity and perfectivity. In S. Rothstein (ed.), *Theoretical and crosslinguistic approaches to the semantics of aspect*, 217–256. Amsterdam/Philadelphia: John Benjamins.

Galton, A. 1984. *The logic of aspect. An axiomatic approach.* Oxford: Clarendon Press.

Gropen, J., S. Pinker, M. Hollander, R. Goldberg & R. Wilson. 1989. The learnability and acquisition of the dative alternation in English. *Language* 65.2. 203–257.

Habel, C. 1989. zwischen-Bericht. In C. Habel, M. Herweg & K. Rehkämper (eds.), *Raumkonzepte in Verstehensprozessen. Interdisziplinäre Beiträge zu Sprache und Raum*, 37–69. Tübingen: Niemeyer.

Herweg, M. 1989. Ansätze zu einer semantischen Beschreibung topologischer Präpositionen. In C. Habel, M. Herweg & K. Rehkämper (eds.), *Raumkonzepte in Verstehensprozessen. Interdisziplinäre Beiträge zu Sprache und Raum*, 99–127. Tübingen: Niemeyer.

Herweg, M. 1990. *Zeitaspekte. Die Bedeutung von Tempus, Aspekt und temporalen Konjunktionen.* Wiesbaden: Deutscher Universitäts-Verlag.

Herweg, M. 1991a. A critical examination of two classical approaches to aspect. *Journal of Semantics* 8.3. 363–402.

Herweg, M. 1991b. Perfective and imperfective aspect and the theory of events and states. *Linguistics* 29. 969–1010.

Herweg, M. 1991c. Temporale Konjunktionen und Aspekt – der sprachliche Ausdruck von Zeitrelationen zwischen Situationen. *Kognitionswissenschaft* 2.2. 51–90.

Kaufmann, I. 1989. Direktionale Präpositionen. In C. Habel, M. Herweg & K. Rehkämper (eds.), *Raumkonzepte in Verstehensprozessen. Interdisziplinäre Beiträge zu Sprache und Raum*, 128–149. Tübingen: Niemeyer.

Kaufmann, I. 1993. Semantic and conceptual aspects of the insert 'durch'. In C. Zelinsky-Wibbelt (ed.), *The semantics of prepositions. From mental processing to natural language processing.*, 221–247. Berlin: Mouton de Gruyter.

Kaufmann, I. 1995. *Konzeptuelle Grundlagen semantischer Dekompositionsstrukturen. Die Kombinatorik lokaler Verben und prädikativer Komplemente*. Tübingen: Niemeyer.

Klein, W. 1991. Raumausdrücke. *Linguistische Berichte* 132. 77–114.

Krifka, M. 1989a. Nominal reference, temporal constitution and quantification in event semantics. In R. Bartsch, J. van Benthem & P. von Emde Boas (eds.), *Semantics and contextual expression*, 75–115. Dordrecht: Foris Publications.

Krifka, M. 1989b. *Nominalreferenz und Zeitkonstitution. Zur Semantik von Massentermen, Individualtermen, Aspektklassen*. München: Wilhelm Fink Verlag.

Krifka, M. 1989c. Nominalreferenz, Zeitkonstitution, Aspekt, Aktionsart: Eine semantische Erklärung ihrer Interaktion. In W. Abraham & T. Jansen (eds.), *Tempus – Aspekt – Modus. Die lexikalischen und grammatischen Formen in den germanischen Sprachen*, 227–258. Tübingen: Niemeyer.

Krifka, M. 1998. The origins of telicity. In S. Rothstein (ed.), *Events and grammar*, 197–235. Dordrecht/Boston/London: Kluwer Academic Publishers.

Krifka, M. 2012. Some remarks on event structure, conceptual spaces and logical form. *Theoretical Linguistics* 38. 223–336.

Lang, E. 1989. The semantics of dimensional designation of spatial objects. In M. Bierwisch & E. Lang (eds.), *Dimensional adjectives: Grammatical structure and conceptual interpretation*, 287–458. Berlin, Heidelberg, New York: Springer.

Levin, B. 1993. *English verb classes and alternations: A preliminary investigation*. Chicago: University of Chicago Press.

Löbner, S. 1988. Ansätze zu einer integralen semantischen Theorie von Tempus, Aspekt und Aktionsarten. In V. Ehrich & H. Vater (eds.), *Temporalsemantik: Beiträge zur Linguistik der Zeitreferenz*, 163–191. Tübingen: Niemeyer.

Löbner, S. 1989. German schon – erst – noch: an integrated analysis. *Linguistics and Philosophy* 12. 167–212.

Löbner, S. 2011. Dual oppositions in lexical meaning. In C. Maienborn, K. von Heusinger & P. Portner (eds.), *Semantics. an international handbook of natural language meaning (HSK)*, vol. 1, 479–506. Berlin/New York: Mouton de Gruyter.

Rappaport Hovav, M. 2008. Lexicalized meaning and the internal temporal structure of events. In S. Rothstein (ed.), *Theoretical and crosslinguistic approaches to the semantics of aspect*, 13–42. Amsterdam: John Benjamins.

Rappaport Hovav, M. & B. Levin. 1998. Building verb meanings. In M. Butt & W. Geuder (eds.), *The projection of arguments: Lexical and compositional factors*, 97–134. Stanford: CSLI Publications.

Rothstein, S. 2004. *Structuring events. A study in the semantics of lexical aspect.* Oxford: Blackwell Publishing.

Smith, C. S. 1991. *The parameter of aspect.* Dordrecht/Boston/London: Kluwer Academic Publishers.

Vendler, Z. 1957. *Linguistics in philosophy.* Ithaca: Cornell University Press.

Wunderlich, D. & M. Herweg. 1991. Lokale und Direktionale. In A. von Stechow & D. Wunderlich (eds.), *Semantik – ein internationales Handbuch der zeitgenössischen Forschung*, 758–785. Berlin/New York: de Gruyter.

Zwarts, J. 2005. Prepositional aspect and the algebra of paths. *Linguistics and Philosophy* 26.6. 739–779.

Zwarts, J. 2008. Aspects of a typology of direction. In S. Rothstein (ed.), *Theoretical and crosslinguistic approaches to the semantics of aspect*, 79–106. Amsterdam: John Benjamins.

Zwarts, J. & Y. Winter. 2000. Vector space semantics: a modeltheoretic analysis of locative prepositions. *Journal of Logic, Language and Information* 9.2. 171–213.

Author

Michael Herweg
IBM Germany
michael.herweg@de.ibm.com

The purported Present Perfect Puzzle

Anita Mittwoch

Introduction

The Present Perfect Puzzle (Klein 1992) asks why English sentences in the Present Perfect do not allow a specification of the time of the event. The paper suggests an indirect answer to the question: in languages that do allow this, perfect morphology is ambiguous between a use that is semantically a true Perfect and one that corresponds to a Past (Preterit). A further puzzle in Klein's paper relates to the English Past Perfect: what is wrong with *At seven, Chris had left at six*? In this case the present paper suggests a direct answer; it attributes the ill-formedness of this sentence to fact that the English Past Perfect is ambiguous.

Klein (1992) raises two questions.

Question I: Why doesn't the English Present Perfect go with temporal adverbials denoting a definite Past interval?

Unlike German, Dutch, Latin, French and many other languages, English does not allow sentences in which definite temporal adverbials modify a sentence in the Present Perfect:

(1) #She has visited me on Monday / yesterday.

(2) Sie hat mich gestern / am Montag besucht.

1 Underlying assumptions

1.1 Assumptions about the English Perfect

The Perfect is a composite category; it consists of a state and of an event leading up to the state.

One decisive piece of evidence for the stativeness of the Perfect is compatibility with *already* and *not yet*, which occur with lexical statives, with the progressive and habituals, both derived statives, and with the Perfect; they do not occur with episodic readings of the simple forms of dynamic verbs.

(3) a. *She is already here.*
 b. *She is already leaving.*
 c. *She already goes to school.*
 d. *She has already left.*
 e. *#She already left.*[1,2]

The Tense is determined by a time (usually a point) within the state, which for a present Perfect normally contains utterance time.[3] I shall call it P(erfect) E(valuation) Point. PEpt can be expressed overtly by deictic expressions, preferably in initial position, as in (4) or governed by temporal *by* as in (5):

(4) a. *Today I have done my homework.*
 b. *Now I have seen Naples*

(5) *The guests have left by now*

In (4) the time of the event need not be included in the day the sentence is uttered; the utterance can be meant to say *today I am prepared.*

The meaning of a prepositional phrase consisting of *by*, followed by temporal expressions like *three, Monday, June, last week* is 'not later than the time designated by the referent of the NP' and thus marks the terminal point of an interval during which an event has occurred or will occur; in the first case the *by*-phrase corresponds to PEpt. The interval is contextually given.

The event component of the Perfect is contained in a contextually determined interval terminating at PEpt. Its beginning can be marked by the preposition *since*. For a Present Perfect this is McCoard's 'extended now' or XN; but since we need a term that applies to Non-present Perfects as well, I shall call it, following Iatridou

---

[1] For many American speakers, what is said here about *already* does not apply. They have no problem with (3c) often with reverse order of verb and adverb *She LEFT already*, and they may also use *already* with narrow focus: *She already left at FIVE.* In general, use of the perfect seems to be comparatively rare among such speakers. However, judging by the English of the International Herald Tribune, I believe that formal American English does not differ from British English in this respect.

[2] A reviewer notes that the adverb *currently* is also restricted to states, and asks whether it is good with the present perfect. The following sentence, found on the web, answers the question: *14 teams have currently registered.*

[3] The only exception is future reference in *when*-clauses, as in *Call me when you have finished.*

et al. (2001), P(erfect) T(ime) S(pan). The beginning of the PTS can be marked by the preposition *since*. It should be obvious that the temporal *by*-phrase described in the previous paragraph has a special affinity to the Perfect.[4]

The temporal relations are set out in (6) and shown graphically in (6'):

(6)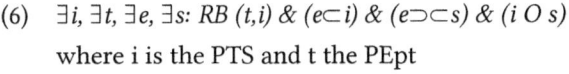
where i is the PTS and t the PEpt

(6')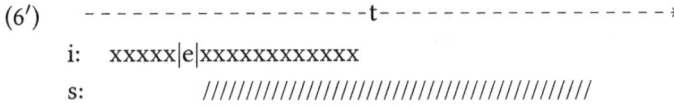

Following Kamp & Reyle (1993), (6) says that e abuts s, but does not specify the nature of the connection between them, which obviously has to be more than just temporal sequence. I take the state *s* to be, at its most basic, the post-state of *e* (Parsons 1990, Vlach 1993), but typically overlaid by an ephemeral state that has some concrete content of its own, depending partly on the use of the Perfect involved, as will be shown below.[5]

1.2 Assumptions about languages that allow what looks like a straightforward translation equivalent of (1)

Perfect morphology is ambiguous in such languages; a form like German *hat besucht* represents either a composite state-event category as in English, or a Past Tense, what Löbner (2002) calls *Non-Past Perfect* or *Past No-Perfect*.[6]

In a later paper Klein (2000) supports this position with the examples in (7) and (8):

---

[4] Many existing treatments of the Perfect focus on either the stativeness of the Perfect or on the PTS interval in connection with the event. I believe that both are needed to account for the interaction between the two components of the Perfect. The stativeness determines the properties of the PEpt. The PTS accounts for the occurrence of indefinite temporal adverbials like *on a Monday* or *formerly*, and for *since*-phrases. It also provides a link between the uses of the Perfect discussed in this paper and the Universal Perfect, as in *I have lived here for ten years / since 2003*.

[5] The term post state is due to Klein (1994). Parsons termed it 'resultant state', a state which lasts forever. But as his characterization of this state suggests that it is a property of the referent of the subject, the question arises whether it can outlive that entity. The idea of the post-state is not new. It is clearly enunciated in a classic late nineteenth century work on Ancient Greek: "The perfect, although it implies the performance of the action in Past time, yet states only that it *stands completed* at the *present* time." (Goodwin 1889) It may well be much older still.

[6] The term 'perfect morphology' stands for an auxiliary corresponding to English HAVE – or BE – plus Past participle; it could also correspond to inflected verbs, as in Latin.

(7) Ich habe im Garten gearbeitet [und muss zuerst einmal duschen].
'I have in the garden worked [and must-PRES first shower].

(8) Ich habe im Garten gearbeitet [und konnte deshalb die Klingel
'I have in the garden worked [and could-PAST therefore the bell
nicht hören].
not hear]

Among additional arguments for this position Löbner mentions temporal *als* 'when', which is restricted to Past (non-habitual) contexts:

(9) Als/*Wenn ich sie gestern traf/getroffen habe erzählte sie
When I her yesterday met/have met told she
mir ...
me (L 17a, 18a)[7]

Note that if perfect morphology not only in German but in many other languages is ambiguous, one well-known 'peculiarity' of the English Perfect becomes less puzzling. The English Present Perfect exhibits a lifetime effect, like sentences in the Present Tense in general.[8] Both sentences in (10) are inappropriate when uttered today:

(10) a. *Einstein is from Ulm.*
  b. *Einstein has visited Princeton*

The German equivalent of (a) is equally inappropriate; but the equivalent of (b) *Einstein hat Princeton besucht* is unproblematic; its perfect morphology can denote a Past.[9]

The simplest answer to Question I would be: A definite temporal adverbial like *yesterday, on Monday* refers to a specific time in the past (ignoring *on Monday* in a future context). Therefore a sentence containing such an adverbial cannot denote simple anteriority, and cannot be absorbed into an Extended Now, the PTS for the Present Perfect. It has to be evaluated at the time specified by the

---

[7] Other scholars arguing for the ambiguity of the German perfect include Fabricius-Hansen (1994), Dahl (1995), Pancheva & von Stechow (2004).

[8] Mittwoch (2008a) argues that lifetime inferences are presuppositional.

[9] Klein (2000) treats it as a perfect. He explains the difference between English and German by the claim that in German an operator POST can apply to the predicate alone or to the whole sentence including the subject. English has only the first option, which means that a present property is attributed to the referent of the subject. Since his examples do not appear in a context in which they are unequivocally Perfects, I cannot evaluate this argument.

adverbial. The presence of such an adverbial in a sentence evaluated at speech time would therefore lead to a clash. The German sentence in (2) is not subject to this restriction because its perfect morphology does not encode a semantic Perfect, and therefore *hat besucht* in (2) is not a Present Tense form, despite appearances. If this is true for ambiguous 'perfects' in general, then English-like languages would not be out of the ordinary; the puzzle would disappear or be replaced by historical questions: why did so many languages allow the state component to fade together with the confinement of the event to anteriority, and why did English and the mainland Scandinavian languages not follow suit? I believe that this is in fact a large part of the answer to Klein's question, but perhaps not a full answer.

This answer has also been challenged by Löbner with what he calls a non-argument for the ambiguity of the German 'Perfect', i.e. perfect morphology in the terminology used here. Löbner, following work by Klein (1992) and Herweg (1990), denies the widely-held assumption that semantic perfect is inherently incompatible with co-occurrence of a specification of event time by means of a definite temporal adverbial:

(11)   *Jetzt wo   Karla gestern   hier eingezogen ist, brauchen wir einen*
       Now where K.   yesterday here moved-in   is   need   we a
       Schlüssel fürs   Klo.
       key   for the loo.
       #'Now that K. has moved in here yesterday we need a key for the toilet.'
       (Löbner 2002: (13); I have added the hash)

Since the embedded clause modifies *jetzt* the italicised verbal phrase must be a semantic perfect. The presence of the adverbial is facilitated, I suggest, by the fact that it is in an embedded clause which does not contain new information, but at most a reminder to which it makes a minimal contribution. One difference between German and English that might also be relevant is the position of the adverb in its clause, and the effect of this on prosody. *Gestern*, between subject and predicate, requires no prosodic prominence; the English equivalent has the adverb in clause-final position immediately before resumption of the matrix, and would require a slight rise.[10]

---

[10] One of my informants rejected an analogous sentence (*Jetzt wo ich den Film gestern gesehen habe kann ich ihn dir sehr empfehlen*) because of the presence of *gestern*, but did not know why. Others were happy with it. Since I thought that the presence of the adverb was also facilitated by its position in a place where it does not require prosodic prominence, I tried the sentence with the

If Löbner's claim reflects a robust German phenomenon, then semantic perfect in German is obviously very different from Perfect in English and English-like languages. In the next section I will show why the relevant temporal adverbial are incompatible with two of the main uses of he English Perfect.

2 How would temporal adverbials affect Resultative and Experiential Perfects?

Descriptions of the English Perfect usually distinguish a number of 'uses'. In what follows I shall discuss two of these, the Resultative and the Experiential Perfect, and show that for each of them there is a different factor at work that blocks co-ocurrence with definite temporal adverbials. Before presenting examples I must make it clear that the distinction is between uses of sentences rather than meanings; many sentences in isolation could belong to either category. A hash in the examples below is to be read as 'unacceptable as a Resultative Perfect'. This will be explained more fully and exemplified at the end of this section.

2.1 The Resultative

The Resultative is the oldest and still the prototypical use of the Perfect. It involves an episodic event and a clearly defined result state. In what I have called Strong Resultatives the result state is the target state of a telic event, and can be read off the event sentence (Mittwoch 2008b). The target state of the untensed VP *lock the door* is *the door be locked*. From an utterance of (12a) one can normally infer (12b):

(12)   a.   *Jill has locked the door.*
       b.   *The door is now locked.*

If the speaker has reason to suspect that someone else has meanwhile unlocked the door again, the Perfect is inappropriate; the Past Tense is called for: #*Jill has locked the door, but I am not sure whether it is still locked.* For Weak Resultatives the nature of the result state is not dictated by the meaning of the verb, but has to be inferred from the extra-linguistic context: for example, from an utterance of *I've had lunch*, the hearer may infer that the speaker is not going to have lunch right now, or simply that s/he is not hungry.

---

addition of *schon* before the adverb, which would then require focal stress. Two informants were not bothered, one would have preferred *schon* before *eingezogen*.

For the Resultative Perfect the definite temporal adverbial is only one of a series of constituents that is excluded. Thus

(13) a. *Jane has translated the poem #quickly/literally.*
b. *They have sealed the door #noisily/hermetically.*
c. *I've had lunch #in the cafeteria/#with Anne.*

Any adverbial that modifies only the event VP is out. For the Strong Resultatives in (13a and b) the acceptable adverbials *literally* and *hermetically* modify the target state, witness *a literally translated version of the text, a hermetically sealed door.*[11] Even the subject position of change of state verbs is affected, inasmuch as it cannot be the focus of a question or a cleft sentence, unless it is relevant to the target state:

(14) a. *Who has #broken/ taken my umbrella?*
b. *It's John who has #broken /taken your umbrella.*

A broken umbrella is not expected to show signs of the culprit; but there is a good chance that the person who has taken my umbrella has it now.

The Resultative Perfect is state-oriented. A definite temporal adverbial has to be excluded from this Perfect because it would modify only the event.

2.2 The Experiential Perfect

In contrast to the Resultative, the event component of an Experiential Perfect is non-specific. A sentence in this type of Perfect merely says that an event type is instantiated in the PTS. The state component may be no more than the 'post-state'; or it may allow inferences based on world knowledge, what is called the 'present relevance' of the Present Perfect.

Many examples of such Perfects explicitly refer to a plurality of events by means of adverbs of quantity like *sometimes, three times*, etc.

(15) *We have often dined in that restaurant with guests.*

In other cases it is left vague whether a single event is involved or a multiplicity of instantiations. The beginning of the PTS may be marked by the preposition *since*:

(16) *Since graduating, she has (already) been back in Cambridge twice.*

---

[11] According to two informants the facts are the same in Swedish.

The post-state being somewhat nebulous, the Experiential Perfect gives the impression of being event-oriented. But as the event component is purely quantificational, a definite temporal adverbial is incompatible with an Experiential Perfect as we know it, because by its nature such an adverbial would individualize the event and make it specific.

2.3 The relationship between Resultative and Experiential

Semantically, this relationship is asymmetrical. Although the Resultative is more basic and perhaps more common, Resultative one-sidedly entails Experiential. If there is a specific token of an event type, the type is obviously instantiated. (McCawley 1981, Mittwoch 2008b). Sentences that out of the blue are likely to be interpreted as Resultative can in suitable contexts be interpreted as Experientials, but the reverse is not true. For example, if you see a policeman approaching, and say to the person sitting next to you in the car

(17)   *(Oh dear!) I've left my driving license at home.*

the Perfect is likely to be a meant as a Resultative. But if you complain to your doctor that you have been unusually absent-minded lately and say

(18)   *I've forgotten to lock the front door, I've left my driving license athome, I've taken the wrong turning on my way to work.*

all three Perfects are Experiential; at utterance time the door need not be open, the speaker is not driving, and the license may be in his pocket. On the other hand, (15) and (16) above cannot be used as resultatives.

3   The Past Perfect and Klein's second question

In the Past Perfect a temporal adverbial can refer either to the PEpt or to the time in which the event occurred, a notorious problem for Reichenbach's analysis of 'the tenses of verbs' (Reichenbach 1947: 290), in particular his R(eference time). (19) is ambiguous (as printed) between these readings, as shown when it is placed in contexts in (20a and b):

(19)   *Chris had left at six.*

(20)   a.   *Mary came home at six. Unfortunately Chris had already left at six.*
       b.   *Yesterday, Mary came to Chris's office at seven. But Chris had left at six.*
            (Klein 1992: 40)

In terms of information structure these sentences are very different. In (20a) *six* is old information, *left* is new and carries focal stress; in (20b) *left at six* is new, and focal stress is on *six*. Consider also

(21) John had left the house when I arrived.

On the reading corresponding to (20a) John was no longer in the house at the time of my arrival. On the reading corresponding to (20b) the event of John's leaving is likely to have occurred a short time - perhaps only a minute – after the event of my arrival. (This is not a necessary inference, however; if my arrival would serve as a signal for John's leaving, and if he saw me coming from a distance, the two events could be simultaneous.)

Question II: Why can't two temporal adverbials occur together in one clause, with one marking the evaluation time and the other the event time, as in (22)?

(22) #At seven, Chris had left at six. (Klein 1992: (41) and (44))

Klein's answer to Question II: The reason is neither syntactic nor semantic. (22) is true if (20b) is true. The reason is pragmatic: "it gives the somewhat unfortunate impression that at some other time yesterday Chris had not left at six."[12] This leads him to postulate the constraint in (23):

(23) POSITION (p) - definiteness constraint:
 In an utterance, the expression of TT Topic Time= (Evaluation Time) and the expression of TSit (Situation Time= Event Time) cannot both be independently p-definite. (Klein 1992: (43))

He points out that this constraint also covers the ban on definite temporal adverbials in the Present Perfect, since utterance time is also a 'topic time'.

Klein's answer to the question he has posed, and the constraint based on it are correct. But there is also solid semantic evidence for the ill-formedness of (22).

In spite of pointing out the two different temporal positions to which the adverbial can belong, Klein assumed that the perfect morphology in (20a and b) has the same function.[13] The examples below, from Mittwoch (1995), show that there are 'Past Perfects' that are incompatible with definite temporal adverbials:

---

[12] In the paper's concluding remarks Klein says that "the solution to the present perfect puzzle has a semantic component – the meaning of the English perfect construction – and a pragmatic component"; but the paper does not make it clear how the semantic component operates.

[13] The assumption is shared by many recent discussions of the English Perfect, (Katz 2003, Portner 2003, Reyle et al. 2007, Schaden 2009). On the other hand, Kamp & Reyle (1993) and Kiparsky (2002) discuss the ambiguity at length. Kiparsky, who, contrary to the position taken here, believes that the difference between Experiential and Resultative is truth-conditional, relates the PPerf reading to the former and the Resultative reading to the latter.

(24) a. *I phoned at 7, but Mary had #already left at six that morning.*

b. *Since leaving Cambridge, Mary had been back #last summer.*

Already in (24a) and *since* in (24b) are markers of semantic Perfect. The trouble with both sentences is exactly the same as the trouble with present Tense sentences like (1): *She has visited me on Monday / yesterday*. Past perfect morphology in English can correspond to a Past of a Perfect or to an iterated Past. In Mittwoch (1995) these are called PPerf and PPast respectively.

The two uses cannot be mixed in one sentence. Klein's own example in (22) is in fact another case of such illegitimate mixing.

Neither can they be conjoined with ellipsis of the auxiliary:

(25) a. *John had already arrived, and #(had) gone to the dining room at seven.*

b. *John had arrived at seven and #(had) already gone to the dining room.*

In coordinations where Past Tense morphology stands for the same type the auxiliary can be omitted:

(26) a. *Mary had already finished her degree and started work.*

b. *Mary had finished her degree and started work last October.*

These examples provide clear evidence that the auxiliaries have different functions in the two conjuncts in (25a and b).

In the following example the PPast reading is recognized not only by the temporal adverbial in the introductory sentence, but also by its containing a narrative sequence, which would be incompatible with a true Perfect (cf. Kamp & Reyle 1993: 594 and Michaelis 1994, who makes this point about the Present Perfect):

(27) *(John had come in at five.) He had switched on the TV, opened a can of beer and settled down in his armchair.*

Apart from the adverbs *already* and *not yet*, temporal *by* is a sure diagnostic for a PPerf. It is probably commoner than the prepositions *at, in, on* to mark PEpt in PPerf:

(28) *The workers had finished the job by 4/ Friday afternoon/ June.*

Past perfect morphology in English displays basically the same ambiguity as present perfect morphology in German, Latin and many other languages. Perfect morphology can represent a true Perfect or function as a stand-in for Past, in this

The purported Present Perfect Puzzle

case the 'Inner' Past in the scope of the Past operator that is spelled out in the case of *have* as *had*.

The two readings of (19) given in (20a and b) are shown in (29):

(29) a. *May came home at 6. Chris had already left.*

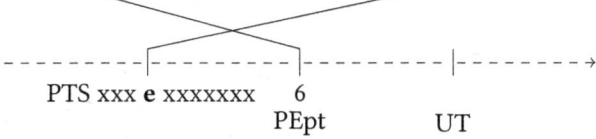

```
--------|---------|---------|-------→
    PTS xxx e xxxxxxx    6
                       PEpt        UT
```

b. *Mary came ... at 7[.] Chris had left at 6.*

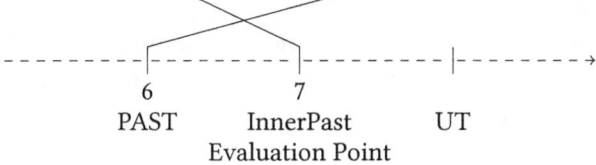

```
--------|---------|---------|-------→
             6           7
           PAST      InnerPast    UT
                  Evaluation Point
```

There is one apparent difference between the Past Perfect in its PPerf function and the Present Perfect. Several authors who regard only the Present Perfect as puzzling support this position by denying that the Past Perfect exhibits a lifetime effect, citing the well-formed sentence

(30) *Einstein had visited Princeton.*

Needless to say, (30) is not a counterexample to the position adopted here since its perfect morphology can denote a PPast. For a lifetime effect we would need a clear PPerf sentence, with PEpt later than Einstein's death. Suppose a famous Russian scientist, after escaping from the Soviet Union, visited Princeton or some other famous Western university in 1960. Suppose further that we had just heard about this event, and we knew that Einstein died in 1955. Would we react to (31) as to the corresponding Present Perfect sentence?

(31) *Einstein has already visited Princeton.* (=(10b))

It sounds pretty unlikely, quite apart from the fact that the function of *already* is unclear. Or, supposing that we knew that Columbus died in 1506, would we be disturbed by (32)?

(32) *In 1510 when the Portuguese conquered Goa, Columbus had already discovered America.*

I find it only slightly more likely that there would be a lifetime effect. I suspect that the explanation for the absence of such an effect in the Past Perfect is that historical knowledge does not have the same impact as knowledge about well-known figures in our own temporal environment.

4 Other Non-Present Perfects

The ambiguity of the Past Perfect is paralled in all non-present perfects. On one reading they are true Perfects, with a PEpt in the Past or future (or Present in infinitivals). On the other reading they denote an Inner Past relative to a Past a modal or an infinitive.

(33) illustrates a mixed perfect morphology *to*-infinitive, (35) an illegitimate conjunction of bare infinitives governed by an epistemic modal, and (34) a similar mixture involving future *will*:

(33) We seem to have already found a suitable candidate #yesterday.[14]

(34) John may have changed his mind since then, and #(have) spoken to the Dean yesterday.[15]

(35) Anne will arrive the day after tomorrow. Everybody else will have already arrived #yesterday, today or tomorrow.

5 Concluding remarks

I have argued that the temporal adverbial in (1) #*I have visited her yesterday* is in conflict with the Present Tense of the sentence. The Tense that such an adverbial is related to can only be a Past. In a Perfect of Result such a temporal adverbial would also share the constraint barring other adverbials that do not modify the result state. In an Experiential Perfect they would impose a specific singular interpretation of the event. Non-Present Perfects in English are ambiguous in the same way as Present Perfects in German and many other languages. I have given examples showing that the two readings of sentences in Non-Present Perfects cannot be mixed in one clause. This applies in formal English; for many speakers, especially American speakers, the line dividing these readings may well

---

[14] The ambiguity of infinitives with perfect morphology was pointed out by Hofmann (1976)

[15] This example sounds better to my ear with repetition of *may* as well as *have*.

be blurred, or they may not have Non-Present Perfects at all. I suspect that the same is true for speakers of German with regard to the Present Perfect.

Bibliography

Dahl, Ö. 1995. The tense system of Swedish. In *Tense systems in European languages*, vol. II, Tübingen: Niemeyer.
Fabricius-Hansen, C. 1994. Das norwegische und dänische Tempussystem im Vergleich mit dem deutschen. In R. Thieroff & J. Ballweg (eds.), *Tense systems in European languages*, Tübingen: Niemyer.
Goodwin, W. W. 1889. *Syntax of the moods and tenses of the Greek verb*. London: Macmillan.
Herweg, Michael. 1990. *Zeitaspekte. Die Bedeutung von Tempus, Aspekt und temporalen Konjunktionen*. Wiesbaden: Deutscher Universitätsverlag.
Hofmann, T. 1976. Past tense replacement and the modal system. In J. D. McCawley (ed.), *Syntax and semantics 7: Notes from the linguistic underground*, 86–100. New York: Academic Press.
Iatridou, S., E. Anagnostopolou & R. Izvorski. 2001. Observations about the form and meaning of the perfect. In M. Kenstowicz (ed.), *Ken Hale: A life in language*, chap. 6. Cambridge, Mass.: MIT Press.
Kamp, H. & U. Reyle. 1993. *From discourse to logic*. Dordrecht: Kluwer.
Katz, G. 2003. A modal account of the present perfect puzzle. In R. Young and Y. Zhou (eds), SALT XIII, 145–161 , Ithaca, NY: Cornell University.
Kiparsky, P. 2002. Event structure and the perfect. In Beaver D. I., L. D. C. Martinez, B. Z. Clark & S. Kaufmann (eds.), *The construction of meaning*, CSLI publications.
Klein, W. 1992. The present perfect puzzle. *Language* 68. 525–552.
Klein, W. 1994. *Time in language*. London: Routledge.
Klein, W. 2000. An analysis of the German perfect. *Language* 76. 358–382.
Löbner, S. 2002. Is the German perfect a perfect perfect. In I. Kaufmann & B. Stiebels (eds.), *More than words: A festschrift for Dieter Wunderlich*, 369–391. Berlin: Akademie Verlag.
McCawley, J. 1981. Notes on the English present perfect. *Australian Journal of Linguistics* 1. 81–90.
Michaelis, L. 1994. The English present perfect. *Journal of Linguistics* 30. 111–158.
Mittwoch, A. 1995. The English perfect, past perfect and future perfect in a neo-reichenbachian framework. In P. M. Bertinetto, V. Bianchi & Ö. Dahl (eds.),

Temporal reference, aspect and actionality: Typological perspectives, vol. 2, 255–267. Torino: Rosenberg and Sellier.

Mittwoch, A. 2008a. Tenses for the living and the dead: Lifetime inferences reconsidered. In S. Rothstein (ed.), *Theoretical and crosslinguistic approaches to the semantics of aspect*, Amsterdam: Benjamins.

Mittwoch, A. 2008b. The English resultative perfect and its relationship to the experiental perfect and the simple past tense. *Linguistics and Philosophy* 31. 323–351.

Pancheva, R. & A. von Stechow. 2004. On the present perfect puzzle. In K. Meulten & M. Wolf (eds.), *Proceedings of NELS 34*, .

Parsons, T. 1990. *Events in the semantics of English. a study in subatomic semantics.* Cambridge/Mass.: MIT Press.

Portner, P. 2003. The (temporal) semantics and (modal) pragmatics of the perfect. *Linguistics and Philosophy* 26. 459–510. Issue 4.

Reichenbach, H. 1947. *Elements of symbolic logic.* London: Collier-Macmillan.

Reyle, U., A. Rossdeutscher & H. Kamp. 2007. Ups and downs in the theory of temporal reference. *Linguistics and Philosophy* 34. 565–635. Issue 5.

Schaden, G. 2009. Present perfects compete. *Linguistics and Philosophy* 32 (2). 115–141.

Vlach, F. 1993. Temporal adverbials, tenses and the perfect. *Linguistics and Philosophy* 16. 231–283.

Author

Anita Mittwoch
English Department
The Hebrew University of Jerusalem
anita.mittwoch@mail.huji.ac.il

Phase quantification and frame Theory

Ralf Naumann

Introduction

In my contribution I will provide an outline of how two major strands in Löbner's work can be combined in a dynamic game-theoretical semantics: phase quantification (PQ) and frame theory (FT). In a first step a formal analysis of PQ in (dynamic) arrow logic is presented. Based on this analysis it is shown in the second step that frame theory must not be understood as being an alternative to standard Tarskian semantics. Rather it must be seen as an *extension* of such a semantics. The extension developed in this contribution combines the formal frame theory developed in Petersen (2007) with the analysis of PQ in arrow logic developed in this paper. In contrast to other dynamic formalisms like Dynamic Predicate Logic, the dynamic aspect is already located in the lexicon. For example, although adjectives like 'late' are basically interpreted as properties of states, they admit in addition of an interpretation where they denote relations between states (or, to be precise, basic frames representing partial descriptions of objects in the sense of Löbner 2012, 2014 and Petersen 2007).

The paper is organized as follows: In sections 1 and 2 the empirical data used by Löbner for his account of PQ as well as counterexamples discussed in Mittwoch (1993) are presented. In section 3 the formal analysis of PQ in Arrow Logic is developed. In the final section it is outlined how this formal analysis can be used to arrive at a satisfying formal theory of frames.

1 Phase quantification as a major module in natural language semantics

According to Löbner (1987, 1989, 1999), quantification in natural language is not restricted to the semantics of noun phrases but applies to a wide range of semantic phenomena including for instance adverbs of quantification like *already* or *still*, intensifiers like *too* and *enough*, scalar adjectives like *few* (*small*) and *many* (*big*) and phasal verbs like *begin, continue* and *stop*. Some examples are given in (1).

(1) a. *He sometimes/always/never manages to be friendly.*
     b. *In China you can buy Coca-Cola somewhere/everywhere/nowhere.*
     c. *The dollar is already/still/not yet/no longer high.*
     d. *This house is big enough/too big for us.*
     e. *In the weather forecast they said it will continue to rain/start raining/stop raining.*

Löbner is aware of the fact that traditionally the above examples are not normally covered by the term 'quantification'. However, according to him, this term nevertheless refers to a seemingly very comprehensive range of phenomena which are syntactically and grammatically rather diverse but semantically closely enough related to form a class of their own (Löbner 1987: 53). Löbner refers to this broadened view of quantification as *phase quantification* (PQ). PQ is characterized by the following five constraints: (i) the interpretation of PQ expressions is always based on a (monotone) scale. This scale is either temporal (the time line in the case of the *already*-group) or non-temporal, i.e. a dimension like width or height (scalar adjectives);[1] (ii) PQ-expressions contain an implicit parameter which models a particular perspective taken by the speaker; (iii) semantically, these expressions take two arguments: a predicate P which defines a positive phase or range of values on the scale and the parameter from (ii); (iv) sentences containing PQ-expressions are about admissible developments which are defined in terms of two adjacent phases (called a "double-phase") on the underlying scale. The two phases differ with respect to the fact of whether the truth conditions imposed by the predicate are satisfied on them (positive) or not (negative); (v) the existence of an admissible development is a presupposition of sentences containing a PQ-expression.

These constraints are best explained by means of an example. Consider *schon* ('already').[2]

---

[1] The use of *schon* is not restricted to temporal uses, as shown by (i).

   (i)   *Basel liegt schon in der Schweiz.*

   Löbner (1987: 81) interprets (i) as follows: "Walk along any relevant path to Basel and you will cross the border of Switzerland."

[2] This use of *schon* is only one of three different uses of this expression distinguished by Löbner; see below for details.

(2) a. *Es ist schon spät.*
    It is already late

  b. *Es ist spät.*
    It is late

In this case the scale is the time line and the parameter point is a temporal reference point t. The logical expression is 'schon(t,late)' and an admissible development (or interval) consists of a phase during which it is not late followed by a second phase during which it is late. The parameter point t is required to fall into the second (positive) phase. Figure 1 is a pictorial representation of an admissible interval. The truth conditions for 'schon(t,P)' are given in (3).

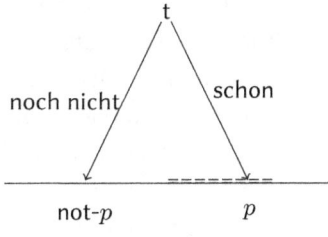

Figure 1

(3) Truth conditions for 'schon(t,P)'

  a. 'schon(t,P)' triggers the presupposition that there is a phase of not-P starting before t and that up to t at most one change between not-P and P occurred.

  b. 'schon(t,P)' is true iff the presupposition in (a) is satisfied and P(t) is true.

  c. 'schon(t,P)' is false iff the presupposition in (a) is satisfied and P(t) is false.

  d. If the presupposition in (a) is not satisfied, 'schon(t,P)' is undefined.

The presuppositions of the *already*-group are displayed in (4), where '⇒' means presupposes.

(4) a. schon p at t ⇒ not p before t

  b. noch p at t ⇒ p before t

  c. noch nicht p at t ⇒ not p before t

In what exactly does the semantic contribution of expressions like *already* consists? Or, more generally, what is the innovative feature of PQ? Let's consider another example.

(5) a. *Das Licht ist an.*
     The light is on.

   b. *Das Licht ist schon   an.*
     The light is already on.

According to Löbner (1999: 51), modifying *spät* with *schon* "adds a sense of temporal dynamics". He comments: "While (5a) is a stative predication about the implicit evaluation time t, sentence (5b) represents the same state as the result of a development from a previous state of affairs with the light not on to the present state with the light now on." The notion of "temporal dynamics" is explained in terms of a presupposition. (5b) presupposes that the light was not on some time before t, i.e. (5a) was false on a relevant interval before t. By contrast, for (5a) no such presupposition is triggered. For Löbner, this has the effect that the meaning of a sentence involving a PQ-expression cannot be reduced to its truth conditions. In addition to the truth conditional dimension such expressions have both a procedural (or dynamic) and a cognitive dimension. Expressions involving phase quantification require information about the way in which the truth conditions came about. Löbner illustrates this view by the following procedural definition of 'schon spät': one starts from within the first (negative) semiphase, no matter where but, say, from its leftmost point. Next, one runs along the scale until one reaches the parameter point, which is required to lie in the double phase, and checks whether one is in the second (positive) semiphase. The conceptual dimension is described by Löbner as follows: in order to process and comprehend a sentence containing a PQ-expression, a speaker has to have the concept of the different admissible cases because otherwise (s)he is not able to mentally process its propositional content. As Löbner (1989: 180) notes: "Making sense of any such sentence means constructing a specific alternative on the basis of the alternative cases as a first step, and only then, as a second step, checking (or registering, or asking, or whatever) which alternative applies."

Empirical evidence for this analysis comes from data like the following (Löbner 1989: 181f.).

(6) a. *Zwei plus zwei ist #schon/#noch vier.*

   b. *Sie ist #schon/#noch nicht jung/Jungfrau.*

c. Sie ist #noch/#nicht mehr alt.

d. Es ist schon/#noch spät.

e. Es ist #schon/noch früh.

Common to all examples in (6) is the fact that it is not possible to construct the required succession of two different phases, either a positive phase followed by a negative one or vice versa. (6a) is an example of an 'eternal' or timeless statement. (6b) and (6c) show that for temporally contingent statements, all irreversible states are incompatible with the perspective presupposed by *noch*, and conversely *schon* excludes those states which cannot be preceded by a contrary state. (6d) and (6e) are not admissible because the underlying scale is ordered by *früh* < *spät*. From this it follows that there is no phase of lateness preceding *früh* and no phase of earliness following *spät*. Thus, for both sentences the presupposition is not satisfied.

Löbner (1989: 182) hypothesizes that the sentences in (6) are refuted *already at a level of conceptual analysis which precedes any reference to actual situations*. To quote Löbner: "To put it in terms of the analysis suggested: in these cases we know by the very conceptual content of the sentence that the set of admissible cases is degenerate." (Löbner 1989: 182)

1.1 Standard quantification and phase quantification

In contrast to Generalized Quantifier Theory (GQT), Löbner analyzes standard quantifiers like *all* or *some* not solely in terms of set-theoretic relations. For example, on the GQT view the meaning of a quantifier Q(P) can be described as follows: Q(P) is true just in case P is an element of the denotation of Q. This view is criticized by Löbner on the following ground: "Such a picture is natural in a semantic framework which has in view the truth conditions of sentences and does not consider the way truth or falsity comes about." (Löbner 1987: 79) The advantage of a procedural semantics is primarily seen in the fact that it provides criteria to choose among alternative formulations of truth conditions which are equivalent when viewed from their results but not from the way they come about.

Standard quantifiers can be analyzed as an instance of phase quantification in the following way. Using the fact that quantifiers live on their domain of quantification, it follows that no other elements of the domain are relevant for the evaluation procedure. If one assumes in addition that the domain of quantification is finite, it is possible to define a linear order on the elements the quantifier lives on so that those elements which have a certain property (say the property of being human) come first. If defined in this way, the sentence *Some A are P* is analyzed similarly to a sentence with *schon*: "start with elements of A for which P does not hold (if there are any), run through A, and you will eventually enter P, or, shorter, A reaches into P" (Löbner 1987: 81). In Löbner (1987) this idea of relating standard quantification to phase quantification is made more precise in terms of semantic automata.

1.2 Phase quantification and semantic automata

In Van Benthem (1986) the following two theorems are proved (see also Sevenster 2006 for details).

(7) a. The first-order definable quantifiers are precisely those which can be recognized by permutation-invariant acyclic finite state machines.

b. The first-order additively definable quantifiers are precisely those which can be recognized by push-down automata.

In the second theorem first-order additive logic is first-order logic extended with the ternary + relation and two constants *a* and *b*. The constant *a* is interpreted as the number of zeros and *b* as the number of ones. Formulas in this extension of FOL, then, are statements from standard arithmetic. According to these theorems, quantifiers like *all*, *some* or *at least* are recognized by acyclic finite state automata whereas quantifiers like *an even number of* require for their recognition finite state automata with loops. The relation to natural language semantics is described by Van Benthem (1986: 151) as follows: "Viewed procedurally, the quantifier has to decide which truth value to give when presented with an enumeration of the individuals in the universe of discourse marked for their (non-)membership of A and B." Below in Figures 2 and 3 the two automata for computing *all* and *some* are depicted.

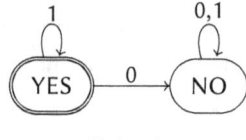

Figure 2

By unfolding such an automaton, one gets a tree (assuming that there is a unique initial state) of possible runs (or computations) (see e. g. Khoussainov &

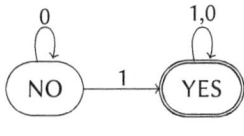

Figure 3

Nerode 2001 and Hollenberg 1998 for details). The automaton begins its run at the initial state, which is the root of the tree, and proceeds until it either reaches an accepting or a refuting state. Thus, edges of the tree correspond to possible moves (or behaviour) of the automaton while reading the input.

A relation between semantic automata and PQ is established by Löbner (1987: 82) in the following way. The automata in Figures 2 and 3 can be considered as representing a simple notion of border-crossing, either from p to not-p or from not-p to p. The automaton for *all* can also be used for representing *noch* ('still'): "Start from a given, contextually determined point t' where p holds (e. g. p = früh with YES the accepting state) and keep to it as long as you stay in p, but change irreversibly to the refuting state NO as soon as you encounter a time at which not-p holds, (e. g. at which it is no longer early)." However, as conceded by Löbner, these automata fail to capture the presupposition triggered by elements of the *schon*-group. He suggests that presuppositions can be modeled by indeterministic automata that are defined for the relevant input only, yielding no truth value (i. e. neither true nor false) if the presupposition is not satisfied. One formal possibility of defining this idea, alluded to by Löbner (1987: 83), consists in defining presuppositions as additional automata that are 'inserted' as subroutines into automata like those in the two figures above, calculating the truth value of a corresponding sentence.

2 Some problems for phase quantification

There are a number of critical points that can be put forward against Löbner's arguments for PQ. First, as observed by several authors, there are empirical counterexamples to central claims of PQ. On the theoretical side one has to mention that so far Löbner has never tried to formalize the above ideas, except for the short comparison to the concept of semantic automata explained above in section 1.2, and that the relation between SQ and PQ is not as neat as Löbner takes it.

2.1 Empirical adequacy

Mittwoch (1993) noted that there are obvious empirical counterexamples to the presuppositions in (4).

(8) a. *He/she is already rich.*
 b. *The easy movement of the couplet is already there.*
 c. *The Smiths have had a baby girl; they already have two sons.*

These examples show that the existence of a negative phase is not a necessary condition for *schon* (or 'already') to be admissible. (8a) can be used in a situation in which a baby is born who has come into an inheritance at birth. (8b) is appropriate to express a verdict about a poet's very first work. Finally, what makes *already* appropriate in (8c) is not the existence of a phase in which the Smiths had no children, but rather the contrast between the situation in which they only had two sons and the present situation (Mittwoch 1993: 75). According to Mittwoch (1993: 75), (6a) and (6b) are unacceptable solely due to the pragmatic meaning of *schon* or *already*. This meaning involves temporal comparison of some kind. Whereas in (8a) it is comparison with some norm: one can be richer earlier than other people who attain riches, the state of being young referred to in (6b) starts at birth for everybody. Similar counter-examples can be found for the pair *noch nicht* and *noch*.

(9) a. *Peters Augen waren noch nicht braun, als er geboren wurde.*
 b. *# Peters Augen waren noch blau, als er geboren wurde.*

As noted by Mittwoch (1993: 76), there is a striking difference in acceptability between (9a) and (9b). If (9a) were simply a case of inner negation of *noch*, it should be as odd as (9b). However, (9b) is odd precisely because it suggests that Peter had blue eyes before his birth, which, though undoubtedly true, is irrelevant. This implication is rather due to the presupposition of *noch*. By contrast, (9a) lacks this implication. As a consequence, there is no need to speculate about the prenatal colour of Peter's eyes. Mittwoch concludes that the combination of *noch nicht* is not normally fully compositional and that it lacks the presuppositional meaning component of *noch*. Sentences with 'noch nicht' do not require a preceding phase of not-p. However, as noted by Mittwoch (1993: 76), there are counter-examples to (9b).

(10) a. *Als Taschenrechner neu auf den Markt kamen, waren sie noch ziemlich teuer.*

b. *Als Taschenrechner neu auf den Markt kamen, kosteten sie noch 400 DM.*

A third set of counterexamples concerns the second and third type of uses of 'schon' distinguished by Löbner.

(11) a. *Peter hat schon drei Seiten gelesen.*

   b. *Peter hat drei Seiten gelesen.*

In this use *schon* focuses on a time-dependent predicate. For example, in (11a) the predicate in focus is *drei Seiten* and indicates the amount of text read so far by Peter (Löbner 1999: 48). According to Löbner, the amount of material read at the parameter point t is a time-dependent function f. The meaning of (11a) can then be paraphrased as 'at t, f is already three pages'. When viewed as an instance of PQ, the predicate p is 'f is three pages'. Reading being a cumulative process (the amount of material read increases continuously with time), the negation of p, not-p, is equivalent to 'f is less than three pages'. Thus, if p is true, then there is a (negative) phase preceding the phase at which p is true at which not-p is true. However, exactly the same argument is true for the unmodified sentence (11b).

In the third type of use distinguished by Löbner, the time adverbial in focus specifies the normally implicit evaluation time t_n.

(12) a. *Peter war schon gestern da.*

   b. *Peter war gestern da, ja er war (sogar) schon die ganze Woche da.*

Similarly to the case of (11a), the admissibility of (12a) does not require a preceding phase of not-p, as shown by the example (12b).

2.2 The relation between standard quantification and phase quantification

Löbner's claim that standard quantification involving *all* or *some* is similar to proper PQ is open to criticism. First, there is an asymmetry between the standard (FOL) quantifiers *all* and *some* on the one hand and modifiers like *schon* and *noch* on the other. For example, whereas *some* only requires there to be an element that is in the denotation of A and of B, *schon* requires something stronger: in addition to 'late(t)', there must be a(n initial) preceding phase in the given admissible interval where 'late(t)' is false. Thus, for *all* and *some* there is only one way of how the truth conditions can be brought about. For *all*, one has to show for all elements of the domain (or a given context set) that they satisfy a particular condition (say, being mortal if being human). In the case of *some* one gets: find some element which satisfies the property. In this respect the quantifiers are similar to unmodified *late*, which requires only a simple test to show either its truth or falsity at a given point in time. It is only by modifying this adjective with *already* (or *still* in the case of *early*) that one gets "a sense of dynamic development". By contrast, this component is absent in the case of the two quantifiers. Second, in contrast to cases involving elements of the *schon* group there is in general no presupposition in the case of quantifiers. For both *All humans are mortal* and *Some students come from Italy*, there are no corresponding sentences that can be said to 'add a sense of dynamics' triggering a presupposition similar to that of *schon* in the case of *schon spät*. Thus, there are no pairs corresponding to *Es ist spät* und *Es ist schon spät*. Rather, quantified sentences simply correspond to the unmodified form of *spät*.[3] Third, Löbner's assumption that the domain of quantification can always be linearly ordered in such a way that elements having a certain property, say coming from Italy, are first in the ordering is artificial and, as admitted by Löbner, violates the condition of permutational invariance (i. e. the truth of a quantified sentence is not dependent on a particular order on the domain of quantification) for those quantifiers.[4]

3 An alternative interpretation of phase quantification

If there really is any concept of phase quantification, it must be possible to analyze standard quantification and phase quantification as instances of a general quantificational scheme. I will suggest, building on results from Van Benthem & Alechina (1997), that there is indeed such a general scheme.

3.1 Quantifiers as modal operators

In GQT, a monadic generalized quantifier Q is interpreted as a set of subsets of the domain in such a way that in a model M the formula $Qx\phi$ is true just in case the set of elements which satisfy ϕ belongs to the interpretation of the quantifier. For the existential quantifier one gets that it is interpreted as the set of all non-empty subsets of the domain D underlying M. Similarly, the universal quantifier

---

[3] See below for details on this point.

[4] From this it does not follow that the property of being ordered is cognitively unimportant, as shown by the following example. In a paper-and-pencil experiment Szymanik & Zajenkowski (2010) showed that on ordered domains processing sentences with the quantifier *most* is easier than on unordered domains. The reaction times of people participating in the experiment were significantly faster if the domain was ordered compared to the same sentence on unordered domains.

Phase quantification and frame Theory

is interpreted as the singleton set containing only D. As shown in Van Benthem & Alechina (1997), quantifiers can also be interpreted as a special form of modal operators. Consider the Tarskian truth condition for the existential quantifier (for $\alpha = d$ or $\alpha = y$, $\alpha^{\rightarrow}$ is a sequence of objects or variables, respectively).

(13) $M, [d^{\rightarrow}/y^{\rightarrow}] \models \exists x \phi(x, y^{\rightarrow})$ iff there exists a $d \in D$ with
$M, [d/x, d^{\rightarrow}/y^{\rightarrow}] \models \phi(x, y^{\rightarrow})$

(13) is an instance of the more general scheme (14).

(14) $M, [d^{\rightarrow}/y^{\rightarrow}] \models \diamond_x \phi(x, y^{\rightarrow})$ iff there is a $d \in D$ with
$R(d, d^{\rightarrow}) \wedge M, [d/x, d^{\rightarrow}/y^{\rightarrow}] \models \phi(x, y^{\rightarrow})$

The difference between (13) and (14) is the following. In (14), the element d is required to stand in the relation R to the sequence $d^{\rightarrow}$, where R is an n-ary relation on the domain D so that D can be taken as structured. By contrast, in (13) one has the special case of a flat individual domain admitting of "random access", where R is the universal relation. In view of this, (13) and (14) can also be formulated as (15a) and (15b), where R is a binary relation between elements of D and finite sequences from D.

(15) a. $M, v \models \exists x \phi(x)$ iff there exists a variable assignment v' which differs from v at most in its assignment of a value to x s.t. $M, v' \models \phi(x)$.

b. $M, v \models \diamond_x \phi(x, y_1, \ldots, y_n)$ iff there exists a variable assignment v' which differs from v at most in its assignment of a value to x s.t. $R(v'(x), v'(y_1), \ldots, v'(y_n))$ and $M, v' \models \phi(x, y_1, \ldots, y_n)$ where $y_1, \ldots, y_n$ are all (and just the) free variables of $\diamond_x \phi$ listed in alphabetic order.

Even (15b) can be generalized to (15c) where not only unary but n-ary modal operators are considered.

(15) c. $M, v \models \diamond_{x1, \ldots, xm} \phi(x_1, \ldots, x_m; y_1, \ldots, y_n)$ iff there exists a variable assignment v' which differs from v at most in its assignment of a value to $x_1, \ldots, x_m$ s.t. $R(v'(x), \ldots, v'(x_m); v'(y_1), \ldots, v'(y_n))$ and $M, v' \models \phi(x_1, \ldots, x_m, y_1, \ldots, y_n)$ where $y_1, \ldots, y_n$ are all (and just the) free variables of $\diamond_x \phi$ listed in alphabetic order.

Van Benthem & Alechina (1997: 1) comment: "When generalized quantifiers are viewed as first-order operators binding first-order variables, it becomes clear that a variable bound by a generalized quantifier cannot in general take any possible value. Its range is restricted, and this restriction can be defined using an accessibility relation."

In (15a) the value of the variable x does not depend on the values of other variables, or, in terms of elements of the domain, the value of x can be chosen independently of the choice of the value of any other variable. In this respect 'late' is similar to the existential and the universal quantifier.

(16) $\exists t.late(t)$

However, in contrast to the two standard quantifiers, its interpretation is non-relational in the sense that no dependencies between or accessibility to other time points need to be taken into account. If 'late' is modified by 'already', the perspective changes. One is no longer interested in the property 'late' being simply true at a parameter point t_0, say at speech time. Rather, the interest is restricted to those developments leading up to t_0 such that the truth value of 'late' is distributed on those developments in a particular way determined by 'already'. Thus, one switches from a non-relational to a relational perspective on which not only single points but relations between points (or points and sequences of points) are taken into consideration. The first main thesis now is (17).

(17) Thesis I: The general format for PQ is the quantificational scheme in (15c).

(17) raises the question of what semantic and cognitive restrictions can be put on the accessibility relation R. From what has been said it follows that there are at least two different layers (or dimensions).

(18) a. non-relational: static
 b. relational : dynamic

Consequently, there are basically three types of relations that can be relevant.

(19) a. relations at the static level
 b. relations at the dynamic level
 c. relations between the static and the dynamic level

Relations of type (19c) can be used for zooming in the sense of Blackburn & De Rijke (1997) and Finger & Gabbay (1992). On this perspective, the non-relational layer is used to provide information about the relational layer. At the relational level, objects can be seen as atomic objects with no internal structure, except for those structures that can be defined in terms of relations between those objects,

i. e. in terms of relations of type (19b). By contrast, by using relations of type (19c), objects of the relational layer are described in a more fine-grained way by objects of a different sort.

In the context of *already* and *still* the domain D can be taken to be two-sorted, consisting of a sort of states and a sort of sequences of states.[5] For temporal uses of *already* and *still* the sort of states can be taken to be time points and the sort of sequences are intervals. For spatial uses, as in *Basel liegt schon in der Schweiz*, states are (spatial) points in the topological sense and the sort of sequences consists of paths. The two different sorts can be related in different ways. For example, in the temporal case, 13 possible relations, including equality, during and after, can be distinguished for two different intervals. For time points, there are three different relations: *before, equal* and *after*. Finally, and most importantly, in the present context, there are five relations that can hold between a point and an interval: *before, beginning point, during, ending point* and *after*. In the case of *already* and *still* there are three different types of relations one is interested in. At the level of intervals, the required relation is *meet*. For the relation between points and intervals the two relations are *during* and *ending point*.

For each sort, there is a particular logic (or language) to talk about elements of the domain and relations holding between those elements. In addition, and most importantly, it must be possible to define relations between the two layers. The two layers are connected by two types of shifting operations (see e. g. De Rijke 1994), corresponding to the two possible types of relations in (19c).

(20)   a.   static level → dynamic level: modes (i. e. non-relational properties are analyzed in a 'wider' context, e. g. by describing how they 'develop' on a scale)

         b.   dynamic level → static level: projections (one passes from a relational view to the evaluation at a particular point)

A possible choice for the relational layer is Arrow Logic (Van Benthem 1994)[6]. The basic operation of Arrow Logic is the following composition operation.

(21) Cx, yzx is a 'composition' of y and z (or, alternatively, x can be 'decomposed' into y and z)

The basic modal operator of an appropriate modal propositional language for expressing properties of (sets of) arrows is •, whose satisfaction condition is (22).

---

[5] See Balbiani et al. (2011) and the two appendices for details.

[6] See Appendix A for details.

(22) $M, x \models \phi \bullet \psi$ iff there exist y, z with Cx, yz and $M, y \models \phi$ and $M, z \models \psi$

Having the notion of an arrow together with the possibility of modeling in addition the internal structure of arrows in terms of other sorts of objects, makes it possible to use this notion as a generalization for different types of objects, in particular for Löbner's notion of a phase. Three examples are given in (23).

(23) temporal: intervals
spatial (topological) : physical path
conceptual: property

What type of second layer is used depends on the kind of objects that is modeled by an arrow. For example, in the case of properties only a beginning and an end point are distinguished without any internal structure. Next, I will illustrate this two-layered architecture by analyzing *already*.

The composition operation C can be used to decompose an arrow into two arrows which are sequentially related to each other (relation of type (19b)). Thus, x in (22) is an admissible interval as defined by Löbner, whereas y and z are the two adjacent phases into which this interval can be split. Using C and the relation D (defined in the appendix), 'already' can be defined as (26a). If $p =$ 'late', one gets (24b).

(24) a. $M, s \models already(p)$ iff there are x, y, z s.t.
  (i) Cx, yz,
  (ii) $D(z, s)$,
  (iii) $M, y \models M, y \models Int(G \neg p)$ and
  (iv) $M, z \models Int(Gp)$
 b. $M, s \models already(late)$ iff there are x, y, z s.t.
  (i) Cx, yz,
  (ii) $D(z, s)$,
  (iii) $M, y \models M, y \models Int(G \neg (late))$ and
  (iv) $M, z \models Int(G(late))$

According to (24b), 'already late' is true at a parameter point s just in case s belongs to an arrow (phase) z which is the right part of an arrow x s.t. during z 'late' is constantly true (with the possible exception of the left point) and during the left part y of x 'late' is constantly false (again with the possible exception of the left point). As it stands, (24) is not quite satisfactory. For example, it does not account for a sentence like (25), since in this case there is no phase before the parameter point during which 'not rich' holds.

(25)   Er war schon reich, als er geboren wurde.

This shortcoming can be remedied by using the weak Until-operator. This operator is compatible with the fact that its second argument, here p, constantly holds on the first phase. As a consequence, no border crossing needs to be involved.

(26) $M, s \models already(p)$ iff there are x, y, z s.t. (i) Cx, yz, (ii) $D(z, s)$, (iii) $M, y \models M, y \models Int(\neg pWp)$ and (iv) $M, z \models Int(Gp)$

(26) still makes an assertion about what holds after the parameter point so that *already* has a futurate meaning, which is empirically not adequate (see Löbner 1989 for arguments and details). In this case one requires that the parameter point has to be the end point of the second phase.

(27) $M, s \models already(p)$ iff there is an x s.t. (i) $RP(x, s)$ and (ii) $M, x \models Int(\neg pWp) \bullet Int(Gp)$

Thus, on the present account, *already* and *still* semantically function as lifts (or shifts), i.e. they lift non-relational properties to relational ones. The semantic, or truth-conditional, effect of this lift consists in evaluating a static property not only with respect to a single state but with respect to a sequence of states of which this state is an element.

From what has been said so far it may seem that the relation between the two standard quantifiers and *already* and *still* has been lost. In order to show that this view is not correct, I will begin by considering the semantic automata from section (1.2) again.

3.2   Safety and liveness properties

There is another way of looking at the automata in Figure 2 and Figure 3. In the case of *all* and *still* the "border crossing" leads to a fail state or non-accepting state, i.e. the sentence is false. Thus, this state must not be attained after the automaton started at the initial state. By contrast, for *some* and *already* the border crossing is necessary in order to prove (the truth of) the sentence. Generalizing this observation, one gets:

- a property constantly holds (no "bad" thing happens)   *all, still*
- a property which (possibly) fails to hold during an initial phase eventually comes to hold after some time (a "good" thing happens)   *some, already*

No such border crossing is involved in the case of unmodified *late* (or *early*) because it is a non-relational property. The above two kinds of properties can be defined in Temporal Logic.

A *safety* property is a property stating that "something bad does never happen." These properties are expressed by formulas of the form (28).

(28) $\psi \to G\phi$

In (28) ϕ is a propositional formula, i. e., a formula that does not contain any temporal operators. Intuitively, a safety property says that ϕ constantly or invariantly holds. If $\psi \equiv true$, (28) is reduced to (29).

(29) $G\phi$

A *liveness* property states that "something good will happen". These properties can be defined by (30).

(30) $\psi \to F\phi$

If in (30) $\psi = \neg\phi$, a border crossing occurs. Similarly to safety properties, ϕ must not contain any temporal operators. Not all properties are safety or liveness properties. It is possible to combine the two kinds. An example is given in (31), assuming that W is taken as basic.

(31) $\psi \cup \phi \equiv (\psi W \phi) \wedge F\phi$

In (31) $\psi \cup \phi$ is a safety property whereas $F\phi$ is a liveness property.

Anticipating the discussion in section (3.4), one can say that combinations of safety and liveness properties, in particular if they involve the Until-operator, can be used to express dependence relations because they either say that a property is invariant (over a certain interval) or that its value has changed after some phase during which it didn't hold. They therefore admit to view a property not only at a particular point (or state), i. e. in isolation, but to consider it in a broader context in which its relation to other the valuation at other states is taken into account as well.

3.3 Standard quantifiers as operations on scales

Recall that type $\langle 1 \rangle$ quantifiers in natural language live on a set A (Peters & Westerstahl 2006: 89).

(32) If Q is a type $\langle 1 \rangle$ quantifier, M a universe and A any set, then Q_M 'lives on' A iff, for all $B \subseteq M$, one has $Q_M(B) \leftrightarrow Q_M(A \cap B)$.

This property is a characteristic trait of restricted quantifiers. If Q_M lives on A, knowing for any subset B of M whether or not the quantifier holds of it reduces to looking at those elements of B which also belong to A. For type $\langle 1, 1 \rangle$ quantifiers like *all* or *some*, it is possible to freeze the restriction argument as follows (Peters & Westerståhl 2006: 110).

(33) If Q is any type $\langle 1, 1 \rangle$ quantifier, and A is any set, the type $\langle 1 \rangle$ quantifier Q^A is defined, for all M and all $B \subseteq M$, by $(Q^A)_M(B) \leftrightarrow Q_{A \cup M}(A, B)$.

The effect of freezing is to reduce a type $\langle 1, 1 \rangle$ quantifier to a type $\langle 1 \rangle$ quantifier. By holding the restrictor argument constant (or frozen), it becomes possible to view it as a scale with respect to which elements of B (or $A \cap B$ due to the property of living on) can be checked, whether they satisfy the required property or not. On this scale, either a 'good' thing happens or no 'bad' thing happens. In particular, one gets (34), where p is the property corresponding to the set B.

(34)   a. $\forall : Gp$ (safety property: no border crossing)

       b. $\exists : Fp$ (liveness property: border crossing)

We are now able to characterize the similarities and differences between the various forms of phase quantification.

(35) Thesis II: Common to all types of phase quantification is the fact that the truth conditions can be defined in terms of combinations of safety- and liveness properties of sequences or, more generally, arrows.

The various types differ in at least the following two respects.

- The standard quantifiers $\forall$ and $\exists$ are always defined.[7]
- The standard quantifiers $\forall$ and $\exists$ are permutation invariant.

As I will now show, these two differences are not independent of each other. As was shown in section (2.1), *already* does not require that there be an initial phase during which $\neg p$ holds (36a). However, it is admissible only if this possibility exists, at least theoretically (36b,c). Similarly, *still* imposes the condition that p eventually becomes false, otherwise it, too, is not admissible (37).

(36)   a.   *Er war schon reich, als er geboren wurde.*

       b.   # *Das Auto ist schon neu.*

       c.   # *Es ist schon früh.*

---

[7] Possible counterexamples are empty restrictor sets as in 'All unicorns are tall'.

(37) a. # *Er war noch alt, als er starb.*

b. # *Es ist noch spät.*

These constraints are not imposed by the two standard quantifiers. For example, ∃ is compatible with the fact that all elements of the domain have the property expressed by p, i.e. one has Gp for all enumerations x. By contrast, if Gp holds for all xs, then *already* is not admissible. This difference can be explained if one considers the differences with respect to the cognitive significance of (combinations of) safety and liveness properties. This difference is the topic of the next section.

3.4 The cognitive significance of phase quantification

When viewed from the point of view of cognitive linguistics, the most important question with respect to modifiers like 'already' and 'still' is: what do they add in addition to the simple assertion that p holds at the parameter point t? What are the consequences in processing the modified sentence in the brain? Only getting the information that it is late at the parameter point, solely conveys information about that particular point. It does neither give him/her information about what happened before nor about what is likely to happen afterwards with respect to the property of being late. Thus, there is an epistemic or informational uncertainty for the comprehender about what happened before t and about what is likely to happen after t with respect to the truth value of 'late'. Such information is not provided by (unmodified) 'late'.

What is the cognitive relevance (significance) of resolving such epistemic uncertainties? First, there is a gain in the amount of information the comprehender gets. For example, (s)he not only knows that it is late at the parameter point but that during some interval (phase) before that point it was not late. Second, this gain in information can be used for strategic planning or to revise and adapt one's current projections (or expectations) of how a discourse (or a piece of communication) will continue. Simplifying somewhat, one can summarize the cognitive function of 'already' and 'still' as follows: resolving epistemic uncertainties allows a comprehender to eliminate certain possibilities of how a result came about or how it will continue to hold or develop. This helps reducing both processing and memory load during semantically parsing a sentence in the brain. Let's consider the examples in (38), some of which have been discussed before.

(38) a. *Peter verfügt über ein Millionenvermögen. Er wurde schon reich geboren.*

b. *The Smiths have had a baby girl. They already have two sons.*

c. # *Es ist schon früh.*

d. # *Es ist noch spät.*

When a comprehender comes to know that Peter is rich, he does not know how he acquired his riches.[8] The second sentence in (40a) provides additional information. He might have inherited his money from his parents or some other source. A possible, though defeasible, conclusion that can be derived from this additional information is: probably, his riches are not due to his own achievements. An analogous argument applies to (40b). Upon learning that the Smiths have had a baby girl, I don't know how many children they have. Or, to put it in game-theoretical terms: I don't know the exact number of children in the "Smiths having children" game. In the case of (40c) and (40d) composition of the corresponding game with another game does not result in a gain of information or a reduction in epistemic uncertainty. For example, if it is early in the morning at the parameter point, then it has been early for all other points belonging to the interval denoted by 'this morning' preceding the parameter point. As a consequence, no new information is provided about how this state came about so that this information is redundant at the cognitive level.

Thus, after lifting 'late' to a relational property, its truth value at the parameter point t_0 depends on the truth value assigned to this property on a sequence (or arrow) the end point of which is t_0, or, to put it differently, only those assignments of the value 'true' to the property at t_0 are admissible that also have $y_k = false$ for $1 \leqslant k \leqslant m$ and $y_j = true$ for $m + 1 \leqslant j \leqslant n$ for some m with n the length of the sequence and t_0 being one of the y_j. Thus, the value of t_0 ($true$ in this case) is dependent on the values of the sequence $y^\rightarrow : R(x, y^\rightarrow)$. On this perspective, elements of the *already*-group not only lift a non-relational property to a relational one, but, in addition, they exclude some possible relations. As an effect, the relation R must not be the universal one, i.e. admit of random access, because in that case no (new) information would be added by triggering this lift.

By contrast, for the standard quantifiers, the cognitive relevance does not consist in eliminating epistemic uncertainty but rather in establishing (or building up) relations between the values of different attributes which have been learned in encounters with the world. They express relations between the values of *different* properties, whereas *already* and *still* express relations between the value of a

---

[8] Of course, one has to assume that the comprehender does not already have information about this point of Peter's life. Otherwise, he would get no new information.

single property at *different* states. Therefore, it does not matter whether the domain is ordered and whether some ways of bringing about the truth are excluded. These constraints only apply if a single property is viewed at different states. The above considerations are summarized in the table below.

	type of property	relation
late	atomic	non-relational
all	safety	relation between values of different properties
some	liveness	
still(late)	combination of safety and liveness	relation between the values of a single property at different states
already (late)	combination of safety and liveness	

Table 1

The property of border crossing refers to the type of property. Safety properties forbid such a border crossing, whereas (combinations of) safety and liveness properties require it. For atomic properties, the concept of border crossing does not apply.

4 Phase quantification and frame Theory

In this final section I will relate the analysis of Section 3 to the frame theory that is being developed in the CRC 991 'The Structure of Representations' at the University of Düsseldorf, the huge and international project led by Sebastian Löbner. This theory will henceforth be called the Düsseldorf Frame Model. Following Barsalou (1992), Löbner (2014) argues for the following two claims: (i) the human cognitive system operates with *one* general format of representations and (ii) if the human cognitive system operates with one general format of representations, this format is essentially a Barsalou frame. This Barsalou-Löbner Frame-Hypothesis (BLFH) requires a frame model that is sufficiently expressive to capture the diversity of representations and that is sufficiently precise and restrictive in order to be testable. Given these two constraints, it follows that the gap between cognitive linguistics, brain science and formal semantics has to be filled (Naumann & Petersen 2013). A formalization of the BLFH was presented in Petersen (2007). In this formalization linguistic items, or the concepts expressed by them, like sortal nouns, say *bottle* or *dog*, are modeled as typed feature structures (see Petersen 2007 for details). For example, a possible frame for the sortal noun 'bottle' is given in Figure 4 (this figure is taken from Gamerschlag et al. 2014, see Löbner 2014 for the reference).

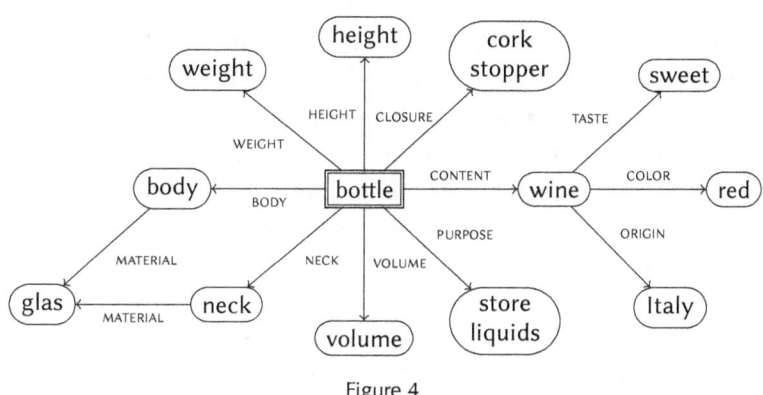

Figure 4

According to Löbner (2014), such a frame is a parameterized description of an object. The basic building blocks are attribute-value pairs. Attributes are functions which are defined for a certain type of possessor and which assign to every possessor of the appropriate type a unique value from a set of admissible values. For example, the attribute COLOR assigns possible colour values to the objects of type 'visible (monochrome) object'. In the specific bottle example above, the attribute CONTENT specifies that the bottle contains wine whose origin is Italy (value of the attribute ORIGIN) and which tastes sweet (value of the attribute TASTE). Value specifications can be more or less specific, depending either on the amount of information that is available about the object or on the level of abstraction at which the object is described. Frames like that in Figure 4 can be taken as representing an atemporal or static (partial) snapshot of a bottle. What is not captured is the possibility that the value of an attribute may eventually be changed, say as the effect of an action or an event, or simply by the passing of time.

In Naumann (2013) frames in the Düsseldorf Frame Model were called Petersen Frames. They were formalized as pointed Kripke-models in the following way.

Given a signature $\langle P, Attr \rangle$, a Petersen Frame Model (PFM) is a triple as given in (39).

(39) $\langle S, \{R_a\}_{a \in Attr}, s_0, V \rangle$ with
- S a (non-empty) set of nodes (or states), the domain of the model,
- each R_a is a (functional) binary relation on S,
- V is a valuation function that assigns to each $p \in P$ a subset of S,
- s_0 is the central node of the frame.

An example of a language for talking about PFMs is an extended modal language (see Naumann 2013 and Naumann & Petersen 2013 for details). However, this formalization of frames raises at least the following two serious issues: (i) if frames can be reduced to a particular type of feature structures, what is *specific* about a theory of frames, or, to put it differently, is there really a *genuine* theory of frames, and (ii) in what exactly does the cognitive significance of frames lie?

From the perspective of the approach developed in Section 3, the situation can be analyzed as follows. In previous formalizations of the BLFH only the truth-conditional dimension of frames has been taken into consideration. However, if truth conditions are taken as primary, the semantic value of a lexical item is reduced to (or is completely determined by) its contribution to the truth conditions of sentences.[9] For example, in standard Tarskian semantics, the meaning of an expression in formal semantics is usually identified with the (constant) contribution it makes to the truth conditions of sentences in which it occurs. For example, intransitive verbs like *run* or adjectives like *late* or *cool* denote sets of entities like persistent objects (*run*) or time points (*late*). By contrast, in a dynamic setting like Dynamic Predicate Logic (DPL), expressions are interpreted as (generalized) relations between (information) states.

(40) $\lambda x \lambda s \lambda s'. \|Expr\|(x)(s)(s')$

However, in DPL atomic predicates like 'run' or 'late' are interpreted as tests, i. e. the input and the output state are identical so that their meaning can be reduced to that in a static (standard) Tarskian framework.

(41) $\lambda x \lambda s \lambda s'. \|Expr\|(x)(s)(s') \wedge s = s'$

In the formal framework developed in section 3 adjectives like *late* or *coo* are basically analyzed as properties of states (or time points). As a consequence,

---

[9] Thus, the additional meaning components do not consists in intersentential relations (anaphora) as in DRT or Dynamic Predicate Logic.

their meaning can be identified with the contribution they make to the meaning (truth conditions) of a sentence in which they occur. However, given the way modifiers like *already* and *still* are analyzed in section 3, those adjectives are usually interpreted in a higher or lifted type. Intuitively, at this level the meaning corresponds to what Löbner calls an admissible interval. Using the distinction between a static and a dynamic component, the question becomes: how can a static component be integrated into a dynamic one?

One way of arriving at such an integration or combination consists in using the technique of combining systems (Finger & Gabbay 1992, De Rijke 1994). In such frameworks a global and a local component (layer) are distinguished. Models have the form $M = \langle S_g, \ldots \rangle$ with the global component given by the '...'. The set S_g represents the local component. S_g is a set $\{m_i\}_{i \in I}$. Each m_i can itself be a model, and thus having a complex structure. In the setting of the Düsseldorf Frame Model the local layer, i.e. S_g, corresponds to the static dimension and therefore consists of a set of PFMs, which captures atemporal snapshots of an object or entity. The global component models the dynamic layer and is given by the arrow-models from section 3. The global-local distinction is paralleled by a (possible) distinction with respect to the languages (or logics) that are used to talk about the two layers (De Rijke 1994: 174). First, there is a global language which talks about global aspects of the structure but not about local ones. Second, there is a local language which is used to describe elements of S_g.

For PQ, a combined model can be defined as follows.

(42) A Dynamic Frame Model (DFM) is a triple $\langle \{P_f\}_{f \in F}, R, AS \rangle$ such that
- the elements of P_g are PFMs[10],
- AS is an arrow structure which is used to describe how the objects denoted by elements of P_g change,
- R is a relation on $P_g \times A \times P_g$ which combines the local with the global layer. Intuitively, $(m, x, m') \in R$ if 'executing' an arrow in input m results in m' as output[11],
- values of attributes in a PFM represent the values of a properties of a possessor before a change occurred. PFMs are static in the sense that only the contribution to the truth conditions of sentences is captured.

---

[10] The domain of Petersen frame models will be ordered by a subsumption relation (see Carpenter 1992 for details).

[11] There will in general be constraints imposed on R. For example, for a pair (m, x), $R(m, x)$ is required to be a singleton.

A PFM is a partial description of an object and this description is true at a parameter point just in case the object exhibits the values of those properties expressed by attributes in the PFM.
- a DMF represents the evolution of a property (or a set of properties) of an object with respect to a particular dimension (or a set of dimensions) and is therefore relational.

In the context of PQ, examples for arrow models are
- events or actions which change the value of a property (or the values of a set of properties) of an object.
- the flow (or passage) of time. On this perspective, arrows can be taken as time intervals.
- physical paths connecting regions (or points) in space (or space-time).

Arrows are a separate domain of the model and must therefore not be identified with binary relations on the domain S_g. Thus, one has $(m, x, m') \neq (m, x', m')$ if $x \neq x'$. By contrast, were R be defined as a binary relation on S_g, one would have $(m, m') = (m, m')$, which trivially holds.

So far no constraints have been imposed on the relation R, i.e. R can be an arbitrary relation on $P_g \times A \times P_g$. A first, and obvious, constraint imposes the correct core frame-semantical meaning. For example, in the case of *late* any admissible transition must end in a PFM for which the value of the attribute TIME is 'late' (or ϕ_{late}). By itself, *late* does not impose any further conditions. As a consequence, it is compatible with any transition that ends in a 'late'-state. The contribution of modifiers like *already* or *still*, then, consists in restricting this model to a submodel where each transition is admissible according to the constraints imposed by the modifier.

When taken together, one arrives at the following four hypotheses.

Hypothesis 1: The core frame-semantical meaning of an expression includes its (standard) static Tarskian meaning which is defined in terms of the contribution it makes to the truth conditions of sentences. This meaning component is captured in terms of PFMs.[12]

Hypothesis 2: The proper frame-semantical meaning of an expression is defined in terms of DFMs, which specify possible ways of how the core feature-semantical meaning, expressing its contribution to truth conditions of sentences, can be

---

[12] This last claim need not necessarily hold for dynamic or action verbs like *eat* or *hit*.

brought about. This is its dynamic meaning component and is part of its cognitive meaning.

Hypothesis 3: The frame-semantical meaning of an expression can be given in terms of DTM-formulas of the form $\pi \rightarrow \diamond_{RP}\phi$ where π is a formula of the global language expressing how the truth came about and ϕ expresses the (static) truth conditions. Such a formula is satisfied by an arrow if it satisfies π and the truth conditions expressed by ϕ are true at its right (end) point (boundary). For example, in the case of *late* one gets (43).

(43) $\quad M, x \models Int(\neg late \; W \; late) \bullet Int(G(late)) \rightarrow \diamond_{RP}late$

(43) expresses a relationship between the dynamic level of an arrow and its static component. (43) can be read as "if an arrow x can be decomposed into subarrows y and z satisfying π, then ϕ holds at the end point of the arrow".

Hypothesis 4: Identical contributions to truth conditions modeled by the same PFM can correspond to different DFMs capturing the dynamic (cognitive) meaning of the expression (or concept).

Core frame-semantical meanings are expressed in terms of the language that is used to talk about PFMs, e. g. an extended modal language (see Naumann 2013 for details). The proper frame-semantical meaning is expressed in terms of the language used for talking about the global layer of a DFM. For phase quantification, this is the language defined in section 3.

Of course, phase quantification is an example of this fourth hypothesis: *It is already late*, *It is still late* and *It is late* have the same truth conditions (it must be late at the parameter point or at speech time), however the constraints they impose at the level of DFM are different. Using Hypothesis 3 their difference consists in the DFM formula π while they all have the same formula $\diamond_{RP}\phi$ in the consequent, expressing the fact that the sentences have the same truth conditions. Depending on π, different types of information about the way the truth conditions have come about are conveyed by the sentences. As a consequence, different (additional) conclusions, like those discussed in section 3.4, can be inferred, reflecting the difference in their cognitive value (or in their cognitive meaning).

Bibliography

Balbiani, P., V. Goranko & G. Sciavicco. 2011. Two-sorted point-interval temporal logics. *Electronic Notes in Theoretical Computer Science* 278. 31–45.

Barsalou, L. 1992. Frames, concepts, and conceptual fields. In A. Lehrer & E. Feder Kittay (eds.), *Frames, fields, and contrasts: New essays in semantic and lexical organization*, 21–74. Hillsdale, NJ: Lawrence Erlbaum Associates Publishers.

Blackburn, P. & M. De Rijke. 1997. Zooming in, zooming out. *Journal of Logic, Language and Information* 6 (1). 5–31.

Carpenter, B. 1992. *The logic of typed feature structures*. Cambridge Tracts in Theoretical Computer Science 32. Cambridge University Press.

De Rijke, M. 1994. Meeting some neighbours. In J. Van Eijck & A. Visser (eds.), *Logic and information flow*, 170–195. Cambridge: MIT Press.

Finger, M. & D. Gabbay. 1992. Adding a temporal dimension to a logic system. *Journal of Logic, Language and Information* 2. 203–233.

Gamerschlag, T., D. Gerland, W. Petersen & R. Osswald (eds.). 2014. *Frames and concept types: applications in language and philosophy*. Studies in Linguistics and Philosophy 94. Dordrecht: Springer.

Hollenberg, M. 1998. *Logic and bisimulation*: University of Utrecht dissertation.

Khoussainov, B. & A. Nerode. 2001. *Automata theory and its applications*. Basel: Birkhäuser.

Kröger, F. & S. Merz. 2008. *Temporal logic and state systems*. Heidelberg: Springer.

Löbner, S. 1987. Quantification as a major module of natural language semantics. In J. Groenendijk, M. Stokhof & D. de Jongh (eds.), *Studies in discourse representation theory and the theory of generalized quantifiers*, 53–85. Dordrecht: Foris.

Löbner, S. 1989. German schon – erst – noch: an integrated analysis. *Linguistics and Philosophy* 12. 167–212.

Löbner, S. 1999. Why German schon and noch are still duals: a reply to van der Auwera. *Linguistics and Philosophy* 22. 45–107.

Löbner, S. 2012. Functional concepts and frames. Ms., University of Düsseldorf. http://semanticsarchive.net/Archive/jl1NGEwO/Loebner_Functional_Concepts_and_Frames.pdf.

Löbner, S. 2014. Evidence for frames from human language. In T. Gamerschlag, D. Gerland, R. Osswald & W. Petersen (eds.), *Frames and concept types: applications in language and philosophy*, vol. 94 Studies in Linguistics and Philosophy, 23–68. Heidelberg, New York: Springer.

Mittwoch, A. 1993. The relationship between schon/already and noch/still: A reply to Löbner. *NLS* 2. 71–82.

Naumann, R. 2013. Outline of a dynamic theory of frames. In G. Bezhanishvili, S. Löbner, V. Marra & F. Richter (eds.), *Logic, language, and computation*, vol. 7758 Lecture Notes in Computer Science (LNCS), 115–137. Berlin, Heidelberg: Springer.

Naumann, R. & W. Petersen. 2013. Frames as strategies. Paper presented at Tbilisi 2013.

Peters, S. & D. Westerstahl. 2006. *Quantifiers in language and logic.* Oxford: Oxford UP.

Petersen, W. 2007. Representation of concepts as frames. *The Baltic International Yearbook of Cognition, Logic and Communication* 2. 151–170.

Sevenster, M. 2006. *Branches of imperfect information: Logic, games, and computation*: ILLC, Universiteit van Amsterdam dissertation.

Szymanik, J. & M. Zajenkowski. 2010. Comprehension of simple quantifiers – empirical evaluation of a computational model. *Cognitive Science* 34. 521–532.

Van Benthem, J. F. A. K. 1986. *Essays in logical semantics.* Dordrecht: Reidel.

Van Benthem, J. F. A. K. 1994. A note on dynamic arrow logic. In J. Van Eijck & A. Visser (eds.), *Logic and information flow*, 15–29. Cambridge: MIT Press.

Van Benthem, J. F. A. K. & Natasha Alechina. 1997. Modal quantification over structured domains. In M. de Rijke (ed.), *Advances in intensional logic*, 1–27. Dordrecht: Kluwer.

Appendix A: Arrow logic and two-layered systems

Arrow Logic[13] is based on the intuition that binary relations can be interpreted as denoting sets of arrows. Examples are arcs in graphs, transitions in Labeled Transition Systems, attributes in attribute-value structures or even preferences if they are used as ranking relations. Arrows can have internal structure so that they need not be identified with ordered pairs because different arrows can have the same source (beginning point) and target (end point). Conversely, there may be points that are not related by arrows. An arrow frame is defined as follows.

(1) Arrow frames are tuples (A, C, R, I) with

    a. A *a (non-empty) set of objects ('arrows')*

---

[13] See van Van Benthem (1994) and the references cited therein for details.

b. C, x, yz x is a 'composition' of y and z

c. Rx, y y is a 'reversal' of x

d. Ix x is an 'identity' arrow

If a propositional valuation V is added to such a frame, one gets an arrow model with the following satisfaction relation.

(2)   a. $M, x \models p$ iff $x \in V(p)$

     b. $M, x \models \neg \phi$ iff not $M, x \models \phi$

     c. $M, x \models \phi \wedge \psi$ iff $M, x \models \psi$ and $M, x \models \psi$

     d. $M, x \models \phi \bullet \psi$ iff there exist y, z with Cx, yz, $M, y \models \phi$ and $M, z \models \psi$

     e. $M, x \models \phi^{\circ}$ iff there exists y with Rx, y and $M, y \models \phi$

     f. $M, x \models Id$ iff Ix

Arrow frames (models) are combined with state frames (models).

(3)   State frames are pairs $(S, \leq)$ with

     1.   a (non-empty) set of states

     2. $\leq$ a partial (or linear) order on S

There are the following mechanisms of interaction (bridges) connecting the two components.

(4)   a. $LP \subseteq A \times S$, mapping an arrow to its beginning (or left) point.

     b. $RP \subseteq A \times S$, mapping an arrow to its end (or right) point.

Both LP and RP are required to be functional, i.e. both $LP(x)$ and $RP(x)$ are singletons. In terms of LP and RP the relation D ('during') between arrows and states is defined as follows.

(5) $D(x, s)$ iff $LP(x) < s \leq RP(x)$

To LP and RP correspond the two modalities defined in (6).

(6)   a. $M, x \models \Diamond_{LP} \phi$ iff $M, LP(x) \models \phi$

     b. $M, x \models \Diamond_{RP} \phi$ iff $M, RP(x) \models \phi$

Since one is mainly interested in the lifting of non-relational properties that can be expressed using one of the variants of the Until-operator, state formulas are evaluated on sequences $\gamma = s_0 s_1 \ldots s_k$ in such a way that an atomic formula p is true on a sequence if it is true at its beginning point s_0, (7a). In (7b)-(7c) the clauses for Int, corresponding to D, as well as for G and F are given.

(7) a. $M, \gamma \models p$ iff $M, s_0 \models p$ for p a state propositional variable
     b. $M, x \models Int(\phi)$ iff $M, D(x) \models \phi$
     c. $M, \gamma \models G(\phi)$ iff for all suffixes γ' of γ: $M, \gamma' \models \phi$
     d. $M, \gamma \models F(\phi)$ iff for some suffix γ' of γ: $M, \gamma' \models \phi$

The definition of the Until-operator U is given in (8a). In (8b) the weak variant W of the Until-operator is defined. It is compatible with ϕ being constantly true.

(8) a. $M, s \models \psi U \phi$ iff there is an s' with $s < s'$ and $M, s' \models \phi$ and for all s'' with $s < s'' < s'$: $M, s'' \models \psi$.
     b. $\psi W \phi \equiv (\psi U \phi) \vee G \phi$

The intuitive meaning of the two variants are given in (9) (see Kröger & Merz 2008: 66).

(9) a. "There is a strictly subsequent state in which ϕ holds, and ψ holds until that state."
     b. "ψ does not become false before a state where ϕ holds is reached." ("ψ waiting for ϕ")

Author

Ralf Naumann
Departement of Linguistics and Information Science
Heinrich-Heine-University Düsseldorf
naumann@phil.hhu.de

Semantic and grammatical aspects of nouns and verbs

She loves you, *-ja -ja -ja*: objective conjugation and pragmatic possession in Hungarian

Albert Ortmann & Doris Gerland

1 Introduction*

Hungarian displays two inflectional asymmetries which pertain to verb agreement and possessor agreement, respectively. One goal of this paper is to provide a thorough description and analysis of both splits. Although each of them is dealt with in quite some detail in the literature, and although the morpho(phono)logical affinities between the two are striking, no analytical link between them has as yet been suggested. As its second goal, this paper suggests a common rationale of the two splits, namely the expression of the presence or absence of a pragmatic component in the anchoring of the object and of the possessor, respectively.

The possessor agreement asymmetry involves an 'inalienable' possessor suffix and an 'alienable' counterpart *-ja* (or, depending on vowel harmony, its allomorph

---

* For many years now, Sebastian Löbner has been an important figure for both authors: as our semantics teacher, colleague, mentor and friend. With this paper, we would like to express our gratitude for his constant generous and open-minded support.

The work reported here was started in the Research Unit FOR 600 "Functional concepts and frames", and subsequently carried out in the Collaborative Research Centre (CRC 991) "The Structure of Representation in Language, Cognition and Science", both sponsored by the German Research Foundation (DFG). We are particularly indebted to two anonymous reviewers for their detailed and helpful criticism. For comments and discussion we would like to thank Liz Coppock, Jens Fleischhauer, Thomas Gamerschlag, Klaus von Heusinger, Lisa Hofmann, Jenny Kohls, and Robert Van Valin. For valuable feedback we would furthermore like to thank the audiences of oral presentations in Düsseldorf (at the workshop 'Nominal and verbal possession' and at 'Concept Types and Frames 2012'), in Graz, and in Saarbrücken (at 'Semantik und Pragmatik im Südwesten 5').

Those Hungarian examples that are not quoted as being taken from the literature were provided by co-author Gerland and were additionally checked by two informants, Attila Hajdú and Barbara Ördög. We gratefully acknowledge their cooperation.

-*je*). It indicates that the possessor is perceived as standing in a contextually established relation to the possessum noun, rather than in a part-whole relation that is inherent to the latter. Consequently, we argue that the alienability split expresses the contrast between semantic and pragmatic possession.

The verb agreement asymmetry consists of the contrast of so-called subjective and objective conjugation, where the paradigm of the latter also comprises the suffix -*ja* (with its front vowel variant -*i*). The distribution of the two conjugations is sensitive for those referential dimensions such as definiteness and specificity that are typically located on the definiteness scale; concretely, we refer to Coppock (2013), who suggests that the decisive notion is partitive specificity coming about by a lexical specification of familiarity. We therefore propose an analysis that draws on differential object marking. The distribution is furthermore sensitive to the category of person, in that 1st and 2nd person trigger the subjective conjugation, even though they are definite. We show that the special status of local person objects has another ramification in Hungarian. The otherwise obligatory accusative case marking of the direct object is being abandoned with local persons, even if these only feature as possessors of 3rd-person lexical objects. We analyse these facts in the light of a typological trend of reluctance to treat local persons as direct objects: local persons are highest on the definiteness scale, and are preferred as subjects acting on 3rd-person objects, but dispreferred as objects. As a common denominator of the non-occurrence of the objective conjugation on the upper end and on the lower end of the scale, we introduce the notion of 'Robust Transitivity'. We argue that the objective conjugation occurs if the object implies a presupposition regarding the identifiability of the referent of the object. Given this, we are able to propose a common explanation for both agreement splits.

The paper is structured as follows: in section 2 we analyse the alienability split in the possessor agreement, and in section 3 the subjective-objective split in the verbal conjugation. Section 4 connects the conjugation split with differential object marking in other languages. Section 5 analyses the person asymmetry in the objective conjugation in view of the special status of local person objects. In section 6, we develop the notion of robust transitivity and suggest a common explanation of the verbal split and the possessor agreement split. Section 7 sums up the key results.

2 A split in the possessor agreement

2.1 Typological context: the morphosyntax of alienability

Cross-linguistically it is very common for languages to show a morphosyntactic split in adnominal possession that has a semantic-conceptual basis (Seiler 1983, Nichols 1988, Chappell & McGregor 1996). The two classes can roughly be characterised as follows:

(i) *inalienable possession* involves a lexically inherent affiliation of the possessum to the possessor, which is unchangeable under normal conditions. It is typically instantiated by those relations that are not subject to choice or control, such as kinship, body parts and part-whole relationships.

(ii) *alienable possession* involves temporary affiliation, where the possessor typically has control over the possessum, and may be dissolved by selling, etc. Accordingly, the purpose or the function of the possessum for the possessor (for example, eating, growing, use as a tool) is of relevance. It is precisely in this area that the notion 'possession' can be understood in the literal sense. Moreover, often the relation between the two individuals is a purely a contextual one, thus, dependent on the speech situation, as in *my chair*, denoting, for example, the chair that I am sitting on right now.

One way of expressing an (in)alienability distinction in contexts of possession is that the marker of possessor agreement is directly attached to inalienably possessed nouns, whereas it is mediated by a possessive connective when used with alienably possessed nouns. This strategy of endowing non-relational nouns (that is, sortal nouns in the sense of Löbner 1985, 2011) with a POSS(ession) connective prior to possessor agreement is illustrated here from Udihe:

(1) Udihe (Tungus < Altaic; Siewierska 2004: 138f)

    a. *bi   anda-i*
       PRON1SG friend-P'OR1SG
       'my friend'

    b. *nuanija:-ŋi-ni*
       cow-POSS-P'OR3SG
       'his cow'

The noun in (1a) is semantically relational, hence 'inherently', or inalienably possessed. Accordingly, it is immediately combined with a possessor prefix or phrase. By contrast, the noun in (1b) is sortal and can therefore be combined with a possessor (in other words: can be made possessable) only after it is extended by the connective suffix -*ŋi*. Thus, some additional material is required, hence we are dealing with the marked variant. This way, the relators are sensitive for the underlying semantics of the noun in that they typically occur only with underlyingly sortal nouns, which they transfer into relational concepts (cf. Löbner 2011 for an analysis of the conceptual shifts between different types of nouns).

We construe the conceptual basis of the alienability dichotomy as the opposition of semantic possession and pragmatic possession. By the former, it is meant that the relation between possessor and possessum is inherent to the lexical semantics of the head noun, the argument structure of which accordingly contains the possessor. Pragmatic possession, on the other hand, implies that the POSS relation is contextually established, thus coming about from world knowledge or from the speech situation rather than being derived from the lexical semantics.[1] The opposition is parallel to that of semantic and pragmatic definiteness, or more precisely (since we reserve the latter term for the corresponding syntactic feature), semantic uniqueness and pragmatic uniqueness in the sense of Löbner (1985, 2011) and Ortmann (2014). The uniqueness of *the sun* and *John's mother* is guaranteed by the lexical semantics of an individual noun and a functional noun, respectively. By contrast, with definite descriptions involving a sortal noun such as *the dog*, unique reference comes about by anaphoric or deictic use, hence pragmatic uniqueness.

2.2 Possession and alienability in Hungarian

In Hungarian, the head noun of a possessive noun phrase always bears a morphological specification of the possessor (*ház-am* house-P'OR1SG 'my house', *ház-ad* house-P'OR2SG 'your house', etc.).[2] The possessor morphology displays an alienability split that was first investigated in Kiefer (1985) and subsequently mentioned by Elekfi (2000) and Moravcsik (2003). The split occurs almost only with 3rd-person possessor suffixes. In addition to the "unmarked" *-a/-e* (singular) and

---

[1] This dichotomy differs from that in Jensen & Vikner (2004: 5f) in that these authors subsume both inalienable and alienable possession under semantic interpretations, thus, also including ownership. The difference arises from the fact that Jensen & Vikner consider Qualia roles as part of the lexical semantics, whereas the present approach considers only those relational components which are also manifest in the argument structure, hence make the noun a relational noun.

[2] In addition, the possessor can be realised by a personal pronoun for emphasis (*az én ház-am*, DEF PRON1SG house-P'OR1SG, 'MY house'). Lexical possessors can either be in the unmarked nominative (*Péter ház-a*, Péter house-P'OR3SG, 'Péter's house') or in the dative (*Péter-nek a ház-a*, Péter-DAT DEF house-P'OR3SG, 'Péter's house'); see Szabolcsi (1994: 198ff) and É. Kiss (2002: 157f) for empirical and analytical details.

-uk/-ük in the plural (the distribution of the allomorphs being governed by the backness/frontness of the final stem vowel), there is also a variant with an additional -j; thus, -ja/-je and -juk/-jük, respectively. This is illustrated in (2):

(2) a. inalienable: *ablak-a*   *ablak-uk*
                       window-P'OR3SG   window-P'OR3PL
                       'its window'   'their window'

     b. alienable: *ablak-ja*   *ablak-juk*
                       window-ALIEN_P'OR3SG   window-ALIEN_P'OR3PL
                       'his/her window'   'their window'

The contrast is also apparent when the possessed noun is in the plural, thus *ablak-a-i* window-P'OR3SG-PL, 'its windows', vs. *ablak-ja-i* window-ALIEN_P'OR3SG-PL, 'his/her windows', and *ablak-a-i-k* window-P'OR3-PL-P'OR.PL, 'their windows', vs. *ablak-ja-i-k* window-ALIEN_P'OR3-PL-P'OR.PL, 'their windows'. An example with front vowels is *keret-e-i-k* frame-P'OR3-PL-P'OR.PL vs. *keret-je-i-k* frame-ALIEN_P'OR3-PL-P'OR.PL, 'their frames'. For simplicity, we will only use examples with a singular possessum here.

Conceptually, the forms in (2a) usually represent inalienable possession, thus, the window standing in a part-whole relation to a house or a door. By contrast, the forms in (2b) with the additional -*j* in the possessor suffix express alienable possession; typically, the possessum is literally possessed by a person in the sense of ownership. (Note that although for some speakers the -*j*-less variant can also be used with alienable possession, the -*j*-full variant cannot be used with inalienable possession; Elekfi 2000: 154f.) Kiefer (1985: 108) characterises this semantic differentiation as an ongoing change, and states: "In general, the suffix -*ja/-je* can be used to render conspicuous the relation of real possession whereas the other *habeo* relations are indicated by means of the suffix -*a/-e*."[3] Consider the following examples of alternating nouns, taken from the exhaustive description in Elekfi (2000: 154–168):

---

[3] Like Kiefer, we hesitate to ascribe a separate morpheme status to -*j*, even though our use of Moravcsik's terminology of '-*j*-full and '-*j*-less' possessor suffixes may suggest such an analysis. The reason is that its presence and segmentation is obscured by allomorphy. For example, it fails to occur with nouns that end in *ő* or *ö* and are used as plural possessees, as in *szülő* 'parent', with *szülei* 'his/her (e. g., a child's) parents' and *szülői* 'its parents (e. g., of a school)'. Contrarily, with many nouns the -*j* sometimes occurs invariantly in the possessor suffixes for reasons of the phonology rather than of the semantics.

(3) inalienable: alienable:

üveg-e 'its glass (of a window)' *üveg-je* 'his/her glass'
zseb-e 'its pocket (of a coat)' *zseb-je* 'his/her pocket'
taréj-a 'its crest (of a cock)' *taréj-ja* 'his/her crest'
keret-e 'its frame (of a picture)' *keret-je* 'his/her frame'
anyag-a 'its material (of something)' *anyag-ja* 'his/her material'
talp-a 'his/her sole (of a person's foot)' *talp-ja* 'his/her sole'
játék-a 'his/her play (of an author)' *játék-ja* 'his/her toy'
test-e 'his/her/its body (of sb./sth.)' *test-je* 'his/her geometrical solid'
küszöb-e 'its threshold (of a house)' *küszöb-je* 'his/her threshold'
bőr-e 'his/her/its skin (of a person)' *bőr-je* 'his/her leather'
gép-e 'its machine (of a car)' *gép-je* 'his/her machine'
fonal-a 'thread (of a ball of wool)' *fonal-ja* 'his/her thread'

This alienability split, then, implies that one and the same noun may be 'temporarily' assigned to either construction according to whether it is construed as standing in a part-whole relation, or in a contextual relation to the possessor.[4] The *-j*-less variant *-a/-e* expresses semantic possession, whereas the *-j*-full variant *-ja/-je* expresses pragmatic possession. This is in line with the typological generalization that less conceptual distance between possessor and possessum is mirrored by less structural markedness (Seiler 1983, Chappell & McGregor 1996).

---

[4] Typologically, it is very common for there to be so-called 'temporary' (or 'fluid') assignment that comes about in terms of different conceptualisations. Consider the following minimal pair:

(i) Patpatar (Oceanic < East Malayo-Polynesian; Papua New Guinea; Chappell & McGregor 1996: 3)

a. *a kat-igu*
ART liver-P'OR1SG
'my liver'

b. *agu kat*
1SG liver
'my liver (that I am going to eat)'

The inalienable variant in (i)a requires a possessor suffix on the head noun whereas the alienable variant (which involves a shift from relational to sortal concept) is expressed by a free possessor pronoun.

It is the alienable use of a relational noun which is marked additionally, while a noun in the inalienable use takes the less marked possessor suffix.[5]

The example list shows that the alternating nouns denote meronyms, thus, their lexical meaning involves a part-whole relation. Furthermore, most of them are artefacts. These two criteria exclude, for example, such nouns as *honap* 'month' or *ötlet* 'idea', which may well be regarded as relational, from the alternation. Note especially that kinship terms do not alternate either (the only exception being *szülő(k)* 'parent(s)'). There are very few alternating nouns which cannot be classified as meronymic artefacts. One of them is *játék* as mentioned in (3), another is *pincér* 'waiter', with the inalienable variant *pincére* referring to the waiter of a restaurant and the alienable variant *pincérje* referring to the employee of the restaurant owner. The inalienable variant refers to the waiter as a member of an organisation, thus, as a part of a whole, albeit not denoting an artefact.[6] Some nouns fail to exhibit two different variants for phonological reasons. Some phonological environments in Hungarian do not allow for *–j* altogether, others require it invariably in the possessor suffix irrespective of (in)alienability. Stems ending in one of the strident or palatal consonants [s, z, ʃ, j, ɲ, ʒ] allow only the *-j*-less variant; conversely, stems ending in a vowel require the *-j* as an epenthetic segment in the suffix (Olsson 1992, Siptar & Törkenczy 2000). Furthermore, most nouns ending in a voiced stop ([b, d, g]) invariably exhibit the *-j* in the suffix: *család-ja*, 'his/her family', *darab-ja*, 'its/his/her piece', *hang-ja*, 'his/her voice'.

To generalise, we can state the following two input conditions for alternating nouns:

---

[5] There are only a few counterexamples to this generalisation. These end in a vowel and consequently display *-j* in the inalienable use as well, as a result of epenthesis. However, these nouns still exhibit a contrast in that the final vowel alternates (Elekfi 2000: 157):

(i) a. stem: *ajtó* 'door'   *ajta-ja*   *ajtó-ja*
                              'its door' (of a house)   'his/her door'
    b. stem: *tüdő* 'lung'   *tüde-je*   *tüdő-je*
                              'his/her/its lung' (of a person   'his/her lung' (in the soup)
                              or animal)

In a sense, then, it is the inalienable rather than the alienable variant that involves a marking. The behaviour in (i) is, however, idiosyncratic.

[6] As for the two other exceptions, *titkár* 'secretary' behaves analogously to *pincér* 'waiter', with *titkára* referring to a person working for a party or an association, and *titkárja* referring to a person as an employee of some boss; conversely, *füzet* 'exercise book' denotes an artefact but is not meronymic (where *füzete* refers to a pupil's exercise book and *füzet-je* to, for example, the exercise book in a stationery shop).

(4) Input conditions for Hungarian nouns displaying the alienability alternation

- Semantic input condition: The noun is relational; specifically, it denotes a meronymous artefact.
- Phonological input condition: The noun ends in a consonant other than a strident or palatal consonant, or in vowel other than [a].

Pursuing the approach of concept types and type shift set out by Löbner (2011), using a meronym with an alienable possessor implies the following: an underlyingly relational noun is used as a sortal noun which is then again shifted to a relational noun, where the relation at issue is different from its inherent relation, thus RC → SC → RC. With a –j-less possessor suffix, the relational concept is maintained as such, namely a part-whole relation in accordance with the lexical semantics of the noun. For the –j-full possessor suffix, a relation between possessor and possessum is established which is contextually instantiated; hence we are dealing with pragmatic possession. We represent this contrast as follows:

(5) a. Representation of semantic and pragmatic possession in Hungarian
scheme for RCs: $\lambda y\ \lambda x\ [((\text{SortalComponents}(x)))\ ...\ \&\ \text{RelationalComponent}(x,y)]$
instantiation by *ablak*: $\lambda y\ \lambda x\ [\text{WINDOW'}(x)\ ...\ \&\ \text{PART-OF}(x,y)]$
b. semantic possession: –j-less form simply saturate the p'or argument:
applied to -*a* "it": $\lambda x\ [\text{WINDOW'}(x)\ ...\ \&\ \text{PART-OF}(x, \text{"it"})]$
c. pragmatic possession: –j-full forms indicate a shift RC → SC → RC and at the same time saturates the p'or argument:
-*ja* applied to (5a): $\lambda \text{RC}\ \lambda x\ \exists y\ [\text{RC}(x,y)\ \&\ \text{POSSCONTEXT}(\text{"s/he"},x)]$
applied to *ablak*: $\lambda x\ \exists y\ [\text{WINDOW'}(x)\ ...\ \&\ \text{PART-OF}(x,y)\ \&\ \text{POSS}_{\text{context}}(\text{"s/he"},x)]$

The general scheme for relational nouns in (5a) shows that they entail sortal components and relational components. The latter require the saturation of the possessor argument and specify the kind of relation between the respective noun's referential argument and the possessor. For artefacts such as *ablak* 'window', this kind of relation consists of a part-whole relation. The –j-less possessor suffix saturates the possessor argument and specifies it as a 3rd-person pronoun.[7]

---

[7] Strictly speaking, all possessor suffixes are ambiguous between pronominal and non-pronominal agreement markers. The latter variant is chosen in combination with a prenominal possessor phrase (see footnote 2 as well as 3.2.5). Formally, one can simply assume a person specification that must

She loves you, -ja -ja -ja: objective conjugation and pragmatic possession in Hungarian

The *-j*-full suffix represented in (5c) has the additional status of an operator. It introduces a relation of possession other than the lexically inherent meronymic relation, and existentially binds the second argument of the latter. This way, the inherent relation, over which we abstract by using 'RC' as a variable for two-place relations, is "suppressed" (rather than remaining at issue as in (5b)). The newly introduced relation POSS presupposes that its precise instantiation can be determined from the context. The relation also implies that the possessor is animate, or in fact human, which is indicated in the somewhat informal representation of the pronominal argument.

For some nouns, the alternation has given rise to two different lexicalized meaning variants:

(6) a. *csillag-a*   *csillag-ja*
'its star' (of the sky)   'his star' (star-shaped insignia of soldiers)

b. *szőlő-je*   *szőle-je*
'its grape'   'his/her vineyard'

c. *nej-e*   *nő-je*
'his wife'   'his/her woman'

d. *férj-e*   *férfi-je*
'her husband'   'his/her man'

e. *fej-e*   *fő-je*
'his/her/its head' (of a person/animal)   'its head' (leader of a group)

(6a–d) show minimal pairs one variant of which is an RC and the other is underlyingly an SC.[8] Significantly, in (6c–e) the *-j* is reanalysed as belonging to the stem of the RC variant. Although for (6e) both variants, 'head' and 'leader', are relational, the latter can be assumed to involve less conceptual closeness between possessum and possessor since it involves neither a meronymic nor a kinship relation.

---

     be unified with that of the possessor phrase, rather than saturation of the possessor argument as the pronominal variants in (5).

[8] Note that (6b) does not show the exceptional markedness behaviour discussed in footnote 5, but rather the expected pattern in that the inalienable variant corresponds to the stem *szőlő*, whereas the alienable variant is derived.

The lexicalization of the -*j* as part of the stem is also found with a sub-group of body part terms: *száj* 'mouth', *máj* 'liver', *haj* 'hair', *fej* 'head', *ujj* 'finger'. Contrary to the above examples (6c-e), these nouns do not alternate. Their non-alternating behaviour cannot, however, be explained on phonological grounds: a geminate [jj], as it would result from suffixing *-ja/-je*, is attested in Hungarian, both in general (as in *ujj* 'finger', contrasting with *új* 'new') and in the morphological context at issue (as in *taréj-ja* 'his/her crest'; this is the only example, though). We therefore consider this invariant behaviour as a sub-pattern within the Hungarian alienability asymmetry. With body parts, the *-j* indicates (vacuously, without performing an operation) an inherent rather than a contextually established relation; hence, in this case it represents semantic rather than pragmatic possession.

Interestingly, most of those body part terms that do not end in *-j* do not alternate either, although, again, this is not excluded for phonological reasons. Examples are *kar* 'arm', *láb* 'leg', *comb* 'haunch', *fül* 'ear', *vér* 'blood', *veríték* 'sweat', *köröm* 'nail', all of which allow only for one variant of the possessor suffix. (The only exceptions are *bőr* 'skin', *velő* 'marrow', *taréj* 'crest', *talp* 'sole', *test* 'body', and *tüdő* 'lung', thus, *bőre* vs. *bőrje*. These six nouns either refer to butcher's goods or exhibit two different meaning variants such as 'skin/leather'; see the list in (3)). Thus, although body parts denote meronyms, most of them do not alternate. We explain this by the fact that they are not artefacts in the sense of artificial objects. The role of artificiality and animacy in the possession split is further evidenced by the fact that kinship terms also fail to alternate. As with *láb* 'leg', *kar* 'arm', etc., kinship terms do not exhibit reanalysis of *-j* into the stem (for example, *báty* 'big brother', *nővér* 'big sister', *húg* 'little sister', etc.; the only apparent exceptions are *férj* 'husband' and *nej* 'wife' (6c,d), which are lexicalised variants of the sortal nouns *férfi* 'man' and *nő* 'woman'). Taken together, the entirety of the facts corroborates the above generalisation that nouns that undergo the alienability split denote meronymic artefacts.

One may wonder why the split is only found with 3rd person and not with 1st and 2nd person possessors. Our explanation is that for 1st and 2nd person, such a split would have no functional load because they hardly ever occur as inalienable possessors of inanimate artefacts. In other words, if the part is inanimate, then the whole will be inanimate too, and thus 3rd person. It follows that 1st and 2nd person possessors of artefacts are necessarily alienable possessors, which renders an alienability distinction in terms of additional possessor suffixes absurd. Note in this connection that the lack of contrast also holds for 1st and 2nd person as verbal objects, namely in the verbal agreement system. Later we will return to the lack of contrast in both environments.

2.3 Conclusion

To sum up, the Hungarian alienability split involves an interaction of morphological and semantic distinctions which is well in harmony with typological generalisations, though instantiating a particular sub-kind. Meronymic artefacts which are used in congruence with their inherent relationality take the *-j*-less possessor suffix variant. If their use involves a relation different from the inherent one, that is, in case of pragmatic possession, they take the *-j*-full variant. The latter denotes, apart from specifying the possessor, two type shifts, namely RC → SC → RC. The status of *–j*-full suffixes with alternating nouns is thus that of an exponent of relationality that bears on the pragmatic character of the relation.

The contrast of two suffixes with and without the occurrence of *-j* has its parallel in the paradigm of the verbal conjugation and is dealt with subsequently.

3 A split in the verbal agreement

3.1 Basic facts

The verbal agreement morphology of Hungarian comprises two different conjugations, the so-called 'subjective' and 'objective' conjugations. The objective verbal conjugation displays agreement with the subject, and at the same time depends on referential properties of the direct object. It is found in the present and preterite indicative (as well as in the future tense, which is, however, composed of a present tense form of *fog* and the infinitive), and in the imperative. In the present, it involves *-j*-full forms as they also occur with possessed nouns as dealt with in the previous section. The *-j* occurs with subjects of 3rd-person singular as well as of all persons in the plural. The following charts give a survey of objective, subjective and possessor agreement.

(7) a. Paradigm for *lát* 'to see'

	objective present	subjective present	objective preterite	subjective preterite
1SG	lát-om	lát-ok	lát-tam	lát-tam
2SG	lát-od	lát-sz	lát-tad	lát-tál
3SG	lát-ja	lát	lát-ta	lát-t
1PL	lát-juk	lát-unk	lát-tuk	lát-tunk
2PL	lát-játok	lát-tok	lát-tátok	lát-tatok
3PL	lát-ják	lát-nak	lát-ták	lát-tak

b. Possessor agreement paradigm for *ablak* 'window'

ablak-om	'my window'
ablak-od	'your window'
ablak-a/-ja	'its window' (inal.)/ 'his/her window' (al.)
ablak-unk	'our window'
ablak-otok	'your window'
ablak-uk/-juk	'their window' (inal./al.)

It can be seen that the objective conjugation closely resembles the possessor series (more precisely, in the 'alienable' or pragmatic possession variant), with the exception of 1st and 2nd plural subject, where the subjective conjugation looks like the possessor series.[9]

The objective conjugation is obligatorily used when the object is a definite lexical noun phrase as in (8a), including proper names and demonstrative determination, and with 3rd-person pronouns as in (8b).[10]

---

[9] Verbs with a front vowel in their final syllable take *-i* as the front-harmonising suffix variant of *-ja*: *szeret-i* love.3SG.OBJ, *szeret-ik* love.3PL.OBJ. For this class, the similarity between objective conjugation and possessor agreement (*-je*, *-jük*) may not be as obvious as with verbs with a back vowel. Crucially, however, for [i] and [j] we are dealing with the same segment, in a vocalic and a consonantal variant, respectively. The expression '*-j*-full' should therefore be taken to be more abstract, in terms of comprising a suffix with the features [+high, +front].

[10] A note on the gloss of the conjugation suffixes is in order here. We annotate the specification of the subject (e. g., 2nd plural in the case of *-játok* 2PL.OBJ), followed by a dot and the information whether the suffix furthermore indicates an object, thus '.OBJ' if it does and '.SUBJ' otherwise. In specifying two arguments, the objective agreement suffixes crucially differ from the possessor agreement suffixes. The latter invariably specify one argument (the possessor), and are consequently glossed without a dot, thus P'OR2PL in the case of *-atok*. Given this difference, 2PL.OBJ as we use it is, in fact, an abbreviation of SUBJ2PL.OBJ3, which would be a more accurate gloss.

(8) a. *Lát-játok   a   kutyá-t.*
    see-2PL.OBJ DEF dog-ACC
    'You (pl.) see the dog.'

  b. *Lát-játok   ő-t.*
    see-2PL.OBJ PRON3SG-ACC
    'You (pl.) see him/her.'

  c. *Lát-tok.*
    see-2PL.SUBJ
    'You (pl.) see.'

  d. *Lát-tok   egy   kutyá-t.*
    see-2PL.SUBJ INDEF dog-ACC
    'You (pl.) see a dog.'

Conversely, objective agreement is incompatible with intransitive verbs (or intransitive verb uses, as opposed to 'dropped' objects in elliptic contexts, which exhibit the objective conjugation), or with (unpossessed) objects featuring the indefinite article; see (8c,d). It is therefore commonly analysed as being triggered by the definiteness of the object. This is the key notion of numerous descriptions and accounts, in informal terms (Comrie 1977, Kenesei, Vago & Fenyvesi 1998, Coppock & Wechsler 2010), in terms of syntactic (DP-)structure (Bartos 1997, 1999, É. Kiss 2002), as well as in terms of a feature [+DEF] that is either purely formal (den Dikken 2004, Coppock & Wechsler 2012) or semantically motivated (Coppock 2013). Accordingly, the objective conjugation is often referred to as the 'definite conjugation'. In the following, we list the complexities of the conjugation split; that is, those contexts where the choice of the conjugation does not clearly follow from the rule of thumb in terms of definiteness.

3.2 Complexities of the distribution

3.2.1 'Local' object

The most prominent distributional peculiarity that is not explicable in terms of (in)definiteness of the object is that 1st- and 2nd-person pronouns, that is, the local person objects, trigger the subjective rather than the objective conjugation:

(9) a. *Engem   lát-sz/*-od.*
    PRON1SG.ACC see-2SG.SUBJ/2SG.OBJ
    'You see me.'

b. *Téged   szeret/*-i.*
   PRON2SG.ACC love.3SG.SUBJ/3SG.OBJ
   'S/he loves you.'

c. *Lát-unk/*-juk   téged.*
   see-1PL.SUBJ/1PL.OBJ PRON.2SG
   'We see you.'

d. *Lát-unk/*-juk   titeket.*
   see-1PL.SUBJ/1PL.OBJ PRON.2PL.ACC
   'We see you-guys.'

As (9c,d) show, the combination 1st-person plural subject and 2nd-person object requires the subjective conjugation just like other local-object combinations do. For 1st singular subject and 2nd-person object, however, there is a particular exponent, namely the portmanteau suffix *-lak/-lek*.

(10) a. *Lát-lak   (téged).*
        see-1SG→2 PRON.2SG.ACC
        'I see you.'

   b. *Lát-lak   titeket.*
      see-1SG→2 PRON.2PL.ACC
      'I see you-guys.'

The examples show that object pro-drop is possible with *-lak/-lek* for 2nd singular, but not for 2nd plural objects; see (10b). For the latter, the pronoun serves the function of disambiguating, since the number of the object is not specified by the portmanteau suffix.

Any analysis of the conjugation split is furthermore confronted with a series of other subtleties regarding the distribution, which will be discussed successively now.

3.2.2 Objects with wh-words: interrogative pronouns and relative pronouns

Hungarian exhibits several interrogative pronouns. Two of them are distributed according to [±human], namely *ki* with reference to human and *mi* to non-human. Both of them combine with the subjective conjugation. By contrast, the variant *melyik* and the indefinite pronoun *bármelyik*, which can be used with referents of either sort, trigger the objective conjugation.

(11) a. *Ki-t / mi-t lát-sz/*lát-od?*
 who-ACC what-ACC see-2SG.SUBJ/*2SG.OBJ
 'Who/what do you see?'

 b. *Melyik vázá-t vesz-ed/*vesz-el?*
 which vase-ACC buy-2SG.OBJ/*2SG.SUBJ
 'Which vase do you buy?'

 c. *Bármelyik váza-t megvesz-em/*megvesz-ek.*
 whichever vase-ACC buy-1SG.OBJ/*1SG.SUBJ
 'I buy any vase.'

In contrast to the 'simple' indefinite wh-pronouns in (11a), those in (11b,c) involve a partitive component, in that they operate against the background of some superset. This generalisation is informally stated in Comrie (1977: 9), Trommer (1995: 23), and more formally in Coppock (2013). The latter account, which we will use as a major point of reference, relies on the lexical-semantic foundation of the syntactic feature [+DEF]. It is this specification which is assumed to cause the objective conjugation. It is assumed to be present if the semantics of a nominal entails that its referent is familiar, in the sense of D(iscourse)-linking and partitive specificity (see von Heusinger 2011 for an overview of the various kinds of specificity). On the other hand, a negative specification of an item with respect to familiarity ([−DEF]) implies that the referential argument is new. Coppock posits a 'Lexical Familiarity Hypothesis', stating that "If the referential argument of a phrase is *lexically specified* as familiar, then the phrase triggers the objective conjugation" (2013: 7). This way, the choice of the conjugation follows "under the assumption that *melyik* 'which' imposes a familiarity requirement on the referential argument and *mit* 'what' does not" (2013: 17). Thus, whereas the latter is treated as equivalent to 'something', *melyik* is lexically specified as familiar, since its referential argument is mereologically related to a presupposed entity.

The distribution of the conjugation with respect to relative pronouns is analogous to that with interrogative pronouns. There are three different relative pronouns. Two of them, human *aki* and non-human *ami*, require the subjective conjugation as in (12a). The third relative pronoun *amelyik*, which is used with referents of either sort, optionally occurs with either the subjective or objective conjugation as shown in (12b) (see also Trommer 1995: 22).

(12) a. *A férfi, aki-t / A ház, ami-t ott lát-sz*
 DEF man who-ACC DEF house which-ACC there see-2SG.SUBJ
 'the man who / the house which you see over there'

b. *A   férfi / A   ház,   amelyik-et   ott   lát-sz/-od*
   DEF man   DEF house   which-ACC   there   see-2SG.SUBJ/-2SG.OBJ
   'the man / the house you see over there'

Unlike with (11a), the NPs in (12) are all clearly definite. This is obvious from the determination of the relativised head nouns. Why, then, do *aki* and *ami* not trigger the objective conjugation? The reason lies in the morphological source of the relative pronouns, namely interrogative pronouns, whose referents are of necessity not familiar. Observe the parallel in the morphological structure and the choice of the conjugation between interrogative *ki, mi, melyik* on the one hand, and the relative pronouns *aki, ami, amelyik* on the other. As mentioned above, the *ki* and *mi* stems pass their non-familiarity on to the entire noun phrase, hence the choice of the subjective conjugation.[11] By contrast, *amelyik* comprises the suffix –*ik*. É. Kiss (2002: 154) observes that this suffix generally triggers objective agreement. The fact that it has the function of deriving ordinal from cardinal numbers, as well as turning *egy* 'one, a' into a quantifier with a presupposed superset, *egy-ik* 'one of them', lends further support to the role of a partitive component. These morphological differences, then, are decisive for the choice of conjugation.[12]

3.2.3   Objects with indefinite pronouns and quantifiers

The indefinite pronouns *néhány* and *valamennyi* 'some' and the quantifier *minden* 'every' trigger subjective agreement, whereas *valamennyi* 'each' triggers objective agreement.[13]

(13)   a.   *Lát-ok/*-om   néhány / minden / valamennyi gyerek-et.*
             see-1SG.SUBJ/1SG.OBJ some   every   some   child-ACC
             'I see some / all children.'

---

[11] This is notwithstanding the fact noted by É. Kiss (2002: 243f) that the initial *a-* is a remnant of the demonstrative pronoun *az*. É. Kiss considers the *a-* to be optional; its omission, however, appears to be a colloquial feature.

[12] Note in this connection that coordinate object NPs call for some technical amendment to any formal analysis of the conjugation split, namely with respect to linearity. Regardless of whether the coordinate object is pre- or postverbal, it is generally the constituent closest to the verb that decides the choice of the conjugation; see Trommer (1995:28, 44ff).

[13] Thus, *valamennyi* is polysemous, with the meaning 'some' in addition to that of 'each', the former calling for the subjective and the latter for the objective conjugation (Csirmaz & Szabolcsi 2012). See also Kenesei, Vago & Fenyvesi (1998: 324) for some other quantifiers and indefinite pronouns.

b. Lát-om/*-ok   valamennyi gyerek-et (az osztály-ból).
   see-1SG.OBJ/1SG.SUBJ each   child-ACC DEF class-ELATIVE
   'I see each child (of the class).'

The different behaviour of *valamennyi* 'some', *néhány* and *minden* in (13a) on the one hand, and *minden*'s only apparent equivalent *valamennyi* 'each' in (13b) (as well as the obsolete *mind*) on the other is conditioned in the same way as the contrast between the two types of interrogative pronouns. The lexical semantics of *valamennyi* 'each' involves a partitive component. Recall that Coppock's (2013) familiarity analysis explicitly hypothesises a specification in the lexical semantics to be responsible for triggering objective agreement. Accordingly, she explains the contrast of *minden* and *néhány* to *valamennyi* by assuming a presuppositional component of the lexical entry of the latter but not of the former, namely the sum of all entities with the property denoted by the noun. As a result, *valamennyi* 'each' receives a familiarity specification that gives rise to [+DEF].

The same partitivity contrast is also found with possessed indefinite objects, which will be discussed in 3.2.5.

3.2.4 Infinitival and clausal objects

Complement clause objects trigger the objective conjugation, whereas infinitival complements trigger the subjective conjugation.[14] Compare (14) and (15):

(14) *Tud-ta,   hogy Péter csal-t   egy*
     know-PRET.3SG.OBJ COMPL Péter cheat-PRET.3SG.SUBJ INDEF
     vizsgá-n.
     exam-SUPERESSIVE
     'He knew that Péter cheated in an exam.'

(15) *János szeret   mosogat-ni   ebéd után.*
     John like.3SG.SUBJ   wash_dishes-INF dinner after
     'John likes to do the dishes after dinner.'

The motivation for this contrast unquestionably lies in the fact that complement clauses are (onto)logically affine to individual terms and, as such, to definite NPs. Note that subordinate clauses tend to be nominalised, especially in SOV languages with central-embedding VPs. By contrast, infinitives can be seen to instantiate

---

[14] Intriguingly, though, if the infinitive comes with an object, the matrix verb can show objective agreement provided that it is transitive. This is, for example, the case with *akar* 'want', as opposed to *igyekez* 'make efforts to'; see É. Kiss (2002: 50). Den Dikken (2004) accounts for this contrast in terms of clause union with the former class.

the logical type of properties, not of individuals, hence they do not correspond to definite NPs. Starting from the assumption that clauses, just like DPs, have a referential argument in the sense of a discourse referent, Coppock (2013: 24) hints at a formal explanation of the use of the objective conjugation in terms of a part-whole relation between atomic possibilities and multiple possible worlds: "A clause could then be analyzed in a parallel fashion to a definite description, with maximization over possibilities rather than individuals." The CP complementiser *hogy* is consequently analysed as a quantifier over possibilities.[15]

3.2.5 Possessed and specific indefinite objects

We will now illustrate that the objective conjugation is also found with indefinite objects, provided that these are either possessed or specific. First, consider the possessive NPs in (16). Only (16a) is definite, but all of them obligatorily trigger the same agreement.

(16) a. *egy   magyar   író   első könyv-é-t   olvas-om*
       INDEF Hungarian author first book-P'OR3SG-ACC read-1SG.OBJ
       'I read the first book by a Hungarian author.'

   b. *János egy   könyv-é-t   olvas-om*
       János INDEF book-P'OR3SG-ACC read-1SG.OBJ
       'I read one of János's books.' (lit.: I read a book of János's.)

   c. *egy   könyv-em-et   / könyv-ünk-et   olvas-om*
       INDEF book-P'OR1SG-ACC book-P'OR1PL-ACC read-1SG.OBJ
       'I read one of my books / of our books.'

---

[15] É. Kiss (2002) mentions a group of optionally transitive verbs such as *telefonál* 'telephone', for which the complement clause is associated with an accusative pronoun in their transitive use. The pronoun is optional, or, in É. Kiss's analysis "dropped in post-verbal position. Nevertheless, its presence can be reconstructed from the objective conjugation of the matrix verb" (2002: 242). For intransitive sentence-embedding verbs such as *szól* 'call out', which take the subjective conjugation, the status of the *that*-clause is that of an adjunct clause. Consequently, É. Kiss analyses the objective conjugation as being triggered by the associated pronoun. Obviously, the association of complement clauses with pronouns is another effect of their ontological affinity to individuals. Coppock & Wechsler (2012: 725) argue explicitly against the idea of complement clauses adopting a syntactic DP specification mediated by a correlative pronoun. On the basis of extraction asymmetries, they conclude that "complement clauses trigger the objective conjugation, yet are CPs rather than DPs", without further motivating the choice of the conjugation.
It is not clear to us whether any of the approaches mentioned will also account for the obligatoriness of objective agreement on the matrix verb of direct speech complements (see Trommer 1995: 20). In particular, we are not sure whether it is legitimate to assume a null complementiser or a dropped pronoun in connection with direct speech.

d. *egy   magyar   író   könyv-é-t   olvas-om*
     INDEF Hungarian author book-P'OR3SG-ACC read-1SG.OBJ
     'I read a book by a Hungarian author.'

In view of (16b,c), which exhibit indefinite head nouns with a definite possessor, one might be tempted to put forward an analysis in terms of a definiteness effect, according to which the referential uniqueness of the entire noun phrase would be warranted by that of the possessor. However, such an explanation would not work in the light of (16d), in which not only the head noun but also the possessor is indefinite. This example seems to show that the presence of any possessor suffices to trigger the objective conjugation.

One other possible speculation would be that it is syntactic complexity rather than uniqueness that makes the difference. However, that this cannot be the case is clear from the fact that the objective conjugation is neither found with indefinite objects modified by relative clauses or by complex APs, nor with coordinated indefinite NPs. For that reason, such notions as complexity or 'heaviness' of the NP are not relevant here. Much rather, what is significant beyond definiteness and possession is a certain kind of specificity. Bartos (1997) observes the contrast in (17):

(17) a. *Olvas-tuk   Péter (öt) vers-é-t*   (Bartos 1997: 368)
        read-PRET.1PL.OBJ Péter five poem-P'OR3SG-ACC
        'We have read Péter's (five) poems.'

   b. *Olvas-tunk   Péter-nek (öt) vers-é-t.*
      read-PRET.1PL.SUBJ Péter-DAT five poem-P'OR3SG-ACC
      'We have read (five) poems by Péter.'

Neither is (17a) formally marked by the definite article *a(z)*, nor is (17b) formally marked as indefinite by a quantifier or *egy*. So how does the different choice of the conjugation come about? Significantly, (17a) implies totality in the sense that Péter wrote no more than the (five) poems that are at issue, whereas (17b) makes no such commitment. In other words, although the NP is referentially anchored by the speaker (the speaker knows which poems were read) and, hence, epistemically specific, it is not partitive-specific.

Partitive specificity has indeed been well-known for being a relevant criterion for object case marking since Enç (1991), who refers to the notion of D(iscourse)-linking. Enç shows that in Turkish indefinite objects are marked by accusative only if the referent is included in a set that was previously established in the discourse. For Hungarian objective agreement, however, this does not fully suffice. This can be seen from (18), the translation of Enç's (1991: 6) corresponding example in which the Turkish noun displays accusative.

(18) (Several children entered my room ...)
... két lány-t ismer-ek / *ismer-em
two girl-ACC know-1SG.SUBJ / know-1SG.OBJ
'I know two girls'

We conclude that partitive specificity as such is not a sufficient condition for Hungarian objective agreement, but rather overt partitive specificity, meaning that it is carried either by one of the above-discussed indefinite pronouns and quantifiers or by a possessor. Our conclusion is furthermore underpinned by the fact (pointed out to us by an anonymous reviewer) that not only the lexical-semantic specification but also the syntactic structure plays a role. Notice that the subjective agreement in (17b) depends on a syntactic configuration under which the possessor is marked by dative case and furthermore extracted from the possessed noun phrase. As long as it is realised locally – that is, according to É. Kiss (2002: 168f), adjoined to the DP – it triggers objective agreement. This is obvious from the difference in word order that arises when further material such as an adverb is added:[16]

(19) a. *Olvas-tunk*   *Péter-nek$_i$ tegnap*   [$_{DP}$ *(öt) vers-é-t t$_i$*].
read-PRET.1PL.SUBJ Péter-DAT yesterday   five poem-P'OR3SG-ACC
'Yesterday we read (five) poems by Péter.'

b. *Olvas-tuk*   *tegnap*   [$_{DP}$ *Péter-nek$_i$* [$_{DP}$ *(öt) vers-é-t t$_i$*]].
read-PRET.1PL.OBJ yesterday   Péter-DAT   five poem-P'OR3SG-ACC
'Yesterday we read Péter's (five) poems.'

To account for this asymmetry, Bárány (2013) proposes that the feature [+DEF] (used in the sense of Coppock 2013) is located in D, therefore triggered by a 'local' possessor (that is, either a nominative possessor or a non-extracted dative possessor), this way inducing specificity. The correlation between the location of the possessor and specificity is also manifest in other syntactic environments, especially, as pointed out in Szabolcsi (1994: 223ff) and É. Kiss (2002: 172–175), with the verb *szület* 'be born' and the existential verbs *van* 'be' and *nincs* 'not be', which

---

[16] The specificity contrast in (19b) appears to be somewhat less strong than in (17), in the sense that the totality can in principle be cancelled. We suspect that this has to do with the position of the possessor, namely adjoined to DP rather than embedded in the DP.

can only be combined with extracted possessors, hence non-specific arguments. Equally, overt partitive specificity is the criterion for objective agreement, and the local realisation of the possessor argument (in [Spec, D] or adjoined to DP, or purely in terms of pronominal agreement as in (16c)) ensures overtly expressed partitive specificity.

Taken together – and disregarding local person objects for the moment – the objective conjugation is triggered by objects that are either definite or overtly partitive-specific. Note that, stressing the parallel in the referential anchoring of partitive-specific (or D-linked) NPs to that of definite NPs, Özge (2013) builds on the notion of 'presuppositionality' of the object – in other words, a pragmatic component just like in the case of the *-j-*full forms in the possessor agreement split. We follow Coppock (2013) in essential regards, who draws on the notion of familiarity by proposing the above-quoted Lexical Familiarity Hypothesis. This way, the trigger of the objective series is explicitly based in semantic terms rather than in a mere feature specification. As for possessed nouns, Coppock explains the choice of objective behaviour by ascribing to the possessor suffix the lexical information that the possessor is part of the presupposed universe, which is tantamount to our assumption that possessed nouns are explicitly partitive-specific.[17]

Given that definiteness is only a sufficient but not a necessary condition for Hungarian objective agreement, we replace the syntactic feature specification [+DEF] as commonly assumed in this context by [+PARTSPEC]. Furthermore, although otherwise in harmony with Coppock (2013), our account will depart from hers at one point. While she explains the behaviour of 1st and 2nd person as illustrated in 3.2.1 by positing that they incur no familiarity since they are not anaphoric, we will later bear on the marked status of local objects, and argue for the role of presuppositionality in referential anchoring. Before that, however, we will examine the conjugation split from a typological point and explain why, in the first place, specificity of the object can play such a major role here.

---

[17] Bartos (1999) notes that in some dialects possessed nouns determined by non-partitive *néhány* 'some', which otherwise trigger the subjective conjugation as illustrated in (13a), allow for both conjugations:

(i) *(i)Ismer-ek/%-em néhany könyv-ed-et* (Bartos 1999: 99)
know-1SG.SUBJ/1SG.OBJ some book-P'OR2SG-ACC
'I know some of your books.'

This variation can be interpreted as following from the conflict of the non-specificity of *néhány* and the partitive specificity indicated by the presence of a possessor. See Coppock (2013: 22ff) for a proposal along these lines.

4 The conjugation split in a typological context: differential object marking in Hungarian

The sensitivity for referential dimensions such as definiteness and specificity speaks for the role that 'salience', or 'prominence' plays for the object. This encourages an analysis of the split in the light of the well-established typological notion of DOM ('differential object marking').

4.1 The realisation of object agreement

Although in some languages, such as Basque and Greenlandic, object case and object agreement are employed across the board to all sorts of objects, in most languages they are differential. Basically, they are restricted to noun phrases either with human (or animate) referents, or with a definite (or specific) interpretation. To mention a classical example, object agreement in Swahili is confined to objects that are definite or human, whereas indefinite non-human objects trigger only subject agreement. Similarly, in Palauan, direct object agreement in the perfective aspect is, according to Woolford (1995), restricted to human and specific non-plural objects (the particle *a* marks NPs, and *el* licenses modifiers of the noun):

(20) Palauan (Austronesian; Woolford 1995: 658ff)

    a. *Te-'illebed   a bilis a   rengalek*
        SUBJ3-hit.PERF DET dog DET children
        'The kids hit a dog / the dogs / some dog(s)'

    b. *Te-'illebed-ii   a bilis a   rengalek*
        SUBJ3-hit.PERF-OBJ3SG DET dog DET children
        'The kids hit the dog.'

The motivation of DOM asymmetries is that object agreement (and, likewise, object case) is restricted to those objects which display properties that are typical of subjects, hence to 'marked' objects. It is generally assumed in the typological literature that DOM splits are related to 'topicality' or 'salience' hierarchies; see especially Siewierska (2004: 149) for five explicit sub-hierarchies. Of these, those in (21a-c) are of particular relevance, as well as the definiteness hierarchy suggested by Aissen (2003).

(21) a. Person hierarchy: 1st > 2nd > 3rd

      b. Animacy hierarchy: Human > Animate > Inanimate > Abstract

c. Focus hierarchy: not in focus > in focus
d. Definiteness Scale: Pronoun > Name > Definite > Indefinite Specific > Non-Specific

Notice that 1st- and 2nd-person pronouns are located on top of three of the scales because of their necessarily definite and human reference. It is a language-specific option whether the cut on the scale is marked by definite and indefinite, or human and non-human, or specific and non-specific. The fact that object linking splits follow these hierarchies – in the sense that a language will choose some step as its threshold of which sort of objects are morphologically marked and which are not – can be functionally explained by the requirement for an economic and efficient linking system. The distribution of object marking is economic since the morphological markers are avoided in cases of little concrete individuation.

If it is possible to show that the Hungarian verb inflection paradigm as illustrated in chart (7) above should best be analysed as involving object agreement, then the subjective–objective asymmetry can indeed be readily explained as an instance of DOM.

4.2 The Hungarian objective conjugation as object agreement

Given that the objective series does not distinguish the person and number of the object, it would appear natural to assume (as in fact many authors do[18]) that Hungarian has only subject but no object agreement. This way, one would not speak of verb-object agreement since the object itself is not specified in terms of its phi features, but only as to its mere presence plus the feature [+DEF], which is indeed the position taken by Coppock & Wechsler (2012). We will assume, by contrast, that the objective series includes a specification of the category of person, hence qualifies as object agreement. We analyse the Hungarian objective conjunction 1.) as object agreement, 2.) as being restricted in terms of DOM, 3.) with [±PARTSPEC] marking the lower bound. This explains why the distribution of would-be subject agreement is governed by object properties. Evidence for our proposal comes from the following considerations:

(i) With 2nd-person objects, in view of the portmanteau affix *-lak/-lek* for the combination 1SG→2 as illustrated in (10), it is obvious that there is an agreement specification. This holds regardless of whether one segments *-lak/-lek* into *–l-* for the object and *-ak/-ek* for the subject, as Bartos (1997: 364), É. Kiss

---
[18] For example, Nikolaeva (1999: 336) and Siewierska (1999: 244f).

(2002: 54, 2005: 113, 2013: 9) and den Dikken (2004) as well as Trommer (2003) do, or not.[19]

(ii) For 1st person, a specification of the object is excluded as an effect of the person hierarchy 1 > 2 > 3. For the combinations 2→1 and 3→1, the object would be higher than the subject, which amounts to a less natural scenario (see section 5). For these combinations, Hungarian has neither a portmanteau suffix in store, nor inverse morphology (see section 5.1). It is precisely this strategy of non-realisation, the gap in the object agreement and the resort to mere subjective agreement, that is symptomatic for most Uralic languages.

(iii) Finally, with 3rd person there is an agreement specification in the sense of paradigmatic contrast since the whole rest of the objective series indicates that the object is neither 1st nor 2nd person. Among others, this is also a key feature of the analysis by É. Kiss (2005: 113), who states: "The object agreement morpheme does have a person feature after all. The allomorphs -(j)a/-j/-i/-e mark a 3rd-person object, whereas the -l- marks a 2nd-person object." Even if one does not subscribe to this segmentation and assumes -om, -juk etc. to be impartible suffixes, the specification still follows from the paradigmatic contrast, on the assumption that -lak/-lek belongs to the objective paradigm.

The upshot is that although the Hungarian objective conjugation apparently displays only subject agreement, we are in fact dealing with object agreement. The objective conjugation series displays the specification [1/2/3→3rd-person object]. Apart from that, there is only the portmanteau form -lak/-lek for the scenario 1SG→2. For object agreement it is cross-linguistically the rule rather than the exception that it is restricted in terms of DOM, thus to be avoided in those cases where the object is least 'salient', in the sense of having little affinity to prototypical subjects.[20] In Hungarian, the threshold for objective agreement is marked by [±PARTSPEC].

---

[19] Trommer (2003) advocates an abstract and strictly featural-compositional analysis. In accordance with the framework of Distributed Morphology, morphemes are construed of as syntactic feature bundles. Trommer assumes zero morphemes for the object part of objective agreement, in order to keep them distinct from the subject part, thus denying the status of portmanteau for Hungarian verb agreement altogether, not only for -lak/-lek.

[20] Quite in the same vein, Szamosi (1974) already observed that Hungarian objective agreement is typologically in line with clitic doubling with respect to the definiteness restriction. Accordingly, Szamosi proposes analysing the former as an instance of clitic doubling and clitic placement.
  The opposite view is taken by Bárány (2012), who argues that "typical criteria of DOM [...] cannot explain the distribution of the Hungarian conjugations" (p3). The person asymmetry and the assumed redundancy resulting from the fact that Hungarian displays accusative case marking

What still needs to be explained is how the person split (ii), illustrated above in 3.2.1, fits into the picture. In the following, we will therefore motivate the person sensitivity, that is, the restriction at the upper end of the definiteness hierarchy.

5 The person asymmetry, or: 1st- and 2nd-person pronouns are 'bad' direct objects

We have pointed out in the previous section that the absence of the objective agreement with local pronouns is not motivated in terms of DOM, in fact is the opposite of what DOM predicts. Note that it is not the existence of a second split as such that is unusual. Such splits are very common, especially in terms of a tripartite case system ergative–nominative/absolutive–accusative. Here, however, we are dealing with just two different markers, but a seemingly unexpected distribution in that only a segment in the middle of the scale is singled out for objective agreement.

We would like to put forward the claim that the person sensitivity arises due to the tendency of local person pronouns not to display the full range of object properties.

5.1 Typological context: why local person objects are dispreferred

The rationale behind the dispreference of 'normal' object marking with 1st and 2nd person, that is, the reluctance to treat them like 3rd-person objects, lies in the prototypical properties of 'good' and 'bad' objects. It is, in a way, the other side of the coin of DOM. The most natural and 'unmarked' objects are low in salience, animacy, definiteness, which means that 1st and 2nd person are the most 'marked' objects – the worst, so to speak. There are several strategies by which languages react to this markedness, regarding grammatical relation, morphological linking, and the syntactic processes they undergo.

First, it may give rise to DOM in the usual sense. By this we mean that if it comes to the realisation of 1st and 2nd person as a genuine object, then accusative case and object agreement cannot be left out unless it is left out for less salient objects (hence, all other objects) as well. This is an instance of person hierarchy-driven DOM effects, observed elsewhere but not in Hungarian. For example,

---

in addition lead Bárány (2012: 21) to conclude that with respect to the DOM status, Hungarian objective agreement "is a peculiar kind that does not adhere to principles seen in other languages".

in the Papuan language Yimas only the local persons are realised by designated object agreement, as opposed to neutralisation to 'nominative' agreement prefixes with 3rd; see Wunderlich (2001b) for references and closer analysis.

Second, that local objects are challenging is corroborated by languages that employ distinctive morphological linking devices such as the inverse marking system as found in Algonquian languages, for example, Fox, Cree, and Potawatomi. As long as the agent is higher on the person scale (2 > 1 > 3 in the case of Algonquian) than the patient, the unmarked 'direct' scenario will hold. If the agent is lower on the person scale than the patient, the same person-number affixes are employed, but with an inverse marker in addition, rather than with the direct marker.

(22) Cree (Algonquian; Siewierska 2004: 150f)

    a. *Ki-wapam-i-n*
       2-see-DIRECT-1
       'You see me.'

    b. *Ki-wapam-iti-n*
       2-see-INVERSE-1
       'I see you.'

    c. *Ki-wapam-ikw-ak*
       2-see-INVERSE-3PL
       'They see you.'

Third, it is not uncommon for languages with otherwise transparent combinatorial systems of subject and object agreement markers to exclude some of the combinations of 1st and 2nd person (see also Heath 1998). This may give rise to gaps in the paradigm, or to repairs such as portmanteau forms. Both are found in Yimas, for which Wunderlich (2001b: 331) notes: "In all 1Ag/2Th settings, the expected transparent combination of prefixes is blocked. There exists a fused morpheme for 1Ag/2sgTh (namely *kampan-*); in the other instances, 2Th is expressed by a prefix, while 1Ag can only be expressed by a free pronoun". In the Northern Australian language Dalabon, it is the combination 2→1 that calls for a repair, namely neutralisation, in the sense that a subject prefix of 3rd rather than 2nd person is used. Most significantly, however, in Dalabon's rich system of pronominal prefixes, a 1st-person singular object cannot be morphologically expressed at all (Wunderlich 2001a).

She loves you, -ja -ja -ja: objective conjugation and pragmatic possession in Hungarian

Fourth, one other reaction to local objects is to deny them their object status, thus excluding them from (all or some) object privileges: (i) In Selkup (a Samoyedic language, thus remotely related to Hungarian), 1st- and 2nd-person pronouns do not trigger objective agreement either, and furthermore, according to Polinsky (1992: 415f), they fail to show direct object status altogether since they are not 'passivisable'. In other words, they are incapable of occurring as subjects of a passive structure, while 3rd-person pronouns trigger objective agreement and do occur as passive subjects. (ii) Bresnan et al. (2001) base their framework of stochastic OT syntax on the following observations. If the agent is lower on the person scale (here: 1st, 2nd > 3rd) than the patient, the passive is preferred or even obligatory, depending on the language. Conversely, if the agent is higher the passive is dispreferred, if at all possible. In fact, in Lummi (Salish) 1st and 2nd person are precluded as passive agents, just as 3rd person cannot be used for active subjects when the object is 1st or 2nd. And in languages like English, although 1st and 2nd person are not excluded altogether from being passive agents (*He is seen by me* is possible), it is much more common to say *I see him*.

We would like to propose that the Hungarian person asymmetry should be seen in the same vein, namely the trend that objects should not be too high compared to subjects. Of course, Hungarian local persons do not fail to show direct object status; this is corroborated by the fact that none of the criteria discussed here apply. However, there are two areas with respect to which Hungarian clearly is just as 'reluctant' as the languages mentioned in this section to treat local person objects parallel to 3rd-person pronoun and lexical objects. These areas are accusative case marking and also objective agreement, the subject of this paper.

5.2 Accusative marking and object agreement in Hungarian

The first piece of evidence for Hungarian's special response to local persons as direct objects comes from the omission of case marking in certain environments. Direct objects usually bear the accusative suffix *-(V)t*, which is, however, often omitted with (i) 1st and 2nd pronominal objects, and (ii) 3rd-person lexical objects when preceded by a possessor suffix of 1st or 2nd person. As for the first context of omission, Hungarian had developed unusually complex accusative forms for the local pronouns. These forms consist of the base, *én* and *te* respectively, which is extended by a final velar before the possessor suffix is attached; finally, the case suffix that is also used with nouns occurs. The old-style forms are thus *eng-em-et* PRON1SG-P'OR1SG-ACC, literally 'my I/me', and *tég-ed-et* PRON2SG-P'OR2SG-

ACC 'your you'. From a functional point of view, the accusative marker on local pronouns is entirely redundant, since the stems *engem* and *téged* PRON2SG.ACC clearly differ from the nominative (the mere base) and the dative and, hence, are already indicated as accusative objects. Significantly, the accusative suffix on 1st- and 2nd-person pronouns is obsolete, at best optional, in the contemporary language; see (23). It is, however, still maintained in poetry as in (24), a passage from a traditional old folk song.[21]

(23) a. *Téged(-et)   szeret.*
    PRON2SG.ACC-ACC love.3SG.SUBJ
    'She loves you.'

  b. *Eng-em(-et)   látsz.*
    PRON1SG.ACC-ACC see.2SG.SUBJ
    'You see me.'

(24) Excerpt from the folk song "Tavaszi szél" ('Spring wind'):
   Hát én immár ki-t   válassz-ak,   virág-om,   virág-om.
   so   1SG now   who-ACC choose-1SG.SUBJ flower-P'OR1SG flower-P'OR1SG
   *Te **engem-et**   's én **téged-et**,   virág-om,*
   2SG PRON1SG.ACC-ACC and 1SG PRON2SG.ACC-ACC flower-P'OR1SG
   virág-om.
   flower.P'OR1SG
   'Who should I choose now? My flower, my flower. You me and I you, my flower, my flower.'

The morphological structure in terms of possessor and possessed provides the link to the second context of omission. As a speciality of Hungarian, the reluctance against local person as regularly case-marked objects increasingly extends

---

[21] Also note the strong contrast to accusative marking of the 3rd-person pronoun, which does not involve a possessor suffix. Accordingly, omission of the accusative suffix is not possible with these forms, thus, *ő* PRON3SG – *ő-t* PRON3SG-ACC, *ők* PRON3PL – *ők-et* PRON3PL-ACC.
  The structure of the accusative plural forms of the local persons is fully parallel to the singular: *mi-nk-et* PRON1PL-P'OR1PL-ACC 'us' and *ti-tek-et* PRON2PL-P'OR2PL-ACC 'you (pl.)' (the segmentation is suggested in den Dikken 2004). The corresponding nominative forms are *mi* PRON1PL 'we' and *ti* PRON2PL 'you (pl.)'. With these plural forms the accusative marker cannot be omitted; see footnote 23 on the role of number in object marking asymmetries..
  For pronouns in the dative as well as for all semantic cases, the stem is (notably, in all three persons) not the pronoun stem as such, but rather the morpheme that otherwise functions as the suffix indicating the respective case with nouns: e. g., *nek-em*, DAT-P'OR1SG, 'to me', *vel-ed* INSTR-P'OR2SG 'with you', and *nál-uk*, ADESSIVE-P'OR3PL, 'by/at them'. É. Kiss (2002: 194) points to the parallel composition of postpositional phrases with a pronominal complement.

She loves you, -ja -ja -ja: objective conjugation and pragmatic possession in Hungarian

from local person as objects to 'locally possessed' nouns, so that even with lexical objects the accusative suffix is not always obligatory: it is optionally omitted on lexical objects provided a 1st- or 2nd-person possessor suffix precedes.[22] This is evidenced by the contrast of (25a) with local possessors and (25b) with a 3rd-person possessor, where the accusative suffix is obligatory.

(25) a. *Elveszt-ettem   a   toll-am(-at)   / toll-ad(-at)*
         lose-PRET.1SG.OBJ DEF pen-P'OR1SG-ACC pen-P'OR2SG-ACC
         'I lost my/your pen.'

   b. *Elveszt-ettem   a   toll-á-t   /* toll-a*
       lose-PRET.1SG.OBJ DEF pen-P'OR3SG-ACC   pen-P'OR3SG
       'I lost his/her pen.'

For 1st and 2nd plural, the omission of the accusative suffix is somewhat less common, but still possible. Crucially, the same contrast between local and 3rd person applies; see (26a) vs. (26b).

(26) a. *Elveszt-ettem   a   toll-unk(-at)   / toll-atok(-at)*
         lose-PRET.1SG.OBJ DEF pen-P'OR1PL(-ACC) pen-P'OR2PL(-ACC)
         'I lost our/your(PL) pen.'

   b. *Elveszt-ettem   a   toll-uk-at   /* toll-uk*
       lose-PRET.1SG.OBJ DEF pen-P'OR3PL-ACC   pen-P'OR3PL
       'I lost their pen.'

For possessed nouns and the phrases they project, we are, of course, dealing with 3rd-person objects. We assume that the Hungarian reluctance of treating 1st and 2nd pronouns as objects with full object status has analogously extended to the morphological context '1st or 2nd within the lexical object', regardless of its actual status of a 3rd-person NP.

5.3 The rank of subject and object on the person hierarchy

Given that all those direct objects that fail to exhibit accusative case in Hungarian involve a local person p'or suffix which would appear immediately preceding the accusative suffix, let us state as a mere generalisation about the data that this combination as such is dispreferred. As an explanation of this generalisation, we suspect that the cease of realising the accusative in combination with local person objects is an analogy to the person sensitivity of the conjugation split. It

---

[22] This is especially common in oral speech, but also found in written language.

is precisely with these combinations where we see the link to the trend discussed in 5.1: local persons are so unsuitable as objects that they are likely to fail to fulfil all structural grammatical properties of objects, be they morphological or syntactic.

Some languages afford this markedness for the sake of expressivity, and provide the full paradigm. To give an example from Uralic, the Finnic language Mordvin displays portmanteau suffixes for all except the reflexive combinations (Zaicz 1998). In contrast, Hungarian has neither portmanteau affixes nor inverse marking for 2→1, 1PL→2, 3→1 and 3→2. These combinations as such are, of course, not precluded (cf. the examples in (9) and (23)). The point is that the object can only be syntactically specified, not morphologically.

To conclude, (i) local person arguments are 'bad' objects. The unavailability of objective conjugation is just one ramification of this status, the decline of accusative marking is another. (ii) Portmanteau suffixes are one typological strategy of reacting to the challenge of dealing with local objects. To the extent they exist in Uralic, they should be analysed as belonging to the objective series since by their nature they specify the object. (iii) Hungarian resolves the conflict of faithfulness ("morphological marking of the object should be realised") and markedness ("avoid bad objects") by allowing for just one combination with a 'bad' object, namely the least marked one in terms of the person hierarchy 1 > 2 > 3, in the morphological inventory, namely the combination 1SG→2, with -lak/-lek, as in lát-lak (téged) 'I see you'.[23] (iv) As an effect, the objective series can functionally be interpreted as portmanteau forms for the 'unmarked' combinations in which the object does not outrank the subject on the hierarchy: 1→3, 2→3, and 3→3 (the consequence being that it specifies the feature value 3rd person of the object). The 'bad' scenarios (3→1, 3→2, 2→1, 1PL→2) are ignored in the objective conjugation. Instead the subjective series can only be employed.

As for combinations of equally high (or low) subject and object, anaphor scenarios defy any obvious integration into the scale because subject and object have the same referent, which typically calls for some morphosyntactic device

---

[23] Recall from the above examples in (9c,d) that the combination 1plural→2 requires the subjective conjugation, rather than the portmanteau affix -lak/-lek, which is restricted to 1singular→2. We attribute this to the fact that singular entities are conceptualised as being more prominent, or salient, than plural entities. This difference gives rise to DOM effects in other languages as well; an example is Palauan object agreement as illustrated in 4.1. The individual number values are therefore assumed to occupy different positions on the salience scale, with 1[−pl] > 1[+pl], and mutatis mutandis for 2nd and 3rd person. With respect to Hungarian this means that 1st person plural is not considered higher than 2nd person. Accordingly, the version adopted by É. Kiss (2005: 112, 2013: 8) is 1SG > 1PL/2 > 3.

of its own. In Hungarian, all anaphors trigger objective agreement: *magam-at lát-om*, myself-ACC see-1SG.OBJ, 'I see myself'; *magad-at lát-od*, yourself-ACC see-2SG.OBJ, 'you see yourself', *magá-t lát-ja*, him/herself-ACC see-3SG.OBJ, 's/he sees him/herself'. Notice, crucially, that the reflexive pronouns morphologically consist of the stem *mag* 'kernel' and a possessor suffix with the person/number specification of the referent. We therefore assume with É. Kiss (2005: 112) that the choice of the objective series follows from the reflexive's morphosyntactic status of a possessed noun. This status is, in fact, more obvious than in the case of the accusative pronouns discussed above; for example, it is possible to realise a free pronoun in addition, as with possessor constructions in general. While accounting for reflexive anaphors, however, the possessive analysis does not apply to the reciprocal pronoun *egymás*. This form is composed of *egy* 'a, one' and *más* 'other'. Evidently, the fact that *egymás* also triggers objective agreement does not follow from the morphological structure of the word (see note 27 on the matter). The most appropriate generalisation in terms of the person hierarchy would therefore appear to be: objective agreement is restricted to the unmarked scenarios; more precisely, subject and object having the same rank is 'still alright', while a scenario with the object higher than the subject, and in addition 1PL→2, is not – hence our absolute (rather than relative) generalisation in terms of the restriction to non-local objects except 1SG→2.

In referring to the person hierarchy, our proposal shares an essential feature with that of É. Kiss (2005, 2013) who also draws a connection between the person asymmetry and the portmanteau suffix *-lak/-lek*. Her generalisation, named the 'Inverse agreement constraint', is that object agreement is only licit when the object is lower than the subject on the hierarchy 1SG > 1PL/2 > 3, rather than including equal ranking. The major difference between this and our proposal is, however, that É. Kiss refers to the inverse systems as they are also found in Eurasia, namely in Kartvelian and Paleo-Siberian languages (see also the example from Cree in 5.1). Given that objective agreement also occurs in combination with 3rd-person subjects although these are lowest, É. Kiss refines her generalisation by adding a stipulation concerning the lowest rank. (The additional stipulation that we need, incidentally, concerns the combination 1SG→2, as the 'best of the worst', thus, in this case referring to the relative rank of the two arguments). Note that if one were to integrate definiteness and specificity into É. Kiss's scale (parallel to animacy in other inverse languages) this would yield an incorrect prediction, namely that objective agreement should not occur with specific objects but with non-specific objects, since these are lowest.[24]

5.4 The person asymmetry as a by-product of familiarity?

We would finally like to compare our analysis to that by Coppock (2013) with regard to whether her analysis actually copes with the person asymmetry and the partitivity-driven asymmetry in terms of one single explanation based on familiarity. Coppock emphasises that of all the proposed explanations, hers is the only one from which the person asymmetry follows, rather than treating person as a separate factor. She argues that "[u]nder the present account, the reason that first and second person non-reflexive, non-reciprocal pronouns do not trigger the objective conjugation is that they are not anaphoric; they are purely indexical" (2013: 25).[25] The reason why we do not subscribe to this claim is that in Coppock's theory, anaphoricity is understood in the sense of familiarity being modelled in Discourse Representation Theory, for these are the concepts that are made use of formally. Notably, the referents of local person pronouns, though they are not anaphoric, are indeed familiar. This is actually implied by the definition that Coppock (2013: 8) provides, thus conflicting her explanation of the person asymmetry: "Crucially, 'familiarity' is broader than 'anaphoricity': Familiar discourse referents do not necessarily have a linguistic antecedent, so long as the discourse referent can be found in the associated context". The referential arguments of local person pronouns would therefore seem to be no less familiar than those of nouns determined by indefinite pronouns operating over a presupposed domain, or by demonstratives pronouns.[26] After all, the speaker and hearer of an utterance are among the discourse referents in the common ground, thus

---

[24] For further criticism of É. Kiss's (2005) inverse analysis, see also Coppock & Wechsler (2010: 177f). They provide a historical motivation based on incorporation of pronouns that only involves 3rd-person pronouns. Consequently, they also deny a connection between the person asymmetry and the portmanteau suffix -*lak*/-*lek*.

[25] This solution is also considered by Bartos (1997: 370), who notes in a footnote: "É. Kiss (p.c.) suggests that one might toy with the idea of taking 1st and 2nd person pronouns to be non-specific, in a discoursal sense, on the grounds that they can never be co-indexed with a syntactic antecedent – the sole way of rendering an NP specific." Bartos does not pursue this idea any further, preferring a syntactic account in terms of the categorical difference between DP and NP. He finally admits the person asymmetry as a problem and points to the possibility that 1st and 2nd person pronouns might be "less-than-DP" (1997: 382).

[26] With regard to demonstratives, Coppock (2013: 12f) argues to the contrary. She posits that also in case of purely deictic use, demonstratives involve familiarity, just as in their anaphoric use, by virtue of the accompanying gesture. This gesture is assumed to introduce the referent into the discourse, unlike with the purely indexical local pronouns.

fulfilling one of the two alternative conditions on the referential argument of a lexical item to be classified as familiar (2013: 8), at least to the same extent that uniques such as *the sun* do. Accordingly, they carry the feature [+DEF] which is responsible for objective agreement. In short, as long as familiarity – which is explicitly assumed to be a broader, thus, less restrictive concept compared to anaphoricity – is the key criterion, the failure of object agreement to occur with local persons does not follow from their non-anaphoricity.[27]

A familiarity analysis of the person split, moreover, does at least not gain further plausibility in the light of dialects of the closest relatives to Hungarian, namely the Ob-Ugric languages Khanty and Mansi (also known as Ostyak and Vogul, respectively). In Northern Mansi and Northern Khanty, the objective conjugation also occurs with (non-focus) local person objects as in (27b).

(27) Northern Khanty (Ob-Ugric; Nikolaeva 1999: 337):

    a. *ma năŋ-en   / năŋ   xot-en   wan-s-əm*
       I   PRON2SG-ACC PRON2SG house-P'OR2SG see-PRET-1SG.SUBJ
       'I saw YOU / YOUR HOUSE.'

    b. *ma năŋ-en   / năŋ   xot-en   wan-s-em*
       I   PRON2SG-ACC PRON2SG house-P'OR2SG see-PRET-1SG.OBJ_SG
       'I saw you / your house.'

This extended use has to do with the fact that these languages no longer exhibit a morphological person specification of the object; instead, only number is specified (into singular, plural, and dual). One can therefore assume, as Coppock & Wechsler (2010: 170f) explicitly do in an LFG format analysis, that the objective agreement markers of Northern Khanty, in contrast to Eastern Khanty, have lost the 3rd-person specification of their lexical entry. The authors suggest that the same loss occurred in Hungarian too (counter to our assumption made in 4.2 that we are dealing with the specification [1/2/3→3rd-person object]), but for this language the condition of objective agreement was reanalysed from topicality to [+DEF]. This latter feature is assumed not to be predictable from the meaning, which enables them to stipulate that non-reflexive 1st and 2nd person are not specified as [+DEF]. Now Coppock's familiarity analysis, which aims at a semantic foundation of this stipulation, appears to fare well with the fact

---

[27] As far as reflexive and reciprocal pronouns are concerned, Coppock's explanation is successful, because these are necessarily anaphoric, thus correctly predicted to trigger objective agreement. On the other hand, as stated above, in the case of reflexives the choice of agreement also follows from their morphological status of possessed nouns.

that in Northern Khanty the objective conjugation is not found with local objects that are focal (which we indicate by capital letters in the translation of (27a)) but only with non-focus objects, in fact those that are secondary topics according to Nikolaeva (1999: 372).[28] On the other hand, given this very opposition, and especially the existence of a grammaticalised pattern for local objects that are familiar (namely the occurrence of objective agreement as in (27b)), it is even questionable whether non-reflexive local person pronouns should strictly be conceived as non-anaphoric.

In fact, under the assumption that the person asymmetry is a by-product of the 'lexical familiarity' analysis, differential object marking and the behaviour of local objects would for most languages be subject to conditions strikingly different from those of Hungarian. Either the object would not be required to be familiar, or this specification would not have to result from a lexical item. Note in this connection that Coppock (2013: 7, 14f) regards accusative marking in Turkish, following Enç (1991) and Özge (2013), as also being sensitive to familiarity but in contrast to Hungarian not necessarily in the sense of arising from a lexical item. It is not fully obvious to us how this will account for the fact that Turkish local objects exhibit the same object marking as 3rd-person objects (anaphoric and non-anaphoric). In any case, other DOM languages dismiss local person objects just as little as Turkish from their marking patterns of object case, agreement and clitic doubling.

We conclude that the absence of objective conjugation at the upper end of the definiteness hierarchy on the one hand (the local persons) and at the lower end on the other hand (non-specific objects) does not follow from one and the same featural specification. Instead, the two gaps have so far been given different motivations under our analysis: whereas the gap at the lower end was argued to be an instance of object agreement constrained by factors responsible for DOM (that is, the object is of little salience), the failure of local person pronouns to trigger objective agreement is traced to the typological trend that 1st- and 2nd-person objects are highly marked since in most of the cases they outrank the subject on the person scale.

These two trends are combined in Hungarian so as to circumscribe a medium section of the salience hierarchy, namely from 3rd pronoun down to partitive-specific, the effect being that it is precisely this medium segment which displays

---

[28] Notice that this information-structure-based asymmetry can be captured by making reference to the focus hierarchy in (21c). See, moreover, Marcantonio (1985) on the relevance of the object's topic status for accusative marking and objective agreement in the history of Hungarian.

objective agreement. Similarly, in the other Ob-Ugrian languages Eastern Khanty and Eastern Mansi (in constrast to the above-mentioned Northern varieties; cf. Nikolaeva 1999), as well as in Selkup (Polinsky 1992) and other Samoyedic languages, objective agreement fails to occur, on the one hand, with local pronouns, and on the other with indefinite objects (or non-topical objects, see Coppock & Wechsler 2010 for a historical account of the variation). The question that we eventually investigate is whether it is yet possible to find a uniform rationale for these two restrictions of the distribution of the objective series. The goal will be approached by way of returning to the split in possessor agreement as analysed in section 2.

6 'Robust' transitive scenarios and agreement splits restricted by pragmatic factors

In order to provide a uniform explanation for the non-occurrence of Hungarian objective agreement, we will pursue two questions: how does the distribution fit with typological generalisations concerning subject-and-object scenarios, thus, with transitivity? And why does the objective agreement series, thus, the *-j*-full of the two conjugation paradigms, align with the alienable variant of possessor agreement?

6.1 Restrictions on grammatical 'objecthood' and the notion of robust transitivity

There is ample evidence that object marking is not only constrained by low saliency in the sense of DOM, thus by referential properties of the internal argument such as non-specificity, but also by properties of the event or situation denoted by the verb. Above all, these are the categories of aspect and aktionsart. A case in point from Uralic is Mordvin, whose object agreement is referred to as the 'direct declension' (Zaicz 1998). As already mentioned in 5.3, it consists of portmanteau suffixes for all person and number combinations. Crucially, it is only employed in the perfective aspect, so that in imperfective contexts the definite object combines with the 'indirect' series. The relevance of aktionsart-based transitivity splits is evidenced by the analysis of two-argument activity verbs in Van Valin (1990). For example, in Italian two-argument activities do not allow for a passivisation variant while their accomplishment counterparts do, similar to the contrast of *eat spaghetti (#in five minutes)* and *eat the spaghetti (in five minutes)* in English. Still more conclusive is the behaviour of two-argument activity verbs in ergative languages such as Samoan or West Caucasian as mentioned by Van Valin & LaPolla (1997: 122ff). In Samoan, the ergative-absolutive case pattern that is typical of transitive verbs is not available when the verb is taken to denote an activity rather than an accomplishment. Instead, the pattern absolutive-locative must be used, that is, absolutive case for the otherwise ergative-marked argument. This implies that in these languages a two-place activity is treated as an intransitive rather than a transitive scenario.

Besides, as Van Valin & LaPolla (1997: 122ff) point out, when the internal argument is non-specific or non-referential it can be thought of as an inherent argument, in the sense of inherent to the lexical semantics of the verb. One important characteristic is that it can be omitted in many languages (including English and Hungarian, as in *speak/beszél*). Another characteristic is that it is incorporated, especially in languages such as Lakhota and Samoan, whose verbal morphology exhibits a regular pattern of object incorporation.

Overall, these findings show that object marking can be further restricted to the effect that the internal argument of a two-place verb fails to fulfil all morphological and syntactic properties of direct objects. In fact, it may not enjoy the status of a direct object at all. This status can be affected by referential properties as well as by situational properties. Like with local pronouns, this also holds true of 3rd lexical NPs in scenarios of too little transitivity. This leaves us, for the Samoyedic and the Ob-Ugrian languages including Hungarian, with a middle part of the hierarchy that delimits those scenarios for which we would like to introduce the term robust transitivity. By this we mean that the likelihood is highest for an internal argument to star as a bona fide direct object. What does it take, then, to be a robust transitive scenario?

6.2 The role of presuppositionality for the internal argument

Situational properties such as aspect, tense and mood are, for those languages in which they play a role in the above sense, just as relevant for robust transitivity as object properties such as animacy and discourse saliency. Unlike the latter, the former cannot be readily be ranked in terms of salience hierarchies such as the ones in (21). A hard and fast account that combines all the various dimensions involved would go beyond the present scope.

As regards Hungarian, the distinction that is responsible for the agreement splits is not simply transitive vs. intransitive. This is clear from the fact that indefinite NPs do not only bear accusative case but can also be passivised, hence are clearly treated as direct objects. Apparently, it is in the case of high, but not too high, saliency of the object that the object is specified with respect to person. The relevance of the robustness of transitivity for Hungarian is further corroborated by the fact that the objective conjugation requires the internal argument to have the grammatical status of a direct object, while that of an oblique object does not suffice. Two-place verbs such as *segít* 'help' and *örül* 'look forward to' that assign dative or local case rather than the accusative exhibit the subjective conjugation throughout, even if the internal argument is possessed and definite (*örülök a nyaralásomra* 'I look forward to my holidays'). This excludes the possibility of basing an approach merely on the presence of a semantic relation between two individuals. Furthermore, since the object has to be at least [+PartSpec], objective agreement signals more than merely transitivity in the sense of involving a direct object.

What is therefore essential is our assumption of a conceptually grounded scale that elaborates on the person and definiteness hierarchies (21a,d), and the definition of the two cut-off points for Hungarian. This scale is indicated on the left-hand column in (28). To more precisely define how the middle segment of the scale, which delimits objects of robust transitivity for Hungarian, can be positively characterised, we make use of the concept of presupposition. More concretely, we specify the contents of the involved presupposition for each step on the scale. It turns out that from local pronouns down to proper names on the one hand, and from non-referential NPs up to proper names on the other, each step on the scale subsumes the information of the previous step. The increase of presuppositional contents towards the objects of robust transitive scenarios is explicated in the right-hand column in (28).

The use of any NP upwards from [+PartSpec] NPs includes a presupposition concerning the anchoring of the referent.[29] For local pronouns, the anchoring is purely indexical, that is, determined by the context of utterance. No coherence

---

[29] In making use of the notion 'referential anchoring' we draw on von von Heusinger (2011), who conceives this notion to be the common denominator of the various different kinds of specificity.

The non-specific segment of the scale, that is, those nominals that are not referentially anchored, is largely equivalent to those which Chung & Ladusaw (2004) propose to analyse in terms of 'predicate restriction'. As an additional mode of composition next to argument saturation (modelled as function application), predicate restriction involves a modifier that conjoins with the verb predicate, thus leaving the latter unsaturated and still allowing for subsequent saturation or existential closure.

Furthermore, the term 'identifiability' as we use it should be understood as non-ambiguity of reference, in the sense of individual and functional concepts as employed in Löbner's (1985, 2011) Concept Type and Determination approach.

(28) Scale according to the referentiality of internal arguments and their presuppositional contents

	Status of internal argument in terms of definiteness and referentiality	Illustration or example reference	Presuppositional contents	
subjective	definite personal pronouns local pronouns	(9)	identifiability only in speech situation	indexical
objective: robust transitivity	non-local (= 3rd) person pro-nouns	(8b)	identifiability via coherence in discourse set (previous mentioning)	anchoring via coherence in discourse
	unique concepts, proper names	*Látom a napot/ Jánost* 'I see the sun / John'	identifiability via utterance-independent common ground and discourse	
	anaphoric (including ellipsis)	(8a)	identifiability via coherence in discourse set (previous mentioning)	
	indefinite: possessed	(16b-d)	existence and coherence; anchoring via superset that contains the referent	
	[+PartSpec]	(11b,c), (12b), (13a)		
subjective	[−PartSpec]: epistemically or scopally specific	(8d), (11a)	(existence asserted, not presupposed)	no referential anchoring
	not referentially anchored:	*Nem üt (egy) kutyát.* 'He doesn't beat dogs.'	(no anchoring, only warranted by speaker)	
	non-specific indefinite (pseudo-)incorporated arguments[30]	*fagylaltot eszek* 'I ice-cream-eat'	(no anchoring, only modificational restriction on verb meaning)	
	no genuine exponent: inherent objects	*beszélek* 'I speak' *szólok* 'I call out'		
	existentially bound arguments	(8c)		
	no internal arg.(monadic verbs)	*megyek* 'I walk'		

---

[30] The notion of pseudo-incorporation comes from Dayal (2011). Dayal shows that the notion also applies to Hungarian. It characterises such instances as *fagylaltot eszek* 'I ice-cream-eat', where the incorporated nominal is syntactically vigorous. In Hungarian, it may bear number and accusative case morphology, while in Hindi it may even be phrasal; that is, NP rather than only N°.

or discourse knowledge is presupposed, so that the referential anchoring is only 'locally' warranted. This is in opposition to the anchoring of non-local (= 'talked about') NPs, which presuppose some background of coherence. For one thing this involves identifiability in the discourse set, especially the resolution of anaphoric NPs and 3rd-person pronouns. Moreover, the identifiability of non-deictic definite NPs generally presupposes some common ground that is independent of the utterance. This also holds for the felicitous use of proper names (including NPs of which the name is not the head) and other semantically unique concepts. (Note that the existence of the referent is not presupposed in all cases. This is obvious from non-specific definites such as *the owner of the car with the license plate xyz, the winner of the next championship.*) Coherence in discourse is also at issue here, presupposing, for example, that names will be assigned referents in a one-to-one fashion.

Utilising the concept of coherence, partitive-specific indefinites are positively circumscribed since they presuppose an identifiable superset to which the referent belongs. By contrast, the reference of merely epistemically or scopally specific and other [−PARTSPEC] indefinites is only warranted by the speaker, thus, not anchored in the common ground of speaker and hearer. Note that the amount of descriptive content is low with pronouns and non-referentially anchored NPs, and highest 'in the middle', namely with common (as opposed to proper) nouns, and especially with so-called 'establishing' modifiers such as restrictive relative clauses as they are typically employed in first-mention use of sortal nouns. In this sense, syntactic complexity corresponds to descriptive complexity, and to more presuppositional contents in terms of common ground.

The different behaviour of 3rd and local pronouns is now straightforwardly captured. We propose that objective agreement signals the need for discourse coherence in the anchoring of the referent. For local pronouns anchoring is possible without any knowledge of previous discourse. This means that the context for objective agreement is not met, and, consequently, subjective agreement is employed.[31] Overall, for Hungarian robust transitivity implies a presupposition of coherence with respect to the referent of the object.

---

[31] As an anonymous reviewer rightly points out, the present analysis does not account for the existence of the portmanteau suffix *–lak/-lek* for the particular combination 1st singular subject and 2nd object, thus, an overt object agreement specification for a local object. In this respect, our approach does not fare better than the familiarity explanation which we contrast to ours in section 5.4. At this stage, we can offer no more than the assumption that this suffix, with its special morphological status, does not underlie the same coherence presupposition as the rest of the objective series. See also the discussion in 5.3 on the status of this particular combination, and on the 'inverse' analysis by É. Kiss (2005, 2013) in terms of the relative ranking of subject and object on the peron hierarchy.

6.3 Pragmatic factors in verb and possessor agreement splits

That the crucial factor for the choice of verbal agreement is not simply the presence of a relation (denoted by a transitive verb), but rather a pragmatic relation involving the notion of presupposition, has an equivalent in the choice of the possessor agreement morphology. Remember that in section 2 the possessor split was analysed as an opposition of semantic and pragmatic possession. The forms of the objective paradigm, most of which feature *-j* as a component, indicate a presupposition pertaining to the relation denoted by the verb and its internal argument. Much in the same way, the forms of the alienable sub-paradigm, which also regularly involve the ingredient *-j*, indicate that the possessor is in a pragmatically established relation with the possessum, usually presupposing context or world knowledge.

Recall further from section 2 that just like with verb agreement, the morphological contrast in possessor agreement is found with 3rd person but not with 1st and 2nd person. We explained this by the fact that an artefact-denoting meronym cannot exhibit an alienability distinction with local person possessors, since it cannot be inalienably possessed by the latter (it cannot be, so to speak, a part of speaker or hearer). 3rd-person possessors, by contrast, can either be alienable or inalienable possessors; thus a morphological contrast 'makes sense' here and only here, given the restriction to meronymic artefacts. On the basis of the analysis in this section, we suggest that the role of discourse coherence that is indicated by the verbal conjugation contrast is just as immaterial for local person objects as for local person possessors. Local person objects are invariant with respect to their referential status, whereas 3rd-person objects may exhibit the full range from non-referential/non-specific to anaphoric pronouns.

In sum, the '*-j*-full' suffixes that crop up in possessor agreement and in verb agreement are indicators of a relation involving presuppositional contents. As far as possession is concerned, the *-j*-full possessor is construed as standing in a pragmatically established relation with the possessum. As regards objective agreement, it is triggered by the middle segment of the definiteness scale from 3rd pronoun down to partitive-specific. In semantic-pragmatic terms, this segment is characterised as presupposing speech situation-independent identifiability. For definite and partitive-specific 3rd-person objects, the anchoring of the referent or of a superset presupposes coherence.

7 Conclusion: pragmatic restrictions on agreement morphology

This paper has connected two inflectional splits of Hungarian, one pertaining to possessor agreement and the other to verbal agreement. Both splits display an obvious morphological parallel. For possessed nouns, the split was analysed as expressing the contrast of semantic versus pragmatic possession, the latter being marked by an additional *-j* in the agreement suffix. This '*-j*-full' morphological make-up constitutes the link to the objective conjugation, where its occurrence is analogously limited so as to indicate a relation with certain pragmatic conditions.

Specifically, we argued that Hungarian objective agreement is restricted by a refined definiteness hierarchy. Two facts have been given particular reference and were accounted for in their typological context: first, the objective conjugation is also used with indefinite objects, provided that these are (either definitely or indefinitely) possessed. Second, if the object is a local pronoun the subjective rather than the objective conjugation is used. We are therefore dealing with a combination of the two dimensions of 'not too low' referentiality – in terms of [+PartSpec], and in line with differential object marking – and of speech situation-independent identifiability. Taking these two restrictions affecting the upper and the lower end together, an intermediate segment on a refined definiteness scale is circumscribed which encompasses what we refer to as robust transitive scenarios. Which segment it is that exactly triggers objective agreement in Hungarian (roughly: 3rd Pronoun > Proper Name > Definite > Partitive-specific, therein slightly different from that of other Uralic languages) was characterised in terms of a restriction regarding the presuppositional contents in the referential anchoring of the objects.

The morphological parallels between the two splits could thus be given a conceptual rationale by analysing both the alienable and the objective paradigm as involving a restriction in terms of a pragmatic component in the anchoring of the referent of the internal argument: for possessed nouns, in the sense that pragmatic possession presupposes a contextual instantiation which is not presupposed for semantic possession; for transitive verbs, in the sense of including a presupposition concerning the anchoring via discourse coherence.

Bibliography

Aissen, J. 2003. Differential object marking: Iconicity vs. economy. *Natural Language and Linguistic Theory* 21. 453–483.

Bartos, H. 1997. On 'subjective' and 'objective' agreement in Hungarian. *Acta Linguistica Hungarica* 44. 363–384.

Bartos, H. 1999. *Morfoszintaxis és interpretáció: a magyar inflexiós jeleségek szintaktikai háttere.* Budapest: ELTE dissertation.

Bresnan, J., S. Dingare & C. D. Manning. 2001. Soft constraints mirror hard constraints: voice and person in English and Lummi. In M. Butt & T. Holloway King (eds.), *Proceedings of the LFG 01 conference*, The University of Hong Kong.

Bárány, A. 2012. Hungarian conjugations and differential object marking. In *Proceedings of the first central European conference in linguistics for postgraduate students*, 3–25. http://cecils.btk.ppke.hu/cecils1proceedings.

Bárány, A. 2013. The Hungarian subjective paradigm and possessed DOs. Abstract for the 11th International Conference on the Structure of Hungarian (ICSH). http://icsh11.nytud.hu/abs/ICSH13abstract17.pdf.

Chappell, H. & W. McGregor. 1996. Prolegomena to a theory of inalienability. In H. Chappell & W. McGregor (eds.), *The grammar of inalienability: a typological perspective on body part terms and the part whole relation*, 3–30. Berlin: Mouton de Gruyter.

Chung, S. & W. A. Ladusaw. 2004. *Restriction and saturation.* Cambridge (MA): MIT Press.

Comrie, B. 1977. Subjects and direct objects in Uralic languages: a functional explanation of case-marking systems. *Études Finno-Ougriennes XII*, 5–17.

Coppock, E. 2013. A semantic solution to the problem of Hungarian object agreement. *Natural Language Semantics* 21. 345–371. Issue 4.

Coppock, E. & S. Wechsler. 2010. Less-travelled paths from pronoun to agreement: the case of the Uralic objective conjugations. In M. Butt & T. Holloway King (eds.), *Proceedings of the LFG 10 conference*, 165–185. Stanford: CSLI Publications.

Coppock, E. & S. Wechsler. 2012. The objective conjugation in Hungarian: agreement without phi-features. *Natural Language and Linguistic Theory* 30. 699–740.

Csirmaz, A. & A. Szabolcsi. 2012. Quantification in Hungarian. In E. Keenan & D. Paperno (eds.), *Handbook of quantifiers in natural language*, 399–466. Dordrecht: Springer.

den Dikken, M. 2004. Agreement and 'clause union'. In K. É. Kiss & H. van Riemsdijk (eds.), *Verb clusters: A study of Hungarian, German and Dutch*, 445–498. Amsterdam: John Benjamins.

É. Kiss, K. 2002. *The syntax of Hungarian*. Cambridge: Cambridge University Press.

É. Kiss, K. 2005. The inverse agreement constraint in Hungarian: A relic of a Uralic-Siberian sprachbund? In H. Broekhuis et al. (ed.), *Organizing grammar. linguistic studies in honor of Henk van Riemsdijk*, 108–115. Amsterdam: John Benjamins.

É. Kiss, K. 2013. The inverse agreement constraint in Uralic languages. *Finno-Ugric Languages and Linguistics* 3. 2–21.

Elekfi, L. 2000. Semantic differences of suffix alternates in Hungarian. *Acta Linguistica Hungarica* 47. 145–177.

Enç, M. 1991. The semantics of specificity. *Linguistic Inquiry* 22. 1–25.

Heath, J. 1998. Pragmatic skewing in 1 ↔ 2 pronominal combinations in native American languages. *International Journal of American Linguistics (IJAL)* 64. 83–104.

von Heusinger, K. 2011. Specificity. In K. von Heusinger, C. Maienborn & P. Portner (eds.), *Semantics. an international handbook of natural language meaning*, vol. 2, 1024-1057. Berlin: de Gruyter.

Jensen, P. . & C. Vikner. 2004. The English prenominal genitive and lexical semantics. In J.-Y. Kim, Y. A. Lander & B. H. Partee (eds.), *Possessives and beyond: semantics and syntax*, 3–27. Amherst: GLSA.

Kenesei, I., R. M. Vago & A. Fenyvesi. 1998. *Hungarian*. London: Routledge.

Kiefer, F. 1985. The possessive in Hungarian: a problem for natural morphology. *Acta Linguistica Scientiarum Academiae Hungaricae* 35. 139–149.

Löbner, S. 1985. Definites. *Journal of Semantics* 4. 279–326.

Löbner, S. 2011. Concept types and determination. *Journal of Semantics* 28. 279–333.

Marcantonio, A. 1985. On the definite vs. indefinite conjugation in Hungarian: a typological and diachronic analysis. *Acta Linguistica Hungarica* 35. 267–298.

Moravcsik, E. 2003. Inflectional morphology in the Hungarian noun phrase. In F. Plank (ed.), *Noun phrase structure in the languages of Europe*, 113-252. Berlin/New York: de Gruyter.

Nichols, J. 1988. On alienable and inalienable possession. In W. Shipley (ed.), *In honor of Mary Haas. Haas festival conference on native American linguistics*, 557–609. Berlin: Mouton de Gruyter.

Nikolaeva, I. 1999. Object agreement, grammatical relations and information structure. *Studies in Language* 23. 331–376.

Olsson, M. 1992. *Hungarian phonology and morphology*. Lund: Lund University Press.

Ortmann, A. 2014. Definite article asymmetries and concept types: semantic and pragmatic uniqueness. In T. Gamerschlag, D. Gerland, R. Osswald & W. Petersen (eds.), *Frames and concept types. applications in language and philosophy*, 293–321. Dordrecht: Springer.

Özge, U. 2013. What does it mean for an indefinite to be presuppositional? In G. Bezhanishvili, S. Löbner, V. Marra & F. Richter (eds.), *Logic, language, and computation. 9th international tbilisi symposium on logic, language, and computation, TbiLLC 2011*, 138–154. Berlin/Heidelberg: Springer.

Polinsky, M. 1992. Verb agreement and object marking in Sel'kup: interaction of morphology and syntax. In C. P. Canakis, G. P. Chan & J. Marshall Denton (eds.), *Papers from the 28th regional meeting of the Chicago Linguistic Society*, vol. 1, 412–425.

Seiler, H. 1983. *Possession as an operational domain of language*. Tübingen: Narr.

Siewierska, A. 1999. From anaphoric pronoun to grammatical agreement marker: Why objects don't make it. *Folia Linguistica* 33. 225–251. Special issue "Agreement", ed. by Greville G. Corbett.

Siewierska, A. 2004. *Person*. Cambridge: Cambridge University Press.

Siptar, P. & M. Törkenczy. 2000. *The phonology of Hungarian*. Oxford: Oxford University Press.

Szabolcsi, A. 1994. The noun phrase. In F. Kiefer & K. É. Kiss (eds.), *The syntactic structure of Hungarian. syntax and semantics*, 179–274. San Diego/New York: Academic Press.

Szamosi, M. 1974. Verb-object agreement in Hungarian. In M. W. La Galy, R. A. Fox, and A. Bruck (eds.) *Papers from the 10th regional meeting of the Chicago Linguistic Society*, 701–711.

Trommer, J. 1995. Ungarische Verb-Objekt-Kongruenz im Rahmen einer Unifikationsgrammatik. In *Arbeitspapier der Forschungsstelle Artikulationsprozesse (FORSA) 1: Verbale Kategorien und Aktantenkonfiguration*, 17–66. Osnabrück: Universität Osnabrück.

Trommer, J. 2003. Hungarian has no portmanteau agreement. Ms., University of Osnabrück.

Van Valin, R. D. Jr. 1990. Semantic parameters of split intransitivity. *Language* 66. 221–260.

Van Valin, R. D. Jr & Randy LaPolla. 1997. *Syntax: structure, meaning and function.* Cambridge: Cambridge University Press.

Woolford, E. 1995. Object agreement in Palauan: Specificity, humanness, economy and optimality. In J. Beckman, S. Urbanczyk & L. Walsh (eds.), *Papers in Optimality Theory,* 665–700. University of Massachusetts Occasional Papers in Linguistics 18, Amherst: GLSA.

Wunderlich, D. 2001a. A correspondence-theoretic analysis of Dalabon transitive paradigms. In G. Booij & J. van Marle (eds.), *Yearbook of morphology 2000,* 233–252. Dordrecht: Kluwer.

Wunderlich, D. 2001b. How gaps and substitutions can become optimal: the pronominal affix paradigms of Yimas. *Transactions of the Philological Society* 99. 315–366. Special issue on Morphological paradigms, ed. by James P. Blevins.

Zaicz, G. 1998. Mordva. In Daniel Abondolo (ed.), *The Uralic languages,* 184–218. London: Routledge.

Authors

Albert Ortmann
Doris Gerland
Departement of Linguistics and Information Science
Heinrich-Heine-University Düsseldorf
{ortmann,gerland}@phil.hhu.de

Black and white Languages

Leon Stassen

1 Introduction

Seen from a certain perspective, the cross-linguistic variation which language typologists aim to elucidate can be distinguished into two different kinds. First, there are parameters of cross-linguistic variation whose distribution is most likely to be rated as *free*, be it geographically, or typologically, or both. An often cited example of such a parameter is the distribution of the dual across languages. As is well known, there are languages which mark their noun phrases (or at least some of them) for dual number, whereas in other languages no such marking is available. Now, it seems that the languages which do have such dual marking do not, in all probability, form a natural class, neither with respect to their general typological status, nor with respect to their geographical distribution. Thus, dual marking appears to occur in languages that are widely different from each other in their typological make-up. Hence, there are no language features on the basis of which the occurrence or non-occurrence of dual marking in a language can be predicted, and, conversely, the occurrence or non-occurrence of dual marking in a language does not seem to predict any other structural characteristics. Moreover, the spread of the phenomenon of dual marking does not correspond to geographical patterns: dual marking seems to be 'sprinkled' across the globe without any discernible regularity, and there are hardly any major language families in which dual number marking is mandatory for all members. For these reasons, at the present state of our knowledge it seems best to view the phenomenon of dual number marking as some typological 'extra'. That is, it is a feature that languages may 'want' to have, but its occurrence is probably not licensed by any considerations of a genetic, areal, or typological nature, and it is therefore largely unpredictable, if not to say whimsical.

In contrast, linguistic typology has also identified quite a few parameters whose settings do seem to fit into more general typological or areal pictures. In such cases, the particular setting on a given parameter can be shown to be correlated to the setting on one or more other parameters, so that an implicational relation between various different linguistic features can be established. To give just one simple example, the following implicational statement, originally formulated in Greenberg (1963), appears to hold between the options that languages have in their encoding of verb placement and adpositional phrases:

(1) If a language has verb-initial word order, it will have prepositions.

Clearly, by statements such as these the randomness of parameter setting in the encoding of a certain grammatical construction (in this case, adpositional phrases) is constrained to a certain degree: if statement (1) is true – and it seems that it is; no counter-example has been found as yet – we can conclude that, for some reason, at least some languages are 'forced' to have prepositions instead of postpositions. Thus, verb-initial word order and prepositional phrases appear to 'go together'. Another way of formulating this insight is to say that these encoding options form a typological *cluster*. Discovering typological clusters can be seen as the descriptive core business of language typology. In the last fifty years a considerable number of statements such as the one in (1) have been proposed and, in many cases, their validity has been established on the basis of extensive documentation.

When typological parameters form a cluster, it will commonly be the case that one of the parameters can be seen as *primary* or 'first-order'. That is, the value settings on this parameter do not seem to be determined by anything else, and they therefore represent some sort of 'basic structural decision'. Again, basic word order can be used as an instance of such primary parameters. As far as we know, there is nothing in the structure of a language which 'forces' that language to select verb-initial word order instead of, say, verb-final word order. All we can say is that, from the word order options available, a language has to choose at least some option, but the actual choice which a language (or a language family) makes in this respect is probably random. On the other hand, a typological cluster will also contain one or more *secondary* or 'second-order' parameters whose value settings can be said to be determined by the value settings on some other parameter. A case in point here is the value setting on the adposition parameter described above. In constructing adpositional phrases, a language may opt for prepositions or postpositions, but this choice is not completely random. As the correlation formulated in (1) illustrates, the choice between prepositions and postpositions is restricted to prepositions for those languages which have selected the verb-initial option on the primary parameter of basic word order. In the following sections, we will encounter several other parameter settings which appear to be determined by a 'previous' value setting on a primary parameter. Thus, it turns out, for example, that the choice between verbal or nonverbal encoding of predicative adjectives is not random for a language: instead, this choice is determined by the value setting of that language on the (primary) tensedness parameter (see Section 3).

Since settings on primary parameters are essentially selected at random, it is commonly assumed that primary parameters cannot form clusters among themselves. Thus, if a language has a value setting A on one primary parameter (say, basic word order) and a value setting Z on another primary parameter (for instance, tensedness), the collocation of these two particular value settings is usually rated as a matter of coincidence: the combination of the features A and Z in this language might, in principle, have been otherwise. Now, the point of the present paper is to cast some doubt on this assumption, by demonstrating that the settings on at least a number of primary parameters show mutual restrictions and interdependencies to such a degree that the idea of random value selection on these parameters becomes highly unlikely.

In the following sections, I will discuss five typological parameters which, at the present state of our knowledge, are commonly held to be primary. These parameters will be defined in a binary fashion, so that for each parameter a choice between a "yes" and a "no" option is available. Basing my analysis on a sample of 410 languages, selected from families and areas from all over the globe, I will assign a value setting for the sampled languages on all five parameters, and plot the results for each parameter on a world map. A surprising conclusion that can be drawn from these maps is that these five parameters, which are generally understood to be structurally independent, show a remarkable similarity in the geographical distribution of their positive and negative settings. This result suggests interesting consequences for areal linguistics and linguistic typology alike; further discussion will be presented in the final section of this paper.

2 The basic word order parameter

The first of the parameters to be considered here is in many ways 'iconic' to the typological enterprise as a whole: it was the subject of the classic studies by Greenberg (1963, 1966) which are commonly seen as the starting point of modern-day linguistic typology. In these studies, Greenberg and his associates examined possible word order variation in a wide range of constructions and attempted to formulate correlations between the options which languages may choose across these constructions: the above statement (1) is, of course, an example of such a correlation. For the purposes of the current study, I will restrict myself to just a fragment of the domain of word order variation, namely, the options which languages may choose in arranging their basic word order.

Basic word order can be defined as the linear ordering of the main parts of the sentence, viz. the verb (V), the subject (S) and the direct object (O); an additional part of the definition is that basic word order is limited to the ordering of these elements in declarative main clauses. Given the fact that a linear ordering of three elements can, in theory, give rise to six permutations, we conclude that the typology of basic word order will maximally consist of six different types. However, in our study I will reduce this number of options by leaving the position of the subject out of consideration. This decision is motivated by the fact that, as has been argued extensively in the literature that followed Greenberg, subjects have 'a mind of their own' when it comes to ordering principles. Most importantly, their behaviour in word ordering appears to be governed largely by their special status as sentential topics, and hence they are subjected to special motivations which do not hold for the other two basic elements. As a result, the parameter that will be considered here deals only with the ordering of the verb and the direct object. In this way, we arrive at a binary parameter with the orderings V-O and O-V as its possible options. It should be remarked that the VO/OV parameter is not an isolated typological distinction: it forms part of a typological cluster in that it can be shown to determine the settings of various other typological parameters. Above, we have seen that VO/OV settings at least partly determine the options in other realms of word order, such as the choice between prepositions and postpositions. Moreover, it has been suggested that the choice between OV order and VO order is an important determinant factor in the choice between prefixation versus suffixation of agreement items on verbs (Siewierska & Bakker 1996).

Both of the options on the VO/OV parameter can be shown to occur as the exclusive choice in at least some of the languages of the sample. Examples of the

V-O option (which covers the basic word order Types SVO, VOS, and VSO) are the following:

(2) English (Indo-European, West Germanic)
John bought a newspaper.

(3) Scottish Gaelic (Indo-European, Celtic)
Chunnaic sinn an tarbh.
saw   we   the bull
'We saw the bull.'

In contrast, Turkish is an example of a language in which the O-V option is mandatory:

(4) Turkish (Altaic, Turkic)
Hasan okü-zü aldi.
H.   ox-ACC bought
'Hasan bought an ox.'

English, Scottish Gaelic, and Turkish are clear representatives of their respective types, in that their ordering of verbs and direct objects is rigid: divergence from the norm is virtually impossible, or acceptable only under highly marked circumstances. On the other hand, we find languages in which verb-direct object order (and often, word order in general) can be much less restrictive: Classical Latin, Hungarian, and many of the languages of Australia, are well-known cases in point. For some of these languages, a frequency count in text may help to establish the predominant ordering option, but there are also cases in which one has to concede that, apparently, both options are equally possible. Moreover, a different sort of typological indeterminacy may arise from the fact that languages may have undergone a diachronic change: this is, for example, the common analysis for a number of Western branches of Indo-European, where a drift from OV to VO has been hypothesized.

Map 1 shows the geographical distribution of the two possible parameter settings with respect to verb-object order. On the map, areas marked in black contain those languages in which OV is the only, or the clearly dominant option. Areas in which VO is the only or dominant option are marked in white. Shaded parts of the map indicate either areas in which both parameter settings are possible, or areas in which a drift from OV order to VO order can be argued with some degree of plausibility. Looking at this map, we see that there are at least three large, and

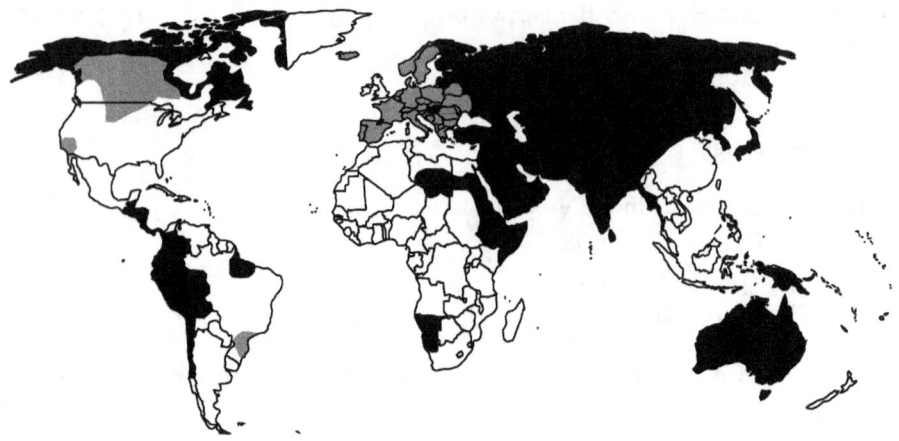

Map 1: Distribution of OV word order

practically uninterrupted, black areas. First, OV ordering is the norm in the mega-area which I will call Eurasia here, and which consists of North and Central Asia (including Japan), India, Iran, and Turkey, and eastern parts of Europe (including the languages of the Caucasus). The Eurasian black area spreads into America on its north-eastern flank, due to the immigration of Asian Eskimo-Aleut speakers into the north of Canada. The area on the western flank of Eurasia, the European peninsula, is mainly shaded, due to a possible diachronic OV-VO drift; exceptions here are Basque (which is clearly OV) and the Celtic languages, which have (and presumably always have had) basic VSO word order.

Apart from Eurasia, other notable 'black' areas are the mega-area which consists of Australia and New Guinea, and an area which covers the southern part of Middle America and the western part of South America (with the Andes mountain range as its eastern border). Smaller OV areas include the territory of the Southern Semitic, Cushitic, and Saharan languages in North-East Africa, the Khoisan languages of South-West Africa, and the Carib languages in the north-western part of South America; these latter languages have the extremely rare OVS pattern as their option for basic word order.

Opposed to these 'black' OV areas, there are also a number of vast areas where VO order reigns supreme. First, we have the 'white' area of East and South-East Asia, which also includes the islands of the Indian and Pacific Ocean. The Middle East and Africa are also predominantly 'white', as is the case with almost the whole of North America (including Mexico and Guatemala), and the centre and south of South America. With regard to this latter area, the Tupi languages of Brazil and Paraguay need some special mention. Of the nine sampled members of this family, eight clearly have OV order. However, the ninth member, the Paraguayan language Guaraní, has more than ninety-five percent of the total of Tupi speakers, and it definitely has VO order, which may or may not be attributed to influence from Spanish.

3 The tensedness parameter

The second parameter to be examined in this study concerns the notion of tensedness. Since this notion is not a standard one in linguistic typology, some explanation may be in order. The notion was introduced in Wetzer (1996) and Stassen (1997). This latter author provides the following definition:

(5) Definition of a tensed language (Stassen 1997)
A language is tensed if

a) predicates in main sentences are obligatorily marked for a past/non-past distinction, and
b) this distinction is encoded by means of bound verbal morphology.

Thus, in order to be rated as tensed, a language must meet two structural conditions at once. First, it needs to make a systematic and obligatory distinction in its finite verb forms between marking for present (or non-past) time reference and marking for past time reference. (Of course, for one of these time references the marking may be zero; this is often the case for the present tense). Furthermore, this distinctive present-past marking must be effectuated by morphological means, rather than by, for example, adverbs, independent particles, or other non-morphological devices. In other words, a language is tensed if, by looking at the form of a finite verb, one can always decide unequivocally whether this verb form refers to present or past time.

A language which clearly meets the requirements of the definition in (5) is English. Here, we see that simplex finite verb forms come in two paradigms. In one of these paradigms, which is used for present time reference, the verb appears in its unmarked stem form. In the other, the past tense, the verb appears in a form which is morphologically marked, either by a suffix – *ed* (for so-called 'weak verbs') or by some internal alteration of the stem (for so-called 'strong verbs').

(6) English (Indo-European, West Germanic)
   a. *John sees the dog.*
   b. *John saw the dog.*

There is only one way in which a language can be tensed, but non-tensed languages come in a number of different varieties. First, there are languages like Mandarin Chinese, which have no (or hardly any) verbal morphology at all. Secondly, languages like Choctaw that do have distinctive verbal paradigms, but the distinction expressed by these paradigms is aspectual in nature rather than temporal. In a language like Burmese, verbal suffixation is used to distinguish a future form from a non-future form, which, in all probability, represents a modal distinction rather than a temporal one. And finally, a language like Tigak does have an obligatory marking for past versus non-past in all of its declarative main sentences, but this marking does not involve bound verbal morphology: it is effectuated by the use of two different sets of so-called 'subject pronouns'. As a result, all of these languages fail to meet the conditions stated in (5), albeit for different reasons.

(7) Mandarin Chinese (Sino-Tibetan, Sinitic)
   Ta   pao.
   3SG run
   'He/she runs/ran/will run.'

(8) Choctaw (Muskogean)
   a. *Pisa   - li.*
      look.at.PERF - 1SG.ACT
      'I see/saw it.'
   b. *Pinsa   - li.*
      look.at.IMPERF - 1SG.ACT
      'I am/was looking at it.'

(9) Burmese (Sino-Tibetan, Burmese-Lolo)
   a. *Ein   pyan   -thwa-te.*
      home return-go -NONFUT
      '(He) goes/went home.'
   b. *Li?   - me.*
      vanish - FUT
      '(I) will vanish.'

(10) Tigak (Austronesian, Melanesian)

    a. *Gi   ima.*
       3SG.PRES come
       'He is coming.'

    b. *Ga   ima.*
       3SG.PAST come
       'He came.'

There is evidence to show that tensedness is not an isolated parameter. In particular, Stassen (1997) has shown that it functions as a predictive factor in the cross-linguistic encoding of adjectival predicates: if a language is tensed, its adjectival predicates are almost always encoded in the same way as predicate nominals, whereas in non-tensed languages adjectival predicates are, in the overwhelming majority of cases, treated on a par with verbs.

It should be remarked that the distinction between tensed and non-tensed languages is not a completely discrete one: there can be 'undecided' or 'diffuse' cases. A main source for this diffusion is the fact that aspectual distinctions (mainly, the one between perfective and imperfective aspect) show a tendency of evolving into a temporal past/non-past distinction over time (see Bybee & Dahl 1989), but this diachronic process does not need to have reached its full completion in all languages. In Map 2, areas with languages in which such an 'intermediate' value on the tensedness parameter has been documented are represented as shaded. In contrast, areas with clearly tensed languages are marked in black, whereas areas with clearly non-tensed languages are marked in white.

There are striking similarities between this tensedness map and the map of OV/VO word order. Most importantly, the three black mega-areas on the word order map (viz. Eurasia, New-Guinea-Australia, and Meso-American-Andean) by and large repeat themselves as black areas on the tensedness map, while the major white areas on the Word Order map (viz. East-South East Asia and the Pacific, North America, the heartland of South America, and sub-Saharan Africa) turn up as white areas on the tensedness map as well. There are a number of discrepancies between the two maps (Hebrew and Arabic, two Semitic languages of the Middle East and Northern Africa are VO, but tensed; the languages of North-East Siberia, and the Eskimo-Aleut languages of North-America, are OV, but non-tensed, as are the Khoisan languages of South-West Africa), but it can be seen that these 'conflicting' areas are typically situated on what might be called 'fault lines' , that

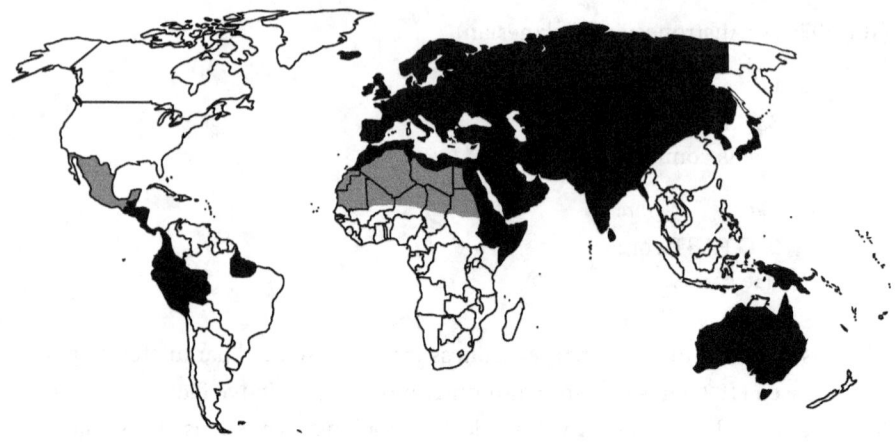

Map 2: Tensed vs. non-tensed languages

is, places where major black and white areas meet and 'bump into each other', so to speak.

4 The casedness parameter

Like tensedness, casedness is not a generally employed notion in typological linguistics. It has been devised specifically for this study, and it can be defined as follows:

(11) Definition of a cased language
A language is cased, if it has morphological (dependent) marking to indicate the difference between subjects and direct objects, at least for pronouns.

Casedness thus represents a specific strategy that languages may employ to keep the two core grammatical functions (Subject vs. Direct Object, or Agent vs. Patient) apart and identifiable. As is well known, the differentiation between these two functions can be effectuated by a number of different means. Some languages, such as Bahasa Indonesia, use fixed word order to this effect, as is shown in example (12):

(12) Bahasa Indonesia (Austronesian, West Indonesian)
   a. *Saya memeluk dia.*
      1SG embrace 3SG
      'I embrace(d) him/her.'

b. *Dia memeluk saya.*
   3SG embrace 1SG
   'He/she embrace(d) me.'

Other languages use a 'head marking' strategy (Nichols 1992), in which core functions are made identifiable by means of a system of agreement affixes on the verb. Casedness is the opposite of this head marking strategy: here, the function of a core argument can be identified in isolation, by looking at the specific form which the two relevant argument NP's have. In languages which are 'cased' in this sense, it frequently happens that one of the core arguments (typically, the subject) remains formally unmarked, whereas the other has overt marking. The specific way of marking may take different formal forms: some languages have an affixational case system, whereas others use structurally independent case markers or adpositions to achieve the discriminatory effect. Examples are:

(13) German (Indo-European, West Germanic)
   Der   Mann sah den   Hund.
   ART.MASC.SG.NOM man   saw ART.MASC.ACC dog
   'The man saw the dog.'

(14) Japanese (Altaic, Japanese)
   Taroo ga   tegami o   katta.
   T.   SUBJ letter OBJ wrote
   'Taroo wrote a letter.'

A special feature of definition (11) is that dependent case marking on pronouns is specified as the minimal requirement for casedness. The reason for this is that dependent case marking systems show a cross-linguistic tendency to 'wear off' over time: an example of this development can be found in various Germanic languages such as English, Dutch, or Swedish, where an erstwhile case marking on noun phrases has gradually vanished. Now, it turns out that the abandonment of core case marking takes place earlier and more radical with full nominal arguments than with pronominal arguments: the above-mentioned Germanic languages no longer differentiate full lexical subjects and direct objects by case marking, but when the subjects and/or direct objects are pronominal they still do.

(15) Dutch (Indo-European, West Germanic)
   a. *Het meisje zag de hond. / De hond zag het meisje.*
      the girl   saw the dog   the dog saw the girl
      'The girl saw the dog. / The dog saw the girl.'

b. *Het meisje zag mij.   / Ik   zag het meisje.*
   the girl   saw 1SG.ACC 1SG.NOM saw the girl
   'The girl saw me. / I saw the girl.'

Pronouns thus appear to be the 'nec plus ultra' of dependent case marking. If they are not marked for grammatical function (as is the case in Bahasa Indonesia; see example (12) above), the language will be rated accordingly as non-cased.

As far as I am aware, the casedness parameter cannot yet be brought into connection with other typological parameters. That is, I do not know of any typological correlations in which the cased or non-cased status of a language predicts anything else, and neither do I know of any correlation in which the cased or non-cased status of a language is predicted by anything. It has sometimes been suggested that the presence of dependent case marking makes it easier for a language to have relatively free word order, and that, conversely, absence of such marking will lead to stricter and more rigid sentential word order. It remains to be seen, however, whether this idea, attractive though it may sound initially, will stand the test of thorough typological examination. Map 3 pictures the distribution of cased and non-cased languages in my sample. Cased areas are marked in black, and non-cased areas are marked in white.

Map 3: Cased vs. non-cased languages

As was the case with the two previous maps, we see that the geographical distribution of the settings on the casedness parameter corresponds to a patterning in mega-areas, and that this patterning is conspicuously similar to the one depicted in Map 1 and Map 2. Again, we find a split between the same major 'black' areas (Eurasia and North Africa, New-Guinea-Australia, and Meso-American-Andean) and major 'white' areas (East and South-Asia, North America, sub-Saharan Africa and Central South America). Areas that are 'white' on the tensedness map but black on the casedness map cover the Khoisan languages of South-West Africa, and the North-East Siberian languages (including Eskimo-Aleut). A change from black to white can be seen in the Carib languages of North-East South America: these languages are OV and tensed, but they do not have a dependent case system.

5 The AND-WITH parameter

The AND-WITH parameter, which was proposed in Stassen (2000), has to do with the cross-linguistic variation in the encoding of noun phrase conjunctions. It entails a distinction between AND languages and WITH languages, and can be defined as follows:

(16) Definition of AND languages and WITH languages (Stassen 2000)

a. A language is an AND language if
there is a structural or lexical distinction between the encoding of noun phrase conjunctions and the encoding of the comitative case.

b. If there is no such distinction, the language is a WITH language.

An obvious example of an AND language is English. In order to express a situation in which two participants are involved together in one action, this language has the choice of using either one of the following constructions. In the first, the two participants, encoded here as full noun phrases, are constructed on the same structural rank. Thus, they form – in this language at least – constituents of a conjoined noun phrase and are – again, in this particular language – connected by the conjunctional particle *and*. In the second construction, there is no equality of structural rank between the two noun phrases: while one of these noun phrases is a core argument (in this case, the subject), the other noun phrase is constructed as part of an adverbial phrase, marked by the comitative preposition *with*.

(17) English (Indo-European, West Germanic)

a. *John and Mary went to see a movie.*

b. *John went to see a movie with Mary.*

In contrast to AND languages such as English, there are languages in which only one option is available. To be specific, such languages have only the second option – that is, the option in which the two noun phrases are not of equal rank – at their disposal; an equivalent way of stating this situation is that such languages lack the option of conjoined noun phrases. Examples of languages which are to be rated as WITH languages on this criterion are:

(18) Samoan (Austronesian, Polynesian)
 Ua   sau   Paulo ma   Maria.
 PROG come P.   and/with M.
 'Paulo and Maria are coming / Paulo is coming with Maria.'

(19) Akan (Niger-Kordofanian, Kwa)
 Kwasi nye   Amba a-ba.
 K.   and/with A.   PAST-come
 'Kwasi and Amba have come/Kwasi has come with Amba.'

Like the casedness parameter, the AND-WITH parameter is not known to participate in any established typological clustering. Moreover, just like the other three parameters discussed so far, settings on the AND-WITH parameter are not necessarily discrete: 'intermediate' values can be observed for quite a few languages in the sample. The motivation behind this indeterminacy is, again, mostly of a diachronic nature. Stassen (2000) discusses a number of cases in which an erstwhile WITH language gradually reanalyses its WITH strategy into something that resembles a 'true' conjunctional construction to a lesser or greater degree. In such languages, an additional *and* structure can be seen to arise, although typically the same conjunctional item will continue to be used in both constructions. Furthermore, several WITH languages seem to have borrowed an additional AND construction from neighbouring dominant languages. This is apparently the case in a number of languages from Siberia, which have added the Russian conjunction *i* 'and' to their repertoire of conjunctional strategies.

Map 4 shows the AND languages in my sample marked in black. Areas that contain WITH languages are marked in white, and intermediate cases are shaded.

I trust that, by now, the stratification of this map will look familiar to the reader. We see the same major 'black' and 'white' areas here as we have seen on the three previous maps, and what is more, we also note the same 'swing' areas. North-East Siberia and Eskimo-Aleut are shaded on this map, for reasons that were exposed above. Khoisan is back as a black area here, but Carib and Tupi

Black and white Languages

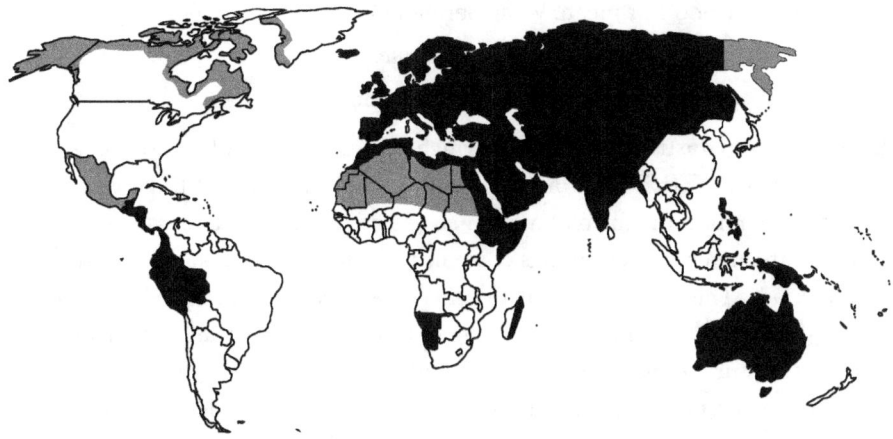

Map 4: AND vs. WITH languages

in South America are white, as they are definitely WITH languages. Newcomers to the 'black' areas are to be found among Austronesian languages. Malagasy (the westernmost Austronesian language, spoken in Madagascar) is an AND language, as are the languages of the Philippines: all these languages are 'white' on the three previous maps. Conversely, Japanese and Korean are 'white' on this map, whereas they are 'black' on all other maps presented thus far.

6 The absolute parameter

The final parameter to be discussed in this study can be called the absolute parameter. This parameter has to do with the morphosyntactic variation which languages exhibit in the encoding of clause linkage. This is a structural domain in which several parameters interact. For our present purpose we do not have to consider all these parameters, and we can restrict ourselves to a somewhat simplified picture, in which we will take into account only those constructions in which the linked clauses at issue have different subjects.

If two such clauses are linked in, for example, a sequence that expresses the simultaneous occurrence of two events, a distinction can be made between two different strategies of encoding. In the first strategy, the predicates in the two clauses both have the form that predicates in main clauses have, the so-called 'finite form'. English examples of sequences in which this situation holds are the following:

(20) English (Indo-European, West Germanic)
   a. *Mary sang and John played the piano.*
   b. *While Mary sang, John played the piano.*

In the English constructions in (20), which represent cases of clause linkage between two clauses that have different subjects, we can see that the predicates in both clauses retain the form of a main clause predicate. Since Stassen (1985) the term 'balancing construction' has come into use for clause linkage constructions of this kind. This term is meant to reflect the fact that both predicates in the construction have main predicate form and thus 'balance' one another in terms of their structural rank within their clause.

Unlike encoding in a balancing construction, clause linkage may also be achieved by a strategy that was labelled 'deranking' in Stassen (1985). Under this strategy, one of the predicates in the sequence keeps its main predicate form, but the predicate in the other clause takes a non-finite form which is typically reduced in its verbal categories when compared to finite verb forms. Such 'deranked' predicates take a number of different morphosyntactic shapes across languages and the terminology to refer to them has not been standardized; we find labels like 'participle', 'gerund', 'infinitive', 'action nominal', 'converb', and several others in the literature. For our purposes, the cross-linguistic variation in the morphosyntactic encoding of deranked predicates need not detain us. What is important for us here is the fact that all deranked predicates, irrespective of their actual morphosyntactic make-up, have a form which cannot be used for a predicate in a main clause.

In addition to its balancing option, English also has the option of deranking for linked clauses, but this option is restricted to sequences in which the two clauses have the same subject. This is demonstrated by the examples in (21). We see that in sentence (21a), where the two clauses have the same subject, it is possible to derank one of the predicates by means of a non-finite verb form called the present participle. If, however, the two clauses have different subjects, deranking of one of the predicates leads to ungrammaticality (see example (21b)).

(21) English (Indo-European, West Germanic)
   a. *Mary was up on the stage, playing a violin.*
   b. ** Mary was up on the stage, John playing a violin.*

In traditional grammar, deranked sequences with different subjects are known as 'absolute constructions'. Sentence (21b) demonstrates that English is a language that lacks the possibility to form constructions of this kind. On the other hand, however, quite a few languages in my sample actually allow such absolute constructions, be it as the only option for different-subject sequences, or as one of the options in addition to a balancing construction. Examples of languages in which absolute constructions are particularly frequent are Classical Latin and Finnish.

(22) Classical Latin (Indo-European, Italic)
Serva cantante dominus
slave.girl.ABL.SG sing.PCP.PRES.ABL.SG master.NOM.SG.
bibit.
drink.PRES.IND.3SG
'The master drinks and/while the slave girl sings'

(23) Finnish (Uralic, Fenno-Ugric)
Kalle-n tu -le -ssa Pekka lahti.
K.-GEN come -INF -INESS P.-NOM leave.PRES.IND.3SG
'When Kalle came, Pekka left.' (lit. 'In Kalle's coming Pekka left.')

On the basis of this contrast between languages like English, on the one hand, and languages like Classical Latin and Finnish, on the other, the concepts of absolute and non-absolute languages can now be defined as follows:

(24) Definition of absolute and non-absolute languages

   a. A language is an absolute language if, in a sequence of two clauses with different subjects, one of the predicates can take a deranked form.
   b. A language is non-absolute if deranking in a sequence of two clauses with different subjects is not possible.

There is ample evidence to suggest that the absolute parameter, and clause linkage encoding in general, constitutes an important primary parameter. Options in clause linkage encoding play a determinant role in the typologies of other construction types, such as the encoding of comparative constructions (Stassen 1985), the encoding of predicative possession constructions (Stassen 2009), and the encoding of various constructions of secondary predication, such as the formation of manner adverbials (Loeb-Diehl 2006) and resultatives (Verkerk 2009).

Map 5 documents the geographical distribution of absolute and non-absolute languages. Here, a by now familiar caveat must be repeated. Assigning a value on the absolute parameter can be problematic for some languages, and again, this indeterminacy is mainly due to diachronic developments. In the Indo-European languages of Europe in particular one can notice a gradual demise of the absolute construction in favour of balancing encodings, to the effect that absolute formations, if they are still in use at all, are seen as 'old-fashioned', 'bookish', or 'formal' in comparison to their balancing counterparts. Languages in which this diachronic drift towards balancing clause linkage can be made plausible are represented by shading in Map 5. For the clear cases, we will use the same colouring as on the other maps. Areas with a positive value on the absolute parameter (that is, areas with absolute languages) are marked in black, whereas areas with a negative value on the parameter (that is, areas with non-absolute languages) are marked in white.

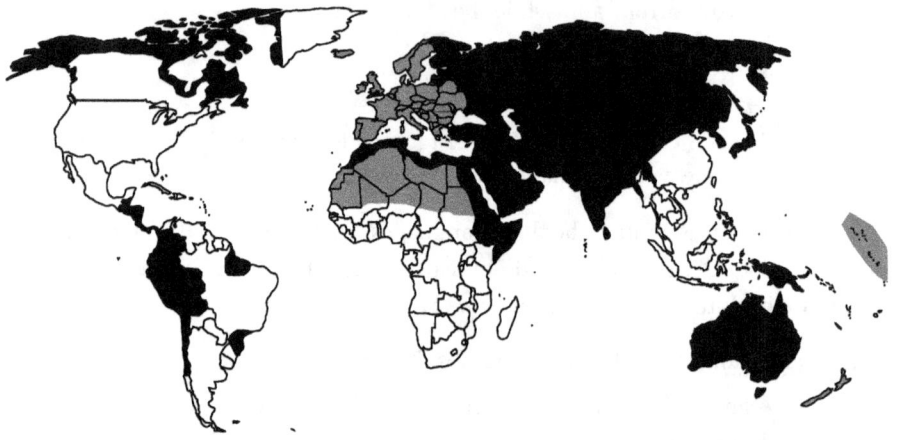

Map 5: Absolute vs. non-absolute languages

As is clear from Map 5, the geographical distribution of the 'black' and 'white' values on the absolute parameter does not differ greatly from the distributions that are depicted on the other maps. Eurasia (including Japanese, Korean, North-East Siberia and Eskimo-Aleut, the Middle East, and North-East Africa) is again a black area here, with the exception of Europe, which, as we have seen above, is a shaded area on this parameter. New-Guinea-Australia and Meso-America-Andean are again the other two steadfast black areas. The same consistency can, by and large, be attested for the major 'white' areas on this map. North America, the heartland of South America, sub-Saharan Africa, and East and South-East Asia all contain clearly non-absolute languages, the only exception being the Polynesian languages, which happen to allow for absolute constructions and therefore show up on this map as a 'black' area for the first time. As for the 'swing areas',

Black and white Languages

we can note that the South-American Carib and Tupi languages turn up marked in black on this map. The South-West African Khoisan languages, on the other hand, do not tolerate absolute constructions and are therefore represented as a 'white' area here.

7 Discussion

As I see it, the results of the cross-linguistic investigation of the five parameters in the previous sections, and the maps that are based upon these results, raise some intriguing questions for both linguistic typology and areal linguistics. Starting with the typological side of things, we can conclude that the combination of value settings on these five parameters is almost certainly not random, even though all the parameters considered are, to the best of our knowledge, 'primary', and hence structurally independent of one another. However, if languages were free to select their value settings on these five parameters, the predicted number of different language types would be $(2*2*2*2*2 =)32$. Now, we can see that this number of logically possible language types is severely restricted empirically. In fact, it appears that there is a strong tendency towards a dichotomy into 'mega-types', in which languages tend to align themselves into two sides which, on each parameter, have opposite settings. In keeping with the terminology used in the previous sections, I will call these two language types 'black languages' and 'white languages'. For these two types, the following clustering of parameter settings can be observed:

(25) Value settings for black and white languages

	White Languages	Black Languages
Word Order	VO	OV
Tensedness	Non-tensed	Tensed
Casedness	Non-cased	Cased
Nominal Conjunction	WITH	AND
Absolute Converb	Non-absolute	Absolute

What these results suggest is that the typological variation between languages may be far more restricted than has been assumed so far. It may be the case that languages align themselves in 'optimal' collocations of settings on a rather restricted set of 'primary' parameters, which largely determine the type to which the language belongs. In fact, based on the results of this study one might even venture the – admittedly, totally wild – hypothesis that there are only two basic language types in the world, which are characterized by taking opposite choices on a number of fundamental structural decisions. At the same time, however, it should be conceded right away that the results obtained in this study raise various questions of their own, both of a descriptive and an explanatory nature. First, we can ask whether the five parameters that cluster in the way which is presented in (25) are all truly independent of one another: it may very well be that the empirically established cluster of these five parameters can be shown to have (some degree of) internal structure after all, so that some of these parameters are actually secondary. Furthermore, one can ask why it is just this set of parameters which gives rise to the differentiation into two structurally opposite language types. It should be kept in mind that the parameters discussed in this study were selected largely on the basis of my personal typological domains of interest, and that there is absolutely no guarantee that the list of these clustering parameters is complete; in fact, the opposite seems far more likely. In other words, the results obtained in this study can only be considered as a starting point for much more thorough further research, and the best one can say at the moment is that these results are intriguing and potentially promising.

Turning now to issues of areal linguistics, we can conclude that the results of this study have potential consequences for our conception of language areas as well. In the previous sections we have seen that the typological distinction between black and white languages tends to converge with the definition of black and white 'mega-areas'. In Map 6, I have summarized the five maps for the separate parameters, according to the following format:

- If a language appears 4 or 5 times on a map as a black language, it will be marked as a black language on Map 6.
- If a language appears 0 or 1 times on a map as a black language, it will be marked as a white language on Map 6.
- If a language appears 2 or 3 times on a map as a black language, it will appear as shaded on Map 6.

As a result, the map of black and white language distribution looks like this:

As we have already noticed in our discussions of the various parameter maps, the distribution of black and white languages across the globe gives rise to the identification of a number of clear black and white mega-areas, which form relatively homogenous, uninterrupted stretches. The largest black area is Eurasia (or 'The Old World').which, in its maximal extension, covers Central and Northern

Black and white Languages

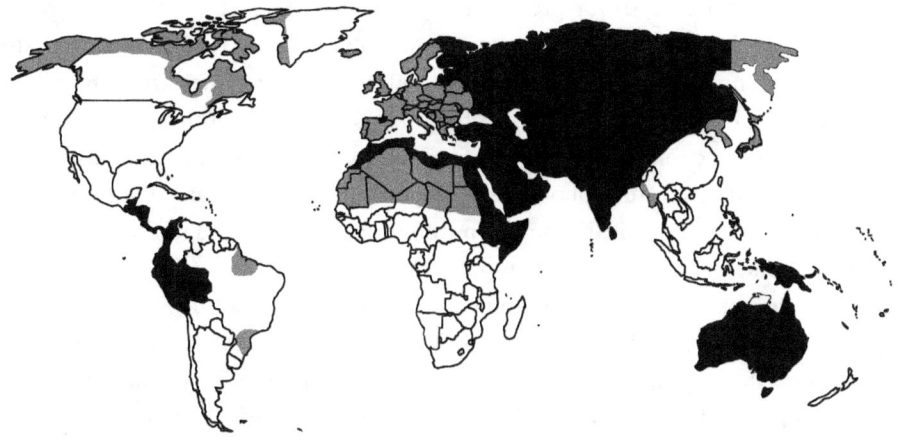

Map 6: Black vs. white languages

Asia, India, Pakistan, The Middle East, Northern Africa, and North-East Africa. Further mega-areas which have a consistent (or almost consistent) black encoding are New Guinea/Australia and the Meso-American-Andean area, which covers the south of Central America and the north-west of South America. In opposition, consistently white areas are found in North America/Mexico, most of South America, sub-Saharan Africa, China and South East Asia, and the Indic and Pacific Ocean. A further remarkable feature of Map 6 is that the shaded 'in-between areas' or 'swing areas' are commonly found at the edges of the Eurasian black area. First, there is Europe, which constitutes the far-western tip of the Eurasian land mass. (The exception here is the isolated Basque language, which is a steadfast black language). At the south-western border of the Eurasian mega-area we find the intermediate, 'shaded' area covered by the North-African Berber languages. Moreover, at the very north-eastern fringe of Eurasia, there are the so-called Paleo-Siberian languages, Japanese, Korean and Eskimo-Aleut which constitute a transitory area between 'black' and 'white' encoding. 'Swing areas' that are not situated at the borderline between black and white mega-areas do occur, but they are scarce and tend to consist of one language family only: in South America we can point to the Tupi languages and the Carib languages, and in South-West Africa we have the relatively small Khoisan family.

What this map suggests is that geographical contact may have been much more extensive than has been assumed up to now. The possibility of linguistic 'macro-areas', which supersede current genetic classification, should be seriously considered, and the time-depth for presumed geographical contact should perhaps be extended much further than is commonly accepted now in areal linguistics. Alternatively, one might reconsider the possibility that there exist 'mega-families' of the type proposed by Joseph Greenberg in various publications. Thus, Map 6 may provide some renewed credibility for concepts like 'Amerind' and 'Nostratic'.

Whatever one may think about these suggestions, I feel it is safe to draw at least one general methodological conclusion from the data presented in this study.

In the generally accepted view, typological linguistics and areal linguistics are seen as two separate enterprises, and one should take care not to confound them. Although I agree that, in principle, this is sound practice, there are nonetheless indications that typological collocations and areal configurations of linguistic parameters have a tendency to converge, especially when macro-areas are considered. Therefore, the two linguistic sub-disciplines of language typology and areal stratification may be beneficial to one another to a degree that is much higher than is usually thought possible.

List of abbreviations

In the glosses of the example sentences the following abbreviations have been used:

1,2,3	first, second, third person
ABL	ablative case
ACC	accusative case
ACT	actor case
ART	article
FUT	future tense
GEN	genitive case
IMPERF	imperfective aspect
IND	indicative mood
INESS	inessive case
INF	infinitive
MASC	masculine gender
NOM	nominative case
NONFUT	non-future tense
PAST	past tense

PCP   participle
PERF   perfective aspect
PRES   present tense
PROG   progressive aspect

Bibliography

Bybee, J. & Ö. Dahl. 1989. The creation of tense and aspect systems in the languages of the world. *Studies in Language* 13-1. 51-103.
Greenberg, J. H. 1963. Some universals of grammar with particular reference to the order of meaningful elements. In J. H. Greenberg (ed.), *Universals of language*, 73-113. Cambridge: MIT Press.
Greenberg, J. H. 1966. *Language universals*. The Hague: Mouton.
Loeb-Diehl, F. 2006. *The typology of manner expressions*. Nijmegen: Radboud University dissertation.
Nichols, J. 1992. *Linguistic diversity in space and time*. Chicago: University of Chicago Press.
Siewierska, A. & D. Bakker. 1996. The distribution of subject and object agreement and word order type. *Studies in Language* 20.1. 115-161.
Stassen, L. 1985. *Comparison and Universal Grammar*. Oxford: Blackwell.
Stassen, L. 1997. *Intransitive Predication*. Oxford: Oxford University Press.
Stassen, L. 2000. AND-languages and WITH-languages. *Linguistic Typology* 4. 1-54.
Stassen, L. 2009. *Predicative possession*. Oxford: Oxford University Press.
Verkerk, A. 2009. *Secondary predication in a typological context*. Nijmegen Radboud University MA thesis.
Wetzer, H. 1996. *Nouniness and verbiness: a typological study of adjectival predication*. Berlin: Mouton De Gruyter.

Author

Leon Stassen
Faculteit der Letteren, Taalwetenschap
Radboud Universiteit Nijmegen
l.stassen@let.ru.nl

Variations of double nominative in Korean and Japanese

Dieter Wunderlich

Preface

A personal note. Once Sebastian Löbner and I tried to climb Mount Fuji, the king of mountains. Because of heavy rainfall, we were forced to turn back, and ended in a sauna with a sake bar. The double ascent had became a kind of double passivity; and both of us were disappointed by this failure. The king of cases is the nominative; a double nominative has two kings of different descent, sometimes emerging in the passive voice (*Leideform* in German). This doubling experience made me ultimately decide to write this article.

An observation. The double nominative is a very popular subject for Japanese and Korean linguists. There are, presumably, hundreds of papers discussing how it interacts with various fields of Japanese and Korean syntax, mostly parallel in these languages. Not wrongly, Japanese and Korean linguists consider the double nominative to be a unique feature of their languages.

A prejudice. A double nominative is not spectacular in itself. Some linguists believe that nominative is assigned in a specific context, say SpecT. In that case, one has to ask: and what assigns the second nominative? Alternatively one might believe that nominative is the default case (often unmarked), and so a double nominative may be more frequent than was previously believed. In many languages, if (for some reason) accusative is blocked for an object, nominative becomes the automatic case instead by default.

A brief abstract. In this paper, various types of alternations bringing about double nominatives are discussed. Nominatives in particular invite focus or topic interpretations, dependent on further circumstances. They also result when more complex structures are formed by extraction. Sometimes, double accusatives and double genitives with similar functions are found. These case-doubling and case-stacking alternations appear as a key to major areas of Korean and Japanese grammar as well as to the historical, often parallel, development of these languages. Many alternations are lexically triggered. Sometimes the double-nominative emerges because the accusative is forbidden in a stative context. A lexical constraint-based framework might be fruitful to account for the interaction between vocabulary classes, information structure and constructional properties.

1 Introduction: Possessor-raising as a source for double-nominative

Japanese and Korean exhibit the same type of double-nominative (NOM-NOM) construction, which relates to a more 'basic' GEN-NOM construction by 'possessor raising': the possessor 'moves' out of a nominal domain into a higher verbal domain – such a variation might be described as syntactic movement or by a lexical rule adding a possessor argument to the verb: $\lambda x V(x) \Rightarrow \lambda x \lambda y [\text{POSS}(y,x) \& V(x)]$. In a sentence such as (1b) or (2b), the first NOM-NP (=N1) stands in a relational or functional *inalienable* relationship with the second NOM-NP (=N2) – as the 'possessor' of a body part, an illness, a relative, a piece of clothing, etc. While the combination GEN-NOM forms a single syntactic constituent, NOM-NOM does not, as shown by the fact that N1 and N2 can be separated by a sentence adverb (Nakamura 2002). However, the order of the two NOM arguments cannot be changed, similarly to the fixed order in the GEN-NOM constituent. In the following, J=Japanese, K=Korean. Note that Korean NOM is either realized by /-ka/ (after vowel) or by /-i/ (after consonant).

(1) a. *Syusyoo-no   byooki-ga   saikin   omo-i.*   J
 [Prime Minister-GEN illness-NOM] recently serious-PRES

 b. *Syusyoo-ga   saikin   byooki-ga   omo-i.*
 Prime Minister-NOM recently illness-NOM serious-PRES
 'The Prime Minister is seriously ill.'

(2) a. *Swungsang-uy   pyeng-i   choykun simha-ta.*   K
 [Prime Minister-GEN illness-NOM] recently serious-DECL

 b. *Swungsang-i   choykun pyeng-i   simha-ta.*
 Prime Minister-NOM recently illness-NOM serious-DECL
 'The Prime Minister is seriously ill.'

In addition, both Japanese and Korean have a number of related structures which also exhibit some sort of 'possessor raising': among them are NOM-NOM objects in Japanese dative-subject verbs (3), and ACC-ACC objects in Korean (4), see Nakamura (2002) and Kim (1989). Similar to NOM-NOM, the ACC-ACC construction is not possible with an alienable possessor, see (4b).

(3) a. *Hanako-ni(wa) kono hon-no naiyoo-ga yoku waka-ru.* J
 H.-DAT(TOP) [this book-GEN content-NOM] well understand-PRES

 b. *Hanako-ni(wa) kono hon-ga yoku naiyoo-ga waka-ru.*
 H.-DAT(TOP) this book-NOM well content-NOM understand-PRES
 'Hanako understands the content of this book well.'

(4) a. *Mary-ka John-uy/-ul tali-lul cha-ess-ta.* inalienable, K
 Mary-NOM John-GEN/ACC leg-ACC kick-PAST-DECL
 'Mary kicked John's leg.'

 b. *Mary-ka John-uy/*-ul cha-lul cha-ess-ta.* alienable, K
 Mary-NOM John-GEN/*ACC car-ACC kick-PAST-DECL
 'Mary kicked John's car.'

Concerning the constructions (3) and (4), the counterpart in the respective other language is odd. In Korean, something like *content (book)* doesn't seem inalienable enough (or, affected enough) to enter the ACC construction, see (5). In Japanese, the ACC-ACC construction is only accepted if the two ACCs are separated by adverbs (Kim 1989), see (6b), or if the possessor is scrambled (6c), clefted (6d), or associated with a focus-inducing element (6e) (examples from Hiraiwa 2010).

(5) *Hanna-eykey(-nun) i chayk(-uy) nayyong-i cal ihaytoy-n-ta.* K
 Hana-DAT(-TOP) this book(-GEN) content-NOM well intelligible-PRS-DECL
 'Hana understands the content of this book well.'

(6) a. *Mary-ga John-no/*-o asi-o ketta.* J
 M.-NOM J.-GEN/*-ACC leg-ACC kicked
 'Mary kicked John's leg.'

 b. *Mary-ga John-o kinoo undoozyo-de asi-o ketta.*
 M.-NOM J.-ACC yesterday playground-LOC leg-ACC kicked
 'Yesterday, Mary kicked John's leg at the playground.'

 c. *John-o Mary-ga asi-o ketta.*
 J.-ACC M.-NOM leg-ACC kicked
 'John, Mary kicked (his) leg.'

d. *[Mary-ga asi-o   ketta-no]-wa John-o da.*
   M.-NOM leg-ACC kicked-C-TOP J.-ACC COP
   'It was John that Mary kicked the leg of.'

e. *Mary-ga John-mo/dake/sae/wa asi-o   ketta.*
   M.-NOM J.-also/only/even/TOP leg-ACC kicked
   'Mary also/only/even kicked John's leg.'

The first question is: Why does the case pattern NOM-NOM appear, rather than NOM-ACC or DAT-NOM? Answer: All predicates that allow NOM-NOM as an alternation are static, and static predicates are excluded from having ACC arguments in both Japanese and Korean. (Note, by the way, that German adjectives, which form a class of stative predicates, also exclude ACC arguments.) A binary verb construction with dative would have to be lexically marked, as is the case with *wakaru* 'understand' in (3). That dative-subject verbs have a NOM object is conditioned by the universal constraint (7a). Since 'understand' is stative, ACC is excluded, while 'kick,' a nonstative verb, allows ACC. Finally, Korean allows ACC-ACC objects, but Japanese does not; this is because UNIQUENESS(ACC) is specifically highly ranked in Japanese.

(7) a. DEFAULT. Each case domain contains the default case NOM. (universal)
   b. *ACC/+stative. Accusative is not possible with stative verbs. (Jap./Kor.)
   c. UNIQUENESS(ACC). ACC occurs only once in a case domain. (Jap.)

These constraints are part of the package proposed in Wunderlich (2001), a first attempt to extend the analysis of optimal case patterns in German and Icelandic (Wunderlich 2003) to a typologically different language such as Japanese. None of the individual constraints given in (7) is new, but what may be new is that each of these constraints can be violated when they are part of a ranked system of constraints. A case domain is governed by a lexical head (such as a verb, or a noun, or some other argument-taking entity), it is thus more specific than Chomsky's concept of *phase*. Both (7b) and (7c) are well-known in Japanese linguistics: (7b) was observed by Kuno (1973), and (7c) has been called *double-o constraint*, first described by Harada (1973).

Poser (2002) distinguishes between underlying and surface double-o constraint; it is the latter that is captured by (7c). The underlying double-o constraint forbids ACC on the causee of a causativized transitive verb; such a constraint is unnecessary under the assumption that the medial argument of a 3-place predicate is underlyingly dative. In fact, many of Poser's observations are predicted by Lexical Decomposition Grammar (Wunderlich 1997), for example, that "the verbs that take dative objects permit accusative causees, while those that take accusative objects do not" (1997: 12) (they instead require dative causees) – note that in both instances an optimal NOM-ACC-DAT pattern results, although in different distributions. According to Poser, path-adverbials, which are realized by accusative, can co-occur with an ACC object. Thus, there exist exceptions to the double-o-constraint; in other words, this constraint might be dominated by an even more specific one.

Hiraiwa (2010) explicitly restricts the domain of the double-o constraint to a phase, and also discusses the possibilities for escaping this constraint, as shown in (6c) - (6e) above. Hiraiwa does not discuss what seems to be important, namely that the escape structures have their own functions. A scrambled object possessor like in (6c) could be a topic, while a clefted possessor as in (6d) is in focus. Moreover, the particles added to *John* in (6e) are focus-inducing. The cleft construction (6d) is certainly biclausal, but whether the scrambled version (6c) as well as the focus-particle version (6e) constitute an extra phase (an extra case domain) might be questionable. It could well be the case that these constructions count as exceptions to the double-o-constraint for other than structural reasons.

Another question is: Why does the Korean object-possessor construction show ACC-ACC rather than DAT-ACC? Some authors assume a requirement of case sharing (*case concordance, case-agreement*). The Korean passive, however, speaks against *case sharing* as a rule, because NOM-ACC is possible alongside NOM-NOM (8a,b, Yang 2000). (Note that DEFAULT (7a) does not require more than one NOM.) Similarly, the raised possessor of a dative-marked object can be DAT or NOM (8c, Maling & Kim 1992), thus, case sharing can, but doesn't have to apply. Inversely, in the nominal predicate construction, where German shows case sharing (NOM-NOM: er_{NOM} wurde nicht als $Idiot_{NOM}$ angesehen 'he wasn't considered a fool,' ACC-ACC: *man sah ihn_{ACC} nicht als $Idioten_{ACC}$ an* 'one didn't consider him a fool'), Korean does not, as shown in (8c).

(8) a. *John-i/*-ul   tali-ka/-lul   cha-i-ess-ta.* K
John-NOM/*ACC leg-NOM/ACC kick-PASS-PAST-DECL
'John's leg was kicked.'

b. *John-i   tali-lul   kkuth-ul cha-i-ess-ta.*
John-NOM leg-ACC end-ACC kick-PASS-PAST-DECL
'The end of John's leg was kicked.'

    c. *John-i Yumi-lul papo-ka/*lul   an-i-la-ko   mit-ess-ta.*
       J.-NOM Y.-ACC   fool-NOM/*ACC not-be-SUSP-COMP believe-PAST-DECL
       'John believed Yumi not to be a fool.'

Note that 'possessor raising' is recursive (regardless of whether it is considered a lexical or a syntactical operation).

(9) a. *Mary-ka   John-ul   tali-lul olunccok-ul   cha-ss-ta.*   K
       Mary-NOM John-ACC leg-ACC right.side-ACC kick-PAST-DECL
       'Mary kicked the right side of John's leg.'

    b. *Mary-ka John-uy/ul elkwul-ul sacin(-ul)   ccik-ess-ta.*
       M.-NOM J.-GEN/ACC face-ACC picture(-ACC) take-PAST-DECL
       'Mary took a picture of John's face.' (Cho 2003: 346)

It has been extensively discussed in the literature whether NOM-NOM constructions have two subjects (as suggested by the usually used notion of 'double subject'), or, if they have only one subject, which NP it is. Kuroda (1978) proposed the structure [N1 [N2 PRED]$_{S1}$]$_{S2}$ for the double-subject. Regretfully, the most common subject tests (such as binding of Japanese *zibun*, resp. of Korean *caki* 'self,' honorific agreement with the verb, or plural agreement with an adverb or verb in Korean) yield unclear results. Yet if one uses [N1.NOM [N2.NOM PRED]] in a raising-to-object construction, one would expect N1 to be raised.

Yoon (2009) states that in the multiple subject construction (with iterative NOM doubling), only the final NOM-NP is the grammatical subject (which is predicated of), while all the preceding NOM-NPs are major subjects related to the grammatical subject. More precisely, in my words: each of these NPs fills a gap in the respective subsequent NP, which expresses a relational (or even functional concept). But why something which, for example, gives a value for a body part function such as *someone's leg* should have the same grammatical function as the body part itself, remains a mystery.

What is interesting here is the fact that something which in English is processed from an innermost body part up to a large area ('the [leg of the [president of the [parliament of the [European Union]]]] is broken'), becomes a reversed chain '[European Union [parliament [president [leg is broken]]]]' in Japanese and Korean. In English, an expectation about a property and the possessor of some leg is built up, while in Japanese a piecemeal zooming-in takes place.

A more specific question is: Which relations allow 'possessor raising'? According to Bak (2004), there is a split low in the inalienable hierarchy *body parts* >

family member > *clothing* > **equipment*, compare (10a,b). The restriction is the same with intransitive predicates, see (10c,d), friendship is alienable in the same way that shoes are (10e) (Sun 2013).

(10) a. *Youngsu-ka Chelsu-uy/lul phal-ul ttayli-ess-ta.*   K
     Y.-NOM   C.-GEN/ACC   arm-ACC hit-PAST-DECL
     'Youngsu hit Chelsu's arm.'

    b. *Youngsu-ka Chelsu-uy/*lul cup-ul ttayli-ess-ta.*
     Y.-NOM   C.-GEN/*ACC   cup-ACC hit-PAST-DECL
     'Youngsu hit Chelsu's cup.'

    c. *Mary-uy/ka nwun-i yeyppu-ta.*
     M.-GEN/NOM eye-NOM pretty-DECL
     'Mary's eyes are pretty.'

    d. *Mary-uy/*ka sinpali-i yeyppu-ta.*
     M.-GEN/*NOM shoe-NOM pretty-DECL
     'Mary's shoes are pretty.'

    e. *Mary-uy/*ka shinkwu-ka yeyppu-ta.*
     M.-GEN/*NOM friend-NOM pretty-DECL
     'Mary's friend is pretty.'

Cho (2003) claims that possessor raising is only possible when an *entailment* of the following sort holds (which clearly is too a narrow restriction because it wrongly excludes family members):

John's leg was kicked   ⇒   John was kicked.   (NOM-NOM is possible)
John's friend was kicked   ⇏   John was kicked.   (*NOM-NOM)
John's father was kicked   ⇏   John was kicked.   (but NOM-NOM is possible!)

(Those who consider the raised possessor as a second subject sometimes seem to have such an entailment in mind.) A further question is: Which predicates allow the possessor of their subject to be raised? Above, it has been suggested that the predicates must be stative. Evidence is given by (11): the genitive possessor allows two interpretations, while the raised possessor is restricted to the stative interpretation (Sun 2013). An interpretational asymmetry like that in (11) tends to trigger bifurcation: NOM-NOM ↔ generic, GEN-NOM ↔ episodic interpretation.

(11) *Mary-uy/ka atul-i chwukku-lul ha-n-ta.*   K
       M.-GEN/NOM son-NOM soccer-ACC do-PRES-DECL
       (i) 'Mary's son is playing soccer (now).'   GEN *NOM
       (ii) 'Mary's son is a (professional) soccer player.'   GEN NOM

Note, however, that the possessor of an *object* of a dynamic verb like 'kick' or 'hit' can be raised (see the examples above). There is obviously a complex (and somewhat mysterious) interaction between the kind of predicate, the sort of noun, the relationship between noun and possessor, the fixed word order between possessor and noun, the role of the noun (whether it is subject or object), the domain of the possessor (whether it belongs to the nominal or the verbal domain), the case marking of the noun and possessor, and the three constraints given in (7) (and possibly more). The raised possessor of an object is a further object (and thus marked accusative by default), while the raised possessor of a subject is not an object (and thus marked nominative by default) – this seems simple, yet I think the rigid case-marking of the raised possessor is the most embarrassing problem. All these factors (at least the ways they interact) could vary due to historical contingencies. The constraints mentioned above, *ACC/+stat (7b) and UNIQUENESS(ACC) (7c), could be the product of some development conditioned by accidental variation in the domain of possessor raising.

It is extremely surprising that Japanese and Korean, considered to be genealogically unrelated by most linguists, ended up with nearly the same system (except for UNIQUENESS(ACC)). Many linguists are tempted to seek the common properties within Universal Grammar, identified by (some sort of) syntax. Therefore, they have a syntactic account in mind, and in the process of elaboration they tend to narrow down the empirical domain. I am skeptical about achieving any progress along these lines, and so I would like to propose another treatment: (i) identify all the connections within the possessor-raising net, (ii) determine lexical contributions and compositional semantic interpretations, (iii) study (perhaps via simulation) how the various factors in this net react to some disturbances, (iv) estimate a reasonable value for the relatedness of Japanese and Korean. Languages that share most of their basic vocabularies (like Indo-Aryan, Quechuan or Alor-Pantar languages) are often quite distinct in parts of their grammars, like those concerned with argument structure and case. Why are Japanese and Korean so different – distinct in their vocabularies but very similar in their grammars?

Independently, one can ask for the functional potential of double-NOM. Does the pattern NOM-NOM (or ACC-ACC) constitute any processing advantage (for instance in the sense that every NOM occurrence triggers a new syntactic borderline)? Kwon's (2006) results clearly contradict such an assumption: this author showed in *self-paced* reading experiments that NOM-NOM causes significant delays. Is it perhaps spoken language in which an advantage is present, or because the expressive power is enhanced?

Let us consider a hypothesis: The advantage of shifting the possessor from an argument of the noun to an argument of the governing verb is to make a better use of it: (i) in creating information structure, or (ii) in forming more complex sentences.

In the following, I will discuss a number of constructions and interpretations connected with the double nominative. I do not have an integrating theory in mind from which all of this could follow, but along my way I will stress a number of points having to do with lexical contribution and semantic representation, sometimes neglected but worth taking note of. In the process, I have chosen a suite with 12 dances of different length. My polonaise in 2 is a numeration of the NOM-NOM types found in Korean. In 3, case stacking in Korean is introduced as a means of inducing focus, while in 4, nominatives are studied as enabling topic or focus interpretations. The Korean topic clauses in 5 are followed by Japanese scope variations in 6. Then two Japanese dances follow: potential and passives in 7, and genitive subjects in 8, followed by a very short Korean *tough*-constructional melody in 9. A first summarizing cadence is given in 10, which is then followed by a saxophone's double-NOM passive in 11. That Korean is a little less sensitive than Japanese comes out in 12, and finally we end with the great Korean-Japanese harmony in 13.

2 Types of NOM-NOM constructions

For Korean, I have found the following list of NOM-NOM predicates (Lee 2003). Probably, one might come up with a similar list for Japanese. Let us introduce these types step by step.

Type I comprises predicates with GEN/NOM alternation. N2 (which is predicated of) is a relational noun whose open argument is filled by N1 – which is either the usual GEN possessor or its possessor-raised NOM-variant.

(12)   a. Part-whole relationship (or inalienable possession)   K
          ohn-uy/-i   son-i   cakta.
          John-GEN/NOM hands-NOM small
          'John's hands are small/John has small hands.'

      b. Relational concepts (e. g. *kinship*)
          John-uy/-i   atul-i   cakta.
          John-GEN/NOM son-NOM short
          'John's son is short/John has a short son.'

c. Alienable possession (it is unclear how far the alternation is possible)
   John-uy/-i   cip-i   cakta.
   John-GEN/NOM house-NOM small
   'John's house is small/John has a small house.'

d. Argument of a verbal noun
   i   mwunce-uy/-ka   haykeyl-i   swipta.
   this problem-GEN/NOM solution-NOM easy
   'The solution of this problem is easy/This problem has an easy solution.'

Type II includes predicates with two separately required arguments. There are three subtypes.

IIa. A LOC or DAT argument can get a NOM-alternative:

(13) a. *i   san-ey/-i   namwu-ka manhta.*   K
     this mountain-LOC/NOM trees-NOM abundant
     'There are many trees on this mountain/This mountain has many trees.'

   b. *John-eykey/-i komin-i   saynggi-ess-ta.*
      John-DAT/NOM worry-NOM become-to-exist
      (lit.) 'To John, there happen to be some worries/John has gotten some worries.'

IIb. *Simple* [+stative] predicates (such as psych adjectives or copula verbs) have a NOM-object, and therefore show the NOM-NOM pattern just from the start.

(14) a. *John-i   Mary-ka   cohta.*   K
     John-NOM Mary-NOM be fond of
     'John is fond of Mary.'

   b. *nay-ka tongsaying-i mipta*
      I-NOM brother-NOM hate
      'I hate my brother.'

(15) a. *John-i   kasu-ka   anita.*   K
     John-NOM singer-NOM be-not
     'John is not a singer.'

   b. *Mary-ka   uysa-ka   toyessta.*
      Mary-NOM doctor-NOM became
      'Mary became a doctor.'

IIc. A *complex stative predicate* formed with the verb 'want' (or, with the potentialis suffix 'can' in Japanese) again shows ACC/NOM alternation (Shekar & Agbayani 2003).

(16) a. *Nay-ka sakwa-lul/*ka   mekkessta.* K
     I-NOM apple-ACC/*NOM ate
     'I ate an apple.'

  b. *Nay-ka sakwa-lul/ka   mekko sephta.*
     I-NOM apple-ACC/NOM eat   want
     'I **want** to eat an apple.'

(17) a. *John-ga   huransugo-ga/*o   deki-ru.* J
     John-NOM French-NOM/*ACC capable-PRES
     'John is capable of French.' ('John speaks French.')

  b. *John-ga huransugo-ga/-o hana-se-ru.*
     J.-NOM French-NOM/ACC speak-POT-PRES
     'John **can** speak French.'

This alternation can be captured by the assumption of optional verb complex formation:

- ACC is licensed by the embedded verb in the structure [[ACC eat] want], while
- NOM is accepted by the stative verb complex [NOM [eat want]].

A similar result might be achieved by assuming that the feature [+stative] is optional.

Type III includes two special cases, namely specifications and numerals with classifiers.

(18) a. *Specification.* If N2 is more specific than N1 (|N1| ⊃ |N2|), NOM-NOM is obligatory: K
     kwail-i/*uy   sakwa-ka   masissta.
     fruit-NOM/*GEN apples-NOM tasty
     'As for fruit, apples are tasty.'

  b. *Numerals with classifiers.* If the quantifier is floating, i. e. shifts into a postnominal position to the noun, NOM-NOM is obligatory:

    i. *twu-kay-uy   sakwa-ka   ssekessta.*
       two-**CLF-GEN** apples-NOM rotten
       'Two apples are rotten.'

ii. *sakwa-ka twu-kay-ka ssekessta.*
  apples-NOM two-CLF-NOM rotten
  'Two of the apples are rotten.' (floating quantifier)

Obviously, 'tasty' in (18a) and 'rotten' in (18b) remain intransitive (even if they combine with a NOM-NOM pattern), which may explain why these two special cases show strict *case-sharing* – in contrast to the alternation cases found before. Further tests are the application of passive in the ACC-ACC construction, or *raising-to-object* in the NOM-NOM construction: do both nominals shift their case, or not? In the two special cases, both nouns shift their case – see (19) and (21a). Otherwise, *case-sharing* is optional – see (20) and (21b).

Specification under passive compared with a body part construction under passive (Sim 2006).

(19) a. *Chelswu-ka koki-lul phiraymi-lul cap-ass-ta.* K
  C.-NOM fish-ACC small.fish-ACC catch-PAST-DECL
  'As for fish, Chelswu caught small ones.'

  b. *koki-ka phiraymi-i/*-ul cap-hi-ass-ta.*
  fish-NOM small.fish-NOM/*ACC grab-PASS-PAST-DECL
  'As for fish, small ones were caught.'

(20) a. *Leia-ka Yoda-lul son-ul cap-ass-ta.* K
  L.-NOM Y.-ACC hand-ACC grab-PAST-DECL
  'Leia grabbed Yoda's hand.'

  b. *Yoda-ka son-i/-ul cap-hi-ass-ta.*
  Y.-NOM hand-NOM/ACC grab-PASS-PAST-DECL
  'Yoda's hand was grabbed.'

Floating quantifiers under *raising-to-object* compared with a part-whole-relation under *raising-to-object*:

(21) a. *John-un haksayng-ul sey-myeng-ul/*-i pwuca-lako mitnunta.* K
  John-TOP student-ACC 3-CL-ACC/*NOM rich.be-COMP believe
  'John believes three students to be rich.'

  b. *Mary-nun panana-lul kkepcil-i/?-ul twukkepta-ko mitnunta.*
  Mary-TOP banana-ACC skin-NOM/?-ACC thick.be-COMP believe
  'Mary believes a banana's skin to be thick.'

Summing up, type III predicates are characterized by two case-identical constituents, which encode one and the same argument under different perspectives,

Variations of double nominative in Korean and Japanese

while type IIb predicates are stative and clearly have two distinct NOM arguments. Type IIa and IIc predicates have one argument that can alternate with NOM under specific conditions. Type I predicates have a relational argument, which in turn has an argument by itself alternating with NOM by possessor-raising. The question is, what factors usually trigger the NOM-alternatives?

3 Case-stacking in Korean as a means of inducing focus-interpretation

Korean differs from Japanese in that it allows *case stacking*, where a noun bears two different case suffixes in sequence. The first case encodes argument structure under normal circumstances (including appropriate semantic conditions), while the second case encodes an additional structure, which often has to do with information status. Both Japanese (*-ni-wa* 'DAT-TOP') and Korean (22) show a sequence of case marker and topic marker.

(22) Ce   haksayngtulk-eykey-nun mwuncey-ka taytanhi-tul manh-ta.   K
      Those students-DAT-TOP   problem-NOM extremely-PL much-DECL
      'Those students have a lot of problems.'

There is no focus marker in these languages, but a stacked NOM or ACC invites a focus *interpretation*. Yoon (2004) discusses three types of case-stacking in Korean.

Type 1: DAT+NOM, LOC+NOM, INSTR+NOM. Here, case-stacking is an alternative to case-alternation. As we have seen, DAT and LOC often alternate with NOM; in the case-stacking case they are realized together (23a,b). The instrumental generally does not alternate with NOM, but interestingly, case-stacking is possible, see (23c). This is an obvious innovation in which two different functions are separated: semantic encoding + structural encoding in favor of a discourse-interpretation.

(23) a. *Cheli-eykey/ka/eykey-ka ton-i   philyoha-ta.*   K
         C.-DAT/NOM/DAT-NOM   money-NOM necessary-DECL
         'It is Cheli who needs money.'
      b. *Semyukongcang-eyse/i/eyse-ka   pwul-i   na-ss-ta.*
         textile.factory-LOC/NOM/LOC-NOM fire-NOM break.out-DECL
         'It was in the textile factory that a fire broke out.'

c. *Ku kongkwu-lo/*ka/lo-ka   na-eykey-n cha-lul kochi-ki-ka*
that tool-INST/*NOM/INST-NOM I-DAT-TOP car-ACC fix-NML-NOM
elyepta.
difficult
'It is that tool with which I find it difficult to fix the car.'

Type 2: DAT+ACC. (24a) contains a ditransitive verb with a dative recipient, while (24b) is an instance of *raising-to-object*. One can see that the object (with a facultative focus particle) is augmented with a focus interpretation.

(24) a. *John-i Mary-eykey-(man)-**ul** chayk-ul cwu-ess-ta.*   K
J.-NOM M.-DAT-(only)-ACC book-ACC give-PAST-DECL
'It was only to Mary that John gave the book.'

b. *Na-nun Cheli-eykey-(man)-ul kulen   mwuncey-ka iss-ta-ko*
I-TOP C.-DAT-(only)-ACC that.kind problem-NOM exist-DECL-COMP
sayngkakhan-ta.
think-DECL
'I think that only Cheli has that kind of problem.'

Type 3: DAT+GEN. Here, DAT encodes *goal* interpretation, and GEN is the case licensed by the noun.

(25) *Mary-uy John-eykey-uy phyenci*   K
M.-GEN J.-DAT-GEN   letter
'Mary's letter to John'

It is unclear whether (25) has focus interpretation, but the case-stacking types 1 and 2 certainly have.

[_]$_{N}$-CASE-/CASE ⇒ [_]$_{N:\ Focus}$

Schütze (2001) assumes that the Korean suffixes *ka* and *lul* are ambiguous between case (NOM or ACC) and focus marking. Yoon (2004), however, argues that focus interpretation is contextually determined rather than lexically encoded. In general, focus as well as topic interpretation are available on the basis of a simple NOM or ACC marking. According to Yoon, a *stacked* NOM is base-generated in SpecT and characterizes the presence of a *major subject*.

4 Nom-NPs are accessible to topic and focus interpretation

Both Korean and Japanese show intonational peaks signaling contrastive topic (CT) or focus; the phonetic details can be found in Lee (2006) for Korean, and Venditti et al. (2007) for Japanese. Within the N-domain only intonational focus is possible, while outside of it the NOM-NOM construction enables additional marking for topic and focus.

The topic-marker (Kor. *nun*/ Jap. *wa*) marks *about*-topic or contrastive topic (CT). The *about*-topic is an element in the beginning of a sentence; both arguments and adverbials can be moved into that position. All non-initially topic-marked elements function as CT: they are contrastively selected from the set of elements denoted by a preceding topic, which itself, however, does not need to be introduced explicitly as a topic.

The following dialogue nicely shows how CT functions. The CT on *Sue* in line d was prepared by *nwukwu-lul* 'someone-ACC' in line b: somebody (out of the set of kids including Sue) seems to have been hit. CT is a focus within a given topic. Thus, the answer to a question does not need to be a pure focus; it can also be a CT.

(26) ⟨conversation⟩ (Bak 2004: (3.8))

    a. A1: *Jina-ka way honna-ko   issni?*
           J.-NOM why be_scold-COMP be
           'Why is Jina scolded?'

    b. B1: *ung, nwukwu-lul   ttayli-ess-na   boa.*
           Um, someone-ACC hit-PAST-COMP seem
           '(Jina) seems to have hit somebody.'

    c. A2: *Jina-ka nwukwu-lul ttayli-ess-ni?*
           J.-NOM whom-ACC hit-PAST-Q
           'Whom did Jina hit?'

    d. B2: *ung, Jina-ka* **Sue-nun**   *ttayli-ess-na   boa.*
           um, J.-NOM S.-TOP(CT) hit-PAST-COMP seem
           'Jina seems to have hit **Sue**.'

The about-topic, the first element of a series of topics, has the most comprising denotation ('from the whole to the parts'). When the elephant becomes an about-topic in (27a,b), the parts of the animal can advance to CTs. Intonationally, the initial *about*-topic in (27a,b) remains flat, while the following CT-marker *nun* (27b) is strongly stressed (by pitch and duration) – interestingly, it is not the topicalized element but the topic marker itself that is stressed (Lee 2006). By contrast, the first nominal (N1) of a NOM-NOM construction (27c) gets a focus reading regardless of whether it is stressed.

(27) a. *khokkiri-nun kho-ka   kil-ta.*   TOP - NOM   K
  elephant-TOP nose-NOM long-DECL
  '(As for) elephants, their noses are long.'

  b. *khokkiri-nun kho-**nun**   kil-ta.*   TOP – CT
  elephant-TOP nose-TOP(CT) long-DECL
  '(As for) elephants, their noses are long, but ....'

Kim (2000) states that only the initial NOM of a sentence expressing a *kinship*-relation can get a focus reading, while the initial NOM of a sentence expressing a *body part* relation does not, see (28a,b). These are at best preferred readings. My tests showed that, in principle, both types of relations enabled a focus or a non-focus reading. In fact, it would be surprising if *kinship* and *body part* were more than gradually different.

(28) a. *Mary-ka   son-i   yepputa.*   topic   K
  Mary-NOM hands-NOM pretty
  'Mary's hands are pretty.'

  b. *Mary-ka   emeni-ka   yepputa.*   focus
  Mary-NOM mother-NOM pretty
  'It is Mary whose mother is pretty.'

There is a surprising amount of realizational and interpretational alternatives. Even in a topic- or a focus-preferring context a GEN-NP can be found.

Hoye (2003) says about Japanese that, in the GEN-NOM construction, the predicate can be stressed (29a). If N1 is topic-marked, either an *about*-topic reading or a CT reading results, dependent on whether the topic-phrase is stressed (29b). Similarly, N1 in the NOM-NOM construction gets a focus reading regardless of whether the noun is stressed (29c).

(29) a. Neutral or stress on the predicate   GEN - NOM   J
  *Zoo-no   hana-ga   **nagai**.*
  Elephant-GEN nose-NOM long
  'An elephant's nose is long.'

    b. Possessor-topic   TOP - NOM
        ***Zoo**-wa   hana-ga   nagai.*
        Elephant-TOP nose-NOM long
        'As for an elephant, it has a long nose.'

    c. Possessor with contrastive focus   NOM (=FOC) - NOM
        ***Zoo**-ga   hana-ga   nagai.*
        Elephant-NOM nose-NOM long
        'It is an elephant that has a long nose.'

The same distribution is found in type II NOM-NOM constructions resulting from DAT/NOM or LOC/NOM alternations.

(30)   a. Neutral or predicate stress   DAT - NOM   J
           Ken-ni butsuri-ga   wakaru.
           Ken-DAT physics-NOM understand
           'Ken understands physics.'

        b. Subject-topic   TOP - NOM
           Ken-wa butsuri-ga   wakaru.
           Ken-TOP physics-NOM understand
           'As for Ken, he understands physics.'

        c. Subject with contrastive focus   NOM (=FOC) - NOM
           ***Ken**-ga   butsuri-ga   wakaru.*
           Ken-NOM physics-NOM understand
           'It is Ken who understands physics.'

Obviously, not only the case systems but also the topic-focus systems of Korean and Japanese are very similar. Although many more details have to be studied, one can see how double-NOM and the topic-focus system closely interact in producing the zooming effect, which is characteristic for processing in these languages.

    In contrast to the fixed ordering of a GEN-NOM pattern, the order of the constituents of a NOM-ACC or a DAT-NOM pattern can be reversed without any change of meaning. This is not possible for a TOP-NOM or a NOM-NOM pattern, where argument structure is overridden by information structure. In other words, the zooming effect is possible only with a fixed word order.

5 Topic clauses (in Korean)

Topic clauses are similar to relative clauses. In a topic clause, an item is extracted from a clause and put into the beginning, while in a relative clause an item is extracted and put into the end. This can lead to *long-distance* or *unbounded dependencies*, where the item is extracted from a farther embedded clause.

(31) a. topic$_i$ [[e$_i$]]
      b. [[e$_i$]] rel-head$_i$

The symmetry is complete: if an element can be extracted to the right, it can also be extracted to the left, and vice versa (Lee 2004: 177, 179).

(32) *I fell asleep while reading* K

   a. [nay-ka [ilk-taka]   camtu-n]   ***chayk***   relative clause
      [I$_i$-NOM [e$_i$ e$_k$ read-while] fall_asleep-REL] book$_k$
      'The book that I fell asleep while reading (it)'

   b. *ku **chayk-un** [nay-ka [ilk-taka]   camtul-ess-ta].*   topic clause
      that book$_k$-TOP [I$_i$-NOM [e$_i$ e$_k$ read-while] fall_asleep-PRES-DECL]
      'As for the book, I fell asleep while reading (it).'

Relative clause formation and topicalization can also be combined (Lee 2004: 144). In the following example, the position of the adverb 'yesterday' indicates that 'that woman' is extracted. Moreover, this example shows that also an *about*-topic can be realized by NOM. More precisely, in (33) the topicalized N1 binds a gap in the relative clause headed by N2 : N1$_i$ [[e$_i$ REL] N2].

(33) *Ku yeca-ka   ecey   salangha-nun   naca-ka   cwuessta.* K
      that woman$_i$-NOM [yesterday [e$_i$ e$_k$ love-REL] man$_k$-NOM died]
      (lit) 'That woman, yesterday the man who (she) loved died.'
      [In German, 'Gestern starb der Frau ihr geliebter Mann.']

The topic can simply be marked by NOM rather than by the topic marker (so that double NOM can result). Actually, sentences like these are sometimes ambiguous in whether an initial NOM-phrase has to be viewed as extracted or not; note that (34a) and (34b) are surface-identical but differently structured, and so get different interpretations. (34c) again shows that the extracted topicalized item of (34b) can instead also serve as extracted head of a relative clause.

(34) a. *chinkwu-ka salko iss-nun aphatu-ka   acwu khuta.* K
         [friend-NOM e$_k$ live is-REL] apartment$_k$-NOM very big
         'The apartment where the friend lives is very big.'

b. *chinkwu-ka salko iss-nun   aphatu-ka   acwu khuta.*
   friend$_i$-NOM [[e$_i$ e$_k$ live is-REL] apartment$_k$-NOM very big]
   (lit.) 'As for the friend, the apartment where (he) lives is very big.'

c. *salko iss-nun   aphatu-ka   acwu khu-un chinkwu*
   [[e$_i$ e$_k$ live is-REL] apartment$_k$-NOM very big-REL] friend$_i$
   (lit.) 'The friend whose apartment where (he) lives is very big'

Similar effects are found with raised possessors. By extraction, they either precede or follow the clause in which the possessed NP occurs, as shown by the examples in (34d,e) (Nakamura 2002). The double-NOM construction just fits nicely into the constructional toolkit of these languages.

(34) d. *hon-ga   Hanako-ni naiyoo-ga   waka-ru*   J
        book$_i$-NOM [H.-DAT [e$_i$ content-NOM] understand-PRES]
        'As for the book, Hanako understands (it's) content.'

    e. *Hanako-ni naiyoo-ga   waka-ru   hon*
        [H.-DAT [e$_i$ content-NOM] understand-PRES] book$_i$
        'The book the content of which Hanako understands'

Note that, for general semantic reasons only, the non-relational possessor can be extracted in this way, but not the relational possessee. The latter would be impossible also in English (*As for the content, Hanako understands the book, *the content which Hanako understands the book).

6 Scope variation (in Japanese)

Differences in information structure are connected with scopal differences. The elder literature on Japanese sometimes mentions this fact, but it is not dealt with very systematically. In some verbs (such as Jap. *suki* 'like,' *kirai* 'dislike') as well as verb complexes (formed with *-tai* 'want' or *-(ar)e* 'can' = potential) the object can alternate between ACC and NOM. An object realized as NOM triggers focus interpretation on the object. Compare (35a) with NOM-object and (35b) with ACC-object.

(35) a. Object in focus   J
        Ken-ga/wa ***mizu**-ga   nomi-tai.*   NOM/TOP – NOM (=FOC)
        Ken-NOM/TOP water-NOM drink-want
        'It is water that Ken wants to drink.'

b. Predicate in focus
    *Ken-ga/wa   mizu-o   **nomi-tai**.*   NOM/TOP – ACC
    Ken-NOM/TOP water-ACC drink-want
    'Ken wants to *drink* water.'

When the object is in focus, the scopal conditions shift: the NOM-object becomes wide scope (Tada 1992, Koizumi 1994). That is compatible with the assumption that the entity in focus is semantically highest; consider the paraphrase 'it is only his right eye that John can close' for ONLY > CAN. Since ONLY > CAN is the only interpretation of (36b) with a NOM-object, CAN > ONLY remains the more interesting interpretation of (36a) with an ACC-object – such an entailment could be grammaticalized by bidirectional optimization.

(36) a. *John-ga migime-dake-o   tumur-e-ru.*   J
         J.-NOM right_eye-only-ACC close-CAN-PRES
         'John can close only his right eye.'   CAN > ONLY, ONLY > CAN

     b. *John-ga migime-dake-ga   tumur-e-ru.*
         J.-NOM right_eye-only-NOM close-CAN-PRES
         'John can close only his right eye.'   *CAN > ONLY, ONLY > CAN

Potential constructions generally show the alternation ACC/NOM on the object, see (37b).

(37) a. *Yamada-ga miruku-o/*ga   nom-u.*   NOM – ACC   J
         Y.-NOM   milk-ACC/*NOM drink-PRES
         'Yamada drinks milk.'

     b. *Yamada-ga miruku-o/ga   nom-(ar)e-ru.*   NOM - ACC/NOM
         Y.-NOM   milk-ACC/NOM drink-CAN-PRES
         'Yamada can drink milk.'

If the verbal meaning is embedded under a nominal like the suffix *-koto* 'fact' in (38), the subject can also be realized as genitive (GEN), besides being realized as NOM. With the simple verb, the object remains ACC (38a), whereas with a potential verb the object can be ACC, NOM or GEN (38b), see Nakamura & Fujita (1998).

(38) a. *Yamada-no miruku-o/*ga/*no   nom-u-koto*   GEN – ACC   J
         Y.-GEN   milk-ACC/*NOM/*GEN drink-PRES-fact
         'The fact that Yamada drinks milk'

     b. *Yamada-no miruku-o/ga/no   nom-(ar)e-ru-koto* GEN – ACC/NOM/GEN
         Y.-GEN   milk-ACC/NOM/GEN drink-CAN-PRES-fact
         'The fact that Yamada can drink milk'

The combination 'drink-CAN' opens 2 alternatives for the object, while the combination 'drink-CAN-fact' opens 3 alternatives. It is reasonable to assume that ACC-objects are in the V-domain (VP), NOM-objects in the tensed CAN-domain (IP), and GEN-objects in the N-domain (NP). Consequently, the nominal suffix directly takes a (saturated) IP, or a VP plus one argument, or the verb plus two arguments; CAN in turn takes a (saturated) VP plus one argument, or a verb plus two arguments (recall the remark below (17) in section 2). This yields the five possible structures shown in (39). (Miyagawa 1993 argues that structures of this kind belong to LF, the logical form on which case features are checked. This is exactly what a lexicon- or semantics-based account predicts.)

(39) a. [NP [IP X_{NOM} [VP Y_{ACC} VERB] CAN-PRES] NOUN]   IP-embedding
    [NP [IP X_{NOM} Y_{NOM} [VERB] CAN-PRES] NOUN]
   b. [NP X_{GEN} [IP [VP Y_{ACC} VERB] CAN-PRES] NOUN]   VP-embedding
    [NP X_{GEN} [IP Y_{NOM} [VERB] CAN-PRES] NOUN]
   c. [NP X_{GEN} Y_{GEN} [IP [VERB] CAN-PRES] NOUN]   V-embedding

Interestingly, GEN on the object is only possible if the alternation with NOM is possible, i. e., double-NOM enables double-GEN. In other words, argument extraction (if one considers it syntactically) is a local operation: the object moves first to the CAN-domain, and then to the N-domain. The GEN-NOM alternation played an important role in the history of Japanese. Notice that Jap. *ga* (=NOM) was a GEN-particle in the 13th century, that later was recategorized. Only in contexts where such a recategorization did not take place, an explicit GEN remained in the form *no*.

Scopal differences between NOM- and GEN-*subjects* give evidence for the distinction between IP- and VP-embedding. A GEN-subject can have scope over the head noun, while a NOM-subject cannot (Ahn 2006, Hiraiwa 2010, see also Miyagawa 1993):

(40) a. *Gakusee-tachi ga/no   yon-da   yon-satsu no   hon   wa*
    [student-PL   NOM/GEN read-PAST] 4-CLASSIF GEN book TOP
    tsumarana-i.   J
    boring-PRES
    'The four books that the students read were boring.'
    NOM: books > students, *students > books
    GEN: books > students, students > books (=each of the students read 4 books)

b. *[Rubii ka shinju] ga/no   yasu-ku   na-ru   kanousei   ga*
   [ruby or pearl] NOM/GEN cheap-CONT become-PRES probability NOM
   50% ijou   da.
   50% more COP
   NOM: PROB > OR, *OR > PROB
   GEN: PROB > OR, OR > PROB
   PROB > OR: 'The probability that rubies or pearls become cheap is over 50%.'
   OR > PROB: 'The probability that rubies become cheap or the probability that pearls become cheap is over 50%.'

The assumption that a NOM-subject remains in the V-domain implies that it cannot have scope over the nominal head, while a GEN-subject within the N-domain may or may not have scope over the nominal head.

7 Potential and passive in Japanese

The two sentences given in (41a,b) are very similar, in particular, the common suffix *-ni* suggests that the Japanese potential construction involves a passive effect. Historically, the potential and the passive morphemes were identical, and only became different by partial reduction (*are* < *e* in the potential).

(41) a. *Kono syatu-ga   sensei-ni   araw-are-ru.*   passive   J
        this shirt-NOM teacher-BY wash-PASS-PRES
        'This shirt is washed by the teacher.'

   b. *Kono syatu-ga   sensei-ni   araw-(ar)e-ru.*   potential
        this shirt-NOM teacher-DAT wash-CAN-PRES
        'This shirt can be washed by the teacher.'

However, in fact the two constructions are very different. In the passive, the subject is existentially bound: it can neither be an antecedent for *zibun* 'self', nor can it undergo honorific agreement with the verb (42a). By contrast, in the potential the subject is still present: it can control *zibun*, and it can agree with the verb (42b), see Nakamura & Fujita (1998).

(42) a. **Kono syatu-ga   sensei-ni   go-jibun-de*
        this shirt-NOM teacher-BY HON-self-BY
        *o-araw-**are-ninar**-u.*
        HON-wash-**PASS-HON**-PRES   passive   J
        'This shirt is washed by the teacher (HON).'

b. *Kono syatu-ga sensei-ni go-jibun-de*
   this shirt-NOM teacher-DAT HON-self-BY
   *o-arai-**ninar-e-ru**.*
   HON-wash-**HON-CAN**-PRES   potential
   'As for the shirt, the teacher (HON) can wash it.'

The two *ni*'s have different function. In the passive (42a), *ni* marks an oblique adverbial, whereas in the potential (42b), *ni* marks a dative subject (similarly to experiencer constructions) – therefore the object can occupy the nominative. The dative itself is optional: if the subject precedes the object, a NOM-NOM construction is possible, too (similarly to what has been shown for Korean in (13b) above). Double-NOM in turn makes double-GEN possible, as we have seen in the preceding section. This scenario suggests a possible historical path: when *are* was split into the passive on the one hand and the potential on the other, two different interpretation possibilities arose for a subject-*ni*-phrase along the ways just sketched. In the end, the potential construction was able to become a generator for NOM-NOM (alternating with GEN-GEN).

The actual process by which double-NOM was generated might have been more complex. Modern Japanese shows the tendency of giving up GEN-subjects in favor of NOM. Harada (1971) already pointed out that older people (above forty) were more likely to accept GEN-ACC in the nominal construction (38b), while younger people (below forty) refuted GEN-ACC in favor of either GEN-NOM or NOM-NOM – a process that seems to be continuing (Ahn 2006). Thus, the differences between the five constructions shown in (39) are increasingly flattened. In Korean, all GEN-subjects have been lost since middle Korean.

8 More genitive subjects in Japanese

As already argued above in section 6 for the bound suffix *-koto* 'fact,' the subject of a clause embedded under a noun (a complement or an object-relative clause) can alternate between NOM and GEN (Ahn 2006). (43) shows a complement clause of the noun 'fact,' while (44) shows relative clauses with several kinds of extraction.

(43) Complement clause of a noun   J
    John ga/no   ki-ta   koto wa sira-na-katta.
    J.   NOM/GEN come-PAST fact TOP know-not-PAST
    '(I) didn't know (the fact) that John came.'

(44) a. Object extracted
   John ga/no   kai-ta   hon wa omosiro-i.
   [J. NOM/GEN write-PAST] book TOP interesting-PRES
   'The book that John wrote is interesting.'

b. BY-subject extracted in the passive
   Boku wa keeki ga/no   tabe-rare-ta   inu o   mi-ta.
   I TOP [cake NOM/GEN eat-PASS.PAST] dog ACC see-PAST
   'I saw the dog by whom the cake was eaten.'

c. Object extracted in the causative
   Ichiro ga/no   musuko ni   s-ase-ta   shukudai wa
   [I. NOM/GEN son   DAT do-CAUS-PAST] homework TOP
   yasashi-katta.
   easy-PAST
   'The homework that Ichiro made his son to do was easy.'

d. Causee extracted in the causative + passive construction
   Shinbun   ga/no   yom-ase-rare-ta   kodoma wa joozuni
   [newspaper NOM/GEN read-CAUS-PASS-PAST] child   TOP skilled
   yom-ana-i.
   read-NEG-PRES
   'The child who was made to read the newspaper does not read well.'

If we follow the spirit of section 6, we can describe the NOM/GEN alternation as induced by different structurings. For instance, the subject of (44a) can be integrated within the domain of 'write' (yielding NOM) or within the domain of 'book' (yielding GEN):

[$_{NP}$ [$_{IP}$ x_{NOM} WRITE(x,y)] BOOK(y)]
[$_{NP}$ x_{GEN} [$_{IP}$ WRITE(x,y)] BOOK(y)]

9 Once again, argument gaps in Korean

Lee (2003) considers Kor. *tough*-constructions such as (45b) as a subspecies of NOM-NOM constructions of type 1 (46b): N2 has an argument gap, which is filled by N1.

(45) a. *[[i   sacen-ul   sayongha]-ki] -ka   swipta.*   ACC-NOM K
       this dictionary-ACC use-NML   -NOM easy
       'It is easy to use this dictionary.'

b. i   sacen$_k$-i   [_$_k$ sayongha-ki] -ka   swipta.   NOM-NOM
     this dictionary-NOM   use-NML   -NOM easy
     'This dictionary is easy to use.'

(46) a. [i   sacen-uy   sayongpep] -i   swipta.   GEN-NOM   K
        this dictionary-GEN usage   -NOM easy
        'The usage of this dictionary is easy.'

  b. i   sacen$_k$ -i   [_$_k$ sayongpep] -i   swipta.   NOM-NOM
     this dictionary -NOM   usage   -NOM easy
     (lit.) 'The usage of this dictionary is easy.'

(45) and (46) only differ in the way the verb 'use' is used: in (45) it is combined with the nominalizer *ki* (translated as 'to use'), while in (46) a lexical noun derived from 'use' is taken.

10   Cadenza or a first summary

There is a tradition, especially in Korean linguistics, to consider NOM-NOM as 'double-*subject*,' with N1 = *major* (or *extra*) *subject*, and N2 = *minor* (*real* or *grammatical*) *subject*. In principle, both N1 and N2 can show honorific agreement with the verb, and (in Korean) both can agree with the verb (or adverb) in number. There are a number of contradicting opinions concerning these issues, and possibly there are also dialectal differences. Other subject tests concern the control of *zibun/caki* 'self' and the control of a dependent subject in connection with control verbs, and finally the option of *raising-to-object*.

How can one integrate these 'double subjects' within syntactic theory? One possibility is to assume that these subjects (related to each other) belong to different domains or phases, and that they are assigned nominative in their respective domains. The other possibility is to assume that they belong to the same domain, which has the property to assign (or to license) nominative more than once. Both have been proposed. Ura (1996) assumes a parameter to the effect that PROCRASTINATE might be violated, and therefore more than one NOM can be checked by the same finite T. Sun (2013) assumes that NOM of the grammatical subject is licensed by the finite T, while NOM of the raised possessor is licensed by the gnomic (generic) aspect, considered as an extra structure (recall (11) in section 1: the raised possessor only admits the generic interpretation, while it excludes the episodic one). Similarly, topic and focus nominatives might be licensed by an additional, again different structure. I think that all these proposals are construction-specific: each construction in which double-NOM appears has its own licensing condition.

A more general solution is to distinguish between case domains like those proposed in (39). These domains have a lexical head which determines how many arguments have to be realized and how they are ordered, and sometimes also specifically assigns lexical case. Everything else is determined by argument hierarchy features and additional constraints, according to the program of *Lexical Decomposition Grammar* (LDG, Wunderlich 1997). In this account, NOM is considered to be the default case, and there is no need for a particular constellation of NOM-assignment. (Another question is why the nominative in languages like Japanese and Korean is marked rather than unmarked phonologically.)

Possessor-raising means that N1 does not belong to the domain defined by N2 but rather to the domain of the predicate; in other words, N1 becomes co-argument of N2. Whenever there is a double-NOM, or a double-ACC, or a double-GEN construction, the two entities involved either are co-arguments, or are explicitly distributed into two different domains. Thus, it depends on the respective head and further general constraints whether such a combination of two identical cases is licensed. One important factor is that the two entities that make up a double-case construction mostly respect a strict linear ordering, by which they are distinguished.

All the alternations yielding NOM make the respective NP accessible to one of the following operations: (i) the NP can be marked in situ for topic (by Jap. *wa*, Kor. *nun*), but doesn't have to be in order to get interpreted as topic; (ii) the NP can serve in situ for 'explicit' focus (just by the NOM-suffix, which in Korean might be stacked upon another case-suffix); (iii) the NP can undergo *raising-to-object* as well as *unbounded extraction* (relative clause or topic clause formation). As we have seen, a topic-marked constituent isn't necessarily the highest topic, and topic-interpretation might be possible even on the basis of simple NOM-marking.

There seem to be lexical triggers for all these alternations: in the case of GEN/NOM alternation it is the inherent relational (or functional) character of N2 together with the higher predicate that integrates the further NOM argument; in the case of DAT/NOM alternation it is the predicate that predicates on that argument from the start (which, however, might be less clear with local adverbials). Therefore, a lexical analysis (such as the HPSG analysis of Lee 2004) seems to be on the right track.

11 The double-NOM passive is somewhat special

Having failed to climb Mount Fuji, we experienced with the common *Leideform*. (47a) is an example of the double-NOM passive (slightly changed from Washio 1995: 224), which goes back to the structure shown in (47b).

(47) a. *watashi-tachi-ga/wa   (gakusei-tati-ni) tyosyo-ga waruku*
me-company-NOM/TOP (student-PL-BY) book-NOM badly
yom-are-te   i-ru.   J
read-PASS-PROG be-PRES
'As for us, our books have been read badly by the students.'

b. *gakusei-tati-ga watashi-tachi-no   tyosyo-o waruku yon-de*
student-PL-NOM me-company-GEN book-ACC badly   read-PROG
i-ru.
be-PRES
'The students have been reading our books badly.'

Two derivations are conceivable: (i) possessor-raising followed by passive, or (ii) passive followed by possessor-raising. The former would lead to the virtual intermediate stage of double-accusative, which as such cannot surface in Japanese, yet, a derivation doesn't have to be blocked by virtual stages. I assume that passive binds the highest argument existentially (so that it can only be referred to indirectly, e. g., by means of an optional *by*-phrase) (Wunderlich 2012). Furthermore, possessor-raising regarding the subject yields the possessor as the highest argument, while possessor-raising regarding the object yields the possessor as a medial argument. PR(S) is realized by the topmost possessor (Wunderlich 2001), while PR(O) is realized by a specific kind of applicative (Wunderlich 2012). In route (i) from above we have to start with the applicative, while in route (ii) the topmost possessor must apply with respect to the highest unbound argument (which is the object); thus we get similar results. (Although '&' is asymmetric, namely internally structured as '(A (& B))', in the results yielded in (48d,e) no difference appears in the relative ordering of u > y.)

(48) Operations for deriving the double-NOM passive
  a. passive(V): $\lambda V[\exists x V(x)]$
      All lower arguments of V are inherited to the result by functional composition
  b. topmost possessor(V): $\lambda V \lambda x \lambda u[\text{POSS}(u, x) \& V(x)]$

c. possessor-applicative(V): $\lambda V \lambda y \lambda u \lambda x [V(x, y)$ & POSS$(u, y)]$
d. route (i): $\lambda y \lambda u \exists x [\text{READ}(x, y)$ & POSS$(u, y)]$ with $u > y$
e. route (ii): $\lambda y \lambda u [\text{POSS}(u, y)$ & $\exists x \text{READ}(x, y)]$ with $u > y$

Both the topmost and the medial possessors are also found in German. In (49a), the possessor is medial and regularly takes the dative, while in (49b), the possessor is highest (according to the ordering of indefinite pronouns shown in (49c)) and is lexically marked for a dative.

(49) Possessors in German

a. *Sie verband ihm den Fuß.*
she bandaged he.DAT the.ACC foot
'She bandaged his foot.'

b. *Ihm schmerzte der Fuß.*
he.DAT hurt.PAST the.NOM foot
'His foot hurts.'

c. *weil wem was schmerzte*
because somebody.DAT something.NOM hurt.PAST
*weil was wem schmerzte

There remains an empirical problem. Double-NOM constructions are restricted to stative predicates. However, it is not so evident that passive is stative, even if it often elicits a stative version (the stative passive).

12 Korean is a little less sensitive than Japanese

Washio (1995, appendix) shows that the Japanese double-NOM passive is possible under two conditions: (i) with a relational noun (such as *osiego* 'student of', *imooto* 'sister of', *syuto* 'capital of') in the progressive (*-te iru*) or with simple tense, (ii) or with a body part noun in the progressive provided that the resulting state continues. The progressive contains a stative component. Tying someone's foot results in a state that can continue (50a), while stomping on someone's foot usually is not seen as a continuing action, hence, (50b) is problematic. In other words, the double-passive only arises in a stative scenario.

(50) a. *Takashi ga asi-ga koteis-are-te i-ta.* J
T. NOM foot-NOM fix-PASS-PROG be-PAST
'Takashi had his foot tied (to something).'

b. ?? *Takashi ga   asi-ga   hum-are-te   i-ta.*
   T.   NOM foot-NOM stomp-PASS-PROG be_on-PAST
   'Takashi had his foot stomped.'

Korean is not sensitive to those niceties; double-NOM passive is possible with all body parts independent of verb form and resulting state.

(51) *Jang-Ho-ka pal-i   palp-i-ess-ta.*   K
      J.-NOM   foot-NOM stomp-PASS-PAST-DECL
      (lit.) 'Jang-Ho was stomped on his foot.'

Since Kor. /i/ is ambiguous between causative and passive (where the latter is possible only with inalienables, Kim & Pires 2003), a sentence such as (52) has both a causative and a passive reading.

(52) *John-i/nun Mary-eykey meli-ul   kkakk-i-ess-ta.*   K
      J.-NOM/TOP M.-DAT   hair-ACC cut-CAUS/PASS-PAST-DECL
      (i) 'John had Mary cut the hair.' (John's or someone else's hair)   causative
      (ii) 'John had his hair cut by Mary.'   passive

The causative cannot be stative, but a passive can. The particular contrast between causative and passive readings may establish a stative interpretation of passives as the most natural one. Passives can refer to states that result from certain events, while causatives refer to the dynamics of events.

13   The great Korean-Japanese harmony

Interestingly, the causative-passive suffix *i* in (52) is one of the verbal markers whose etymologies were investigated by Robbeets (2007, 2008). Comparing Japanic, Koreanic, Tungusic, Mongolic and Turkic, she reconstructs the morpheme *ki as an element of the common proto-Transeurasian (another name for 'greater' Altaic), the ancestor of the individual branches: in Mongolic and Turkic it was the independent verb 'do, make,' in Tungusic it switched to a causative-passive auxiliary or a suffix *ki*. Korean has the suffix variants *ki*, *hi*, and *i*, Old Japanic has (C)i, which induces vowel change (e. g., *aga*-(C)*i* → *age* 'rise→raise'). It seems that the periphrastic *ki substituted for an elder *ti (Old Japanic *t*, Korean *t*, *chi*), which also expresses causative-passive and can be found in a number of lexicalized verbs.

   Summarizing the constructional data discussed in this paper, one has to conclude that most of the structural properties are shared by Japanese and Korean. If one looks at examples such as (1) and (2) at the very beginning, one realizes: yes, these sentences are identical, but have different vocabularies. (Although there are some obvious lexical similarities: Kor. -*ka*, Jap. -*ga* NOM; Kor. *choykun*, Jap. *saikin* 'recently'; Kor. *pyeng*, Jap. *byooki* 'illness'; Kor. *swungsang*, Jap. *syusyoo* 'Prime Minister.') Both Korean and Japanese are agglutinative; nearly every morpheme of one language finds it's counterpart in the other, in the same ordering, with similar restrictions and similar polysemies. The differences are extremely marginal.

It has always been debated whether Korean and Japanese are genealogically related, and what their relationship is to the Altaic languages (Tungusic, Mongolic and Turkic). The ancestor of Korean was originally spoken in the southeastern part of the Korean peninsula (Silla kingdom), the ancestor of Japanese (the language of the Yayoi who spread between 4th century BC and 7th century AD to the Japanic islands) was spoken in the southwestern parts of the Korean peninsula. There must have been intensive contact (during the time of the three kingdoms, during the Yayoi immigration and during the Silla extension, which Koreanized the whole peninsula), hence, in principle it is possible that pre-proto-Japanese and proto-Korean formed a sprachbund. Janhunen (1999), propagating this scenario, confesses that people who share morphosyntactic structures are expected to share phonological structures, too, which Japanese and Korean obviously do not. In particular, Korean roots are typically CVC-syllables (producing medial consonant clusters when they are combined), while Japanese roots are mostly CV or CVCV. Janhunen assumes Altaic origin for Korean, but Sinitic origin for Japanese.

Both Samuel Elmo Martin (1924-2009) and Roy Andrew Miller (born 1924) from Yale, excellent researchers of Korean and Japanese, published various papers to show the lexical and morphosyntactic relatedness of these languages. Miller also advocated the Altaic hypothesis, according to which Korean and Japanese belong to the Altaic family. It is assumed that the branches of this family separated 6000 years ago, earlier than Indo-European and Uralic. Over such a long time, many traces of a common origin are erased. All the more surprising that a number of verbal roots and morphemes, such as diathesis operators, nominalizers, and participle-forming suffixes (Robbeets 2009), can still be reconstructed as having the same origin.

Japan colonized Korea for 35 years (1910-1945), thereby propagating a common identity. It may have something to do with this fact (which has largely been ignored at a political level) that Korean and Japanese scholars who study the parallelisms of the two languages mostly remain silent about the origin of the similarities – a reservation that occurs to me as a sort of political correctness. It is mostly researchers from America, Russia, Germany, Scandinavia or the Netherlands who have cultivated the hot debate. 'Cognates or Copies?' is the content of the controversy (see Johanson & Robbeets 2012). In any case, the double-nominative network, a complex system of interactions between case marking, information structure, extraction and verb complex formation, cannot have emerged independently in the two languages, all the more because they have influenced each other in the last 1400 years only marginally.

Bibliography

Ahn, B. 2006. Nominative-genitive conversion in Japanese. A consequence of the syntax. Ms., Cornell Univ.

Bak, J. 2004. *Optional case marking of the possessor in Korean.* University of Manitoba MA thesis.

Cho, Sungeun. 2003. A conditioning factor in possessor agreement constructions. In Patricia M. Clancy (ed.), *Japanese/Korean linguistics*, vol. 11, 343–351. CSLI Publications.

Harada, S. I. 1971. *Ga-no* conversion and idiolectal variation in Japanese. *Gengo Kenkyu* 60. 25–38.

Harada, S. I. 1973. Counter Equi NP deletion. *Annual Bulletin, Research Institute of Logopedics and Phoniatrics* 7. 113–147. University of Tokyo.

Hiraiwa, K. 2010. Spelling out the double-o constraint. *Natural Language and Linguistic Theory* 28. 723–770.

Hoye, Masako Oku. 2003. *Why Japanese double-ga construction cannot be scrambled.* University of North Texas MA thesis.

Janhunen, J. 1999. A contextual approach to the convergence and divergence of Korean and Japanese. *International Journal of Central Asian Studies* 4. 1–23.

Johanson, L. & M. Robbeets (eds.). 2012. *Copies versus cognates in bound morphology.* Leiden: Brill.

Kim, Hee-Soo & A. Pires. 2003. Ambiguity in the Korean morphological causative/passive. In W. McClure (ed.), *Japanese/Korean linguistics*, vol. 12, 255–266. Stanford: CSLI.

Kim, Jong-Bok. 2000. A constraint-based approach to some multiple nominative constructions in Korean. In Akira Ikeya & Masahito Kawamori (eds.), *Proceed-*

ings of the 14th Pacific Asia conference on language, information, and computation*, 165–176. Tokyo: Logico-Linguistic Society of Japan.

Kim, Young-joo. 1989. Inalienable possession as a semantic relationship underlying predication: The case of multiple-accusative constructions. In Susumu Kuno et al. (ed.), *Harvard studies in Korean linguistics*, vol. III, 445–467. Harvard University Press.

Koizumi, M. 1994. Nominative objects: the role of TP in Japanese. In H. Ura & M. Koizumi (eds.), *MITWPL 24: Formal approaches to Japanese linguistics. Proceedings of FAJL 1*, 211–230.

Kuno, S. 1973. *The structure of the Japanese language*. Cambridge, Mass.: MIT Press.

Kuroda, Shige-Yuki. 1978. Case marking, canonical sentence patterns and counter-Equi in Japanese. In J. Hinds & I. Howards (eds.), *Problems in Japanese syntax and semantics*, Tokyo: Kaitakusha.

Kwon, Nayoung. 2006. Case marking signals more than structure building: processing evidence from Korean double nominative constructions. Paper presented at the 37th Annual meeting of the North East Linguistic Society (NELS 37), NELS 37, University of Illinois, Urbana-Champaign, IL.

Lee, Chungmin. 2006. Contrastive (predicate) topic, intonation, and scalar meanings. In Chungmin Lee, Matt Gordon & Daniel Buring (eds.), *Topic and focus: Crosslinguistic perspectives on meaning and intonation*, 151–175. Dordrecht: Springer.

Lee, Sun-Hee. 2003. Korean *tough* constructions and double nominative constructions. In Jong-Bok Kim & Stephen Wechsler (eds.), *Proceedings of the 9th international conference on HPSG*, 187–208. Stanford University.

Lee, Sun-Hee. 2004. *A lexical analysis of selected unbounded dependency constructions in Korean*: Ohio State University dissertation.

Maling, J. & Soowon Kim. 1992. Case assignment in the inalienable possession construction in Korean. *Journal of East Asian Linguistics* 1. 37–68.

Miyagawa, S. 1993. LF case-checking and minimal link condition. In *Case and agreement II, MIT working papers in linguistics 19*, 213–254. Cambridge, Mass.: MIT Press. Department of Linguistics and Philosophy, MIT.

Nakamura, H. 2002. Double subject, double nominative object and double accusative object constructions in Japanese and Korean. In *Language, information and computation (PACLIC 16)*, 358–369.

Nakamura, H. & T. Fujita. 1998. Case alternations in potential constructions in Japanese and their semantic implications. In *Language, information and computation (PACLIC 12)*, 172–183.

Poser, W. J. 2002. The double-o constraints in Japanese. Ms. http://www.billposer.org/papers.html.

Robbeets, M. 2007. The causative-passive in the Trans-Eurasian languages. *Turkic Languages* 11. 235–278.

Robbeets, M. 2008. The development of passive morphology in Korean. In *Current issues in unity and diversity of languages*, Seoul: LSK. Collection of the papers selected from the CIL 18, Korea University.

Robbeets, M. 2009. Insubordination in Altaic. *Voprosy filologii uralo-altaiskije isledovanija* 1. 61–79.

Schütze, C. T. 2001. On Korean 'case stacking': the varied functions of the particles *ka* and *lul*. *The Linguistic Review* 18. 193–232.

Shekar, C. & B. Agbayani. 2003. Accusative-nominative case conversion and complex predicates in Kannada and Japanese/Korean. SALA 23, UT Austin.

Sim, Chang-Yong. 2006. Accusative case in passives. In *Studies in generative grammar*, vol. 16, 515–533. Walter de Gruyter.

Sun, Jisung. 2013. The derivational nature of external possession. In *University of Pennsylvania working papers in linguistics*, vol. 19, 217–226.

Tada, H. 1992. Nominative objects in Japanese. *Journal of Japanese Linguistics* 14. 91–108.

Ura, Hiroyuki. 1996. *Multiple feature checking: A theory of grammatical function splitting*: MIT dissertation.

Venditti, J. J., K. Maekawa & M. E. Beckman. 2007. Verb prominence marking in the Japanese intonation system. To appear in S. Miyagawa & M. Saito (eds.), *Handbook of Japanese linguistics*, Oxford University Press.

Washio, R. 1995. *Interpreting voice. A case study in lexical semantics*. Tokyo: Kaitakusha.

Wunderlich, D. 1997. Cause and the structure of verbs. *Linguistic Inquiry* 28. 27–68.

Wunderlich, D. 2001. Argument linking in Japanese – some facts and suggestions. Ms., University Düsseldorf.

Wunderlich, D. 2003. Optimal case patterns: German and Icelandic compared. In E. Brandner & H. Zinsmeister (eds.), *New perspectives on case theory*, 331–367. Stanford: CSLI.

Wunderlich, D. 2012. Operations on argument structure. In C. Maienborn, K. von Heusinger & P. Portner (eds.), *HSK: An international handbook of natural language meaning*, vol. 3, 2224–2259. Berlin: Mouton de Gruyter.

Yang, Dong-Whe. 2000. Review article: Three forms of case agreement in Korean. By Sungeon Cho, Ph.D. dissertation, State Univ. of New York at Stony Brook.

Yoon, J. H. 2004. Non-nominative (major) subjects and case stacking in Korean. In P. Bhaskararao & K. V. Subbarao (eds.), *Non-nominative subjects*, vol. 2, 265–314. Amsterdam: John Benjamins.

Yoon, J. H. 2009. The distribution of subject properties in multiple subject constructions. In Y. Takubo, T. Kinuhata, S. Grzelak & K. Nagai (eds.), *Japanese/Korean linguistics*, vol. 16, 64–83. Stanford, CA: CSLI.

Author

Dieter Wunderlich
Zentrum für Allgemeine Sprachwissenschaft Berlin
dieterwdl@t-online.de

Definiteness & perfectivity in telic incremental theme predications

Adrian Czardybon & Jens Fleischhauer

1 Introduction*

Incremental theme verbs such as *eat, drink, write* or *read* are well known for the fact that the referential properties of the incremental theme argument affect the referential properties, i.e., telicity, of the predication (e.g. Krifka 1986, 1998 among others). If the incremental theme argument has quantized[1] reference, as for example in the case of a singular count noun such as *apple*, the whole predication is telic (1a). If the incremental theme argument has cumulative reference, which is the case for bare plurals (*apples*) and mass nouns (*soup*), the whole predication is atelic (1b, c). The contrast in telicity is indicated by the interpretation of the time-span adverbial *in ten minutes*. Only (1a) allows for the relevant telic interpretation in which the time-adverbial indicates the time after which the process of eating is finished. Such an interpretation is not possible with (b) and (c) since neither *apples* nor *soup* indicate a specified quantity that introduces a natural endpoint of the event.

(1)   a.   *Paul ate an/the apple in ten minutes.*
       b.   # *Paul ate apples in ten minutes.*
       c.   # *Paul ate soup in ten minutes.*

---

* We want to thank Sebastian Löbner for his inspiring comments on the topic discussed in the paper and also on other topics ranging from specific questions on linguistics to non-academic topics. He has always provided us with help, support, and inspiring examples. This paper profited from fruitful discussion with John Beavers, Hana Filip, Thomas Gamerschlag, Doris Gerland, Albert Ortmann, Sergej Tatevosov, and Robert D. Van Valin, Jr. We further want to thank our informants Katina Bontcheva, Syuzan Sachliyan, Koen Van Hooste, Nikolai Skorolupov, Natalia Mamerow, Wilhelm and Ursula Czardybon, and Ewelina Lamparska, as well as the audience of CTF 2012 and two anonymous reviewers. The work on this topic was financed by the Deutsche Forschungsgemeinschaft through CRC 991 and was carried out in the member projects B1 'Verb Frames at the Syntax-Semantics Interface' and C2 'Conceptual Shifts: Statistical Evidence'.

[1] The notions of 'quantization' and 'cumulativity' are defined in section 2.

Languages provide different ways for the quantization of otherwise cumulative nouns, three of which are illustrated in (2). The numeral *three* in (2a) is used for the quantization of a plural count noun, while in (b) a container construction (*a bowl of*) is used for the quantization of a mass noun. Numeral constructions are restricted to plural count nouns, while container constructions are typical of mass nouns. In (c) it is illustrated that the definite article can be used for the quantization of plural count as well as mass nouns.

(2)   a.   *Paul ate three apples in ten minutes.*

       b.   *Paul ate a bowl of soup in ten minutes.*

       c.   *Paul ate the apples/the soup in ten minutes.*

Filip (2004, 2008) focuses on the contrast between Germanic and Slavic languages in realizing telicity of incremental theme predications. Most Slavic languages such as Russian, Polish, and Czech lack a grammaticalized definite or indefinite article, but in contrast to the Germanic languages they have a systematic distinction between perfective and imperfective aspect. Due to the lack of a definite article, Slavic languages cannot make use of the strategy illustrated in (2c) for the quantization of nouns. Instead, these languages use the aspectual opposition for the expression of the telicity contrast. As the Russian examples in (3) show, a telic interpretation of an incremental theme argument only arises if the verb is used in the perfective aspect (3a, c). An incremental theme verb in the imperfective aspect only yields an atelic interpretation, no matter whether the incremental theme argument is inherently quantized (singular count noun as in (3b)) or not (as in (3d)).[2]

(3)   a.   *On s"-el$_{PF}$*   *jabloko*   *za čas.*
           he S-eat.PAST apple.ACC in hour
           'He ate a/the (whole) apple in an hour.'[3]

       b.   *On el$_{IMPF}$*   *jabloko*   (*za čas).
           he eat.PAST apple.ACC   in hour
           'He ate/was eating an/the apple.'

---

[2] Throughout the paper we indicate grammatical aspect with subscripts on the verb and do not indicate it in the glossing. The reasons for doing this will be discussed in section 3.1.

[3] List of abbreviations: ACC: accusative, AUX: auxiliary, COP: copular, DEF: definite, GEN: genitive, IMPF: imperfective, LOC: locative, NEG: negation, PART: particle, PF: perfective, PL: plural, PREP: preposition, SG: singular.

c. On vy-pil_PF   vod-u   za čas.
   he VY-drink.PAST water-ACC in hour
   'He drank (all) the water in an hour.'

d. On pil_IMPF   vod-u   (*za čas).
   he drink.PAST water-ACC in hour
   'He drank/was drinking water.'

Filip (2008) states that the Germanic and Slavic languages use two different strategies for realizing telicity of incremental theme verbs. For Germanic languages she proposes an object-encoding strategy, since quantization is marked on the object. Slavic languages on the other hand use a verb-encoding strategy, as the grammatical aspect of the verb triggers a telic reading of the predication.[4] The similarities of the use of the definite article in Germanic languages and the perfective aspect in Slavic languages has been observed by different authors as Wierzbicka (1967) for Polish, Filip (1993/1999) for Czech, and Birkenmaier (1979) for Russian. Others such as Abraham (1997), Kabakčiev (2000), Leiss (2000) and Borer (2005) go even further and assume that the definite article and perfective aspect serve the same semantic function. Leiss (2000:14) explicitly proposes that the perfective aspect and the definite article are realizations of the same grammatical category, the only difference being that they are expressed at different parts of the sentence (on the verb in case of aspect and inside the object NP in case of the article). Filip (1993/1999, 2001) argues against an equation of the definite article and perfective aspect; in her view, both have different semantic functions.

In this paper, we follow Filip's view and argue against the assumption that the definite article and perfective aspect have the same semantic function. Therefore, we are looking at two Slavic languages, the Upper Silesian dialect of Polish and Bulgarian, which have a grammaticalized definite article in addition to the grammaticalized aspectual system. Given the assumption that the definite article and perfective aspect are expressions of the same grammatical category, one would expect that one of the two is redundant in Upper Silesian and Bulgarian for expressing telicity of incremental theme predications. However, we will show that both, the definite article and the perfective aspect, are relevant for realizing telicity of those predications and therefore are neither semantically equivalent nor redundant. We will also demonstrate that there are differences in the entailments of definiteness and totality (which is the semantic contribution of the perfective

---

[4] It is not the case that perfective verbs always express telic predications which will be shown in section 3.1.

aspect) depending on whether a language uses (i) the definite article, (ii) perfective aspect or (iii) both of them for realizing telicity of incremental theme predications. This further supports the view that the definite article and perfective aspect have different semantic functions.

The paper proceeds as following: The next section deals with the aspectual composition of incremental theme verbs. In section 3 we focus on the semantics of the definite article and the perfective aspect. Upper Silesian and Bulgarian data are presented in section 4 to show that the definite article as well as the perfective aspect are required to get a telic incremental theme predication. Section 5 discusses the different entailments provided by the perfective aspect and the definite article. Section 6 provides the conclusion and a short outlook.

2   Aspectual composition of incremental theme verbs

Following Vendler (1957), verbs are distinguished into states, activities, achievements, and accomplishments. For the topic of this paper, only the contrast between activities and accomplishments is relevant. Both accomplishments and activities describe dynamic situations but differ with regard to telicity. Accomplishments are telic and therefore express the attainment of a specific natural endpoint. Activities on the other hand are atelic and do not entail the reaching of such an endpoint. Telic predicates license time-span adverbials that indicate the time after which the endpoint of the event has been reached. In (4a), a change from an unstable to a stable condition is denoted, and it is stated that after two days the physical condition is stable. Atelic predicates do not allow time-span adverbials in the same interpretation (4b), since they do not provide a natural endpoint that has to be reached in order to yield a true predication. Rather time-span adverbials indicate the time after which an event starts. Such an interpretation, however, arises with both atelic and telic predications.

(4)   a.   *The physical condition of the patient stabilized in two days.*

   b.   # *John ran in ten minutes.*

A further property of telic predications is that they do not have the 'subinterval property.' This is reflected by the fact that the progressive does not entail the perfect form of the predication (5a). Not just any arbitrary change makes a telic predication true; rather, only if the changes lead to an attainment of the telos. Atelic predicates, on the other hand, have the subinterval property and therefore license the entailment from the progressive to the perfect (5b). Once the process has started, an atelic verb leads to a true predication.

(5) a. *The physical condition of the patient was stabilizing when he died.* → *The physical condition has stabilized.*
   b. *John was running when he was interrupted.* → *John has run.*

Verkuyl (1972), among others, notes that Vendler's classification does not apply to verbs as such, but rather to verbal predications consisting of a verb and its complements and adjuncts. In case of incremental theme verbs, the referential properties of the incremental theme argument (a term introduced by Dowty 1991 based on Krifka's work) affect the aktionsart of the whole predication. This is illustrated by the English example in (6). The predication in (6) shows the aktionsart properties of accomplishments and hence expresses a telic predication due to the referential properties of the incremental theme argument, which has a quantized reference. (7) is an activity and expresses an atelic predication. The incremental theme argument *apples* has cumulative reference.

(6) a. *Peter ate an apple in ten minutes.*
   b. # *Peter was eating an apple in ten minutes.* ↛ *Peter ate an apple.*

(7) a. # *Peter ate soup in ten minutes.*
   b. *Peter was eating apples when he was interrupted* → *Peter ate apples.*

Basically, three types of incremental theme verbs can be distinguished: (i) verbs of consumption such as *drink, eat*, (ii) verbs of creation like *build* and *write* and (iii) verbs of performance such as *sing* and *read*. Only the first two groups of verbs are strictly incremental (see Krifka 1998), which means that they cannot express a change affecting a single object more than once. In the remainder of the paper we concentrate on the first type of incremental theme verbs. The effect of the referential properties of incremental theme arguments on the whole predication is captured by the rule of aspectual composition as stated in (8).

(8) Aspectual composition of incremental theme predications:[5]
   An incremental theme verb combined with a quantized incremental theme argument yields a telic predication, whereas if it combines with a cumula-

---

[5] With regard to other verbs, for example, degree achievements, aspectual composition proceeds in a different way (cf. Kennedy 2012, among others). Kardos (2012) presents a detailed study of the differences between degree achievements, achievements, and accomplishments on the one hand and incremental theme verbs in aspectual composition in Hungarian on the other.

tive incremental theme argument it yields an atelic predication (e. g. Krifka 1986, 1998, Filip 1993/1999, 2001).

The notions of 'cumulativity' and 'quantization' are defined (based on Krifka 1991) in (9) and (10), respectively. ('⊕' is the mereological sum operator and '<' stands for the mereological part-of relation.)

(9) Cumulativity: A predicate P is cumulative iff
$\forall x, y[P(x) \land P(y) \rightarrow P(x \oplus y)]$
(A predicate P is cumulative iff it applies to two individuals x and y, then it also applies to the sum of both.)

(10) Quantization: A predicate P is quantized iff
$\forall x, y[P(x) \land P(y) \rightarrow \neg y < x]$
(A predicate P is quantized iff it applies to two individuals x and y, none of them is a proper part of the other.)

Singular count nouns such as *apple* have a quantized reference. If something is an apple, no proper part of it is also an apple. But the noun *apple* does not have the property of cumulativity, since the sum of two apples cannot be denoted by *apple* again. Rather the plural form *apples* has to be used. The bare plural *apples* shows cumulative reference, since if one has a set of apples and combines them with a second set of apples, the whole can be denoted by *apples* again. On the other hand, *apples* is not quantized, since a proper subset of more than one apple falls under the predicate *apples* again. Mass nouns have the same referential properties as bare plurals.

In English and German, singular count nouns in referential contexts always require some kind of nominal determination such as the definite or indefinite article (11). Sentence (11b) is not ungrammatical, but only allows a kind-denoting interpretation of *apple*.

(11) a. *Peter ate an/the apple.*
b. # *Peter ate apple.*

Mass nouns in English and German are incompatible with the indefinite article but can take the definite article (cf. Krifka 1991). The article is not required with mass nouns and shifts the noun towards a quantized interpretation. This leads to a telic incremental theme predication (12a). Plural count nouns are compatible with the definite article too, in which case they also yield a quantized interpretation. But if they are used without nominal determination, they have cumulative reference. Such a case leads to an atelic incremental theme predication (12b) as stated in (8).

(12) a. *Peter ate the apples/the soup in ten minutes.*
 b. *Peter ate apples/soup (*in ten minutes).*

For aspectual composition of incremental theme verbs, different semantic analyses have been proposed, such as Krifka's (1986, 1998) mereological approach or the degree-based approach by, for example, Hay et al. (1999), Caudal & Nicolas (2005), Beavers (2006), Piñón (2008) and Kennedy (2012). Krifka's account is probably the most influential one and also served as a basis for the degree-based accounts. The central idea of Krifka's approach is that events as well as objects form a part structure and incremental theme verbs provide a mapping between the part structure of events and incremental theme arguments. Referential properties are transferred from the object on the event via the homomorphic mapping between the two. We do not go into further details of this approach, since we merely focus on the morphosyntactic devices for realizing telicity of incremental theme predications (but see Kardos 2012 for a recent comparison of the mereological and the degree-based approaches).

Turning to the Slavic languages now, in (13) the Russian mass noun *sup* (*soup*) is combined with an imperfective (a) and a perfective (b) verb. A telic reading results only in the latter case. As the example shows, there is no explicit quantization of the mass noun.

(13) a. *Ivan el$_{\text{IMPF}}$ sup   (*za čas).*
  Ivan eat.PAST soup.ACC in hour
  'Ivan was eating/ate soup.'
 b. *Ivan s"-el$_{\text{PF}}$ sup   za čas.*
  Ivan S-eat.PAST soup.ACC in hour
  'Ivan ate (all) the soup in an hour.'

The accusative vs. genitive opposition has an effect on telicity of incremental theme predicates. For a telic interpretation, the incremental theme argument has to be marked with accusative case (13b). If the argument is in the genitive, only an atelic reading is possible (14a). The genitive gives rise to a partitive reading of the direct object.

(14) a. *On s"-el$_{\text{PF}}$ xleb-a   (*za čas).*
  he S-eat.PAST bread-GEN in hour
  'He ate some bread.'

b. * On el_IMPF   xleb-a.
he eat.PAST bread-GEN

Russian restricts this case alternation to perfective verbs as indicated in (14b). Other Slavic languages, like Croatian and Serbian, allow the case alternation even with imperfective verbs (Mendoza 2004: 229). In the following discussion, we restrict ourselves to incremental theme verbs in the accusative and do not further investigate the mentioned case alternation.

By comparing (12a) and (13b) one might be led to the assumption that the definite article in the Germanic languages and the perfective aspect in Slavic serve the same function, namely expressing 'totality'[6], as held by Leiss (2000). Similar views are expressed by Borer (2005) and Kabakčiev (1984a, 2000), who state that the function of both is the same and only differ with regard to their overt realization. If totality is expressed via perfective aspect, it is marked on the verb and if it is expressed via definiteness, it is marked in the noun phrase. So far this is in accordance with Filip's (2008) distinction between object-encoding and verb-encoding languages. This distinction centers on the question as to whether nominal determination or verbal morphology is used for realizing telicity of incremental theme predications. The claim is not that Germanic languages are only object-encoding and Slavic languages are only verb-encoding, but that primarily nominal determination is relevant for realizing telicity of incremental theme predications in the Germanic languages and verbal morphology in the Slavic languages.[7]

Filip explicitly rejects the view that perfective aspect and the definite article serve the same semantic function. In Filip's analysis perfective aspect is an expression of 'totality (of events),' but the definite article is not. We follow Filip's (1993/1999, 2005b) analysis of perfective aspect on the one hand and go with Löbner's (1985, 2011) uniqueness approach of definiteness on the other hand. Both, perfectivity and definiteness, are discussed in more detail in the next section.

3 Perfectivity and definiteness

In this section, we provide a short discussion of the semantic contribution of perfective aspect and the definite article. In the process, we take a special look

---

[6] The notion of 'totality' will be discussed in section 3.1.

[7] There are further morpho-syntactic strategies for realizing telicity of incremental theme predicates as shown by Latrouite & Van Valin (this volume) for Lakhota and Tagalog respectively.

at the interaction between perfective aspect, the definite article, and incremental theme predications.

3.1 Perfective aspect

Grammatical aspect is a conventionalized way of expressing different perspectives or viewpoints on a situation. Often it is also called 'viewpoint aspect,' as, for example, in the work of Smith (1991). There is a general distinction between perfective and imperfective aspect. Perfective aspect is used to denote complete but not necessarily completed situations. Hence it does not express the notion of resultativity (cf. Comrie 1976). Rather, the focus is on the situation as a whole without a distinction of its various phases. The imperfective aspect, on the other hand, is a cover term for different ways of denoting an incomplete or not necessarily complete situation. It comprises the habitual, continuous as well as progressive subtypes (see Comrie 1976).[8]

Germanic languages do not have a grammaticalized aspectual system, but some languages, such as English and Icelandic, have at least a grammaticalized progressive aspect (cf. Thieroff 2000). Other Germanic languages, like the north Frisian dialect Fering and German, are on the way towards grammaticalizing the progressive aspect (see Ebert 2000). All Slavic languages, on the other hand, have a systematic aspectual distinction between the perfective and the general imperfective aspect. The imperfective is used for the expression of the continuous, progressive, and habitual subtypes but also has a so-called 'denotative' use which is truth-conditionally equivalent to corresponding perfective sentences (see e. g., Isačenko 1962). Simplex verbs in Slavic languages are either imperfective, perfective or bi-aspectual (meaning that they allow for both aspectual interpretations depending on the context). There is no uniform marker of the perfective aspect in Slavic languages (cf. Isačenko 1962, Filip 1993/1999). Rather, a set of affixes, but also other devices such as suppletive stems or vowel changes are used for realizing the perfective aspect. Verbal prefixes are derivational affixes since they often alter the meaning of the base verb. Following Filip (1993/1999, 2000), prefixes are used to derive new verbs which can be perfective. This is illustrated by the Russian example in (15a) and the Bulgarian one in (b). (15a) shows the derivation of a perfective verb from a simplex imperfective verb by prefixation. The Bulgarian example in (15b) shows (i) that prefixes can be attached to simplex

---

[8] Filip & Carlson (1997) argue against the view that 'habitual' is a subtype of imperfective aspect.

perfective verbs and (ii) that stacking of prefixes is possible. Bulgarian allows an iteration of up to seven prefixes (e. g., Istratkova 2004), and in cases such as *porazdam* it cannot be said that the prefixes contribute perfective aspect since the verb they attach to is already perfective. Thus, in both cases in (b) the prefix has a semantic but no aspectual effect on the verb.

(15)   a.   *pisat'*$_{\text{IMPF}}$ –   *pere-pisat'*$_{\text{PF}}$
            write   copy/rewrite

       b.   *dam*$_{\text{PF}}$ –   *po-dam*$_{\text{PF}}$ –   *po-raz-dam*$_{\text{PF}}$
            give   pass   distribute a little
            (Istratkova 2004: 309)

According to Filip, the only true aspectual marker in Slavic languages is a suffix indicating secondary imperfective aspect.[9] This suffix attaches to perfective verbs and always yields an imperfective predication. Secondary imperfectivization is illustrated in (16) for the Bulgarian verb *piša* (*write*). The simplex verb *piša* is imperfective, by prefixing *na-* a perfective verb is derived from which one gets a secondary imperfective by adding the suffix *–va*. In the following, we do not take secondary imperfectives into consideration, since they behave differently with respect to definiteness and telicity than nonsecondary imperfectives (cf. Filip 2005a).

(16)   *piša*$_{\text{IMPF}}$ –   *na-piša*$_{\text{PF}}$ –   *na-piš-va-m*$_{\text{IMPF}}$
       write

Following Filip (1993/1999, 2005b), the perfective aspect is semantically represented by means of a totality operator (TOT). Filip (2005b: 134) notes that "[t]he effect of *TOT(P)* is to individuate atomic events in the denotation of a perfective verb, given that it is required that no two events in the denotation set of a given predicate P overlap." Intuitively, TOT applied to a predicate P denotes events conceived as a single whole (Filip 2005b: 134), which means that the events are conceived as atomic and therefore no reference to its various phases can be made. (For the formal definition of the totality operator see Filip (2005b)).

With incremental theme verbs the totality operator sets certain requirements on the incremental theme argument. A perfective incremental theme verb always requires a quantized incremental theme argument. Filip (2005b: 134f.) states:

---

[9] Since affixes cannot be analyzed as aspectual markers, aspect is subscripted to the verb in our examples.

"[g]iven that the perfective verb has total events in its denotation, the [homomorphic] mappings [between the event and the object] dictate that the Incremental Theme argument must refer to totalities of objects falling under its description." If the incremental theme argument is a singular count noun, this constraint is fulfilled. However, in order to achieve this constraint with cumulative nouns, they have to be shifted to a totality interpretation. The totality interpretation of mass nouns would account for the maximal quantity of stuff like for example 'water'. For such a maximal quantity interpretation, a specified context-dependent quantity of the referent of the mass noun is required. In the case of plural count nouns, the totality refers to the maximal group of some specific entities such as 'apples.' A description of the respective type shifting processes, based on Link's (1983, 1987) lattice theoretic logics of plurals and mass terms, can be found in Filip (1993/1999, 2005b).

In the context of the current discussion, it is relevant to note that the primary function of the perfective aspect is to express totality (of events) and that quantization is only secondary by imposing restrictions on the incremental theme argument of the verb. More specifically, quantization is achieved by a totality interpretation of inherently cumulative nouns. This also interacts with definiteness, as can be observed in the Russian examples in (17). Mass and plural count nouns as incremental theme arguments of perfective verbs get a definite interpretation (17a), while they get a partitive (indefinite) interpretation with imperfective verbs (17b).

(17) a. *On vy-pil$_{PF}$ vod-u.*
 he VY-drank water-ACC
 'He drank (all) the water.'
 b. *On pil$_{IMPF}$ vod-u.*
 he drank water-ACC
 'He drank/was drinking (some) water.'

Perfectivity does not induce a definite reading of singular count nouns, as the Russian examples in (18) show. Rather, singular count nouns allow for a definite as well as indefinite interpretation irrespective of grammatical aspect (as seen in (a) and (b)). Perfective aspect only induces a totality interpretation. In (18a) it is expressed that an/the whole apple was eaten.

(18) a. *On s"-el$_{PF}$ jabloko.*
 he S-ate apple.ACC
 'He ate a(n)/the (whole) apple.'

b. *On el*_{IMPF} *jabloko.*
   he ate   apple.ACC
   'He ate/was eating an/the apple.'

As stated above, the effect of the perfective aspect is to mark totality (of events) and neither the quantization of nouns nor the expression of definiteness. Both quantization and definiteness are side effects of the totality interpretation of incremental theme arguments and they only arise in certain contexts, namely with cumulative direct object arguments of perfective incremental theme verbs. To be more precise, definiteness is a side effect of quantization and since singular count nouns are quantized, they are not obligatorily conceived as definite if they occur as the direct object of perfective incremental theme verbs. But it is also crucial to note that we distinguish between perfectivity and telicity, following Borik (2006) among others and in contrast to Kabakčiev (1984b, 2000), for example. As shown in the mentioned literature outside of the domain of incremental theme verbs, imperfective predications can be telic (19a) and perfective predications are not necessarily telic but can be atelic (19b).

(19) a. *Petja uže   peresekal*_{IMPF} *etot kanal   *(za) polčasa.*
       Peter already crossed   this channel   in half-hour
       'Peter (has) already crossed this channel in/*for half an hour.'
       (Borik 2006: 9)

   b. *Petja pro-sidel*_{PF} *v tjur'me   (*za) pjat' let.*
      Peter PRO-sit   in prison.LOC in five years
      'Peter was in prison for/*in five years.'
      (Borik 2006: 11)

3.2 Definite article

All Germanic languages exhibit a definite article (cf. König & van der Auwera 1994) but differ with respect to the morphosyntactic realization. In the West Germanic languages such as English, Dutch, and German, the definite article is a free morpheme while in the Northern branch (Norwegian, Swedish, Danish, Faroese, and Icelandic) a free as well as a suffixed article can be found. The distribution of these articles is influenced by syntactic and semantic factors (Ortmann 2014). The following examples illustrate the syntactically governed distribution of the articles in Danish. The suffixed article is used if the noun is not pre-nominally modified (20a), whereas the free-form article is chosen in case of a modified noun (20b).

(20) a. *hus-et*
 house-DEF
 'the house'

b. *det gamle hus*
 DEF old house
 'the old house'
 (Lyons 1999: 77)

In contrast, for the Slavic languages the lack of a definite article is said to be a characteristic property of this language family. However, there are some exceptions such as the two South Slavic languages Macedonian and Bulgarian, as well as two varieties of West Slavic namely Upper Silesian Polish (Czardybon 2010) and Colloquial Upper Sorbian (Breu 2004, Scholze 2008). Bulgarian exhibits a suffixed definite article which is attached to a noun (21a) or the first prenominal element of an NP (21b). In Upper Silesian on the other hand the definite article is realized as a free morpheme (22).

(21) a. *Papa-ta e glava na cărkva-ta.*
 pope-DEF AUX head PREP church-DEF
 'The Pope is the head of the Catholic Church.'

b. *Toj ima moja-ta červena kniga.*
 he has my-DEF red book
 'He has my red book.' (lit. 'He has my the red book')

(22) *Na tym piyrsz-ym zdjynciu jest Róża.*
 PREP DEF first-LOC photo.LOC COP Róża
 'Róża is on the first photo.'

With respect to the semantics of the definite article there are two main approaches, known as 'familiarity' and 'uniqueness,' which try to explain its function.[10] Here, we follow Löbner (1985, 2011) for whom unique reference is the underlying concept of definiteness. In his analysis of definiteness, Löbner argues that the definite article has only one function, independent of whether it is used with a count or mass noun and whether the count noun is used in the singular or plural (Löbner 1985: 280). Essentially, definiteness expresses unique reference, in the sense of non-ambiguity of reference. Following Löbner (1985, 2011) two types of definite-

---

[10] For an overview of the two approaches, see Lyons (1999) and Abbott (2010).

ness exist: semantic and pragmatic definiteness.[11] A noun has semantic definite reference if its definite interpretation is not dependent on the context of use. Pragmatic definiteness on the other hand arises through the context of use and Löbner (1985: 298) writes that in this case the non-ambiguity of reference essentially depends on the special situation. The noun *Pope,* for example, is semantically definite, since there is only one Pope at one time and therefore the noun refers unambiguously. A similar case is the noun *mother (of)* which has unique reference since each person only has one single mother. The difference between *Pope* and *mother (of)* is that in the latter case a relation between two individuals, the mother and the person who she is a mother of, is expressed. Löbner calls nouns such as *Pope* individual concepts, since they uniquely refer to an individual, while *mother (of)* is a functional concept as it expresses a functional relation (a one-to-one mapping) between individuals.[12]

Pragmatic definiteness is established through the context of use and requires a noun (or use of a noun) that does not provide unambiguous reference through its meaning alone. A case in point is *daughter,* since a person can have more than one daughter or even no daughter at all. If used, for example, in a superlative construction, *daughter* allows for unique reference (23).

(23) my eldest daughter

There are two types of nouns which do not show inherently unique reference, these are relational concepts such as *daughter* and sortal concepts like *woman.* Relational concepts provide a relation, in a similar manner to functional concepts, but no one-to-one mapping. Sortal concepts are non-relational and are clear instances of classifying nouns. The function of the definite article is to indicate that the respective noun is taken as a functional concept (Löbner 1985: 314).[13] It either signals, in a redundant way, semantic uniqueness with individual and functional nouns, or signals pragmatic uniqueness with sortal or relational nouns.

Definite determiners are, as Löbner (1985: 281) argues, neutral with regard to the mass/count distinction. This means that the mass/count distinction is orthogonal to the concept type distinction he proposes (also see Löbner unpublished).

---

[11] Löbner (2011) is speaking of 'semantic' and 'pragmatic uniqueness' since uniqueness is the underlying concept for definiteness.

[12] To be more precise, Löbner does not classify nouns but uses of nouns. The reason is that, for example, *mother* can also be used in a non-functional way as in *Mothers are always helpful.*

[13] Löbner (1985) takes individual nouns to be a subtype of functional nouns, while in Löbner (2011) they are taken as a class of its own.

The class of sortal nouns encompasses, for example, *woman* as well as *water*. Also with regard to relational and functional nouns Löbner (1985: 294) states that they are not necessarily count nouns. Gamerschlag & Ortmann (2007) mention *the blood of an alligator* as an example of a functional use of a mass noun. Clearly, this NP is non-quantized since any part of *the blood of an alligator* can be denoted by the same NP. There is still, however, the question as to whether the NP has cumulative reference. The answer depends on the effect of the definite article on mass nouns. Following Löbner (1985: 282), the "definite article indicates that the DD [definite description] refers to that, possibly complex, object to which the noun, as a predicate, applies in the situation referred to. *The children* refers to the entire complex object to which *children* applies; *the child* to the entire object to which *child* applies (which is necessarily only one child); and *the snow* to the entire object to which *snow* applies". The crucial question is what 'entire object' means. It surely does not mean that *snow* refers to all the snow in the world; rather it refers to a contextually specified portion of snow. *The blood of an alligator* does not need to refer to the entire blood of the alligator but only to, for example, a certain amount in a bottle. In this case we can add a further bottle of blood of the same alligator and refer to the sum of both as *the blood of an alligator*. Surely, the connections between Löbner's concept type distinction and the mass/noun distinction has to be further worked out, but this would go beyond the limits of the current paper.

Nevertheless, the marking of unique reference of cumulatively referring nouns leads to quantization by restricting the reference object of the noun to a specified quantity. While the bare mass noun *water* denotes the substance 'water,' *the water* does not denote the entire substance 'water' but its reference is limited to a specific subportion. The exact quantity is context-dependent and could, for example, be *a glass of, a bottle of,* or *three cups of.* However, *the water,* without further linguistic or contextual specification, does not indicate the exact amount of water. This also applies to plural count nouns as in the case *the books*. With inherently quantized nouns, that is singular count nouns, the definite article only indicates unique reference since the noun already has a specified quantity reading.

4 Telicity strategies in Upper Silesian and Bulgarian

The Upper Silesian and Bulgarian data in this and the following sections are provided by native speakers we consulted. The same holds for all other examples in the paper, where not indicated otherwise.

4.1 Upper Silesian

Upper Silesian, a south-west dialect of Polish, differs from standard Polish with regard to the grammaticalization of a definite article, which standard Polish lacks (Czardybon 2010). Authors such as Piskorz (2011) discuss the article status of standard Polish *ten* and claim that *ten* is on the way to being grammaticalized into a definite article due to its anaphoric use. However, we do not regard *ten* as a definite article since in anaphoric contexts demonstratives as well as definite articles can be used and are interchangeable as stated by Christophersen (1939: 29) and Hawkins (1978: 149). We follow Himmelmann (2001: 833f.), for whom a determiner has developed into a definite article if its distribution is extended to associative-anaphoric or larger situation uses such as *the sun, the Queen*. As described in Chapter 3.2, these contexts are called semantically unique contexts by Löbner (2011). In these contexts, only definite articles can be used but not demonstratives which only mark definiteness redundantly due to the fact that the nouns are already semantically unique by themselves. As Polish *ten* is not extended to such contexts, we do not consider it to be a definite article.

In accordance with standard Polish and the other Slavic languages Upper Silesian has a fully grammaticalized aspect system. As shown in (24) the combination of a singular count noun and imperfective incremental theme verb always leads to an atelic predication. This is the case irrespective of whether a singular count noun such as *jabko* (*apple*) is used without (a) or with nominal determination (b). As (b) shows, the definite article is not sufficient to yield a telic interpretation if the verb is used in the imperfective aspect.

(24) a. Łon jod$_{\text{IMPF}}$ jabk-o   (*za godzina).
       he eat.PAST apple-ACC.SG in hour
       'He ate/was eating (of) an apple.'

   b. Łon jod$_{\text{IMPF}}$ te jabk-o   (*za godzina).
      he eat.PAST DEF apple-ACC.SG in hour
      'He ate/was eating (of) the apple.'

Definiteness & perfectivity in telic incremental theme predications

As (25) shows, if the verb is used in the perfective aspect, the incremental theme predication becomes telic. The definite article is not required if a singular count noun is used as an incremental theme argument. Hence, examples (25a) and (25b) only differ with respect to definiteness of the direct object, but not with regard to telicity of the predication.

(25) a. *Łon z-jod*$_{PF}$ *jabk-o za godzina.*
he Z-eat.PAST apple-ACC.SG in hour
'He ate an apple in an hour.'

b. *Łon z-jod*$_{PF}$ *te jabk-o za godzina.*
he Z-eat.PAST DEF apple-ACC.SG in hour
'He ate the apple in an hour.'

If the incremental theme argument is a bare plural or a mass noun, the definite article is required for a telic predication (26b, 27b). Leaving out the definite article does not lead to ungrammatical sentences but (26a) and (27a) only have a kind-denoting and not a referential interpretation of the incremental theme arguments.

(26) a. # *Łon z-jod*$_{PF}$ *jabk-a.*
he Z-eat.PAST apple-ACC.PL
'He ate [some plurality of the kind] apple.'

b. *Łon z-jod*$_{PF}$ *te jabk-a za godzina.*
he Z-eat.PAST DEF apple-ACC.PL in hour
'He ate the apples in an hour.'

(27) a. # *Łon wy-pioł*$_{PF}$ *woda.*
he WY-drink.PAST water.ACC
'He drank [something of the kind] water.'

b. *Łon wy-pioł*$_{PF}$ *ta woda za godzina.*
he WY-drink.PAST DEF water.ACC in hour
'He drank the water in an hour.'

Plural count nouns and mass nouns can combine with imperfective verbs without a definite article, as shown in (28). But as with singular count nouns (24) only an atelic interpretation is possible.

(28) a. *Łon jod*$_{IMPF}$ *jabk-a (*za godzina).*
he eat.PAST apple-ACC.PL in hour
'He ate/was eating (of) the apples.'

b. *Łon jod*_{IMPF} *cuker* (**za godzina).*
   he eat.PAST sugar.ACC   in hour
   'He ate/was eating sugar.'

Thus, the data show that perfective incremental theme verbs always require a quantized incremental theme argument. Furthermore, a telic incremental theme predication only arises if the incremental theme argument is inherently or explicitly quantized and the verb is used in the perfective aspect.

4.2 Bulgarian

Bulgarian shows the same constraint on the combination of cumulative incremental theme arguments and perfective incremental theme verbs that was demonstrated for Upper Silesian. The examples in (29) show that imperfective incremental theme verbs do not require nominal determination of the incremental theme argument. Like in Upper Silesian, an imperfective verb does not lead to a telic predication if the incremental theme argument is definite (29b). As (c) demonstrates, the imperfective aspect is also compatible with quantized mass nouns, but does not give rise to a telic reading.[14]

(29) a. *Marija jade*_{IMPF} *jabălka/ jabălki/ kaša* (**za edin čas).*
       Maria ate   apple.SG/ apple.PL/ mash   in one hour
       'Maria ate/was eating (of) an apple/apples/mash.'

   b. *Marija jade*_{IMPF} *jabălka-ta* (**za edin čas).*
      Maria ate   apple. SG-DEF in one hour
      'Maria ate/was eating (of) the apple.'

   c. *Marija jade*_{IMPF} *kaša-ta* (**za edin čas).*
      Maria ate   mash-DEF in one hour
      'Maria was eating [some specific portion of] the mash.'

As in Upper Silesian, the combination of perfective incremental theme verbs and singular count nouns always leads to a telic predication (30), irrespective of the presence (30b) or absence (30a) of the definite article.

---

[14] Bulgarian shows a difference between the imperfect past tense and the aorist. Imperfective verbs are mainly used in the imperfect past, while perfective verbs show up mainly in the aorist. But as Kuteva (1995), for example, demonstrates, both past tenses can combine with perfective as well as imperfective verbs (also cf. Kabakčiev 2000).

(30) a. *Marija iz-jade*_{PF} *jabălka za edin čas.*
Maria IZ-ate   apple.SG in one hour
'Maria ate an apple in one hour.'

b. *Marija iz-jade*_{PF} *jabălka-ta   za edin čas.*
Maria IZ-ate   apple.SG-DEF in one hour
'Maria ate the apple in one hour.'

The contrastive pairs of sentences in (31) and (32) show that the combination of a perfective incremental theme verb and a cumulative noun only allows for a kind reading of the nominal.[15] As in Upper Silesian the incremental theme argument needs to be quantized by, for example, the addition of the definite article for a referential and, in this case, also a telic interpretation.

(31) a. # *Marija iz-jade*_{PF} *jabălki.*
Maria IZ-ate   apple.PL
'Maria ate [some plurality of the kind] apple.'

b. *Marija iz-jade*_{PF} *jabălki-te   za edin čas.*
Maria IZ-ate   apple.PL-DEF in one hour
'Maria ate the apples in one hour.'

(32) a. # *Marija iz-jade*_{PF} *kaša.*
Maria IZ-ate   mash
'Maria ate [something of the kind] mash.'

b. *Marija iz-jade*_{PF} *kaša-ta   za edin čas.*
Maria IZ-ate   mash-DEF in one hour
'Maria ate the mash in one hour.'

Upper Silesian and Bulgarian, then, behave alike with respect to the expression of telicity of incremental theme predicates. As claimed by Filip, perfective incremental theme verbs always require quantized incremental theme arguments. This is obvious in Upper Silesian and Bulgarian since perfective verbs cannot combine with referentially used bare plurals and mass nouns.

4.3 Summary of telicity strategies

So far, we have discussed the impact of the definite article and grammatical aspect in realizing telicity of incremental theme predications in Germanic and Slavic

---

[15] Guentchéva (1990: 36) gives a Bulgarian example of a perfective incremental theme verb *izpix* 'drunk' used with a bare mass noun *kafe* 'coffee' which is judged by her as ungrammatical. She does not say anything about a possible kind reading of such constructions.

languages. In Germanic languages, nominal determination, for example in the form of the definite article, is required to yield a telic predication.[16] Nevertheless, the definite article is not sufficient to yield a telic predication, since it is also compatible with an atelic predication as (33) shows. Jackendoff (1996) states that if sentences such as (33) are acceptable with durative time adverbials then they do not imply that the object is totally consumed. Hay et al. (1999) state that examples such as (33) demonstrate that telicity is only an implicature in the case of verbs like *eat* (cf. Kardos 2012 for the view that incremental theme verbs in English and Hungarian show variable telicity similarly to degree achievements such as *to cool*).

(33)　*She ate the sandwich in/for five minutes.*　　　　(Hay et al. 1999: 139)

Kardos (2012: 152) mentions that incremental theme verbs in English only show variable telicity if the incremental theme argument has quantized reference and is combined with the definite or indefinite article (as in (33)). Variable telicity does not arise with cumulatively referring nouns (34a) or if a quantized noun is modified by a numeral construction or measure phrase (34b). This highlights again that the effect of the definite article with inherently quantized nouns only expresses unique reference and does not specify quantity.

(34)　a.　*Mary ate soup for 10 minutes/*in ten minutes.*
　　　b.　*Kate ate three apples/two kg of apples in half an hour/??for half an hour.*
　　　　(Kardos 2012: 152)

Those Slavic languages that do not exhibit a definite article, for example Russian and Polish, make use of the perfective aspect to realize a telic incremental theme predication. The imperfective aspect of incremental theme verbs always leads to an atelic predication. Those Slavic languages that do have a definite article (Upper Silesian and Bulgarian) make primary use of the perfective aspect for expressing a telic incremental theme predication. The definite article is necessary in those cases in which the incremental theme argument is not inherently quantized. Thus, while the perfective aspect induces quantization of the incremental theme argument in Russian and Polish, in Upper Silesian and Bulgarian the ex-

---

[16] As already mentioned, the definite article is not the only way to quantize a cumulative noun, but we are only focusing on this strategy. In particular, we are leaving out a discussion of the indefinite article, which often goes parallel in quantization effects with the definite article but differs in its semantics.

plicit quantization of bare plurals and mass nouns is required. Table 1 summarizes the strategies mentioned above.

Language group	telic incremental theme predication	atelic incremental theme predication
Germanic	+DEF	±DEF
Slavic I (without definite article; e.g., Russian, Polish, Czech, …)	+PF	+IMPF
Slavic II (with a definite article; Bulgarian, Upper Silesian)	+PF (+DEF)	+IMPF ±DEF

Table 1: Summary of the different telicity strategies.

The discussion of the Upper Silesian and Bulgarian data reveals that the combination of the perfective aspect and the definite article is not redundant in realizing telicity.[17] The exception to this are singular count nouns which are inherently quantized and hence do not require quantization via nominal determination. As mentioned in section 3.2 and further indicated above, we do not assume that the main function of the definite article consists in expressing quantized reference, but that quantization is a side effect due to unique reference. We will show in the next section that perfective aspect and the definite article license different entailments and therefore have different semantic contributions.

5 Differences in entailments

In this section we want to demonstrate that the definite article and perfective aspect make different semantic contributions to the overall incremental theme predication. Following Filip, we analyze perfective aspect as a totality operator on events. With respect to incremental theme predications, the perfective aspect entails that the referent of the incremental theme argument is totally affected. The Polish sentence in (35) expresses that the whole sandwich is consumed.

(35) Ona z-jadła$_{PF}$ kanapk-ę.
      she Z-eat.PAST sandwich-ACC
      'She ate a/the whole sandwich.'

---

[17] This result is contrary to Abraham (1997: 60, n. 8), who states that the realization of perfective aspect and the definite article in Bulgarian merely represents a double marking of the same category.

The definite article in Germanic languages does not induce a totally reading on the consumption process. This is demonstrated by the English example in (36) in which it is expressed that the sandwich was eaten but nevertheless something is left over. Hence the referent of *the sandwich* is not affected in totality. The Dutch (37) and Danish (38) examples exemplify the same point, which shows that this interpretation is not a peculiar fact of English. Due to the absence of perfectivity marking in Germanic languages, totality is merely an implicature since it can be cancelled.

(36) *She ate the sandwich but as usual she left a few bites.*
 (Hay et al. 1999: 139)

(37) *Zij at het broodje maar zoals gewoonlijk at ze niet alles*
 she eat.PAST DEF bread but as usual eat.PAST she NEG everything
 op.
 PART
 'She ate the sandwich/the bread but as usual she did not eat up everything.'

(38) *Hun spiste sandwich-en, men som sædvanligt levnede hun nogle få*
 she eat.PAST sandwich-DEF but as usual left she some few
 bidder.
 bites
 'She ate the sandwich but as usual she left a few bites.'

Since the perfective aspect is overtly realized in Slavic languages, totality is not merely an implicature and therefore cannot be negated. This is demonstrated by the Polish (39) and Czech (40) examples. Stating that something of the food/drink is left over leads to a contradiction in Slavic languages, in contrast to the Germanic languages.

(39) # *Ona z-jadła$_{PF}$ kanapk-ę, ale jak zwykle trochę zostawila.*
 she Z-ate sandwich-ACC but as usual a bit left
 'She ate a/the (whole) sandwich, but as usual she left a bit.'

(40) # *Ivan vy-pil$_{PF}$ čaj, ale ne-vy-pil$_{PF}$ [ho/jej všechen].*
 Ivan VY-drank tea.ACC but NEG-VY-drank it all.ACC
 'Ivan drank (up) [the whole portion of] tea, but he did not drink it all.'
 (Filip 2001: 463)

The data above reveal that a totality interpretation is only contributed by perfective aspect but not by the definite article. A further difference is that only the definite article but not perfective aspect leads necessarily to a definite interpretation of the incremental theme argument. This is, for example, shown by the Polish example in (35). The verb *zjeść* (*eat*) is perfective but the direct object *kanapka* (*sandwich*) has either a definite or indefinite reading. Example (41) from Slovak exemplifies the same point. Perfective incremental theme verbs only induce a totality interpretation of their incremental theme arguments, but for singular count nouns this is compatible with an indefinite interpretation. As discussed in section 3.1, plural count nouns and mass nouns always get a definite reading if used with a perfective verb. But as we argue there, the definite reading is only a side effect of quantization due to the totality reading.[18]

(41) Diet'a zjedlo$_{PF}$ JABLKO.
      child eat.PAST apple
      'The child ate an/the apple.'
      (Späth 2006: 8)

As shown above, Germanic languages lack a totality interpretation of the incremental theme argument, but a definite interpretation trivially arises due to the definite article. The fact that Slavic languages induce a totality interpretation of the incremental theme argument, while the Germanic ones induce a definite interpretation that depends on differences in the grammaticalization of the perfective aspect and definiteness in these languages. Those Slavic languages that have a definite article necessarily induce a totality and definite interpretation of the incremental theme argument if the verb is used in the perfective and the definite article is present. The Upper Silesian examples in (42) and (43) show that a perfective verb entails totality. Expressing that a bit of the sandwich is left leads to a contradiction. The presence of the definite article in (42) only allows for a definite interpretation of the incremental theme argument. Its absence in (43) leads to an indefinite interpretation. Since Upper Silesian has a grammaticalized definite article as well as a perfective aspect, both definiteness and totality are semantically contributed, which distinguishes them from the Germanic and other Slavic languages.

(42) # Łona z-jadła$_{PF}$ ta kanapka, ale jak zawsze zostawioła trocha.
      she   Z-ate   DEF sandwich but as usual left   a bit
      'She ate the/*a sandwich but as usual she left a bit.'

---

[18] Capital letters indicate sentence stress.

(43) # Łona z-jadła$_{PF}$ kanapka, ale jak zawsze zostawioła trocha.
 she Z-ate sandwich but as usual left a bit
 'She ate a/*the sandwich but as usual she left a bit.'

6 Conclusion & outlook

In this paper we have discussed the role of the definite article and perfective aspect in the realization of telicity in incremental theme predications. Contrary to Leiss (2000), Borer (2005), and others, we argued that the definite article and perfective aspect serve different semantic functions. This was demonstrated by (i) the non-redundancy of the definite article and perfective aspect in the realization of telic incremental theme predications in Upper Silesian and Bulgarian (if the incremental theme argument is not inherently quantized) and (ii) the differences in the entailments that can be observed in languages that only use the definite article (Germanic), that only use the perfective aspect (most Slavic) and those languages that use perfective aspect as well as the definite article for realizing telicity (Upper Silesian and Bulgarian). The function of the definite article is to express uniqueness of the noun's referent, which has the effect of quantization as in the case of cumulative nouns. The perfective aspect is used to express totality, which requires quantized incremental theme arguments. To a certain extent, the effect of the definite article and perfective aspect overlap, nevertheless the data revealed that both serve different semantic functions.

One way to derive a perfective verb in Slavic languages is the use of prefixes. But in many cases, as discussed in 3.1, these prefixes change the semantics of the base verb. It is not always clear whether the telicity effect is solely dependent on perfective aspect or whether it depends on the additional lexical content the prefix adds to the base verb. The same effect of prefixes on telicity can also be observed in Germanic languages such as German. (44a) shows that the prefixed verb *aufessen* (*eat up*) forces a telic interpretation of the incremental theme verb. Furthermore, the example in (b) demonstrates that the prefixed verb is not compatible with cumulative nouns.

(44) a. *Der Junge hat das Brot in fünf Minuten/ (*fünf Minuten lang) aufgegessen.*
 DEF boy has DEF bread in five minutes five minutes long up.eaten
 'The boy ate up the bread in five minutes/*for five minutes.'

 b. * *Der Junge hat Brote/ Suppe aufgegessen.*
 DEF boy has breads soup up.eaten

To exclude the possibility that telicity of incremental theme predications basically depends on the lexical content of the prefix and not (or not exclusively) on the perfective aspect, it would be worth investigating languages that express grammatical aspect as a purely inflectional category. One such language, which also has a grammaticalized definite article, is Arabic. An investigation of languages of such a type will be left open for the future.

Bibliography

Abbott, B. 2010. *Reference*. Oxford: Oxford University Press.

Abraham, W. 1997. The interdependence of case, aspect and referentiality in the history of German: the case of the verbal genitive. In A. van Kemenade & N. Vincent (eds.), *Parameters of morphosyntactic change*, 29–61. Cambridge: Cambridge University Press.

Beavers, J. T. 2006. *Argument/oblique alternations and the structure of lexical meaning*: Stanford University dissertation.

Birkenmaier, W. 1979. *Artikelfunktionen in einer artikellosen Sprache. Studien zur nominalen Determination im Russischen*. München: Wilhelm Fink.

Borer, H. 2005. *The normal course of events*. Oxford: Oxford University Press.

Borik, O. 2006. *Aspect and reference time*. Oxford: Oxford University Press.

Breu, W. 2004. Der definite Artikel in der obersorbischen Umgangssprache. In M. Krause & C. Sappok (eds.), *Slavistische Linguistik 2002. Referate des XXVIII. Konstanzer Slavistischen Arbeitstreffens. Bochum 10. - 12.9.2002*, München: Sagner.

Caudal, P. & D. Nicolas. 2005. Types of degrees and types of event structures. In C. Maienborn & A. Wöllstein (eds.), *Event arguments: Foundations and application*, 277–299. Tübingen: Max Niemeyer Verlag.

Christophersen, P. 1939. *The articles. A study of their theory and use in English*. Copenhagen: Munksgaard.

Comrie, B. 1976. *Aspect: An introduction to the study of verbal aspect and related problems*. Cambridge Textbooks in Linguistics. Cambridge: Cambridge University Press.

Czardybon, A. 2010. *Die Verwendung des definiten Artikels im Oberschlesischen im Sprachvergleich*. University of Düsseldorf MA thesis.

Dowty, D. 1991. Thematic proto-roles and argument selection. *Language* 67 (3). 547–619.

Ebert, K. 2000. Progressive markers in Germanic languages. In Ö. Dahl (ed.), *Tense and aspect in the languages of Europe*, 605–653. Berlin: Mouton de Gruyter.

Filip, H. 1993/1999. *Aspect, eventuality types and noun phrase semantics.* New York/London: Garland.

Filip, H. 2000. The quantization puzzle. In C. Tenny & J. Pustejovsky (eds.), *Events as grammatical objects*, 39–96. CSLI Publications.

Filip, H. 2001. Nominal and verbal semantic structure - analogies and interactions. *Language Sciences* 23. 453–501.

Filip, H. 2004. The telicity parameter revisited. In R. Young (ed.), *Proceedings of SALT XIV*, 92–109. Ithaca/NY, Cornell University.

Filip, H. 2005a. Measures and indefinites. In Gregory N. Carlson & Francis Jeffry Pelletier (eds.), *Reference and quantification*, 229–288. Stanford: CSLI Publications.

Filip, H. 2005b. On accumulating and having it all. In Henk Verkuyl, Henriette de Swart & Angeliek von Hout (eds.), *Perspectives on aspect*, 125–148. Dordrecht: Springer.

Filip, H. 2008. Events and maximalization: The case of telicity and perfectivity. In S. Rothstein (ed.), *Theoretical and crosslinguistic approaches to the semantics of aspect*, 217–256. Amsterdam/Philadelphia: John Benjamins.

Filip, H. & G. Carlson. 1997. Sui generis genericity. *Penn Working Papers in Linguistics* 4. 91–110. The University of Pennsylvania. Philadelphia.

Gamerschlag, T. & A. Ortmann. 2007. The role of functional concepts in the classification of nouns and verbs. Handout of a talk presented at the Conference "Concept Types and Frames 07." 21 August 2007. University of Düsseldorf.

Guentchéva, Z. 1990. *Temps et aspect: l'exemple du bulgare contemporain.* Paris: Édition du centre national de la recherché scientifique.

Hawkins, J. A. 1978. *Definiteness and indefiniteness. A study in reference and grammaticality prediction.* London: Croom Helm.

Hay, J., C. Kennedy & B. Levin. 1999. Scalar structure underlies telicity in "degree achievements". In T. Mathews & D. Strolovitch (eds.), *Proceedings of semantics and linguistic theory*, vol. 9, 199–223. Ithaca/NY: Cornell Linguistic Circle Publications.

Himmelmann, N. 2001. Articles. In M. Haspelmath, E. König, W. Oesterreicher & W. Raible (eds.), *Language typology and language universals*, 831–841. Berlin/New York: de Gruyter.

Isačenko, A. 1962. *Die russische Sprache der Gegenwart.* Halle (Saale): Niemeyer.

Istratkova, V. 2004. On multiple prefixation in Bulgarian. *Nordlyd* 32.2. 301–321.

Jackendoff, R. 1996. The proper treatment of measuring out, telicity, and perhaps even quantification in English. *Natural Language and Linguistic Theory* 14. 305–354.

Kabakčiev, K. J. 1984a. The article and the aorist/imperfect distinction in Bulgarian: an analysis based on cross-language 'aspect' parallelisms. *Linguistics* 22. 643–672.

Kabakčiev, K. J. 1984b. Verkuyl's compositional aspects and aspect in the Slavonic languages. *Linguistique Balkanique* XXVII. 77–83.

Kabakčiev, K. J. 2000. *Aspect in English*. Dordrecht: Kluwer.

Kardos, É. 2012. *Toward a scalar semantic analysis of telicity in Hungarian*: University of Debrecen dissertation.

Kennedy, C. 2012. The composition of incremental change. In V. Demonte & L. McNally (eds.), *Telicity, change, and state: A cross-categorical view of event structure*, 103–121. Oxford: Oxford University Press.

Krifka, M. 1986. *Nominalreferenz und Zeitkonstitution. Zur Semantik von Massentermen, Individualtermen, Aspektklassen*. Munich, Germany: Universität München Dissertation.

Krifka, M. 1991. Massennomina. In D. Wunderlich & A. von Stechow (eds.), *Semantik*, 399–417. Berlin: de Gruyter.

Krifka, M. 1998. The origins of telicity. In S. Rothstein (ed.), *Events and grammar*, 197–235. Dordrecht/Boston/London: Kluwer Academic Publishers.

Kuteva, T. 1995. Bulgarian tenses. In R. Thieroff (ed.), *Tense systems in European languages*, vol. II, 195–213. Tübingen: Niemeyer.

König, E. & J. van der Auwera. 1994. *The Germanic languages*. London: Routledge.

Latrouite, A. & R. D. jr. Van Valin. 2014. Referentiality and telicity in Lakhota and Tagalog. In *This volume*, University of Düsseldorf. This volume.

Leiss, E. 2000. *Artikel und Aspekt. Die grammatischen Muster von Definitheit*. Berlin: de Gruyter.

Link, G. 1983. The logical analysis of plurals and mass terms. In R. Bauerle, Ch. Schwarze & A. von Stechow (eds.), *Meaning, use, and interpretation of language*, 302–323. Berlin: de Gruyter.

Link, G. 1987. Algebraic semantics of event structures. In J. Groenendijk, M. Stokhof & F. Veltman (eds.), *Proceedings of the sixth Amsterdam Colloquium*, 243–272. Amsterdam: ITLI. University of Amsterdam.

Lyons, C. 1999. *Definiteness*. Cambridge: Cambridge University Press.

Löbner, S. 1985. Definites. *Journal of Semantics* 4. 279–326.

Löbner, S. 2011. Concept types and determination. *Journal of Semantics* 28(3). 279–333.

Löbner, S. unpublished. The semantics of nominals. Manuscript, University of Düsseldorf.

Mendoza, I. 2004. Nominaldetermination im Polnischen. Die primären Ausdrucksmittel. Habilitation thesis, LMU München.

Ortmann, A. 2014. Definite article asymmetries and concept types: semantic and pragmatic uniqueness. In T. Gamerschlag, D. Gerland, R. Osswald & W. Petersen (eds.), *Frames and concept types. Applications in language and philosophy*, 293–321. Dordrecht: Springer.

Piskorz, K. 2011. Entsteht ein bestimmter Artikel im Polnischen? In M. Kotin & E. Kotorova (eds.), *History and typology of language systems*, 159–168. Heidelberg: Winter Verlag.

Piñón, C. 2008. Aspectual composition with degrees. In L. McNally & C. Kennedy (eds.), *Adjectives and adverbs: Syntax, semantics and discourse*, 183–219. Oxford: Oxford University Press.

Scholze, L. 2008. *Das grammatische System der obersorbischen Umgangssprache im Sprachkontakt*. Bautzen: Domowina - Verlag.

Smith, C. S. 1991. *The parameter of aspect*. Dordrecht, Boston, London: Kluwer Academic Publishers.

Späth, A. 2006. *Determinierung unter Defektivität des Determinierersystems*. Berlin: de Gruyter.

Thieroff, R. 2000. On the areal distribution of tense - aspect categories in Europe. In Ö. Dahl (ed.), *Tense and aspect in the languages of Europe*, 265–305. Berlin/New York: Mouton de Gruyter.

Vendler, Z. 1957. Verbs and times. *The Philosophical Review* 66. 143–160.

Verkuyl, H. 1972. *On the compositional nature of the aspects*. Dordrecht: Reidel Publishing Co.

Wierzbicka, A. 1967. On the semantics of the verbal aspect in Polish. In R. Jakobson (ed.), *To honor Roman Jakobson. Essays on the occasion of his seventieth birthday*, 2231–2249. The Hague: Mouton.

Authors

Adrian Czardybon
Jens Fleischhauer
Departement of Linguistics and Information Science
Heinrich-Heine-University Düsseldorf
{czardybon,fleischhauer}@phil.hhu.de

Referentiality and telicity in Lakhota and Tagalog

Anja Latrouite & Robert D. Van Valin, Jr.

In this paper we look at the way referentiality and telicity are encoded in Lakhota and Tagalog, two unrelated, morphologically rich languages that exhibit both a determiner system and rich verbal marking. The main question centers on how noun phrase marking and verb marking interact in these languages to generate a telic or an atelic interpretation of incremental theme verbs. The analysis by and large supports Filip's (1993/1999) claim that telicity is 'calculated' based on a number of interacting factors.

1 Introduction: referentiality and telicity*

It has been noted time and again that there is a link between the telicity of incremental predicates and the referential status of undergoer arguments (cf. Verkuyl 1972, Krifka 1986, 1989, 1992, Filip 1993/1999, Filip & Rothstein 2005). The acceptablity of time-span adverbials like *in an hour* is commonly viewed as a good test for telicity. As the examples in (1a) and (2a) show, bare plural or mass nouns in object position always yield an atelic reading with incremental verbs and are clearly not compatible with time-span adverbials of the *in an hour* type. They go well with *for*-adverbials, however, which also denote a time-span, albeit without any implication that the event must be completed. In contrast, plural noun and mass noun undergoers with definite articles (cf. (1b) and (2b)) yield a telic reading with incremental verbs and sound better with *in*-adverbials than with *for*-adverbials. Note that the telic reading is not absolutely required by the definite article, how-

---

* We would like to thank two anonymous reviewers for helpful comments on an earlier draft. We would also like to thank our Lakhota language consultant Della Bad Wound as well as our Tagalog language consultants Reyal Panotes, Redemto Batul and Jeruen Dery. This research was supported in part by CRC 991 'The structure of representations in language, cognition and science'.

ever. Atelic readings and thus *for*-adverbials seem to be marginally acceptable, if the undergoer can be understood as denoting a kind rather than a specific and uniquely identifiable object in a given context.[1]

(1) a. *I drank milk *in an hour/ for an hour.*
    b. *I drank the milk in an hour/ ?? for an hour.*

(2) a. *I built wooden houses *in 10 years/ for ten years.*
    b. *I built the wooden houses in ten years/ (?)for ten years.*

Thus the crucial factor is being referential rather than being marked by a definite article *per se*. The explanation as to why there should be a link between referentiality and telicity goes back to Krifka (1986, 1989, 1992), who proposes that for a certain class of verbs (incremental theme verbs) there is a one-to-one relationship between parts of the event and parts of the referent of the related undergoer arguments, e. g. when we drink a particular drink, then parts of this drink decrease in lockstep with the progress of the drinking event. In that way, there is a homomorphism between the undergoer argument and the event, as every part of the drink being drunk corresponds to a part of the drinking event. The homomorphism hypothesis motivates the influence of the undergoer arguments on the interpretation of the verbal predicates. The idea is that if the undergoer (object) argument is conceived as uniquely identifiable, and thus bounded and occurs with a homomorphic predicate, then the event into which it is mapped will be interpreted as bounded, i. e. telic, too. Therefore, undergoer arguments that are expressed by plural and mass nouns require either a specific quantifier or article to be interpretable as referring to a quantized amount, i. e. as a precise amount measuring out the event from the beginning to the end, as exemplified in (3).

(3) a. *I drank their beer for an hour/ in an hour.*
    b. *I drank the milk ??for an hour/ in an hour.*
    c. *I drank three liters of milk *for an hour/ in an hour.*
    d. *I drank the three liters of milk ??for an hour/ in an hour.*

---

[1] An appropriate context for (2b) would be: I have been in the house building business for years and started out with building wooden houses. I built the traditional wooden houses for ten years, then I started building concrete houses like everyone else. For (1b) it is harder to conceive of a context, possibly: They gave me ten liters of goat milk to cure my stomach problems. I drank the milk for an hour, then I turned to beer and whisky again.

The data support the claim that the hallmark of definiteness marking in languages like English is uniqueness, as suggested by Löbner (1985), rather than familiarity, as suggested by Heim (1991). While the possessive NP in (3a) suggests familiarity, it does not impose uniqueness the way the definite article does, and therefore the NP may be interpreted as quantized or not. The possessive NP *their beer* can be interpreted as either unique, e. g. the particular beer that Sam and Bill have in their refrigerator (quantized), in which case *in an hour* is appropriate, or as non-unique, i. e. as any liquid that can be labeled as 'beer' that they happen to have (non-quantized), and in this case *for an hour* works.

Thus apart from inherently atelic and telic verbs, there is a class of verbs that like telic verbs determine a culmination condition, but unlike telic verbs do not imply a culmination requirement, like *write, knit, eat, paint, read, build, drink*, and therefore are understood as atelic, unless further morphosyntactic (or contextual) clues are given.[2] As is well known these markers may differ quite substantially from language to language. Most importantly they may be either found on the verb, e. g. in terms of perfectivity markers (Filip 1993/1999), or within the noun phrase as definiteness or case markers (Ramchand 1997, Kratzer 2004, Filip & Rothstein 2005), leading to the question as to what exactly the components of telicity are (see also Fleischhauer & Czardybon, this volume).

In this paper we explore two unrelated languages, Lakhota and Tagalog, that have also been claimed to employ markers on the verb to yield telic interpretations (cf. Saclot 2011), albeit not perfectivity markers, but rather markers that indicate certain semantic properties of the undergoer argument: in the case of Tagalog the semantic role and in the case of Lakhota the specificity. On top of that both languages exhibit a determiner system. In the main part of the paper we investigate the division of labour between the verb stems and the respective markers to achieve telicity.

---

[2] This is true for dependent-marking accusative languages like English, German and Russian. In many ergative languages, however, the base forms of these verbs are telic and the atelic uses are derived via e. g. antipassivization; see Van Valin & LaPolla (1997), §3.2.3.3 for discussion. Neither Lakhota nor Tagalog fits easily into a simple accusative-ergative dichotomy.

2 The encoding of specificity and definiteness in Lakhota

Lakhota is a Siouan language spoken in the northern Great Plains of North America. It is verb-final, right-branching and thoroughly head-marking. This is exemplified in (4).[3]

(4) a. Wičháša ki hená wówapi ki Ø-wičhá-wa-k'u.
man the those book the INAN-3plANIMU-1sgA-give
'I gave the book to those men.'

a'. Wičháwak'u.
'I gave it to them.'

b. Wičháša ki hená mathó waŋ Ø-Ø-kté-pi
man the those bear a 3sgU-3A-kill-PL
'Those men killed a bear.'

b'. Ktépi.
'They killed him/her/it.'

Basic word order is SOV, and subject and object are cross-referenced on the verb, with the consequence that the verb word alone can constitute a complete clause, as in (4a', b'). Subject cross-reference follows a split-intransitive pattern, with some intransitive verbs taking actor (nominative) coding and others taking undergoer (accusative) coding. As these examples show, the language has definite and indefinite articles, as well as demonstratives. In fact, it has an extremely rich determiner system, with two definite articles, nine distinct indefinite articles, and nine demonstratives (NLD: 815). We introduce each type of article.

Lakhota has two definite articles, ki(ŋ) 'the' vs. k'uŋ 'the aforementioned', e. g. wówapi ki 'the book(s)' vs. wówapi k'uŋ 'the aforementioned book(s)'; like English *the*, they are neutral with respect to number. The basic definite article, ki(ŋ), has both deictic and anaphoric uses. In contrast, k'uŋ 'the aforementioned' has only anaphoric uses, and it can only mark a nominal whose referent has been previously mentioned. Discussion will be restricted to ki(ŋ) from here on, since it is overwhelmingly the most commonly occurring definite article, due to the strong contextual restriction on k'uŋ.

---

[3] Abbreviations: A 'actor', ANIM 'animate', AV 'actor voice', DAT 'dative', GEN 'genitive', INAN 'inani-mate', IPFV 'imperfective', LK 'linker', MOD 'modifier', NEG 'negation', NLD 'New Lakota Dictionary' (Ullrich 2011), NOM 'nominative', NSO 'non-specific object', PL/pl 'plural', POT 'potential', PSA 'privileged syntactic argument', Q 'interrogative marker', RLS 'realis', sg 'singular', STAT 'stative', U 'undergoer', UV 'undergoer voice'.

There are nine indefinite articles, which fall into three major classes: specific, non-specific and negative. Within each class there are distinctions for singular vs. plural, and within the negative class, plural animate (further, human vs. non-human) vs. inanimate, and non-countable are distinguished. Specific indefinites are referential, while non-specific indefinites are not. There is therefore no possible ambiguity in a sentence like *I'm looking for a book* in Lakhota like there is in English; each of the two possible readings of *a book* in English would be signaled by distinct indefinite articles, as in (5).

(5) a. *Wówapi waŋ   o<Ø-wá>le.*   [*olé* 'look for']
    book   a[+specific] look.for <INAN-1sgA>
    'I'm looking for a [particular] book.'

 b. *Wówapi waŋží   o<Ø-wá>le.*
    book   a[-specific] look.for <INAN-1sgA>
    'I'm looking for a book [any book will do].'

The non-specific indefinite articles can occur with intensional verbs like e. g. *want* or *look for*, with verbs carrying the hypothetical-conditional marker *-ktA*,[4] and as the focus of a yes-no question. The negative indefinite articles occur in the scope of negation. The system of indefinite articles is summarized in Table 1, from Rood & Taylor (1996).

	Specific	Non-specific	Negative
Singular	*waŋ*	*waŋží*	*waŋžíni*
Plural Animate			
Human	*eyá*	*etáŋ*	*tuwéni*
Non-human	*eyá*	*etáŋ*	*tákuni*
Inanimate	*eyá*	*etáŋ*	*tákuni*
Non-countable	*eyá*	*etáŋ*	*etáŋni*

Table 1: Lakhota indefinite articles

The specific and non-specific indefinite articles make only a singular vs. plural distinction, while the most distinctions are found among the negative indefinite articles, all of which end in *-ni*, which is clearly related to the negative morpheme

---

[4] The capital *A* indicates that the vowel undergoes ablaut in various contexts (NLD: 754); it can appear as *-a* (before *-hAŋ* 'continuative'), *-iŋ* (before *naŋ* 'and' or *-ktA*) or *-e* (at the end of a sentence or before *(k')éyaš* 'but'). It contrasts with the final *a* in verbs like *yawá* 'read', which is invariable.

-šni. The human and non-human/inanimate forms are based on *tuwé* 'be who, someone' and *táku* 'what, something'.

3 Lakhota verbs, verb morphology and telicity

The verbal systems in Lakhota and Tagalog differ significantly, in that Lakhota lacks voice, while Tagalog has a rich voice system (see § 5). Accordingly with a transitive verb the actor is always the subject and the undergoer always the object. Because Lakhota is a strictly head-marking language, the actor and the undergoer are coded on the verb, as illustrated in (6). What (6a, b) also illustrate is that third person, both actor and undergoer, is not expressed by a phonological form and is represented by 'Ø' in the morphemic segmentation. Only third-person plural animate undergoers have an overt marker, *wičha-*.[5] Despite the lack of a phonological form, Lakhota verbs take specific third-person actors and undergoers and third arguments of three-place predicates as well, as (6) shows.

(6) a. *Ø-Ø-Ø-K'ú.*   [cf. (4a, a')]
     INAN-3sgU-3sgA-give
     'He/she gave it to him/her.'

   b. *Ø-Ø-Kté.*   [(cf. (4b, b')]
     3sgU-3sgA-kill
     'He/she/it[ANIM] killed him/her/it[ANIM].'

The third-person arguments in these sentences have specific discourse referents, as the translations make clear. The third-person argument markers, with or without phonological form, are not pronouns, as argued in Van Valin (2013), for two reasons (see also Austin & Bresnan 1996). First, they can be bound locally, as in (4a, b), while pronouns cannot be so bound, and second, they can cross-reference indefinite NPs, as in (4b) and (5), something which should not be possible with pronouns, which are inherently definite. Van Valin argues that the bound argument markers are specific rather than definite, which makes them compatible with the specific indefinites introduced in § 2; this specific reference can be cancelled only in a small set of grammatical contexts, the same ones in which the non-specific indefinite articles occur, which were mentioned in § 2. The interpretation of the argument markers as pronouns in (6) could be the result of a Gricean

---

[5] The number of plural animate subjects and non-third-person animate objects is expressed by the suffix *-pi*, as in (4b); the number of plural inanimate subjects of stative verbs is expressed by reduplication of the verb.

Referentiality and telicity in Lakhota and Tagalog

implicature: the use of the bound form alone to signal a referent indicates to the hearer that the speaker believes that the hearer is able to uniquely identify the referent. Pronominal affixes are interpreted as definite, when they occur without an accompanying NP, because the implicature is that they refer to an identifiable referent, and identifiability and referentiality are the key ingredients of the concept of definiteness (Löbner 1985).

Lakhota has limited tense-aspect inflection. There is no inflectional coding for past tense, and therefore a verb can be interpreted as either present or past tense, as in (7) below. If one wanted to explicitly indicate that an action was on-going and continuing, then the aspect marker *-hAŋ* 'continuative' could be added to the verb, e.g. *yúta-he* 'he/she is/was eating' [*yútA* 'eat']. Particularly significant for the discussion of telicity is the fact that there is no marker of perfectivity. If one wanted to signal that an action had not yet occurred or was hypothetical, then *-ktA* can be used, e.g. *yútiŋ-kte* 'he/she will/would eat'. (Rood & Taylor See 1996: 474, NLD: 821–22.)

In English and many other languages it is possible with activity verbs like *eat* to simply drop the direct object, but not surprisingly this is not possible in Lakhota, since dropping the object NP does not affect the specificity of the object argument, as shown in (7).

(7) a. *Hokšíla ki   ağúyapiskuyela ki   Ø-Ø-yúte.*
       boy   the   cookie   the INAN-3sgA-eat
       'The boy is eating/ate the cookie.'

   b. *Hokšíla ki   ağúyapiskuyela waŋ   Ø-Ø-yúte.*
       boy   the   cookie   a[+specific] INAN-3sgA-eat
       'The boy is eating/ate a [certain] cookie.'

   c. *Hokšíla ki   Ø-Ø-yúte.*
       boy   the   INAN-sgA-eat
       'The boy is eating/ate it', *'The boy is eating/ate'.

The transitive verb *yútA* 'eat' is interpreted as having a specific object, regardless of whether there is an overt object or not, just as in the examples in (6). If one wants to use a transitive verb intransitively, there are two options. First, it can be prefixed with the non-specific object marker *wa-*, and it cannot have an overt object NP of any kind.

(8) a. *Hokšíla ki   w-Ø-óte.*   [*wa-* + *yútA* = *wótA*]
       boy   the   NSO-3sgA-eat
       'The boy is eating/ate', *'The boy is eating/ate it'.

407

b. * *Hokšíla ki ağúyapiskuyela (ki/waŋ~waŋží) w-Ø-óte.*
   boy   the cookie   the/a[±specific] NSO-3sgA-eat
   'The boy is eating/ate (the/a [certain]) cookie.'

Second, the object noun can be incorporated, yielding an intransitive construction.

(9) *Hokšíla ki ağúyapi Ø-yúte.*
     boy   the bread 3sgA-eat
     'The boy is eating/ate bread.'

According to DeReuse (1994), noun incorporation in Lakhota does not always involve phonological integration of the noun with the verb; rather, the semantic effect of incorporation can be achieved by 'stripping' the noun of all modifiers and placing it immediately before the verb, as in (9). The noun is non-referential and does not have the status of a direct object in a non-incorporated construction like (7a, b).

The standard test for telicity is compatibility with *in* vs. *for* temporal modifiers, as illustrated in (3). Atelic predications are compatible only with *for*-phrases, while *in*-phrases are compatible only with telic predications. This test can be applied in Lakhota, as there is an optional marker corresponding to *in, imáhel* 'in, within, inside of'; there is, however, no marker corresponding to *for*. Temporal expressions can also occur without any marker, and in such instances one must rely on the translation into English for the *in* vs. *for* contrast, as exemplified in (10).

(10) a. *Wičháša ki oápȟe waŋží ağúyapi waŋ   Ø-Ø-yúte.*
        man   the hour one   bread   a[+specific] INAN-3sgA-eat
        'The man ate a (loaf of) bread in/*for an hour.'

     a'. *Wičháša ki oápȟe waŋží imáhel ağúyapi waŋ   Ø-Ø-yúte.*
         man   the hour one   within bread   a[+specific] INAN-3sgA-eat
         'The man ate a (loaf of) bread in/*for an hour.'

     b. *Wičháša ki oápȟe waŋží w-Ø-óte.*
        man   the hour one   NSO-3sgA-eat
        'The man ate for/*in an hour.'

As noted in § 1, it has been claimed that there are verbs which are inherently telic, e. g. *hit*, verbs which are inherently atelic, e. g. *see, think*, and incremental verbs which are unspecified for telicity, e. g. *eat, write*. Based on the analysis of English and other Indo-European languages it has been claimed that the referential status of the direct object of unspecified verbs is crucial to the interpretation of them as telic or atelic. Telicity is claimed to be a property of VPs, not just the verb in these cases. Krifka (1989) claims that the direct object must be "quantized", i.e. either have a specific referent, as in (10a) or signal a specific amount, as in (10a'). This appears to be the case in Lakhota; in (10a) there is a specific direct object and the interpretation of the clause is telic, whereas in (10b) there is a non-specific object, and the interpretation is atelic. In (11) there is an example of a specific quantity, analogous to (10a').

(11) Wičháša ki oápȟe waŋží (imáhel) tȟaspáŋ núŋpa Ø-Ø-yúte.
man the hour one (within) apple two INAN-3sgA-eat
'The man ate two apples in/*for an hour.'

Thus, at first glance Lakhota appears to work like English in this regard.

Unlike English, however, the interpretation of a predication as telic or atelic is not a property of the VP and does not necessarily depend on the undergoer NP alone, for two reasons. First, Lakhota lacks a VP as a constituent in its clause structure, as shown in Van Valin (1987); there is no evidence that the verb and direct object form a constituent, as Lakhota fails all of the constituency tests for VPs. If factors beyond the verb are involved, as seems to be the case, then one would have to describe telicity as a property of the clause rather than the VP. Second, and more important, NP arguments need not occur, due to the head-marking nature of the language, as shown in (4a', b'), (6) and (7c), and therefore in such cases the telicity interpretation of the clause cannot depend on the status of the undergoer as an independent NP. Rather, it is a function of the coding of the argument on the verb, the temporal phrase accompanying it, or an independent expression of completion. A minimal pair based on verb coding is given in (12).

(12) a. Wičhíŋčala ki oápȟe waŋží wa-Ø-yáwa.
girl the hour one NSO-3sgA-read
'The girl read for an hour.'

b. Wičhíŋčala ki oápȟe waŋží Ø-Ø-yawá.
girl the hour one INAN-3sgA-read
'The girl read it in an hour.'

The only difference between these two examples is the coding of the non-actor argument on the verb. In (12a) it is expressed by the non-specific object prefix wa-, which detransitivizes the verb and yields an atelic reading, as indicated by

409

the translation of *oápȟe waŋží* 'one hour' as 'for an hour'. In (12b), on the other hand, the verb is transitive with a specific undergoer, and the translation of the temporal phrase is 'in an hour'.

This effect can be cancelled, however, by the addition of an explicit temporal phrase, as in (13), with the added clause in brackets confirming the (a)telic interpretation of the first clause.

(13) a. *Hokšíla ki oápȟe waŋží imáhel w-Ø-óte   [éyaš w-ól*
       boy   the hour one within NSO-3sgA-eat [but NSO-eat
       Ø-iglúštaŋ-šni].
       3sgA-finish-NEG]
       'The boy ate in an hour [but he didn't finish eating].'

   a'. *Hokšíla ki oápȟe waŋží imáhel w-Ø-ótiŋ   [naŋ w-ól*
       boy   the hour one within NSO-3sgA-eat [and NSO-eat
       Ø-iglúštaŋ].
       3sgA-finish]
       'The boy ate in an hour [and he finished eating].'

   b. *Hokšila ki oaphe waŋží (aǧúyapi ki) Ø-Ø-yúta-hiŋ   [naŋ*
       boy   the hour one   bread   the INAN-3sgA-eat-CONT [and
       Ø-yúl   Ø-iglúštaŋ].
       INAN-eat 3sgA-finish]
       'The boy was eating it (the bread) for an hour [and he finished eating it].'

   b'. *Hokšila ki oaphe waŋží (aǧúyapi ki) Ø-Ø-yúta-he   [éyaš*
       boy   the hour one   bread   the INAN-3sgA-eat-CONT [but
       Ø-yúl   Ø-iglúštaŋ-šni].
       INAN-eat 3sgA-finish-NEG]
       'The boy was eating it (the bread) for an hour [but didn't finish eating it].'

In (13a, a´) *imáhel* 'in, within' is added to the temporal expression together with the detransitivized form of the incremental verb *yútA* 'eat', *wótA*, and one possible reading is atelic, as (13a) makes clear. However, a telic reading is also possible, as (13a´) shows. When *-haŋ* 'continuative' is added to the transitive form with a specific undergoer, as in (13b, b´), one possible result is an atelic reading, as the compatibility with the second clause in (13b´) shows, despite the specific undergoer. The telic reading is still possible, however, as (13b) shows. Hence in

Lakhota a detransitivized verb with the non-specific object prefix is not necessarily atelic, and an incremental transitive verb with a specific undergoer is not necessarily telic. Verb morphology signaling the referentiality of an argument (*wa-* 'non-specific object' prefix) or signaling the temporal properties of the event (*-hAŋ* 'continuative') can affect the interpretation of telicity in Lakhota. To unequivocally indicate that an incremental process is telic, the verb *iglúštaŋ* 'finish' can be added, as in (14).

(14) a. *Hokšíla ki oápȟe čik'ála wikčémna (imáhel) agúyapi ki Ø-yúl*
    boy the hour little ten within bread the INAN-eat
    Ø-iglúštaŋ.
    3sgA-finish
    'The boy finished eating the bread in ten minutes.'

  b. *Hokšíla ki oápȟe čik'ála wikčémna (imáhel) w-ól Ø-iglúštaŋ.*
    boy the hour little ten within NSO-eat 3sgA-finish
    'The boy finished eating in ten minutes.'

Both sentences express that the action of eating was finished in ten minutes, differing in whether the things eaten are specified or not.

There are inherently telic incremental verbs in Lakhota, the prime example being *tȟebyÁ* 'devour, eat up'. It can co-occur with *yútA* as in (15) (NLD: 545).

(15) *Wóyute kiŋ Ø-Ø-yútiŋ naŋ tȟeb<Ø-Ø>yé.*
    food the INAN-3sgA-eat and devour<INAN-3sgA>
    'He ate the food until he consumed it.' [Lit.: 'He ate the food and devoured it.']

Sentences like (13b´) are not possible with *tȟebyÁ* 'devour'.

(16) * *Hokšíla ki oápȟe waŋží tȟaló ki tȟeb<Ø-Ø>yé k'éyaš Ø-yúl*
    boy the hour one meat the devour<INAN-3sgA> but INAN-eat
    Ø-iglúštaŋ-šni.
    3sgA-finish-NEG
    'The boy devoured/ate up the meat but didn't finish eating it.'

Interestingly, *tȟebyÁ* can take the non-specific object prefix *wa-*, yielding *watȟébyA* meaning 'to consume things by eating, eat things up, to devour things' (NLD: 628), i.e. unspecified objects are being eaten to completion. This is similar to the meaning expressed in (13a), in which the things being eaten are left unspecified but the eating is completed.

We have thus far concerned ourselves with transitive incremental verbs and the specificity status of their object, but there are intransitive incremental verbs which enter into telicity alternations, namely verbs of motion like *run* and *walk*. In English such verbs are sensitive to the type of PP that accompanies them, as illustrated in (17).

(17) a. *The boy ran to the park in/for an hour.*
      b. *The boy ran in the park for/*in hours.*

Run to the park is telic, since the motion to a specific goal (*the park*) is completed in an hour. A *for*-PP is not impossible with this form, but it does not have the relevant meaning; it can mean either that the boy ran back and forth to the park for an hour (iterative telic) or that he ran to the park and stayed there for half an hour (length of the result state, not the action of running). *Run in the park*, on the other hand, lacks a goal of any kind and merely expresses the location of the running, which is unbounded, hence the impossibility of an *in*-PP and the possibility of adding *and he's still out there running* felicitously to (17b). Lakhota can code this contrast, but it does not involve a difference in postpositions, as (18) shows.

(18) a. *Hokšíla ki čhaŋwóžupi ki ektá   oápȟe okhíse (imáhel) íŋyaŋg*
          boy   the park   the at/to/in hour half (within)   run
          i<Ø>húŋni.
          arrive.there<3sgA>
          'The boy ran to the park in half an hour.'
      b. *Hokšila ki čaŋwóžupi ki ektá   oápȟe okhíse o-íŋ<Ø>yaŋke.*
          boy   the park   the at/to/in hour half in-run<3sgA>
          'The boy ran in the park for half an hour.'

In both sentences the PP is *čhaŋwóžupi ki ektá* 'at/in/to the park', *ektá* being neutral between location and goal meanings. To express motion to a goal, the manner of motion verb *íŋyaŋkA* 'run' is combined with the verb *ihúŋni* 'to arrive there, reach a destination' (NLD: 209), which expresses the completion of the action by the arrival at the destination. No such verb occurs in (18b), in which the manner of motion verb takes the locative prefix *o-* 'in', yielding a verb meaning 'to run around, run about, to run inside' (NLD: 414). The *o-* prefix and the lack of a destination verb determine the interpretation of *ektá* as 'in' rather than 'to'. The locus of the expression of telicity with verbs of manner of motion in Lakhota is the verbal complex, not the accompanying PP, as in English.

In sum, while the default interpretation of an incremental verb like *yútA* 'eat' is atelic with a non-specific object and telic with a specific object, as coded minimally on the verb itself, these defaults can be overridden by explicit temporal phrases or expressions of completion or non-completion within the clause. With motion verbs telicity is not signaled by the type of PP accompanying them but rather by the verbal complex directly.

4 The encoding of specificity and definiteness in Tagalog

Tagalog is one of the main languages in the Philippines. Basic sentences are predicate-intial. Dynamic and stative predicates usually appear with an affix which indicates the PSA (priviliged syntactic argument, cf. Van Valin & LaPolla 1997) of the sentence. The affixes are commonly divided into actor voice affixes (*maka-, um-, mag-, mang-*) and undergoer voice affixes (*ma-, i-, -in, -an*), as shown in (19a) and (19b). Philippine linguists also designate these affixes as 'focus affix', i. e. affixes focusing on the 'sentence topic' (the *ang*-marked argument) by indicating its thematic role. In addition to voice, verbal predicates may be marked for mood by the realis prefix *in-* (often realized as an infix or fused with a preceding nasal), and for aspect by prefixal CV-reduplication of the verb stem to express imperfectivity. The opposite values for mood and aspect are morphologically unmarked. Undergoer voice forms of realis verbs do not exhibit the undergoer voice suffix *–in*, so that without further voice marker, the realis form of a verb is always understood as undergoer voice, cf. (19b).

(19) a. *Nag-basa ang bata ng libro.*
    AV.RLS-read NOM child GEN book
    'The child read a/some book.'

   b. *B<in>asa   ng bata ang libro.*
    <RLS>[UV]read GEN child NOM book
    'A/The child read the book.'

Kroeger (1993) views the markers as case particles and labels them as *ang*: NOM, *ng*: GEN, *sa*: DAT. Personal names take their own set of markers as Table 2 shows.

It has been a matter of debate whether the common noun-marking particles *ang, ng* and *sa* are truly determiners. Reid (2002) argues against this view, while Paul, Cortes & Milambiling (2012) and Himmelmann (to appear) put forward convincing arguments in favor of the analysis of *ang* and *ng* as determiners. When a language has a number of determiners, it can be suspected that they serve to

	Nominative	Genitive	Dative
Common nouns	*ang*	*ng*	*sa*
Personal names singular	*si*	*ni*	*kay*
Personal names plural	*sina*	*nina*	*kina*

Table 2: Tagalog noun markers

express different degrees of referentiality. At least since Bloomfield (1917), it has been stated that *ang*-marked undergoer arguments tend to be associated with a definite/specific interpretation (cf. 19b), while *ng*-marked undergoers are typically interpreted as indefinite/non-specific (cf. 19a). However, it is not possible to have more than one *ang*-marked argument in a clause. As the sentences in (19) exemplify, the case marking of the arguments correlates with the voice marking of the verb. In actor voice (AV) sentences undergoers are marked by *ng*, and actors are marked by *ang*, while it is the other way around in undergoer voice (UV) sentences

The notions of definiteness and specificity are usually not formally defined in papers on Tagalog, but there seems to be a tacit consensus among Philippinists that definites establish an 'identifiable' and 'familiar' referent and express an assertion or presupposition of existence and uniqueness (cf. Givón 1973, Heim 1991 and others) with respect to their referent, while specificity is viewed as a weaker form of definiteness, in the sense that specific arguments are only associated with a presupposition of existence, but not necessarily with one of uniqueness.

Francisco de San José (1610) is quoted as the first to be associated with the claim that an indefinite undergoer cannot be *ang*-marked, while a definite undergoer has to be *ang*-marked. The latter claim has been refuted repeatedly. A list of contexts and constructions licensing a specific or even definite interpretation of *ng*-marked undergoer arguments can be found in MacLachlan & Nakamura (1997), among others. They mention for example the recent perfective form of verbs (which does not require *ang*-marking on any argument in contrast to other verb forms), applicative constructions (under which they subsume beneficiary voice, recipient voice, instrumental voice) as well as actor sentences, in which the actor precedes the predicate licensing the *ng*-marked undergoer, as in (20a). Further examples of specific and definite undergoers in AV sentences are given in (20b-f).

(20) a. *Siya   ang naka-kita ng aksidente.*
       3sgNOM NOM AV.RLS-see GEN accident
       'He is the one who saw the accident.'
       (Schachter & Otanes 1972)

   b. *At kaya gusto ko-ng   ma-nalo ng award na ito.*
      and so want 1sgGEN-LK AV-win GEN award LK this
      'And so I want to win this award [=Comedy actress award].'
      (http://m.pep.ph/moblie/news)[6]

   c. *Hindi ba kayo   nag-kita   ng asawa ni Col. Adante?*
      NEG Q 2plNOM AV.RLS-see GEN spouse GEN Col. Adante
      'Have you not met Col. Adante's wife?'
      (http://www.pinoyexchange.com/formus/printthreadphp?t=345875&pp=40&page=43)

   d. *Nag-da~dala   siya   ng Bible.*
      AV.RLS-IPFV~carry 3sgNOM GEN Bible
      'He is carrying the Bible.'
      (pc. Royal Panotes)

   e. *Mag-alis   ka   ng (iyon-g) sapatos bago p<um>asok ng*
      AV.IRR-leave 2sgNOM GEN (2sg-LK) shoe   before <AV>enter GEN
      bahay.
      house
      'Take off (your) the shoes before you enter the house.'
      (www.seasite.niu.edu/Tagalog/.../diction.htm)

   f. *K<um>a~kain   sila   ng kanila-ng sandwich.*
      <AV>[RLS] IPFV~eat 3plNOM GEN 3pl-LK sandwich
      'They are eating their sandwiches.'
      (www.rosettastone.co.jp/.../RSV3_CC_Filipino)

The examples (20c) and (20d) exhibit undergoers with a semantically definite reference (Adante's wife, the Bible), while (20e, f) contain possessed undergoers, where the possessors are anaphoric pronouns whose reference is specific due to the argument in the sentence that binds them. Last, but not least (20a), (20b) and (20e) show *ng*-marked undergoers that receive definite reference due to the given context. The data in (20) provide good evidence that the marker *ng* is not restricted to indefinite/non-specific contexts. In particular, (20b) shows that

---

[6] (20)b and c were pointed out in a draft by Sabbagh (2012)

it would not make sense to attribute a lack of specificity to *ng*, when it may cooccur with a demonstrative pronoun. The marker is thus best analysed as neutral with respect to referentiality (cf. Latrouite 2011), as it may be used to mark semantically and pragmatically definite arguments in the sense of Löbner (1985).

But how about the marker *ang*? Based on the data above one could conclude with Schachter (1976) that 'not every definite NP is a [sentence (AL/RVV)] topic, but every [sentence (AL/RVV)] topic is definite.' However, as Adams & Manaster-Ramer (1988), Law (2006) and others have shown the *Definiteness Restriction* seems to be too strong to correctly predict the distribution of *ang*- and *ng*-marked undergoers even in this limited sense, so that it has become common to refer to *ang* as a specificity and not as a definiteness marker (cf. Himmelmann 2005). Law (2006) claims that *ang*-marked arguments do not even consistently fulfill the requirement of specificity. He points out that in the example in (21a) the existence of *ang mali* ('mistake') is not assumed by the speaker. Similarly in (21b) and (21c), the reference of the *ang*-phrase is neither predetermined nor mediated by referential anchoring to another discourse item.

(21) Non-specific *ang*-phrases

a. *Basa-hin mo   ang libro at sabi-hin mo   sa   akin, kung*
   read-UV 2sgGEN NOM book and tell-UV 2sgGEN DAT 1sgDAT if
   ma-ki~kita   mo   ang mali   sa libro.
   UV.STAT-IPFV~visible 2sgGEN NOM mistake DAT book
   'Read the book and tell me, whether you see a(ny) mistake in the book.'
   (Law 2006: 163)

b. *Maari   na niyan-g   sabi-hin ang anuman dito.*
   possible LK 3sgGEN-LK say-UV   NOM whatever here
   'He can say anything here.'
   (May hiyas pa sa liblib, Ronnie M. Halos, Pilipino Star Ngayon, August 12, 2010)

c. *Gamit-in mo   (ang) kahit   (na) anuma-ng   pinggan.*
   use-UV   2sgGEN NOM   any/even LK   whatever-LK dish
   'Use any dish!'
   (Schachter & Otanes 1972: 534)

If *ang* is not a specificity marker, then the question arises as to why *ang*-phrases are preferably understood as specific. In Latrouite (2011), it is suggested that the tendency to interpret *ang*-phrases as specific can be traced back to the interaction of (i) the function of voice marking, (ii) information flow in Tagalog basic sentences, and (iii) the fact that *ang* most likely evolved from a demonstrative pronoun (Reid 1978). All three factors contribute to the preferred interpretation of *ang*-phrases as specific, even if they may not enforce that *ang*-marked arguments must be specific in all contexts, as its primary function is the marking of the PSA. Another approach would be to assume a broader notion of specificity. It should be noted that the quantifiers used in the translations in (21) are high on the Quantifier Hierarchy (cf. Ioup 1975, Kuno et al. 1999) with respect to individuation, so that in a broader sense of the term the respective phrases could still be argued to fit the label 'specific' or at least 'more specific' in comparison to other quantified phrases. Disregarding this debate, if today's *ang*-marking with verbal predicates is analysed as the result of a grammaticalisation process that led to the development of a syntactic pivot marker, then the reasons for the choice of the *ang*-marked PSA are quite naturally based on a number of semantic, syntactic and pragmatic considerations (cf. Latrouite 2011), so that the role of referential properties of the undergoer argument may become less important for their distribution, at least if nothing hinges on the referentiality on a higher level like the level of event-structure. Note that the verbs in this section were not of the incremental type. Important for this paper is the fact that both case markers may mark definites, but that only for the marker *ang* definiteness is the default assumption without further co(n)text.

5 Tagalog verbs, voice marking and telicity

It has long been known that with a number of incremental verbs actor voice forms tend to receive an activity reading, while undergoer voice forms, more specifically patient voice forms, receive an accomplishment reading, as the sentences in (22) and (23) show.

(22) Activity readings with actor voice

    a. *S<um>ulat   si   Pedro ng liham.*
       <AV>[RLS]write NOM Pedro GEN letter
       'Pedro wrote part of a letter/ letters.'

    b. *L<um>angoy ka   sa   ilog.*
       <AV>[RLS]swim 2sgNOM DAT river
       'Swim in the river.'

c. *K\<um\>ain   ako   ng   isda.*
   \<AV\>[RLS]eat 1sgNOM GEN fish
   'I ate (a) fish/fishes.'

d. *\<Um\>akyat   ako   ng/sa   bulog.*
   \<AV\>[RLS]go.up 1sgNOM GEN/DAT mountain
   'I climbed on a/the mountain.'

(23) Accomplishment readings with undergoer voice

a. *S\<in\>ulat   ni Pedro ang liham.*
   \<RLS\>[UV]write GEN Pedro NOM letter
   'Pedro wrote the letter.'

b. *L\<in\>angoy   mo   ang ilog.*
   \<RLS\>[UV]swim 2sgGEN NOM river
   'Swim (across) the river (= from one side to the opposite side).'

c. *K\<in\>ain   ko   ang isda.*
   \<RLS\>[UV]eat 1sgGEN NOM fish
   'I ate the fish.'

d. *\<In\>akyat   ko   ang bulog.*
   \<RLS\>[UV]go.up 1sgGEN NOM mountain
   'I climbed the mountain (= all the way up to the top of the mountain).'

Saclot (2011: 159), who investigates incremental verbs in Tagalog, takes up this point and states that the AV form of these verbs is inherently atelic and therefore "enforces an indefinite/partitive/bare plural interpretation on the patient", while the UV form is inherently telic, and enforces a specific/definite reading of the undergoer and consistently fails her cancellation and continuity tests. Saclot's conclusion ist that "in Tagalog it appears to be telicity [= the telicity associated with the undergoer voice (AL/RVV)] that triggers the interpretation of the patient argument [as definite (AL/RVV)]." Saclot restricts her claim regarding AV-forms explicitly to incremental verbs, which is necessary, since, as we have seen in the previous section, it would not be possible to uphold it with respect to all verb classes. Note, however, that indefiniteness *per se* does not clash with telicity. There is no difference in telicity between *He ate the apple* and *He ate an apple*, so it is not quite clear why an atelic verb form should induce an indefinite reading.

In order to support her claim with respect to the inherent (a)telicity of the voice forms, Saclot (2011) contrasts the two sentences in (24a) and (24b) and finds that the undergoer voice sentence cannot be continued by the phrase *pero hindi niya natapos* ('but he did not finish it') (24b), while the actor voice sentence can be continued by this phrase (24a). The demonstrative pronoun given in brackets was added by our consultants.

(24) a. G<um>awa   si Ben ng   isa-ng bangka pero hindi niya   (ito)
        <AV>[RLS]make NOM GEN one-LK boat   but   not 3sgGEN this.NOM
        na-tapos.
        UV.STAT-finish
        'Ben made a boat, but he did not finish (it).'

   b. #G<in>awa   ni Ben ang isa-ng bangka pero hindi niya   (ito)
        <UV>[RLS]make GEN NOM one-LK boat   but   not 3sgGEN this.NOM
        na-tapos.
        UV.STAT-finish
        'Ben made the one boat, but he did not finish (it).'

In contrast to Saclot's judgements, three of our four consultants accept both sentences as well-formed. One remarked on the fact that the boat relates differently to the event in both cases. For this consultant the AV-form implies that a boat was built from scratch, while the UV-form connotes that Ben worked on a specific boat (e. g. repaired or painted it) that had already existed. This means that the interpretation of the PSA undergoer in the undergoer voice sentence is affected by the subject property of 'independent existence' (Keenan 1976). Interestingly, the UV-form of the verb is then no longer interpreted as one of creation. Note that *matapos* is ambiguous between 'to finish' and 'to stop' so that the test may be not all that conclusive. In case the test is considered conclusive, however, (25) shows that the AV-form, which is always understood as one of creation, may also be interpreted as telic.

(25) G<um>awa   si Ben ng isa-ng bangko at na-tapos   nang mabilis
     <AV>[RLS]make NOM GEN one-LK boat   but UV.STAT-finish MOD quick
     niya   ito.
     3sgGEN this.NOM
     'Ben made a boat, and he quickly finished it.'

Two consultants come to a similar conclusion regarding strictly incremental predicates like the verb for *to drink* in (26), i. e. they accept both voice forms with the reading that the event was not completed. The difference between the verbs for 'to finish', *matapos* and *maubos*, is that the former is temporal, while the latter is about 'exhaustion'.

(26) a. *Um-inom si Ben ng beer pero hindi niya (ito) na-ubos.*
AV[RLS]-drink NOM GEN beer but not 3sgGEN this.NOM UV.STAT-finish
'Ben drank (a) beer, but he did not finish (it).'

b. ?? *In-inom ni Ben ang beer pero hindi niya (ito) na-ubos.*
UV[RLS]-drink GEN NOM beer but not 3sgGEN this.NOM UV.STAT-finish
'Ben drank the beer, but he did not finish (it).'

With respect to the continuation test, our consultants agree with Saclot's judgements regarding the examples in (27). Apparently the continuation phrase of the UV sentence sounds worse, while it sounds slightly better with the AV form. Once again, the undergoer phrase *Nihongo* gets reinterpreted by our consultants. Obviously, in an attempt to get a clearly individuated and bounded reading of the *ang*-marked undergoer, one consultant suggests that *ang Nihongo* is understood as a course (which Ben attended to become fluent). The continuation reading then is weird, as the quantifier 'a lot' is taken to refer to the course and would result in the contradictory reading that 'Ben studied the course, but still has to study a lot (of the course).'

(27) a. *Nag-aral si Ben ng Nihongo pero marami pa ring dapat aral-in.*
AV.RLS-study NOM GEN Japanese but much still also must learn-UV
'Ben studied Japanese, but he still has to learn a lot.'

b. ?? *In-aral ni Ben ang Nihongo pero marami pa ring dapat aral-in.*
RLS[UV]-study GEN NOM Japanese but much still also must learn-UV
'Ben studied (the) Japanese (course), but he still has to learn a lot.'

Saclot compares the two verb forms in the main clause. The undergoer voice form *aralin* in the subordinate clause translated as 'but he still has to learn a lot (a. of Japanese/ b. of the Japanese course)' is of interest, too. One could not have the actor voice form of 'to learn' in this sentence without changing the meaning significantly. The quantifier *marami* can only refer to the argument identified on the verb via the voice affix, so that the actor voice sentence *marami pa ring dapat magaral* can only mean 'many still have to learn.' Therefore, the only way one can get a quantifier like 'a lot' to modify the undergoer argument is by choosing undergoer voice.

There is further evidence that actor voice forms may very well appear in telic predications. The following actor voice sentences in (28a) and (28b) contain phrases introducing a measure for the length of the path traversed by the actor which can be directly mapped onto the run-time of the event. The interpretation therefore is telic. Note that the PSA of the undergoer voice form of 'to run' in (28) may be a path or an event associated with a path like a marathon, but does not have to be. According to Nolasco (2005), the undergoer may just as well denote an object that is conceived as a goal motivating the running event (cf. Latrouite 2012), as in (28d).

(28) a. *Nag-takbo ako* **ng** *marathon.*
AV.RLS-run 1sgNOM GEN marathon
'I ran a/some marathon'

b. *L<um>angoy siya* **ng** *10 miles para maka-rating ng*
<AV>[RLS]swim 3sgNOM GEN 10 miles for AV.POT-arrive GEN
pinakamalapit na beach.
nearest LK beach
'He swam ten miles to reach the nearest beach.'

c. *Takbu-hin mo* **ang** *marathon!*
run-UV 2sgGEN NOM marathon
'Run the marathon!'
(cf. http://www.scribd.com/doc/6784539/salita)

d. *Takbu-hin mo* **ang** *Marlboro.*
run-UV 2sgGEN NOM Marlboro
'(You) run to (get) the Marlboro!'
(cf. Nolasco 2005: 215)[7]

Note that the difference between (28a) and (28c) is one translated in terms of definiteness rather than in terms of telicity, stressing the point made in Filip (1993/1999) that definiteness and telicity should be kept apart as two independent notions (see also Fleischhauer & Czardybon, this volume). The data so far suggest that actor voice forms of incremental verbs are not restricted to atelic predications, while undergoer voice forms of strictly incremental verbs seem to be at least clearly preferred with telic interpretations by many consultants. The very preliminary study in this paper shows that there may be differences depending on whether a verb is or is not strictly incremental. One could then argue that the difference between telic actor voice sentences and telic undergoer voice sentences is that the former require further context knowledge to calculate the telicity, while the latter do not, as telicity is the default for them.

---

[7] According to English (1986), the form would have to be *takbuhan*.

Summing up the findings in this section, it appears to be right that as a default the undergoer argument receives a specific and individuated reading with undergoer voice verbs. This reading may be viewed as 'imposed' by the undergoer voice form of incremental verbs in that the undergoer voice form requires the undergoer to be prominent to become the PSA, and with incremental verbs an undergoer that measures out an event and thereby influences the aspectual reading of the verb, i.e. an undergoer that is event-structurally salient, is more prominent than one that does not have these properties. However, we have seen that the default for *ang*-marked undergoers is also that they get a specific and individuated reading with activity and other non-telic verbs, so the argument that the inherent telicity of undergoer voice forms enforces a specific interpretation is not particularly strong. The judgements in this section seem to suggest that for certain verbs it is possible to cancel the telicity or deny it via co(n)text without changing the referential reading of the undergoer. If this is so then their telicity may best be viewed as an implicature. In the case of actor voice forms it is very clear that they are not inherently restricted to a particular reading, i.e. to atelicity, given that they do not require a particular reading on their undergoer argument which may be specific or non-specific. In terms of a decompositional approach one would certainly assume that the bare verb stem is not specified for (a)telicity, but may be built upon to achieve telic readings, either by marking that the undergoer argument is the most prominent referentially and in event-structural terms via the undergoer voice affix, or in the case of actor voice through co(n)text.

6 Implications for a theory of telicity

This paper has addressed the issue of referentiality and the interpretation of incremental predicates as telic in two unrelated and typologically very different non-Indo-European languages, Lakhota and Tagalog. Our investigation has shown that while having a referential undergoer often, indeed usually, leads to a telic interpretation of an incremental predicate, it does not necessarily generate a telic reading with such verbs. This supports the arguments made in Filip (2004) against the claim by Borer (2004) regarding a purported correlation between definite direct objects and telic interpretations. Filip argues that "articles, possessive pronouns, certain quantifiers or the accusative suffix in the direct object NP/DP in Germanic languages cannot be claimed to encode telicity, because they are not consistently and in all of their occurrences linked to the telicity of a VP, but rather may serve as just one among other contributing factors that together result in a telic interpretation of a VP" (2004: 98–99).

We have found that there are a number of factors that affect the interpretation of a verb as telic or atelic, no one of which is absolutely decisive. In Lakhota, the specificity of the undergoer argument, which may be coded exclusively by affixes on the verb, is a significant factor. In Tagalog, verbal voice also serves as an important factor in the determination of default telicity with incremental verbs. Its primary function, however, is to identify the thematic role of the PSA of the sentence, which, without further context, is attributed all the prototypical properties of subjects such as specificity, individuation and independent existence mentioned in Keenan (1976). In the presence of an undergoer argument as PSA expressed by a noun (phrase) with the appropriate lexical semantic properties to be interpretable as quantized, a telic reading ensues as the default. As we have seen, this default may be overridden by context or grammatico-semantic considerations. Indeed, Filip (1993/1999) argues that incremental verbs like *eat* are aspectually undetermined. One technical solution would be to posit default interpretations in specific grammatical contexts: incremental verb + quantized object/undergoer voice => telic, incremental verb + non-quantized object/actor voice => atelic. These can, as we have seen in both languages, be overridden, and this raises the issue of how robust these defaults are. That would seem to be a function of the lexical semantic properties of the verb and the relevant argument(s), together with pragmatic principles; and thus very much in line with what Filip (2004) notes with respect to the possible interpretation of a mass noun as having a definite quantity, "[i]f a definite description consisting of *the* and a mass or plural noun has a 'quantity' interpretation it is not determined by the grammar, but rather depends on pragmatic principles of interpretation and world knowledge" (2004: 97).

Important throughout the paper was the role of noun phrase interpretation or noun phrase referentiality for the interpretation of the verb. While the referentiality of the undergoer argument may be recognized as a factor influencing – but not finally determining - the verbal interpretation, it was shown for both languages that the interpretation of noun phrase markers may also be subject to default reasoning that can be overridden.

Throughout the paper it was shown that the referentiality aspect of definiteness was important for telic interpretations. This property, referential uniqueness, is indispensable for the quantization of the undergoer, especially with mass nouns and bare plurals, and this supports the analysis of uniqueness as the essential property of definiteness made in Löbner (1985).

Bibliography

Adams, K. & A. Manaster-Ramer. 1988. Some questions of topic/focus choice in Tagalog. *Oceanic Linguistics* 27. 79–101.

Austin, P. & J. Bresnan. 1996. Non-configurationality in Australian Aboriginal languages. *Natural Language and Linguistic Theory* 14. 215–68.

Bloomfield, L. 1917. Tagalog texts with grammatical analysis. *University of Illinois Studies in Language and Literature* 3. 157–278.

Borer, H. 2004. *Structuring sense.* Oxford: Oxford University Press.

DeReuse, W. 1994. Noun incorporation in Lakota Siouan. *International Journal of American Linguistics* 60. 199–260.

English, J. 1986. Tagalog-English dictionary. Manila.

Filip, H. 1993/1999. *Aspect, situation types and noun phrase semantics.* Garland Publishing, Inc. [PhD Thesis 1993].

Filip, H. 2004. The telicity parameter revisited. In R. Young (ed.), *Proceedings of SALT XIV*, 92–109. Ithaca/NY, Cornell University.

Filip, H. & S. Rothstein. 2005. Telicity as a semantic parameter. In J. Lavine, S. Franks, H. Filip & M. Tasseva-Kurktchieva (eds.), *Formal approaches to Slavic linguistics XIV. The Princeton University meeting*, 139–156. Ann Arbor, MI: University of Michigan Slavic Publications.

Fleischhauer, J. & A. Czardybon. 2014. Definiteness and perfectivity in telic incremental theme predications. This volume.

Givón, T. 1973. Opacity and reference in language: An inquiry into the role of modalities. In J. Kimball (ed.), *Syntax & semantics 2*, New York NY: Academic Press.

Heim, I. 1991. Articles and definiteness. In A. v. Stechow & D. Wunderlich (eds.), *Semantics: An international handbook of contemporary research*, Berlin: de Gruyter. Published in German as "Artikel und Definitheit".

Himmelmann, N. 2005. Tagalog. In K. A. Adelaar & N. P. Himmelmann (eds.), *The Austronesian languages of Asia and Madagascar*, 350–376. London: Routledge.

Himmelmann, N. to appear. Notes on noun phrase structure in Tagalog.

Ioup, G. 1975. Some universals for quantifier scope. In J. Kimball (ed.), *Syntax and semantics*, vol. 4, 37–58. New York: Academic Press.

Keenan, E. 1976. Towards a universal definition of "subject". In C. N. Li (ed.), *Subject and topic*, New York: Academic Press.

Kratzer, A. 2004. Telicity and the meaning of objective case. In J. Guéron & J. Lecarme (eds.), *The syntax of time*, 389–424. Cambridge/Mass.: The MIT Press.

Krifka, M. 1986. *Nominalreferenz und Zeitkonstitution. Zur Semantik von Massentermen, Individualtermen, Aspektklassen.* Munich, Germany: Universität München Dissertation.

Krifka, M. 1989. *Nominalreferenz und Zeitkonstitution. Zur Semantik von Massentermen, Individualtermen, Aspektklassen.* München: Wilhelm Fink Verlag.

Krifka, M. 1992. Thematic relations as links between nominal reference and temporal constitution. In I. A. Sag & A. Szabolcsi (eds.), *Lexical matters*, 29–53. Stanford: CSLI.

Kroeger, P. 1993. *Phrase structure and grammatical relations in Tagalog.* Stanford: CSLI.

Kuno, Susumu, Ken-ichi Takami & Yuru Wu. 1999. Quantifier scope in English, Chinese and Japanese. *Language* 75. 63–111.

Latrouite, A. 2011. *Voice and case in Tagalog: the coding of prominence and orientation.* Düsseldorf: University of Düsseldorf dissertation.

Latrouite, A. 2012. Shifting perspectives. Paper read at the 12th International Conference of Austronesian Linguistics. Indonesia: Bali.

Law, P. 2006. Argument marking and the distribution of *wh*-phrases in Malagasy, Tagalog and Tsou. *Oceanic Linguistics* 45. 153–190.

Löbner, S. 1985. Definites. *Journal of Semantics* 4. 279–326.

MacLachlan, A. & M. Nakamura. 1997. Case-checking and specificity in Tagalog. *The Linguistic Review* 14. 307–333.

Nolasco, R. 2005. What Philippine ergativity really means. Paper presented at Taiwan-Japan Joint Workshop on Austronesian Languages, National Taiwan University, Taipei, p. 215 - 238.

Paul, I., K. Cortes & L. Milambiling. 2012. On Tagalog determiners. Talk given at AFLA19 in Taiwan.

Ramchand, G. C. 1997. *Aspect and predication. The semantics of argument structure.* Oxford: Clarendon Press.

Reid, L. 1978. Problems in the reconstruction of proto-Philippine construction markers. In S. A. Wurm & Lois Carrington (eds.), *Second international conference on Austronesian linguistics: Proceedings, fascicle I —western Austronesian.* Pacific Linguistics Series C, No. 61, 33–66.

Reid, L. 2002. Determiners, nouns, or what? Problems in the analysis of some commonly occurring forms in Philippine languages. *Oceanic Linguistics* 41. 295–309.

Rood, D. & A. Taylor. 1996. Sketch of Lakhota, a Siouan language. In I. Goddard (ed.), *Handbook of North American Indians: Language*, vol. 17, 440–82. Washington: Smithsonian Institution: Smithsonian Institution.

Sabbagh, J. 2012. Specificity and objecthood in Tagalog. Manuscript- UT Arlington ling.auf.net/lingbuzz/001647/current.pdf.

Saclot, M. 2011. *Event structure in Tagalog*. University of Melbourne dissertation.

Schachter, P. 1976. The subject in Philippine languages: topic, actor, actor-topic, or none of the above. In C. Li (ed.), *Subject and topic*, 493–518. New York: Academic Press.

Schachter, P. & F. T. Otanes. 1972. *Tagalog reference grammar*. Berkeley, CA.: University of California Press.

Ullrich, J. 2011. *New Lakota dictionary [NLD]*. Bloomington: Lakota Language Consortium. 2nd. Ed.

Van Valin, R. D. Jr. 1987. The role of government in the grammar of head-marking languages. *International Journal of American Linguistics* 53. 371–97.

Van Valin, R. D. Jr. 2013. Head-marking languages and linguistic theory. In B. Bickel, L. A. Grenoble, D. A. Peterson & A. Timberlake (eds.), *Language typology and historical contingency*, 91-123. Amsterdam: John Benjamins.

Van Valin, R. D. Jr & Randy LaPolla. 1997. *Syntax: structure, meaning and function*. Cambridge: Cambridge University Press.

Verkuyl, H. 1972. *On the compositional nature of the aspects*. Dordrecht: Reidel Publishing Co.

Authors

Anja Latrouite
Robert D. Van Valin, Jr.
Departement of Linguistics and Information Science
Heinrich-Heine-University Düsseldorf
{latrouite,vanvalin}@phil.hhu.de

List of Sebastian Löbner's publications

Monographs and edited volumes

2013. *Understanding semantics*. London: Routledge 2nd edn. (1st edition 2002, London: Hodder; German edition 2003, Korean edition 2010).

2013. (with Guram Bezhanishvili, Vincenzo Marra & Frank Richter). *Logic, language, and computation. 9th international Tbilisi symposium on logic, language, and computation, TbiLLC 2011.* Lecture Notes in Computer Science 7758. Berlin/ Heidelberg: Springer.

2012. (with Christian Horn & Markus Werning). Special issue: Semantic contributions to a theory of concepts. *Journal of Semantics* 29(4).

1990. *Wahr neben Falsch. Duale Operatoren als die Quantoren natürlicher Sprache.* Tübingen: Narr.

1979. *Intensionale Verben und Funktionalbegriffe. Zur Syntax und Semantik von 'wechseln' und den vergleichbaren Verben des Deutschen.* Tübingen: Narr.

1976. *Einführung in die Montague-Grammatik.* Kronberg: Scriptor.

Journal papers and book chapters

2014. Evidence for frames from human language. In T. Gamerschlag, D. Gerland, R. Osswald & W. Petersen (eds.), *Frames and concept types: applications in language and philosophy*, 23–68. Heidelberg, Dordrecht: Springer.

2012. Sub-compositionality. In M. Werning, W. Hinzen & E. Machery (eds.), *The Oxford handbook of compositionality*, 220–241. Oxford: Oxford University Press.

2011. Dual oppositions in lexical meaning. In C. Maienborn, K. von Heusinger & P. Portner (eds.), *Semantics. an international handbook of natural language meaning (HSK)*, vol. 1, 479–506. Berlin, New York: Mouton de Gruyter.

2011. Concept types and determination. *Journal of Semantics* 28. 279–333.

2008. Lexical semantics. In P. van Sterkenburg (ed.), *Unity and diversity of language*, 189–200. Amsterdam: Benjamins.

2005. Funktionalbegriffe und Frames – Interdisziplinäre Grundlagenforschung zu Sprache, Kognition und Wissenschaft. In *Jahrbuch der Heinrich-Heine-Universität Düsseldorf 2004*, 463–477. Düsseldorf: Heinrich-Heine-Universität.

2005. Quantoren im GWDS. In Wiegand. H. E. (ed.), *Untersuchungen zur kommerziellen Lexikographie der deutschen Gegenwartssprache II. "Duden. Das große Wörterbuch der deutschen Sprache in zehn Bänden." Print- und CD-ROM-Version*, 171–192. Tübingen: Niemeyer.

2002. Is the German perfect a perfect perfect. In I. Kaufmann & B. Stiebels (eds.), *More than words: A festschrift für Dieter Wunderlich*, 369–391. Berlin: Akademie Verlag.

2000. Polarity in natural language: predication, quantification and negation in particular and characterizing sentences. *Linguistics and Philosophy* 23. 213–308.

1999. Why German *schon* and *noch* are still duals: a reply to van der Auwera. *Linguistics and Philosophy* 22. 45–107.

1992. (with Yoshiki Mori & Katharina Micha). Aspektuelle Verbklassen im Japanischen. *Zeitschrift für Sprachwissenschaft* 11. 189–215.

1989. German *schon – erst – noch*: an integrated analysis. *Linguistics and Philosophy* 12. 167–212.

1988. Ansätze zu einer integralen semantischen Theorie von Tempus, Aspekt und Aktionsarten. In V. Ehrich & H. Vater (eds.), *Temporalsemantik: Beiträge zur Linguistik der Zeitreferenz*, 163–191. Tübingen: Niemeyer.

1987. Natural language and generalized quantifier theory. In P. Gärdenfors (ed.), *Generalized quantifiers: linguistic and logical approaches*, 181–201. Dordrecht: Reidel.

1987. Quantification as a major module of natural language semantics. In J. Groenendijk, M. Stokhof & D. de Jongh (eds.), *Studies in discourse representation theory and the theory of generalized quantifiers*, 53–85. Dordrecht: Foris.

1986. In Sachen Nullartikel. *Linguistische Berichte* 101. 64–65.

1985c. Drei ist drei. In W. Kürschner & R. Vogt (eds.), *Grammatik, Semantik, Textlinguistik. Akten des 19. Linguistischen Kolloquiums Vechta 1984*, 311–318. Tübingen: Niemeyer.

1985. Definites. *Journal of Semantics* 4. 279–326.

1985. Natürlichsprachliche Quantoren. Zur Verallgemeinerung des Begriffs der Quantifikation. *Studium Linguistik* 17/18. 79–113.

1981. Intensional verbs and functional concepts: More on the "rising temperature" problem. *Linguistic Inquiry* 12. 471–477.

List of Sebastian Löbner's publications

Online articles

2012. Functional concepts and frames. Ms., University of Düsseldorf. http://semanticsarchive.net/Archive/jl1NGEwO/Loebner_Functional_Concepts_and_Frames.pdf.

1998. Definite associative anaphora. In S. Botley (ed.), *Approaches to discourse anaphora. Proceedings of DAARC96 - discourse anaphora and resolution colloquium*. UCREL Technical Papers Series, Vol. 8, Lancaster: Lancaster University.

Reviews

1990. Edward L. Keenan & Leonard M. Faltz: Boolean semantics for natural language. *Linguistics* 28. 517–530.

1987. Harry C. Bunt: Mass terms and model-theoretic semantics. *Studies in Language* 11. 491–500.

1987. Wolfgang Hadamitzky: Kanji und Kana. *Studies in Language* 11. 247–252.